LOVELAND PUBLIC LIBRARY

000429121

Withdrawn

D0429501

6/19/07
$26.95
B&T

AS

11/20/07

6/07

BILL & DAVE

BILL & DAVE

How Hewlett and Packard
Built the World's Greatest Company

Michael S. Malone

PORTFOLIO

PORTFOLIO
Published by the Penguin Group
Penguin Group (USA) Inc., 375 Hudson Street,
New York, New York 10014, U.S.A.
Penguin Group (Canada), 90 Eglinton Avenue East, Suite 700,
Toronto, Ontario, Canada M4P 2Y3
(a division of Pearson Penguin Canada Inc.)
Penguin Books Ltd, 80 Strand, London WC2R 0RL, England
Penguin Ireland, 25 St. Stephen's Green, Dublin 2, Ireland
(a division of Penguin Books Ltd)
Penguin Books Australia Ltd, 250 Camberwell Road, Camberwell,
Victoria 3124, Australia (a division of Pearson Australia Group Pty Ltd)
Penguin Books India Pvt Ltd, 11 Community Centre,
Panchsheel Park, New Delhi – 110 017, India
Penguin Group (NZ), 67 Apollo Drive, Mairangi Bay,
Auckland 1311, New Zealand (a division of Pearson New Zealand Ltd.)
(a division of Pearson New Zealand Ltd)
Penguin Books (South Africa) (Pty) Ltd, 24 Sturdee Avenue,
Rosebank, Johannesburg 2196, South Africa

Penguin Books Ltd, Registered Offices:
80 Strand, London WC2R 0RL, England

First published in 2007 by Portfolio,
a member of Penguin Group (USA) Inc.

10 9 8 7 6 5 4 3 2 1

Copyright © Michael S. Malone, 2007
All rights reserved

LIBRARY OF CONGRESS CATALOGING IN PUBLICATION DATA AVAILABLE
ISBN: 978–1–59184–152–4

Printed in the United States of America
Set in Minion with Gotham
Designed by Sabrina Bowers

Without limiting the rights under copyright reserved above, no part of this publication may be
reproduced, stored in or introduced into a retrieval system, or transmitted, in any form or by any
means (electronic, mechanical, photocopying, recording or otherwise), without the prior written
permission of both the copyright owner and the above publisher of this book.

The scanning, uploading, and distribution of this book via the Internet or via any other means
without the permission of the publisher is illegal and punishable by law. Please purchase only
authorized electronic editions and do not participate in or encourage electronic piracy of
copyrightable materials. Your support of the author's rights is appreciated.

To those who follow the HP Way

Contents

BILL & DAVE

Loveland Public Library
Loveland, Colo. 80537

Foreword:
Restoration

In November 2005, in Palo Alto, California, employees of one of the world's most technologically sophisticated companies regularly stopped by to watch professional restorers patiently disassemble, restore, and reassemble the wall and roof timbers of a humble and well-worn, century-old garage.

It was, without question, the most famous garage in the world: Ground Zero of the electronic age, wellspring of the greatest economic revolution of modern times. And it was the universal symbol of an even greater social revolution, entrepreneurship, that continues to sweep the world.

But if the work on the little twelve-by-eighteen-foot Addison Avenue garage was one of preservation, it was also of restoration. As the restorers carefully extracted the nails and lovingly removed the stained and water-damaged Douglas fir clapboards, they were also reaching back to the two young men who worked in this garage for a few months in 1939.

"We took the whole thing apart and are rebuilding it using the original frame and original 52 boards," archivist Anna Mancini told the *Seattle Times*. "We want to do it right. We want to do everything right."

In that garage, Bill Hewlett and Dave Packard founded what would become one of the world's most famous and influential corporations. Innovative, enlightened, adaptive, and fair, Hewlett-Packard under Bill and Dave overshadowed every company of its time, even those much better known and many times larger. The HP of those years still haunts the business world today, as the gold standard few enterprises can ever hope to approach.

But the company haunted most by the old HP is the new HP. In the years since Hewlett and Packard stepped down from direct leadership of the company, and especially since Packard's death in 1996, HP has been led by a succession of CEOs—some competent, others less so—none of them able to re-create the magic of Hewlett-Packard under its two founders. Few were able even to maintain the fabled company philosophy, the "HP Way," as more than a genuflection to the company's prelapsarian glory.

Loveland Public Library
Loveland, Colo.

This has led many observers, from management specialists to academics to even a new generation of HP managers, to question whether the principles embodied in the HP Way are, in fact, anachronistic. That they were a brilliant set of precepts for a business world long gone, a culture long since evolved, and for a company that was much smaller, more integrated, and far nimbler than the 150,000-employee, $90 billion behemoth it would become.

The nadir came in 1999 with the hiring as HP chief executive officer (and later chairman) Carly Fiorina, formerly a senior executive at Lucent Labs. Fiorina, an archetype of the superstar CEO who characterized the dot-com boom of the late 1990s, arrived at faltering Hewlett-Packard prepared to remake it into her vision of a modern company. She saw the HP Way not as a vital tool for turning the firm around, but rather as the biggest obstacle to doing so.

Thus, even as she aggrandized the symbols of the old HP—most notably the garage itself, which became the leitmotif for a corporate branding campaign—Fiorina was actively dismantling almost every institutional legacy of her two now legendary predecessors. The company built on trust, where decision-making was pushed down through the organization, and that was famously conservative about hiring, firing, and entering new markets, suddenly became a top-down, faceless (except for the CEO) corporation chasing after one Big Plan after another, all while jettisoning legions of laid-off employees. Even the name Hewlett-Packard largely disappeared from company signage and collateral, replaced by the simpler and supposedly hipper "HP."

Ironically, it was Fiorina who made the purchase of the Addison Avenue garage a priority after it had been held in private hands for a century. Then she was gone, driven out by the same board of directors that had hired her.

Thus the garage restoration, intended as a launchpad into an uncertain future, became, for HP employees, a portal to the past—to finding their way home to the Hewlett-Packard that for veterans was the lost glory of their early careers, and to newcomers was the place of myth where they had arrived too late to ever know. Behind those wide doors was the source of it all—two young men who had not only founded an empire, but along the way had rethought every traditional business practice.

Now those practices, or at least their degraded descendents, needed to be rethought again. And the question, for everyone from new CEO Mark Hurd to the oldest HPer to the most recent entry-level hire, was: Could only Bill and Dave build a Hewlett-Packard? Or could there be found, within the choices they made in their careers and within the precepts of the HP Way, a road map out of the company's current predicament? Most of all, was it still possible to build a company like the Hewlett-Packard of the era of mainframe computers, calculators, and oscilloscopes in the age of laptops, WiFi, and the World Wide Web?

If these questions obsessed HPers, they did no less the rest of the technology world. In the years since Bill and Dave, it had become increasingly apparent that, while many great companies had risen and fallen in the digital world, none since HP had ever become emblematic of enlightened management, and no David Packard had ever again emerged as the acknowledged spokesperson for the industry and the role model for its leaders. Intel and Microsoft had become more valuable than Hewlett-Packard, but no one ever called them trendsetters in enlightened management. Apple was certainly more innovative, but few young entrepreneurs wanted to be Steve Jobs. And Google attracted as much customer loyalty, but nobody was betting on the company, or its employees, still being around after more than a half century.

No, the Hewlett-Packard of Bill and Dave increasingly seemed sui generis. And that was the tragedy of it all. At least in high tech, but perhaps in all of American industry (and, by extension, the world economy), there was no longer that one great company whose combination of success, longevity, and integrity stood in permanent rebuke to every other organization that instead chose quick returns, or cut ethical corners, or mistreated or exploited its employees. In the early years of the twenty-first century, there was no company to which everyone turned and said, "Why can't we be like *them*?"

For fifty years, Hewlett-Packard was that institution. In retrospect, even the companies that tried to emulate HP—Tandem, Cisco, Silicon Graphics, Dell, Sun, Google, even the early Apple—seemed to take on an added glow from its penumbra. But most of those firms are now either gone or grown rigid with age and success. Thus, not only is the original gone, but even the pale imitations.

What makes this doubly tragic is that now, when technology is a global industry; when virtual organizations, telecommuting, and the rise of armies of contract employees are forcing a radical rethinking of the very idea of what it means to "work" and to be an "employee"; and when employers are desperately seeking ways to retain and motivate a gypsy-like workforce, what may be the best technique ever found for solving these problems has been abandoned—and the two best practitioners of the art are gone. What if Hewlett and Packard were not only the best business theorists of all time, but also the greatest visionaries?

Reclaiming Bill and Dave

Finding the answers to those questions is not only the task of those who restored the garage—and the thousands of HP employees they represent—but also the goal of this book.

This is not a history of the Hewlett-Packard Company—though the story of HP is necessarily connected with this narrative. The events of the last decade of the HP story will only be summarized at the end, and only to show what happened after the founders' departure.

Nor will this be strictly a book of business theory. There are numerous management books out there, some of them classics, that were derived in all or part from studying the HP culture, notably *Theory Z, In Search of Excellence, Built to Last*, and Packard's own *The HP Way*.

Nor will it be a definitive biography of William Hewlett or David Packard. I will give only brief attention to much of the two men's personal lives, and to their childhoods. Those stories can be found in numerous articles, archival materials, and, no doubt in the years to come, other books. Neither will it be a hagiography of the pair. For all of their success, Bill and Dave were human beings—contrary to myth, they didn't even always get along. Like everyone else, they sometimes made bad, stupid, or selfish decisions in both their professional and personal lives. They were also men of their time, exhibiting prejudices and moral blind spots that disappoint us today, even as we ignore our own. And if the descendents of both men were willing to open their hearts and their family files to me in preparing this book, it only came with the understanding that this text was mine, and mine alone.

Having told you what this book is not, I'll now tell you what it is: *Bill & Dave* is that rarer species of book that might be called a "business biography." That is, it deals not just with both men, but their relationship to each other (one of the most enduring friendships in business history) and, most of all, how they met each challenge in their careers—and the creative solutions they found to meet those challenges. For that reason, this book begins on the day the two young college students met on a football field at Stanford University, and, an extended postscript aside, ends six decades later in the Stanford Chapel a few yards away as they made their last good-bye.

I have chosen to write this book as a business biography precisely because of the desperate need the business world has right now for an archetype of enlightened management, enduring quality, and perpetual innovation. It is not enough to simply tell the story of Hewlett, Packard, and their company, listing the key organizational and product milestones and their dates. What is needed are the "why?" and the "how?" Why did this crisis appear? Why did Bill and Dave see this matter differently—and usually earlier—than all of their peers in industry? How did they solve it (or, on occasion, fail to)? Why did they take a different course than anyone before them? How did they implement it? And how well did it work?

Some of the problems that Bill and Dave faced—dealing with GIs returning from a world war, integrating the first women into the workplace, convincing customers of the value of electronics—will likely never again be faced by modern executives. Others—trusting your employees to make the right decisions, short-term profits versus long-term market share, employee loyalty versus the bottom line—will never go away. What is crucial, then, is not focusing upon those things Bill and Dave finally did, but how they came to those decisions. And that in turn, as this book will show, ultimately comes down to character.

Over and over again, Hewlett and Packard faced business decisions that were, in the end, character choices. Because they were men of character, Bill and Dave almost always made great business choices. It was their ultimate fallback position—"What is the right thing to do?"—in the face of ambiguous data and conflicting pressures from investors, employees, and customers. And, in the end, their greatest business decision of all may have been to codify (and yet leave brilliantly imprecise) that character into the HP Way.

Thus, you might think of *Bill & Dave*, at its heart, as a character study of two men—as told by the men and women who worked for them, and by the legacy they left behind. The very notion of a "character study," with its whiff of Victorian moral precepts, is out of vogue these days—which may in fact be the real source of our current difficulties. But Hewlett and Packard *did* believe in character: it shows in how they structured their business philosophy, in the men and women they hired to work for them, and most of all in the power they entrusted to even the lowliest HP employee. And whatever philosophical argument one can muster against this anachronistic approach, the simple and indisputable truth is that it worked brilliantly for Bill and Dave.

This book will have served its purpose if it becomes not just another business history gathering dust on the shelves of corporate libraries and of ex-employees, but a reference text that businesspeople, from young entrepreneurs to corporate senior executives, revisit regularly at key turning points in their careers. That, when faced with some great career challenge, they ask themselves, *What would Bill and Dave do?* and then open these pages to find a comparable event and its resolution. Sometimes the lesson will be a negative one—that is, don't do what Hewlett and Packard did. But far more often the choices Bill and Dave made (or better yet, the path they took to make those choices) will be as applicable today as they were twenty, fifty, even seventy years ago.

For an author, this presents an interesting challenge. On the one hand, you want to present these lessons to the reader (and just as important, the rereader) in a cogent and easy-to-find way. At the same time, this is not a text-book, and I have no interest in creating what would be little more than a fleshed-out outline, or defacing the text with boldfaced axioms or italicized aphorisms. I'm a writer, and the career of Hewlett and Packard is a terrific story, one that deserves to be told in narrative form.

So, how to reconcile the two competing demands? My choice is to indicate the key lessons and decisions of Hewlett's and Packard's career by using an as-terisk (*) placed after the crucial sentence. That way, the reader can race through the text without tripping over font changes or other practices used to designate some key point as "good medicine." Then, for the rereader skim-ming back through the text for some useful advice, I have compiled all of these asterisked messages, with their proper page numbers, into a single ap-pendix at the back of the book. This rereader can then either check the simple messages in this appendix, or go back to the right page in the text to study the larger context.

On another structural question—that of the order in which to present Hewlett's and Packard's learning curve—I have been given a lucky break. As noted earlier, I've chosen to start and finish the main narrative of this book with the beginning and end of Bill and Dave's friendship. Fortunately, their paths from entrepreneurs to start-up executives to small businessmen to cor-porate executives to public corporation CEOs to global business titans to statesmen and philanthropists is exactly the dream career trajectory of every ambitious modern businessperson. This shouldn't be surprising, as Hewlett and Packard were largely the template for this career arc.

Better yet, the two men passed through most of these milestones sequentially—unlike most celebrated careers, there are no great backward loops in Bill's and Dave's adult lives.

Best of all, at least for a writer, is that the big steps in the two men's careers together—and thus of the company they built—rather neatly correspond with the changes of the decades. Hence the simple organization of the chap-ters in this book.

In the course of my career as a journalist, I have known most of the men and women who built the great enterprises (and the even greater fortunes) of the electronics revolution. As a young college student, I was lucky to be at HP when an aged Fred Terman, the godfather of Silicon Valley, arrived for his last board of directors meeting. I first met Bill Hewlett and Dave Packard, and worked for them, when they were at the very zenith of their careers. Twenty years later, well into a career as a journalist, I again spent time with an aged Packard in his last days at the company.

Among all of the powerful men and women I've met, especially those in the first flush of fame and success, nearly all believed they could easily follow the path of Hewlett and Packard. Some even thought they could do it more quickly, or achieve even greater heights of glory—all while still being admired as enlightened leaders and paragons of high character.

And yet, in all of the years since, none have done it. As even these powerful men and women have come to admit, Bill and Dave stand alone. And that makes their story something of a miracle—and one from which we can never stop learning.

This is that story.

Lakewood Public Library
Lakewood, Ohio 44107

Loveland Public Library
Loveland, Colo. 80537

Chapter One:
Friendship

The most momentous first meeting in modern business history took place in the unlikely, but strangely appropriate, setting of a bench beside a football field between two young men in pads and helmets.

It was autumn 1930, and the occasion was the annual tryouts for the Stanford University football team. As always on the San Francisco peninsula, it would have been hot and dry, the grass on the field barely green while that on the surrounding fields was sunburned a pale gold. The air would have smelled of eucalyptus from the nearby groves of gum trees, and manure from the endless miles of orchards beyond. The sandstone walls and red tile roofs of the nearby quad, with its arched entrance and Romanesque chapel beyond, would have throbbed slightly in the heat. Train whistles, from the Palo Alto/Stanford and Mayfield stations, would have marked the passage of the day.

On-field there would have been the usual sounds of young men grunting into their blocks, whistles, cheers for tackles made, shouting coaches, and, because this was still the era of the dropkick, the sound of shoe leather thumping pigskin. And, as this was the age of leather helmets without face masks and unpadded goalposts, there would also have been a lot of blood, lost teeth, and broken noses.

As with most great universities in America, fall football tryouts were already a long tradition at Stanford. By 1930, the school had been playing organized football for almost forty years, had already played in four Rose Bowls, and, just four years before, had won the national college championship.

There had already been enough football history at Stanford by this time for the first legends to begin forming around the Indians team. As a case in point, watching the freshmen try out that day was the varsity coach, a man whose name would one day be well-known to millions of American boys: Glenn S. "Pop" Warner.

What Warner saw that day likely impressed him. Before they graduated, these young men would help win two Pacific Coast championships, and set

Loveland Public Library
Loveland, Colo. 805??

the stage for not only a third, but a near miss at another national championship. Tryouts are always tough, but with this collection of talent, it would have been particularly competitive.

Still, in the midst of this quality, one tryout still would have definitely caught Pop Warner's eye. At six foot five in a five-ten age, David Packard, a freshman from Colorado, would have stood out anyway. But with his thick blond hair and Roman nose, he was also extraordinarily handsome—the very image of a classic campus football hero. And he was a natural athlete, destined to be a three-letter man at Stanford. Football, in fact, was Dave Packard's worst sport—he was destined to play back-up at end behind future College Hall of Famer Jim (Monk) Moscrip. Dave was far better at basketball, and in a few months, in a track meet against rival USC, he would set a school record for scoring the most points ever by a freshman.

That David Packard also had a brilliant mind and was the rising star in the university's hot new electronics department only furthered the notion that for some unknown reason—perhaps to teach humility to everyone else—he had been chosen by the gods to be favored with more than his share of natural advantages. Packard himself, even at that young age, seemed to appreciate his luck and carried himself with dignity, a quiet reserve, and a sense of humor— which of course only made him seem even more impressive.

One tryout player to whom none of the coaches likely gave a second glance was a short, stocky kid with the wide face and cocky grin of a Dead End Kid and a sense of mischief to match. If heart and desire were all it took to make the team, Bill Hewlett would have been a starter, and one can picture him during the tryouts hitting and tackling with wild abandon. But it would quickly have been obvious to everyone, except perhaps Bill himself, that he wouldn't make the team. He was the kind of player coaches think of fondly even as they cross out their names.

William Redington Hewlett would one day be known as the most practical of business titans, but on this day his very act of trying out for the football team was the very embodiment of youthful foolishness. With his poor high school grades, he had only been admitted to Stanford through influence and family connections—and this was the era when Stanford was still well-known as the place where rich farmers' sons could earn "gentlemen's C's."

Underlying Bill's apparent failure as a student was a learning disability— severe dyslexia—that not only hadn't been diagnosed, but wouldn't even be named for another three decades. All that his frustrated mother and teachers knew of Bill's predicament was that he was an indifferent reader—indeed, the boy only seemed to go through the motion of looking at the words on the page because nothing seemed to register. To his credit, Bill seemed to have a real gift—even a spark of native genius—for mechanical things, especially electrical devices. His functional near-illiteracy had forced young Bill to compensate by developing an extraordinary skill at listening to other people (indeed, it was the only thing that got him through school).

But whatever the compensations, a freshman at Stanford University who could barely read should have been devoting all of his time to his classwork, not going out for the football team. Yet on that autumn afternoon, the one young man whom we know for a fact was having second thoughts about losing valuable study time to play football was the one for whom both came easy: David Packard.

Packard, in fact, despite setting school records, would eventually quit the track team, to the horror of his coach (or, as Packard diplomatically put it, the varsity track coach "was very upset with my decision").[1] In time, he would drop basketball too. In the end, he would only stick with football, because, as he would admit many years later, "the peer pressure was so strong."[2] Still, he would write in his memoir, *The HP Way*, the experience of being on the Stanford varsity team "reinforced my ideas on how to build a winning team."[3]

But that was four years into the future. This was freshman tryouts, and each young man sitting on the bench, big or small, talented or maladroit, still had to prove himself.

As always on such occasions, the young men fidgeted in their pads, tried to look cool and experienced, and discreetly sized up one another. And in those moments, Bill Hewlett and Dave Packard saw each other, and heard each other's names called out, for the first time. Hewlett, for his part, must have looked upon the giant Packard and sunk into a silent despair at his chances at making the team. Packard, one might imagine, would have looked upon Hewlett, if he noticed him at all, as just another cocky little guy too small to play at this level; one less competitor to worry about.

And yet it was the quiet giant who best remembered meeting the pugnacious fireplug that day. Hewlett, like most everybody else on the Stanford campus, might be expected to look upon Packard with a certain amount of awe and admiration. But it was Packard who saw in Hewlett a kindred spirit, and perhaps first recognized his lifelong friend.

In the end, Packard made the team; Hewlett did not. And both were disappointed.

The standard version of the Hewlett-Packard legend is that the two men became fast friends that day on the gridiron. It's a nice story, one that fits with our desire for the most famous friendship in American business history to have been perfectly evident to the two protagonists from the very first, as well as with the cliché that "opposite personalities attract."

But in partnerships, as in marriage, opposites attract only if they have shared interests. And at this point in their young lives, Bill and Dave were headed on different trajectories. Though they would run into one another often over the next three years, occasionally finding themselves in the same classes, it wouldn't be until their senior year that the two men would make their lifelong bond. Thus for most of their undergraduate years, the famous friendship of Bill Hewlett and David Packard might best be described as a casual acquaintance.

Such was the beginning of a sixty-year friendship that would become so complete that, in the words of another tech pioneer, antenna maker John V. Granger, "You could ask either of them a question on any matter, any important matter, and you'd be sure that the answer you got reflected the feeling of the other one as well. I mean, they understood one another perfectly. It was really wonderful."[4] It is easy to imagine that it was always that way. But the reality is that Hewlett and Packard had come from vastly different worlds, their years at Stanford were conducted on very different terms, and even their interests, though close, did not yet coincide.

Pueblo Days

Though both Hewlett and Packard became synonymous with Northern California, from the hallways of HP and Stanford University in Palo Alto, to the great ranch they co-owned in the mountains south of the Santa Clara (that is, "Silicon") Valley, to the Packards' Monterey Aquarium, only Hewlett was a native Californian.

David Packard was born in 1912 in Pueblo, Colorado, which in those days was still very much a frontier town. As Packard would recall, "Pueblo was tough and violent, with immigrant workers, a few gangsters, and lots of brothels and saloons. Street fights and shootings were not uncommon."[5]

But that harsh world rarely touched young Dave Packard. His family belonged to what might be described as the local aristocracy. His father was a lawyer and his mother a high school teacher. They had met while attending Colorado College in nearby Colorado Springs. The 1902 yearbook lists Ella Lorna Graber as class vice president, a scholarship student and an honors graduate. The quote below her photograph reads: "She's beautiful and therefore to be wooed." Sperry Packard is listed as the captain of the baseball team, a three letter man, and a debater. His quote is: "He is of a very melancholy disposition." It must have been an interesting match.

The couple settled in nearby Pueblo to build as comfortable a life as possible in a Wild West town where the steel mills and foundries smelted and poured Leadville ore by day and the pianos played in the whorehouses by night.

The Packard house was located on the very north end of town (near modern Highway 50), as far from the bad neighborhoods as possible—so far, in fact, that across the street from the Packard house the prairie began, running north to the towering bulk of Pike's Peak, and east to forever. Young Dave Packard would often wander out into the prairie, sometimes with his sister Ann Louise (born in 1915), often with his buddies, many times just alone. He would look for horned toads and birds, and try to stay away from the rattlesnakes that lurked under the occasional cactus. And he would think about the bigger world out at the edge of that low horizon.

Packard's most vivid memory of his early childhood was a flood that devastated downtown Pueblo in 1921, when a swollen Salt Creek jumped it banks. His father took him down to see mud four feet deep in the shops and "a railroad boxcar stuck in the second-floor window of one of the main buildings."[6] Much of that mud ended up dumped onto the prairie across from the Packard house, which probably didn't sit well with his parents, but provided an endless source of exploration for young David.

The occasional adventures aside, it was a very quiet and genteel life for the Packard family—the front yard with his mother's well-tended lilac bushes and beds of peonies, his father with his well-paying job, and David helping his mother garden, the smartest boy in high school (and, with his mother teaching there, also one of the best behaved), and the pretty girls dreaming about the tall star athlete with the perfect grades.

It would also have been a little dull, especially for a boy with the mind and the ambition of David Packard. The fleshpots and other vices of downtown may have been out of bounds, but that didn't mean he couldn't take a few risks, especially with an older kid living across the street to egg him on.

Lloyd Penrose appears to have been Dave Packard's first real friend, and his life seems as benighted as Packard's was charmed. The Penroses lived across the alley from the Packards, and because both his mother and sister had tuberculosis, Lloyd worked in the evening at the carnival to help support his family. But during whatever little free time he had, he hung out with David—and, as both were mechanically minded, they usually spent their time building models or plotting elaborate schemes.

Most of these schemes, as they often do for boys that age, involve blowing things up. And Pueblo was a perfect place to get both the necessary chemicals, and even, sometimes, the explosives themselves. David, Lloyd, and other boys in the neighborhood even made their own gunpowder, though with ammonium nitrate (from fertilizer) rather than the usual sodium nitrate, which made it even more powerful. They also made ammonium iodide, the stuff of percussion caps, which they could explode with a mere touch. Best of all, at least in their minds, was the discovery in a rubbish heap that the local sand mill regularly left behind a cup or two of residue in the five-gallon barrels they used to store blasting powder. The occasional tossed-away barrel supplied enough explosive for endless carnage.

Stories about boys and explosives almost always end badly, and this one is no different. During one pyrotechnic experiment Packard filled some copper tubing with explosive powder and then tried to crimp one end by pounding it flat with a hammer. Not surprisingly, the homemade pipe bomb exploded, sparing David's eyes, but nearly blowing off his left hand. Lloyd Penrose, who had been party to the scheme, wrapped Packard's gory hand with a strip of cloth (probably from his undershirt) and raced him to the nearest town physician, a Dr. Wise.[7]

It is a telling indictment about life in a frontier town that Dr. Wise proved to be an inept surgeon and botched the restitching of David's hand, leaving him with, in Packard's own words, "a distorted left thumb" for the rest of his life.[8]

As will be seen in the career of Bill and Dave's mentor, Fred Terman, whose own devastating incapacitation was taking place at this same moment a thousand miles way, this sudden, shocking event in young David Packard's life served to divert him from his current path into a new direction he would follow for the rest of his life. In nearly blowing himself up, Dave not only changed his own life, but the world.

His hand incapacitated, his parents furious, and his newfound hobby taboo forever, Dave now had to find something new to fill his time—preferably something both mechanically challenging and safely indoors.

He found it in the miracle of the age: amateur radio.

From this great distance in time, it is almost impossible to imagine the impact of radio not only upon American culture, but on American boys. It was the personal computer, video games, and the Internet rolled into one. Best of all, the technology itself was comparatively simple—you didn't have to be the 1925 equivalent of a Steve Wozniak dreaming in assembly code and bits and bytes to build a state-of-the art radio. All it took was a tuned crystal, a few parts for the tuner and the antenna, and another new miracle—the vacuum tube—along with some rudimentary skill at soldering, and you were on your way.

Thousands of boys throughout the United States took the challenge, not least of whom Dave Packard. And the experience proved to be an epiphany: "I recall my first vacuum tube. I connected this tube with a variable condenser, a coil, a good lead, an A battery, a B battery, and a set of headphones on our dining room table. There was great excitement as my family and I took turns listening to WHO in Des Moines, Iowa, an astonishing six hundred miles from Pueblo!"[9] It was Packard's first real glimpse of a world beyond the mountains and the prairie.

The Lost Boy

If David Packard's childhood is notable for its consistency, a straight path marred by only a few sharp turns, Bill Hewlett's early years are a heartbreaking whipsaw of the most shattering kind—of paradise offered, then snatched away.

And thus, though the Packard myth looms larger among the pair, it is the Hewlett story that is the more inspiring, and from which we mere mortals can learn much more. Dave Packard's life can sometimes seem too easy: like George Washington, to whom he came to bear an uncanny resemblance thanks to his great height, long nose, and imposing forehead, he is the golden giant for whom everything he touches also turns to gold. He is a man you can admire, even revere, but so favored by nature as to be all but impossible to emulate.

Bill Hewlett, on the other hand, is Everyman, a little too short, a little too thick in the waist, always trying to catch a break (and not quite believing it when it comes), and haunted by the fear, based on experience, that it all can disappear at any moment, that failure is always lurking nearby ready to pounce. It is this knowledge of the dark side of the world that makes Bill Hewlett gruff and impatient, but also deeply engaged, forever self-effacing and often astonishingly warmhearted. Packard seems born to greatness, while Hewlett had to earn his way there.

Throughout his life, Bill Hewlett was involved with others in a way the more Olympian Dave Packard could never be. No doubt Hewlett's empathy came in part from knowing what it was like to fail and to fall, and to be flung about helplessly by fate. It was that understanding that enabled him to build HP into the most humane of companies. And that is why, while it is obvious that Bill needed Dave to accomplish all that they did, upon reflection it becomes apparent that Dave needed Bill even more. If Packard is glory, Hewlett is fidelity and the combination is unbeatable.*

It didn't start out that way. Bill Hewlett's childhood was in many ways more idyllic than Packard's.

The view out the Hewlett family window on Union Street wasn't empty prairie, but the bustling, noisy metropolitan world of San Francisco.[10] A year younger than his future partner, William Redington Hewlett was born in 1913, in Ann Arbor, Michigan, where his father, a renowned physician, served on the faculty of the University of Michigan Medical School.

When Bill was three, his father accepted a new post on the faculty of Stanford University, and the family moved to San Francisco, where the medical school in those days was located.

---

* Asterisks refer to the Appendix, p. 393.

Both of Bill's parents were extraordinary people. Not only was his father an eminent figure in his field, but his mother, a formidable personality who soon made her mark in local society, may have been at least her husband's intellectual equal. She owned one of the best private libraries in San Francisco, and corresponded with the likes of Rudyard Kipling.

Because Bill Hewlett wrote little about his childhood, many of its details can only be gleaned from rare photographs and the memories of his older sister, Louise. There survives one unforgettable photo of Bill's father, Dr. Albion Walter Hewlett, taken a few years before Bill was born, that speaks volumes about the man.[11] It shows a small, compact man in a suit and waistcoat, cravat carefully knotted around a high celluloid collar, his hair parted and combed smooth across his head. Dr. Hewlett looks no more than thirty in the photograph, and he has the same tight mouth, sharp eyes, and low brow of his son. His hands are surprisingly large for such a delicate-looking man, and he holds a book—presumably a medical text—open on his crossed legs as he looks boldly at the camera with his eyebrows slightly raised. He is apparently sitting in his examination room, because there is a reproduction of Rembrandt's *The Anatomy Lesson of Dr. Nicolaes Tulp* on the wall behind his left shoulder, and a privacy screen behind his right.

All in all, it is a photograph of a serious and successful young professional looking out at the world with self-confidence—except, as betrayed by the tiniest twinkle in Dr. Hewlett's eye, the photo is also a joke. That's because, atop the sideboard on which Dr. Hewlett's elbow rests, there is a full human skull, with a tobacco pipe clenched in its teeth. Once you notice the skull, you realize the whole photograph is a put-on.

An admired physician, a professor at a great university, and a man who could laugh at his own pretensions: the photograph is a reminder that Bill wasn't the only great Hewlett.

The 1920s were good to San Francisco. Rebuilt after the 1906 earthquake and fire, the city was shiny and new. The port was booming and light and medium manufacturing was springing up all around the Bay Area. San Francisco seemed to enjoy the best of the twenties—the San Francisco Seals baseball team dominated the Pacific Coast League, flappers in their short skirts mixed easily with elegant society ladies in their hats, veils, and gloves on Market Street, money and jobs were everywhere, and optimism and a sense of an exciting future filled the air. And it had escaped most of its worst past excesses— with the old Barbary Coast destroyed by the quake, the Fatty Arbuckle episode leading to a general crackdown on vice, and a casual attitude about Prohibition that made San Francisco the "wettest" city on the Pacific coast, the city was now about as clean and crime-free as it would ever be.[12]

In other words, it was a great time to be a boy in San Francisco. Bill's mother took him to cultural events at the city center or across the bay at UC Berkeley, his father took him along to his office or down the peninsula to the main Stanford campus, and with his buddies Bill could hike the forests and mountains of the nearby Pacific Coast Range, buy cherry bombs in Chinatown, jump rooftops, or explore the ruins of the 1915 Panama-Pacific International Exposition. On school days, Bill rode the streetcar to Potter private elementary school, and in the summer the Hewlett family journeyed to the Sierra Nevada for vacation.[13]

A class picture of Bill, taken at age nine at the Potter school, shows an appealing kid right out of *Peck's Bad Boy*, his neatly combed hair now fallen over his eyes, a too-small belted jacked waiting to be torn off, and a pissed-off look on young Bill's face like he's just been told by his teacher to shut up and stand still. This is a boy who would be the star of every playground and the nightmare of every teacher.

By all accounts, young Bill was a brilliant child, an indifferent student, and something of a hellion. He was constantly getting into fights—including one memorable occasion when he came home covered with a bottle of ink. Not surprisingly then, like his future friend, young Bill too had a near brush with explosives and mortality—twice. On one occasion, he nearly killed himself with shrapnel after setting off a homemade grenade constructed from a brass doorknob stuffed with black powder. As a teenager traveling in Europe, Bill managed to buy an old Luger pistol from an Austrian hotel manager. He brought it home and set up a shooting range for himself and his friends in the basement. Luckily, no one was wounded by ricochets, though they did manage to shoot a hole in the furnace—which they quickly patched before Bill's mother found out.

In all, it would have been the perfect boyhood, complete with a few scars and scary stories to tell the grandchildren—and then it all came apart in the worst way imaginable.

There is a second photograph, taken in 1926 just four years after the first. And though it is clearly of Bill Hewlett, now thirteen, it is also of a very different boy, one who carries a terrible burden. His face is hard and wary, the look in his eyes fearful and hurt, and his body inert, seemingly drained of all of the energy of youth.

In late November 1925, Albion Walter Hewlett, author, head of the Stanford University department of medicine, and father to a brokenhearted twelve-year-old boy, died of a brain tumor. He was fifty years old. The news was carried around the world in the medical community to an entire generation of doctors who had been trained on his six-volume *Monographic Medicine* and his English translation of *The Principles of Clinical Pathology*. The Stanford Academic Council passed a memorial resolution honoring Dr. Hewlett for his devotion to his profession, his unassuming and kindly manner, and "his studious, fruitful and unselfish life"—and, in a glimpse of his final months, expressed admiration for "his equanimity when faced suddenly by tragic events."[14]

His death had been long, lingering, and awful, and Bill had been forced to watch as the man he admired most in the world, a figure of wisdom, authority, and humor, slowly lost his mind and then his life.

Nothing would ever again be the same for Bill Hewlett. Decades later he would confide to Herant Katchadourian, Stanford's professor emeritus of human biology, that had his life gone differently, he might have become a physician like his father.[15]

Now that door was closed. Young Bill Hewlett would have to find a new direction for his life. But before that, he would have to find himself.

Campus Rat

There is a third, crucial figure in this story whose life was now changing direction to converge with those of Bill and Dave. He was a generation older than the two boys, but distinctly similar to them in personality, and he would serve as mentor and father figure to Bill and Dave for a half century.

As the news of Dr. Hewlett's untimely death spread around the main Stanford campus, this young man, Fred Terman, the twenty-five-year-old son of another famous Stanford professor, was lying in bed, encased in sandbags to keep his chest rigid, struggling to survive a devastating case of tuberculosis.

At that moment, Fredrick Emmons Terman was the least well-known Terman on the Stanford campus. His father was the legendary Lewis M. Terman, world-renowned for his studies in human intelligence and gifted children, and, most of all, as the inventor of the IQ test.[16]

The Terman family had moved to Southern California from the Midwest in 1905, where the senior Terman had taken a high school principal job in a warm, dry climate to help recover from his own near-fatal case of TB. In 1910, he accepted a professorship at the School of Education at Stanford University—the university at the time was less than twenty years old, with just 1,442 undergraduates—and the family moved north.[17]

Young Fred, just ten, found his lifelong home at Stanford and in the surrounding hills. He was a serious young man, slightly built, with horn-rimmed glasses and an indifference to details like his personal appearance that would characterize him for the rest of his life. At Palo Alto High School, Fred competed on the debate team, served as student body vice president, ran track well, played rugby adequately, picked mistletoe in the hills to sell to Stanford faculty wives wary of poison oak, and, most importantly, spent much of his spare time hanging around a local business called Federal Telegraph.

By what turned out to be a history-making coincidence, the Bay Area, and especially Palo Alto, had already become a hotbed of early radio. In 1909, a year before the Termans' arrival, a recent Stanford graduate, Cy Elwell, had managed to broadcast a "wobbly" version of "The Blue Danube" from Palo Alto five miles to receivers in Los Altos and Mountain View.[18] By 1911, thanks to a loan from Stanford president David Starr Jordan, Elwell had founded Poulsen Wireless Telephone and Telegraph Company in Palo Alto and had demonstrated a fifty-mile transmission in California's Central Valley between Sacramento and Stockton. A few months after that, the company, now renamed Federal Telegraph, erected three hundred masts and successfully completed a 2,100-mile transmission to Honolulu. Within a year, it was a full-time service.[19]

Elwell wasn't alone. In downtown San Jose, another Stanford grad, Charles David "Doc" Herrold, inaugurated "San Jose Calling"—a potpourri of recorded music, voice-overs by Herrold's wife (the first disk jockey), and commercials—on his new radio station, FN (today KCBS). After many years of dispute, it is generally recognized today as the first commercial radio broadcast in America.[20]

That same year, Federal Telegraph saw the arrival of one of the greatest, and wildest, inventors of the twentieth century. Lee de Forest was one of those geniuses who seems to exist tangentially to the rest of humanity. Five years before, he had invented the first vacuum tube, the three-electrode audion, the first of more than three hundred patents in his career.[21]

The prototype of the scientist-entrepreneur who would dominate American industry in the years to come, de Forest decided to capitalize on his invention by creating a company in New York to manufacture and market it. It wasn't long before the firm went broke, largely through the financial shenanigans of his fellow company officers. Naive about the ways of business, de Forest was left holding the bag—and ended up broke himself (setting yet another precedent in high tech).

Desperate for work, de Forest packed up his mother and the two headed out to the West Coast, where, his reputation preceding him, he was quickly offered the job of research director at Federal Telegraph by his old acquaintance Cy Elwell. It seemed a perfect arrangement for both parties, and de Forest seemed relieved to be away at last from the hustle and bustle of East Coast business.

But the past was already pursuing, and in March 1912 federal marshals stormed into Federal Telegraph and arrested de Forest for stock fraud related to his old New York firm. Only a hastily called meeting of Federal's board of directors and a quick vote to pay the $10,000 bail kept the company's chief scientist out of jail.

With the prospect of a trial and a long prison term hanging over him, de Forest responded in his characteristic way by burying himself in his work, and, knowing that this might be his last research project, set a feverish pace. He had a notion that if he and his two assistants fiddled with his triode audion, rewiring it in different ways, they might find a way to speed up the transmission of telegraph messages.

Instead, by rearranging the location of the three electrodes, de Forest and his team discovered something infinitely more important. Noticing that one particular configuration seemed to intensify the signal passing through it, de Forest hooked that tube up to a telephone transmitter, put on his headphones, and then dangled his "trusty Ingersoll" pocket watch in front of the transmitter.

He nearly blew out his eardrums. When he recovered from the shock, he realized that he had invented the electronic amplifier. It was the signal (literally) invention of the age. Before long, de Forest was off again to settle the case, license his new invention to the phone company, and shout a description of the amplifier into the ear of Thomas Edison, whose incandescent light bulb had been the grandfather of the audio vacuum tube.[22]

For a teenaged Fred Terman—as for all the other young men in the area hooked on amateur radio—the twin seventy-five-foot towers rising over Federal Telegraph were an irresistible magnet. Fred had built his first crystal set radio receiver at thirteen, and within a year was delving ever deeper into radio theory. While attending Palo Alto High School, when he wasn't running track, he hung out with his buddies at Federal, soaking up all of the knowledge he could from the employees (he may even have been there the day Lee de Forest was led off in handcuffs). As an undergraduate at Stanford, he spent a summer working at Federal, and joined a fraternity (Theta Xi) filled with fellow ham radio buffs, many of them also from Palo Alto.[23] He had even started his own amateur radio station, teaming with two other boys, one the son of a Stanford chemistry professor, the other the son of Herbert Hoover.[24] Terman recalled many years later, "I get a big kick to think back to the time when all three of us were neighbors and upon pushing the key of one of our imposing contraptions, would holler out the window to see if it had been received on the other side of the street."[25]

In retrospect, ham radio was the first Silicon Valley boom, and, because the cost of entry was so low and the technology so simple, it was more open to newcomers and technology amateurs than any that followed up until the dot-com boom almost a century later. And, like the latter, ham radio also showed many of the characteristics of a bubble. In the beginning, it was filled with maverick characters, overnight sensations, quick fortunes, and starry-eyed young players. Fred Terman would recall the happy days of running around the residential streets of Palo Alto, looking for the telltale antenna towers in backyards and knocking on the front door, knowing that a kindred spirit lived inside.

But the boom was over almost as soon as it began. Lee de Forest returned from New York not only with a tentative deal with Bell Telephone, but a chorus girl as his new bride. He was now the first superstar of the electronics age, and, not surprisingly given his personality, it quickly went to his head. Within months, he would leave Federal Telegraph and the Bay Area in pursuit of a new job in the movie industry. He would only return once in the next few years, in 1915, to join Doc Herrold in demonstrating wireless radio at San Francisco's Panama-Pacific International Exposition. He would spend the rest of his days living the Hollywood life (he later married a movie actress), inventing new products (though none as important as the triode amplifier), and writing editorials decrying the debasement of his invention (so he claimed): radio.

Federal Telegraph was also destined for bumpy ride. In the decade to come it would enjoy considerable success, including the first intercontinental radio transmission in 1919, between Annapolis, Maryland, and Bordeaux, France. And that success was not just technological: after the sinking of the *Titanic*, the Radio Law of 1913 mandated that all passenger ships install wireless radios and hire operators—a huge financial boon to the company.

But as would be the case with generations of technology companies to come, that huge success quickly drew competitors, and not just from outside the company. As early as 1910, Federal began to lose top talent: in that year, two company engineers, Peter Jensen and E. S. Pridham, both experts in loudspeakers, left to form what would become Magnavox. Others followed, until by 1920, Federal was bleeding personnel from every doorway. Meanwhile, new competitors were springing up everywhere, and the company began to lose its competitive edge. Over the next decade it would suffer the loss of even more personnel, see entire departments spin off to create new companies, and suffer deep financial reversals—ultimately being acquired in 1931 by Marconi, upon which the entire business moved to the East Coast.

Still, by then, Federal Telegraph had left its mark on Stanford and the world. An entire generation, from an adult Fred Terman, to the college-aged Dave Packard and Bill Hewlett, to William Shockley, still just a teenager growing up in Palo Alto, had been swept up by amateur radio and the magical technology that powered it.

But none of that future was obvious to Fred Terman in 1920 when he showed up to work at Federal, his newly printed Stanford diploma (and Phi Beta Kappa key) in hand. He was just twenty years old, having graduated from high school a semester early, enrolled at Stanford, and finished his bachelor's in just over three years. Stanford in those days was a notorious party school, where students, in the words of new president Ray Lyman Wilbur, were "content to do the minimum amount of work and the maximum amount of play."[26] A serious student like Fred Terman was able to roll through the curriculum.

But even as Fred raced through his undergraduate years, Stanford was changing around him. Thanks to his early high school graduation and university admission, he had been on the Stanford campus to see the graduation of the class of 1917, the "War Class," many of the men already in their army uniforms. The genteel orchard era of the Santa Clara Valley was coming to an end, and a new seriousness, driven by Wilbur's efforts, began to change the character of Stanford University.[27] Fred Terman would prove to be its greatest missionary.

Interestingly, the degree Terman carried that day to Federal Telegraph was in chemical engineering. That's because what little electrical engineering Stanford offered was only available in the graduate program. Moreover, one of Terman's friends and fellow ham radio nut, Jack Franklin, was the son of the most famous chemistry professor at the university. Fred had started out at Stanford in mechanical engineering, but apparently found it boring and moved on to something more challenging.

Despite that diversion (and an ominous temporary medical leave from school in his junior year—likely his first bout with tuberculosis) Fred knew what he wanted to do with his life: work as a scientist at Federal Telegraph. And the first step toward that goal was to enroll in the graduate program in electrical engineering at Stanford.

What came next was classic Fred Terman. He may not have wanted to become an academic, but nobody ever loved academia more. Over the course of six quarters, he carried twice the normal course load, impressing every professor in the department—especially the department head, Harris J. Ryan, Cy Elwell's old professor and mentor—and earned himself not only an engineering certificate, but somehow also managed to hike the surrounding hills, develop a much-admired peak-voltage-reading instrument, and find a girlfriend.

Fred Terman in 1920 had been one of the best students at Stanford; Fred Terman the engineer in 1922 was one of the top graduate school candidates in America. But despite the entreaties of both his famous father and Professor Ryan, he wavered. A PhD in electrical engineering conferred little added advantage in the 1920s; rather, the great figures in the field—like Terman's hero Cy Elwell—were all certified engineers who'd gone on to make their mark in the commercial world.

But in the end, probably because he loved going to class so much, and because he rationalized that he was still young enough that he wouldn't lose any time, Fred agreed with his father and Ryan. Within a week after his graduation and certification, he had sent off an application to Boston Tech (soon to be renamed MIT)—he had already taken every EE course available at Stanford. Besides, as Fred would later recall, in those days "a serious young engineer had to go back east to put spit and polish on his education."[28]

It proved to be an inspired choice, not just because MIT had a robust and rigorous electrical engineering program, but because that program also featured some of the most influential figures in that field in the twentieth century. One was Arthur Kennelly, who, before his title was taken by Fred himself, was the most influential electronics educator on the planet. Kennelly was the author or coauthor of a score of books and hundreds of technical papers. He was also the discoverer of the earth's ionosphere. Another of Terman's professors would be Norbert Wiener, the genius of nonlinear systems and one of the greatest mathematicians who ever lived. Terman earned honors awards from both men.[29]

The third important faculty member became Terman's research adviser. This was Vannevar Bush, the grand chancellor of U.S. electronics in the midcentury. In many ways, Bush, ten years senior to Terman, was like an older twin. He too had been a ham radio buff as a teenager, a college track star, an electronics whiz, and a legendary teacher. In time he would become the dean of engineering at MIT, just as Terman would carry the same title at Stanford. But in other ways, the two men were utterly different—to the point that Bush could seem like Terman's mirror image. Whereas Terman was a private person who preferred to work behind the scenes, was indifferent to his dress to the point of being an eccentric, and preferred to promote the successes of others over his own, Bush was smooth, always elegantly dressed, and loved the excitement of politics, be it in Cambridge or Washington, D.C. [30]

Before his career was over, Vannevar Bush would become one of the founding fathers of the modern computer, president of the Carnegie Institution, director of Roosevelt's Office of Scientific Research and Development, the deviser of the National Science Foundation, and, thanks to his theories on what would become hypertext, one of the acknowledged godfathers of the Internet.[31]

Over the years, the two men, initially close, would come to thoroughly dislike each other—as two successful individuals with opposite personalities often do. But at this point in his career, there was probably no one Fred Terman could have benefited more from knowing. Like Terman, Bush was brilliant and had almost superhuman work habits. But unlike Terman, Bush, thanks to a ten-year head start, was already thinking big, looking beyond the walls of MIT to how electronics could revolutionize society. It would prove to be a vital lesson to the man who would build Silicon Valley.*

Fred Terman, now one of the rare individuals on the planet with a PhD in electrical engineering (for a man whose legacy would be microelectronics, it is interesting to note that his dissertation was on the long-range transmission of massive amounts of electric power). He returned to Stanford late in the summer of 1924 fully prepared to finally start his professional career in industry, most likely at Federal Telegraph.

Had he done so, the story of the electronics revolution might have been much different. We can get a glimpse of what Terman's alternate career might have been by looking at the life of his near-contemporary, Charlie Litton. Like the ten-years-younger Bill Hewlett, Charlie was a San Francisco boy, a ham radio buff, and a Stanford student. But, unlike the other characters in this story so far, Litton was also an artist. And his medium was glass.

As a teenager, frustrated with the high cost of vacuum tubes, Charlie took up glassblowing to create his own. By the time he finished high school, he was not only a master at creating vacuum tubes, but increasingly an expert at the interfacing between glass and metal (had he been born thirty years later, he might well have been a founder of the semiconductor industry). By the time he graduated from Stanford in 1924, just as Fred Terman was coming home to California, Charlie Litton may have been the best custom tube maker anywhere.

Such was his reputation that even at age nineteen Litton had enough pending orders for his tubes that he decided to go into business for himself. Four years later, Federal Telegraph hired him to lead the company's assault on giant RCA for leadership in the tube business.

Had Federal been better managed in those latter days, it might well have beaten RCA. But as it was, Litton's tubes were so remarkable—innovative, of the highest quality, and brilliantly conceived to circumvent RCA's many patents, that Federal managed to land the plum contract of the era—with the newly created International Telephone and Telegraph.

Still, it was too little, too late to save the old Federal Telegraph, and by the early thirties the company was searching for a buyer. When it finally found one and moved east, Charlie Litton decided to stay in California. As before, he set up his own company, this time up the road in Redwood City. Called Litton Engineering Laboratories, he went right back to the work he'd always done. He even designed and built his own manufacturing equipment, such as a glass lathe that was so much better than anything else available that he sold the first few to his own giant competitors, RCA and Westinghouse.

It was a different world now. The second electronics era, the age of instruments, was now in full boom—and with the arrival of the Second World War, Charlie's vacuum tubes would be in desperate demand by the U.S. government. As he would recall later, "I woke up one day, and out of the clear blue sky I suddenly found myself the sole owner of a million-and-a-half-dollar concern."

Twenty years later, Litton Industries would be a billion-dollar company, and Charlie Litton, master glassblower, would be one of the richest men in the United States. David Packard, who would spend many days in Charlie's shop, would say, "Charlie Litton was one of the really brilliant engineers." But Charlie, when asked about his success, would merely shrug and say, "I was just a lucky kid."[32]

Fred Terman, who likely would have ended up at the lab bench next to Charlie Litton, might have enjoyed the same "luck," perhaps even at Litton Industries. He might not have been the artisan Charlie was, but he was a better scientist and visionary—and it is hard to believe that, despite his relative indifference to money, he would not have become a very wealthy businessman.

That is certainly the career trajectory Dr. Fred Terman, PhD, imagined for himself as he rode the train from Boston back home to Palo Alto. But even at that moment, he may have already sensed—literally in his bones—that he was about to undergo a trauma so profound that, if he survived, it would change the direction of his life forever.

It was a warm homecoming. Terman's parents, especially his father, had missed him terribly. It was to be a summer of rest, visiting friends, and surveying the business landscape to determine where to apply for work. At Stanford, Harris Ryan had already put in a request to lure Terman back onto campus as an intern, telling President Wilbur, "In my judgment, the best man available in the nation today is Fred E. Terman. If appointed, the good work that he will do should, in my judgment, be one of the outstanding achievements of his generation of Stanford faculty men."[33]

But Fred never had to make the choice between town and gown. He had already run out of time: just three weeks after his arrival, the tuberculosis returned, this time more virulent than ever. He deteriorated rapidly, his weight plummeting, his lungs erupting in severe hemorrhaging.

So severe was Fred's condition that one doctor decided it was fatal and told Professor Terman and his wife to go ahead and let their son do anything he wanted to do, so as to enjoy the last few months of his life. Luckily, the couple got a second opinion, this time from Dr. Russell V. Lee. Lee, who would go on to found the Palo Alto Medical Clinic, proposed an extreme course of treatment: Fred would have to lie in bed, his chest immobilized by sandbags, for at least nine months.[34]

The treatment, along with the continuous attentions of his devoted parents, saved Fred's life. But there were close calls. The following May, just when it seemed Fred was on the mend, his appendix burst, and once again he nearly died. Because of his state, the surgeons couldn't put him under general anesthetic, but had to perform the appendectomy only under local anesthetic. About the same time, Fred also developed an eye infection that would trouble his vision for years to come.[35]

Before it was done, the illnesses and the recovery consumed a year of Fred Terman's life. But it wasn't a wasted year. As is often the case, that extended stretch of isolation and contemplation had also been a blessing, giving him a better sense of who he was and what he wanted to do. He used the time wisely—for one thing, writing a book on electrical transmission based upon his doctoral dissertation at MIT. But more important for the future, he also found himself revisiting his old love of radio.

He began by studying the current state of the art in radio technology, especially the innovative work on circuitry being done by his old MIT professors. He read the core text in the field, John Harold Morecroft's *Principles of Radio Communications*, cover to cover. Then, as his health improved, Fred tried building a radio of his own. To his astonishment, he found that the two distinct worlds of interest in his career had begun to converge:

> Then I discovered that this circuit theory that I learned from Kennelly, telephone things and so on, could be tied with what I knew about vacuum tubes. Bush had taught me circuit theory, too, and all this tied together. I could put the vacuum tube circuits and the non-vacuum tube circuit theory that I had learned there at MIT all together for a nice understanding of amplifiers and tuned amplifiers, and things like that. I worked this out for fun, just recreational reading, and worked out some equations for how much amplification you could get from vacuum tubes.[36]

At the point of this synthesis was modern electronics, and Fred, ironically thanks to being sidelined from the scientific world for twelve months, was one of the very first people to see it. Spinning out its implications would consume the rest of his life.

The long illness had also taught Fred Terman something else: who his real friends were. There had been no real job offers from the commercial world while he lay there encased in sandbags. But the academic world hadn't forgotten him: both Stanford and MIT had kept their offers open to him until he was ready to work again. And that affected Fred deeply. His son Lewis believed that Terman's deep loyalty to Stanford began during this period, because the university had shown him that loyalty first.

That isn't to say that he didn't consider the MIT offer. After all, his mentors were there. Vannevar Bush would have taken him back in a heartbeat. and, despite their later estrangement, an aged Terman would muse, "I had been one of his handymen, and it was good to be tied to the tail of his kite, a good man. . . . I've always wondered what it would have been like if I [had]."[37]

In the end, Stanford landed Fred Terman for the same reason it had his father: the good weather. Wet, cold Boston was no place for a TB patient, his doctors told him. It would prove to be one of the most influential prescriptions ever given.

At Stanford, Fred's old professor, Harris Ryan, hadn't forgotten his star student either. He stayed in regular touch with both Fred and the doctors— and when he learned, in early 1925, that the young man was on the mend, he quickly proposed that Fred teach a half-time course in the fall. The response from the professorship was overwhelming, as other faculty members sent him letters in support of hiring, in the words of one note, "Dear old, brilliant Fred."[38] Not even an appendicitis attack in the spring deterred Ryan, and by summer, when Terman was finally up and around, the young man knew a job was already waiting for him.

Whatever Terman's ultimate reason for going back to Stanford, it was an inspired choice. As was strangely the case many times during the rest of the century, MIT seemed to turn its back on a hot technology, in this case radio, just as it began to boom commercially. Between 1920 and 1925, retail radio sales exploded from $2 million to $325 million—and that was just the hardware; broadcast hours and advertising revenues enjoyed a comparable jump. This was the first great consumer electronics boom, and as with those that followed, anyone who managed to grab its tail, such as Cy Elwell and Charlie Litton, was in for a thrilling (and lucrative) ride.

But at MIT, Terman's mentors were already becoming disengaged from radio: Wiener back to mathematics, Kennelly to retirement, and Bush to national policy. Had Fred returned to MIT, and lived, he might well have been lost in the crowd.

But Stanford was different, and Fred's arrival was treated like the homecoming of a beloved but prodigal son. Better yet, arriving that first day to teach, he looked out across the classroom to discover that one of his students was his childhood neighbor and friend Herbert Hoover Jr. That day they not only rekindled a friendship that would last the rest of their lives, but also restarted their old hobby of building radio transmitters.

Once again, it was perfect timing. While Terman had been at MIT, Stanford had at last committed itself to radio, earning a 100-watt federal radio license in 1922, and another for a 500-watt station, KFGH, in 1924. In the spring of that year, while Terman was recovering from his appendectomy, the university was visited by representatives from AT&T, Western Electric, and Pacific Telephone. They were touring the major universities around the country stumping for the creation of communications engineering departments and degrees in order to find talented recruits in the years to come. At Stanford, industry reps found a receptive audience, especially when they offered to stock a new Communications Lab. Thus when Fred arrived that fall, he found himself working out of one of the best-stocked university radio labs in the world.

The next four years were among the happiest times for Fred Terman. By being careful and shepherding his energy, spending most of the day in bed except for the two hours he taught at Stanford, he slowly regained his strength. As he recovered, he began to take on an ever greater course load, as well as return to hiking the hills around the university. He began to be a regular sight, the young man with a cowlick of hair, glasses, an out-of-style suit, and even more antiquated shoes, striding purposefully around the quad and through the meadows above Stanford.

During this period, Fred and Herbert Jr. jumped back into the radio world like men trying to chase a train leaving the station. Herbert Jr. used Terman's class as an excuse to buy and test numerous radio receivers and then build a transmitter of his own. He installed the transmitter atop his dorm building, and experimental station 6XH became Stanford University's first independent radio station.

Terman, meanwhile, began to use his growing reputation as the go-to faculty guy for radio to lobby the university for a new radio propagation building. And, as was his natural bent, he settled in to write a textbook on the subject. *Radio Engineering*, as it would be entitled, combined all that he had learned as a boy, as a graduate student, and now as a teacher.[39] It was, from the day it was published in 1932, and remains today, numerous editions and translations later, the seminal text on radio. It made Terman famous in the technology world, and its royalties would pay him more than his salary as a university professor—enough to subsidize the research that would earn him thirty-six patents between 1930 and 1947.[40]

Radio Engineering is also a glimpse into the mind of Fred Terman, and what it must have been like to sit in one of his classes. For such a complex subject, the writing is extraordinarily clear and systematic, the mark of a great teacher. And, like all great teachers, Terman knew how to keep things simple, such that even a neophyte can enter the text and make his or her way through.

To aid the reader, Terman even invented "universal" curves to represent the sensitivity of radio circuits—a technique that has been adopted by subsequent texts ever since.

But the strongest impression left by *Radio Engineering* is its precision and economy. Terman was famous for his concentration. As a friend once said about him, "If there are 10 minutes to work on a manuscript, Terman is able to make nine minutes and 30 seconds of it count."[41] His children would remember their father working on manuscripts while they played jazz music, visitors came and went, and he was surrounded by every possible distraction— yet he never seemed to notice.

With this concentration came equally legendary energy. It was as if, having been trapped and immobile for an entire year of his youth, Fred Terman had recharged his batteries to the point where he often seemed superhuman. Once, when asked if he had ever gone an entire day without working, Terman was astonished. "Why no, how could you ask that question?"[42] Joseph M. Pettit, one of his star students, who would go on to become president of Georgia Technological Institute, said, "Terman never took a year off to write a book. Instead, he used to say that if he wrote only a page per day, he would have a 365–page book by the end of the year."[43]

Even other professors held Terman in awe. One recalled that he got used to having the phone ring in the evening, just as he was sitting down to a martini. It was Fred Terman with a question for his latest book.

But Terman described himself best—and with characteristic simplicity. He was asked why he never took a vacation. "Why bother," he replied, "when your work is more fun?"[44]

It wasn't only Terman's professional life that underwent a radical transformation during those years. It was then that he met, courted, and married Sibyl Walcutt, a graduate student in psychology and education at Stanford—that is, one of her father's students. She was as smart as Fred, but a much worse student. She was also much more outgoing and sociable—and a bit wild. It is telling that when she told her family she was marrying "Dr. Terman," one of her cousins automatically assumed she meant Fred's father. "That's what they'll all say," she wrote Fred wearily, "and you might as well warn your father that it will probably be all over the U.S. pretty soon that he has lost/killed/ divorced his wife and is marrying a flapper."[45]

In later years she would say that it was only after a half dozen dates that Fred finally sneaked over to the psych department and looked up Sibyl's IQ score—and decided on the spot that she was the girl for him. They were married in the Stanford Chapel.

Even more than for Fred, marriage seemed to be what Sibyl had been waiting for to give her life a purpose. They would have three sons. Sibyl would become famous on her own as an educator of children with reading problems, and would develop a hugely popular program for teaching phonics. And she and Fred would be together for forty-seven years in a marriage that was, by all accounts, deeply happy. When she died in July 1975, Fred Terman started down a mental and physical spiral from which he never emerged. On his desk calendar, the page for the day Sibyl died appears to have been soaked with tears.[46]

Chapter Two:
Apprentices

Dave Packard's injury, Bill Hewlett's loss, and Fred Terman's illness, all events that took place within a span of just months, had diverted the trajectory of each of their lives toward one another at a meeting place a decade into the future. In the meantime, as the newly married Professor Fred Terman worked to establish his career at Stanford, Bill and Dave still had to finish growing up.

As always, it was much easier for David Packard. His thumb healed, if damaged, and his explosive hobby was replaced by a compelling new one. He rode his horse, Laddie, went trout fishing in the Rockies with a friend's family (regularly catching the then limit of fifty fish per day), took violin lessons, and, increasingly, built and operated ham radios.

By the time he enrolled at Pueblo's Centennial High School, Dave had already made a name for himself as a radio operator. He became secretary of the school's radio club, and like his contemporaries out in Palo Alto, the Packard family's backyard shed soon sported a tall antenna tower to transmit David's ham radio station, 9DRV. In one of his first encounters with the larger technical world, his position with the school club earned him an invitation to the statewide ham radio convention in Denver.[1]

As he would at Stanford, Dave Packard passed through Centennial High trailing clouds of glory, thrilling the girls, and leaving both teachers and fellow students alike in awe. With the exception of Latin, where he struggled (comparatively), Dave found his high school classes a breeze—especially the technical ones: "The math and science courses were easy because I already knew about as much as the teachers did."[2]

He briefly pursued music, playing second violin in the orchestra and tuba in the band, but other interests drew him away. One was school politics: he ran and won election as his class president all four years.

An even bigger draw was athletics, which Dave didn't pursue until he was a junior. But when at last he did go out, he left an indelible mark. Perhaps not surprisingly, Centennial quickly had championship teams in the three sports in which Dave lettered: football, basketball, and track. The basketball team lost the state championship game, but Dave was nevertheless named all-state center.[3]

Track was his best sport. As he wrote in his memoir, "I won the high jump, the broad jump (now the long jump), the low hurdles, the high hurdles, and the discus, setting a new record for the all-state meet."[4] It didn't hurt that a noted hurdler of the era, Gordon Allott, was studying law in Dave's father's office (he would later become a senator and a great friend of HP) and gave the boy some pointers. But the talent was all Dave's.

Looking back on his high school days, Packard remembered most not radio, but his athletic career. And, tellingly, what he cherished in those memories was not the fame or the many awards, but the lessons it taught, especially about teamwork:

> [Pueblo athletic booster Mr. Porter told us] that many times two teams playing for a championship each have equally good players. In this case teamwork becomes very important, especially in the split-second plays: Given equally good players and good teamwork, the team with the strongest will to win will prevail.
>
> I have remembered that advice, and it has been a guiding principle in developing and managing HP. Get the best people, stress the importance of teamwork, and get them fired up to win the game.[5]*

Despite his father's hope that young David would follow him into the law, the boy would have none of it. Ever since he had first played with an amateur radio, Dave had known he wanted to an engineer when he grew up. Once his determination became known, the next question was where he would pursue his engineering degree. To the north, the University of Colorado at Boulder had a solid electrical engineering department, and several of Packard's older ham radio buddies were already attending the program there. It was generally assumed that Dave would do the same.

But in the summer of 1929, before the beginning of his senior year, David joined his mother and sister on a trip to California to visit some of his mother's old friends. They toured through Southern California (probably listening to Lee de Forest's radio station in the car), then drove north through Monterey (where Dave, with his daughter, would one day leave an indelible mark with their aquarium), then up to Palo Alto to visit Mrs. Packard's college friend, a Mrs. Neff. While they were there, the oldest daughter, Alice, who had just finished her freshman year at Stanford, took Dave for a tour of the campus.

It was on that tour that Packard first learned about Stanford's growing reputation in electrical engineering, the Communications Lab, and the brilliant young professor, Fred Terman, who had just been promoted to run it. Young David, very impressed, decided that Stanford was the school for him. He applied the next spring and, "much to my surprise" and nobody else's, he was accepted.[6]

But America was a different place in June 1930 than it had been twelve months before. The stock market had crashed in October, and though the Great Depression had not yet struck in earnest, there was enough bad news coming from Wall Street, the Midwest, and the major trading nations around the world to worry any thoughtful person. Not surprisingly, then, the news of David's acceptance to Stanford was received with some ambivalence: happiness that their son had been accepted into a top-flight university and concern over the cost of tuition at that university—$114 per quarter. That was a lot of money even in good times, and a frightening amount of assumed debt when the world's economy was sliding into the abyss.

But the golden good luck that always surrounded David Packard came through once again. At a time when attorneys were beginning to close their offices, or take eggs and produce in barter payment for their services, Packard's father managed to be appointed as a bankruptcy referee, the one legal career with a big future at the dawn of the Depression. That was enough to underwrite Dave's admission to Stanford, and the young man would have to work to make the rest.

———

For Bill Hewlett, the challenge was just the opposite. Thanks to his father's estate and book royalties, as well as the tuition discount for faculty children, he could afford to go to Stanford. The real question was whether he could get in.

Not long after Albion Walter Hewlett's untimely death, Bill's grandmother shrewdly decided the best thing for the mourning family was to take a long journey. So she packed them up—Bill, his mother, and his sister—for Europe. They stayed for fifteen months. During that time, Bill's sister was enrolled in a school in Paris, while Mom and Grandma tutored Bill privately. This was a second shrewd decision, because it enabled the boy, who had been struggling desperately in school, to learn at his own pace, in his own manner, and learn to navigate around his dyslexia.

There is a photo of young Bill, now about fourteen, in a wool suit, sitting squinting in the sun at what appears to be a Paris café. This is still very much a shattered boy: he looks older than he would in photographs taken five years later.

When the family finally returned, Bill was enrolled in Lowell High, the city's most distinguished college preparatory school. There he restored his friendship with a childhood buddy, Noel "Ed" Porter, and together they plunged into the troubled waters of high school

A Bill Hewlett today would be spotted rather quickly as suffering from a serious learning disability. He was a classic case: in English and history, he struggled gamely, but inevitably failed. He simply couldn't read the textbooks or keep up with his note-taking in class, so he had to rely entirely on his memory of the teacher's words. By comparison, in chemistry, physics, and mathematics, Bill's performance was nothing short of astonishing. This was particularly true when he was allowed to work with his hands. Among other electrical items, he built a pair of crystal radios for himself and his sister, made an electric arc from carbon rods, and even fabricated a Tesla coil. In math, he and some of the other students tore through the curriculum so quickly that they had to beg the teacher to instruct them in college-level calculus.[7]

But Bill's technical brilliance only counterbalanced his miserable other grades—and the resulting median of mediocrity made him less than a good college prospect. It seemed likely that his formal education was at an end, and that he would now have to attend a trade school, or use what talent he had with his hands to make a way in the world.

But Dr. Hewlett had one last gift for his son. Bill himself would look back upon it as a kind of miracle. Since he didn't commit to paper his memories of this period, we have to depend upon Dave Packard's telling of the story:

> Bill likes to tell the story that when it came time to graduate, he, like many of his classmates, asked his high school principal for a recommendation to Stanford. The principal called his mother in and said, "Mrs. Hewlett, your son had indicated he wants to go to Stanford. There's nothing in his record to justify my recommending him. Do you know why he wants to go?" She said, "His father taught there." The principal brightened and asked, "Was his father Albion Walter Hewlett?" She said yes, and he said, "He was the finest student I ever had!" That, according to Bill, was how he got in. He added that the next year the principal retired, "So I just made it!"[8]

Unlike Dave Packard, arriving at Stanford and not knowing a soul on campus, Bill Hewlett came to the university bearing a name known to almost everyone—and the immense expectations that came with it. Thus, it is even more surprising that he would, soon after his arrival, go out for the football team—an attempt that, given his size, was doomed from the start. Even in an environment where it must have seemed that everyone was watching him, Bill Hewlett was still not afraid to fail.*

Classmates

Though posterity would prefer the simpler story of Bill and Dave meeting on the football field and immediately becoming fast friends, the truth is that they spent the next two years as acquaintances and occasional classmates. Both were working toward their bachelor's degrees in engineering, and so regularly found themselves in the same classes and seminars.

But, until he finally dropped most of his outside activities, Dave's extra-curricular life was filled with sports and "slinging hash" for spending money at his fraternity or local cafeteria.[9] In the summer, because he "felt strongly" that he should help contribute to the cost of his education, he would return to Pueblo and take odd jobs, most of them involving heavy physical labor.[10]

One summer that meant work as a hard-rock gold miner near Cripple Creek drilling dynamite holes (he apparently hadn't fully given up his interests in explosives) and helping cart away the shattered rock afterwards. Another summer he unloaded still-hot bricks from kilns, often on days of 100 degrees or more—a job that often left him almost delirious. As if to counter that experience, he also took a job delivering ice in Pueblo, sawing up the big blocks into manageable smaller pieces he could lug on his back into the same beer joints and gin mills he had so studiously avoided just a few years before. And, in his favorite summer job, Packard worked on a construction crew building a road (now Highway 160) over Wolf Creek Pass in the San Juan Mountains of southern Colorado. The best part of this job was the hour of fishing he was free to do each night after dinner.[11]

Needless to say, this kind of work only made Packard stronger and a better athlete, and even more heartbreaking to his coaches as he began to drop out of one sport after another to focus on his classwork.

As for how Bill Hewlett spent those years, the best description comes from another classmate, Fredrick Seitz, who would go on to become president of Rockefeller University. In his autobiography, Seitz described his fellow physics students during those years, among them David Packard, "a major foot-ball hero on campus," and "William R. Hewlett, usually to be found in the library."[12]

It's likely that Bill didn't have much choice but to spend his free hours studying in the campus library. It is also likely that all of that effort had little effect. His classmates, not least of them Dave Packard, noticed that Bill took very few notes in class, but instead paid extraordinary attention to the lecture, taking in what he thought important and filing it away in a memory grown powerful with use. Bill Hewlett, everyone agreed, was somebody who really knew how to *listen* to other people.

What free time Bill did have was usually spent with his childhood pal Ed

Porter, who had also come up to Stanford. Porter was the son of an Episcopal bishop (who would eventually preside over Bill's wedding and the baptisms of most of the Hewlett and Packard children), and the crucial catalyst in bringing the two future partners together. He would spend his entire working career at Hewlett-Packard Company as a senior executive.

While both Hewlett and Packard were very good ham radio builders, they didn't hold a candle to Porter. Recalled Packard, "Ed knew so much about radios that he partially supported himself by repairing them."[13]

It was Porter, in fact, who had introduced Hewlett to the world of ham radio. While they were in high school, he had invited Bill up to the attic of his house to show off his secret laboratory and the handmade transmitter by which he had already connected with five continents. Even a technical tyro like Hewlett could understand enough to be impressed—and a little scared: using electrolytic rectifiers, Porter's transmitter pumped 1,000 volts around the attic, all on bare wire.[14]

Happily, Porter survived to be accepted to Stanford, and there help his old friend through. And if Packard was famous for his gridiron exploits around the rest of the campus, in the engineering department Porter was equally celebrated for having set up a private radio station on campus, W6BOA—hence Porter's nickname, "The Frisco Snake"—that was fully the equal of Fred Terman's over in the Communications Lab.

Being a ham radio buff, Packard often swung by Porter's room to talk shop and see what the whiz was up to—and just as often ran into Bill Hewlett. And it was then, in their junior year, that the real friendship between the two young men actually began.

In the beginning (and perhaps always) this friendship was less about engineering, and more about a common love of the outdoors. And, of course, as thousands of people who would meet them remarked, there was, from the start, an extraordinary complementarity between their two personalities.

But Ed Porter's place wasn't the only ham radio on campus that Packard regularly visited. He also made it part of his regular routine to visit Terman's lab. Like most Stanford engineering undergrads, Dave was intrigued by the young engineering legend with the famous father and the even more famous new textbook.

These had not been easy times for Fred Terman. The Depression had now hit California with full force. Unemployed men were sleeping in Hoovervilles along the creek beside the campus. The Central Valley was overrun with refugees from the Dust Bowl, even as the state's once powerful agricultural industry collapsed in the face of deflating food prices.

Stanford no longer had the money to subsidize side ventures like the

Communications Lab, even though it was little more than a renovated attic over the electrical engineering laboratory. In particular, there was no money to repair the roof, which leaked ever more with each rainstorm. So bad were the conditions that Terman and the students finally built large wooden trays, lined with tarpaper and sealed with tar, to catch the drips. Recalled Terman, "As the trays filled, we walked around them. Our morale didn't suffer. One winter Bill Hewlett added a homey touch by stocking the trays with goldfish."[15]

But it wasn't all amusing anecdotes to tell later during the good times. Some of the desperation of the era can be heard in another Terman reminiscence:

> The Depression years were more difficult than you can imagine. We had nothing, literally nothing, to work with. An accident that burned out a few vacuum tubes or damaged a meter would produce a crisis in the laboratory budget for a month.
>
> As an economy measure, I insisted that the laboratory meters be protected by an elaborate system of fuses. Students often chafed at this, because the fuses frequently got blown and it was always difficult to find a replacement of the right size. But the meters survived.[16]

Fred Terman may have backed into teaching, but once there he had quickly come to love the profession. He was indeed his father's son and wasn't going to let anything, even a global economic depression, drive him from his dream of turning the electrical engineering department at Stanford—and especially the Communications Lab—into an academic powerhouse, a world center for technical innovation in radio, and a magnet for the best students in the country. He fought all through the 1930s, using every trick, connection, and funding source he knew, to keep both the department and the lab alive.

The great irony of Terman's career is that, first with his illness and now with the Communications Lab, just when things seemed their very darkest, he was also on the brink of his greatest breakthroughs. Even as he was fretting about the survival of Stanford's engineering program, already on campus was a group of students who would not only save the place, but change the world, make Stanford one of the best-funded universities on earth, and, not least, put Fred Terman and his lab in the history books.

Building a Friendship

Easily Bill's greatest asset during his undergraduate years at Stanford was that he owned a car, a rarity for a college kid in Depression America. And that car meant freedom: to get away from school and head for the hills to hike and fish and forget one's problems.

Their first trip happened by luck: one of their professors organized a visit to a hydroelectric power plant run by Southern California Edison. Remembered Packard, "Bill and I took the occasion to go fishing and had a wonderful time. That was the precursor of many trips to the mountains."[17]

For the next two years, Bill and Dave took off on outdoor adventures whenever they could. Sometimes Porter came along, but he was less of an outdoorsman and much more chained to campus by his radio station. Others came along as well, but increasingly the core pair was Hewlett and Packard. The biggest trip of all, the one that cemented Bill and Dave's friendship during their separations in the years to come, came right after their graduation in 1934, when Packard, remembering the good fishing he'd enjoyed while working on the road crew, convinced Hewlett to join him in Colorado for a two-week pack trip in the San Juan Mountains. They rented horses (at a dollar apiece) and a mule and spent the fortnight wandering the mountains, talking, and catching endless fish.

It would have been a perfect trip had not Hewlett, on the penultimate day, gotten a terrible toothache and been forced to ride out early in search of a dentist (who would charge Bill one dollar for the extraction). Packard, alone that night, heard the nearby cry of a mountain lion and spent until dawn trying to sleep while clutching his rifle.

Still, in retrospect, both men looked back on the trip as one of the high points of the college years—an extraordinary statement coming from Packard, who played on two Rose Bowl teams. Sixty years later, he would recall, "There is no question that a shared love of the outdoors strengthened our friendship and helped build a mutual understanding and respect that is at the core of our successful business relationship lasting more than a half-century."[18]

There are many famous legacies of the Hewlett and Packard friendship, from Hewlett-Packard Co. to the engineering buildings on the Stanford campus—but to those who knew the two men best, the one that stands out as the most personal statement is the giant ranch that stretches through the mountains south of Silicon Valley, the last great California rancho. The two men purchased it together in the 1950s, not long after the first really big money came in. Its log cabin and growing complex of buildings soon became a retreat from the pressures of the world, a place to spend time with their families, and even to hold corporate off-sites. It was here, in the simpler, more physical world of ranching, fishing and hunting that both men seemed happiest.

The two young men talked about many things on those hikes and camp-outs, as well as with Porter while they hung around the radio station. And, inevitably, those conversations turned to how they each were going to make a living after graduation. That topic, a perpetual discussion among under-graduates, had an added touch of desperation in 1933 and 1934.

The Great Depression was now in full force. Stanford's most illustrious alum, President Hoover, product of the university's very first class, had failed to stem the tide and had been run out of the White House by voters. His successor, Franklin Roosevelt, had offered optimism and a seemingly endless series of new programs—but so far neither his upbeat speeches nor his alphabet soup of agencies had done much to buoy the economy. The young men knew they were facing the worst job market in American history—and in a strange way, it was kind of liberating: if the traditional corporate career paths were all but closed, they were free to try something radical and new. They even mused about teaming up and starting their *own* company, perhaps even in the field of "electronics" (a term so new that it had been coined after they came to Stanford).

But even with their limited experience with the business, the three knew that starting a company required capital, products, and customers—none of which they currently had. The dream would have to be deferred for now.

Meeting their Mentor

Dave Packard was the first of the group to connect with Fred Terman. It was inevitable that one of the campus's best-known scholar-athletes, who spent his free moments hanging around the radio station next to the Communications Lab, would eventually cross paths with the lab's director. And Fred Terman had apparently prepared well ahead for that moment. He wanted Packard in his circle: as he later told his son, "You don't get a seven-foot jumper by hiring two three-and-a-half foot jumpers."[19]

Packard knew none of this. Regularly bumping into Professor Terman at the radio station seemed merely a coincidence. As Dave would later admit, he knew nothing about Terman—or even his famous father. His encounters with the young professor were occasional and, by all appearances, random: "I would occasionally spend time at the radio station, and Professor Terman would stop by from time to time to visit with me."[20]

So young Dave was surprised when Terman seemed to know an astonishing amount about the classes he was taking, his grades, even his football stats. But he assumed it was just an example of the professor's powerful memory at work.

Finally, Terman made his pitch. Recalled Packard:

[On] a spring day in 1933, he invited me into his office and suggested I take his graduate course in radio engineering during my senior year. That was the beginning of a series of events that resulted in the establishment of the Hewlett-Packard Company.

As the first undergraduate to be invited into Terman's graduate course, I felt very honored. It was this class, taught by a now legendary teacher, that really sparked my enthusiasm for electronics.[21]

Terman recruited in this way throughout the engineering department, bringing together the best and brightest for his graduate seminar. As for Packard, he loved the course, despite the heavy burdens already on his time. "Professor Terman had the unique ability to make a very complex problem seem the essence of simplicity."[22] Dave was now hooked forever.

Being selected while still a senior to be part of Terman's graduate class, and thus the youngest in the professor's elite circle, was an honor Packard seems to have held in higher esteem than being recruited for Stanford's varsity football team. It even made him uncharacteristically cocky. And thus when one day a mere junior—worse, the age of a high schooler—a transfer from Cal Tech, appeared in the class, Dave quickly joined the others in predicting that the kid was in over his head and destined to fail. Even Terman had doubts: he told the young transfer student that if he didn't pass the first midterm exam in the course he would have to drop out and wait a couple years to take the course again.

But teenaged Barney Oliver was the smartest person in the room, probably on the entire campus. And when the midterm grades came back, Oliver had not only passed, but had the highest grade in the class—as he would for every other test for the rest of the year. It was the first chapter in the legend of one of the greatest applied scientists of the twentieth century.

It wasn't long before Oliver joined the troika of Packard, Hewlett, and Porter. And, like Ed Porter, Oliver would devote most of his entire professional career to working for Hewlett-Packard, in his case as the chief scientist and director of research and development. Oliver was brusque, arrogant, and impatient with anyone not intelligent as he (in other words, everyone), but he willingly chose to spend the most productive years of his life in the shadow of his two college friends (though, if Oliver's last great endeavor, the Search for

Extraterrestrial Intelligence [SETI] ever succeeds, he may finally eclipse them in the history books).

With Packard, Oliver, and the other graduate students, along with his most talented undergrads, such as Hewlett and Porter, Fred Terman finally had a collection of pupils to match his ambitions for his radio program. Now the task was to not only teach them, but show them how, in hard times, to turn that knowledge into a career. A few, he knew, might find a home in academia—but even that was no longer guaranteed, as few colleges were hiring. Rather, they would have find work in industry; and as most of the big corporations were in even worse straits than universities, Terman knew his "kids" might have to go it alone.

For that reason, he regularly took his students on field trips around the Bay Area to meet their older counterparts: the men running the very first generation of electronic (that is, vacuum tube-based) companies, many of them spin-offs of Federal Telegraph. They toured Charlie Litton's lab, of course, but also Kaar Engineering in Palo Alto, Eitel-McCullough in Burlingame and the great lone and eccentric genius, Philo Farnsworth, the inventor of television.

It was a brilliant move on Terman's part. His students made connections with future employers (and vice versa), they saw the state of the art in electronics, and, most importantly, they came away with a good idea of what it would take to start and run a real technology company. Recalled Packard, "I remember Terman saying something like: 'Well, as you can see, most of these successful radio firms were built by people without much education,' adding that business opportunities were even greater for someone with a sound theoretical background in the field. This got us thinking."[23]

In studying Terman during this era, it is hard not to conclude that he already had in his mind a scenario not unlike the future Silicon Valley and, while nobody else noticed, was slowly putting together the pieces: Stanford, a collection of bright young entrepreneurs, and a network of established companies to provide a skeleton of infrastructure. Why else would he make less-than-subtle hints to his students that, even as the Great Depression raged, they consider not just finding secure jobs, but taking the ultimate risk of becoming entrepreneurs?

William Shockley, the irascible Nobel Prize winner who would come home to the Valley twenty years hence, start a transistor company, then, through his cruel management, drive away his most brilliant employees to seed the local semiconductor industry, is usually credited with being the founder of Silicon Valley. Even Terman agreed with that assessment. And yet a strong case can be made that the Valley really began with Terman's tours for his students of the Bay Area electronics industry.

Going their Own Way

Bill Hewlett, Dave Packard, and Ed Porter graduated in June 1934. Packard, once again, covered himself with glory, graduating with Stanford's equivalent to summa cum laude, and as a Phi Beta Kappa. The trio, plus Barney Oliver, still talked about starting a company, but as graduation approached they realized they would have to abandon their fantasy and get serious. As Hewlett would say, "Thirty-four was not a good year for being employed."[24]

So, as they pondered their options, Bill and Dave took off for their pack trip in Colorado. When they returned, and with no obvious jobs in the offing, the group once again began to talk about striking out on their own. Over the long summer, that talk grew increasingly serious. In another month, they might well have built that company—and created a much different partnership—but another force intervened. Dave Packard received an unexpected job offer from General Electric in Schenectady, New York. When he hesitated, Terman intervened, shrewdly suggesting to Packard that "I would learn a great deal that would prove useful in our own endeavor."[25] Besides, Terman told Packard privately, Bill Hewlett needed another year of seasoning at Stanford.

Packard agreed. He accepted the GE job offer, telling Bill that he was still determined that they build a company together, and went home to Colorado. Once there, because the job wouldn't begin until February 1935, he signed up for courses at the University of Colorado in Boulder. His favorite was a class in engineering mathematics taught by a professor who was also something of an arithmetic savant and could compute huge columns of numbers in a split second. If nothing else, the class was entertaining.

In January, Packard drove with his mother and sister to Pittsburgh to visit some family friends (a common theme in their journeys). When the time came, Dave drove up to Schenectady and General Electric.

If he had any hopes about a career at GE, they were dashed that very first day. He was called into a meeting with the memorably named Mr. Boring, the man who had interviewed Dave at Stanford and offered him a job. The meeting started out bad and went downhill from there. "He knew of my interest in electronics (still called 'radio') but told me that there was no future for electronics at General Electric, and recommended that I concentrate my work and interests in generators, motors, and other heavy components for public utility plants and electrical transmission systems."[26]*

If Boring had told Packard that his job was to dredge the nearby Mohawk River, he couldn't have insulted him more. Dave hadn't put aside a promising sports career and crunched his way through Terman's graduate course as an undergraduate, and made himself into one of the best young electronics engineers in America, to become a glorified mechanical engineer building generators for hydroelectric dams. And if he missed his life in Palo Alto before, on that first day at GE he must have positively despaired. Decades later, he would be uncharacteristically triumphant in his memoir when he noted, "I have often thought of the irony of Mr. Boring's advice because our electronics firm, Hewlett-Packard Company, has become larger than the entire General Electric Company was at the time he gave me that advice."[27]

It only got worse. As was its policy with newly hired grads, GE assigned David to work in a test department—in Packard's case, on the swing shift testing new refrigerators for leaks and other malfunctions. Packard would later politely describe it as "not very interesting," but it must have been a nightmare.[28] Six months before, he had been in the California sun, a campus hero, working with some of the smartest young engineers anywhere, dreaming of starting his own company—and now here he was, in the middle of New York State, in the dead of winter, working at night checking refrigerator coils for leaking coolant. Worse, he was expected to be honored by the opportunity.

Back in Palo Alto, it was a new school year—and a new crop of students in Terman's electronics class. Once again, the professor had been carefully recruiting. Ed Porter was in the class—not surprising, as he knew more about radios than anyone on the Stanford campus, save Terman himself.

But it was on Ed's friend, Bill Hewlett, that Terman focused his attention. Hewlett may have followed Terman's advice to stick around for another year and take his course, but there was still no guarantee that he could pass it.

That Terman had even noticed the spark of talent in the still directionless C student Bill Hewlett is a testament to his genius as a teacher. So is the fact that his approach to the young man was so specifically designed for Hewlett alone. Said Hewlett, "I took courses simply because I was interested. I had no idea of getting a degree. And one day, Terman said, 'You know, I've been looking at your record, and you've been working on an interesting project in the resistance capacity oscillator, and I figure if you write that up as a thesis and pay $25, you could get an engineer's degree.' So I did."[29]

In that one conversation, Fred Terman had given Bill Hewlett, a student he barely knew, (1) a direction in his life; (2) a professional career; and (3) most remarkable of all, the initial step toward Hewlett-Packard Company's first product, the launching point of the modern electronics age. The lonely boy had found a home.

The Bill Hewlett we see in photos taken during this period is no longer the sad boy of his high school pictures. Now, thanks to his friendship with Ed Porter and Dave Packard, as well as his fraternity brothers at Kappa Sig, the nearly adult Bill Hewlett finally grins again. The touch of mischief in his eyes seen in grade school has returned, and it will never again leave him—even showing up in HP annual report photographs decades in the future.

The relationship between Fred Terman and Bill Hewlett is an interesting one. While there is an obvious fit between the single-minded Terman and the blunt, plainspoken Packard, two men dedicated from the very beginning to excellence in all things, none of those factors, at least at first, come into play in the relationship between Terman and Hewlett. Bill Hewlett as an undergraduate at Stanford was a fun-loving, practical-joke-playing, second-rate student who was forever not living up to his potential—in other words, absolutely the opposite of what Fred Terman expected in one of his "select" students.*

It went both ways. The demanding, apparently humorless Terman would have been the type of professor a Bill Hewlett would have usually tried to avoid. Though they would soon come to admire one another, and eventually love each other like a father and son, Hewlett, even as old man, would still marvel at a man whose thought processes were so utterly alien to his own: "[Terman] had no small talk, but he had a really analytical mind. . . . He'd talk your leg off. He had a distinctly one-track mind, when it was on a subject. You might divert him, but he'd come back and say, 'As I was saying,' and he'd jump right back to what he was saying five minutes previous. He clearly thought in a straight line."[30]

Bill Hewlett's mind, by comparison, clearly didn't work the same way. Unlike Dave Packard, whose sojourn through Terman's class was smooth and uneventful, his intelligence was both erratic and impetuous. Spending day after day for a year in that serious, high-pressure, and intellectually overwhelming environment had him climbing the walls.

Literally. Bill had learned to rock-climb and rappel while he was still in high school, and the rough-hewn sandstone walls of the Stanford quad posed a daily challenge. Fellow classmates during that fifth year would remember him clambering up the walls of the quad's engineering corner, especially the Radio Lab. "You could get pretty damn high—if you'd come off you could have banged yourself up," he recalled.[31]

When it turns out that Bill and his fellow climbers had different routes up the outside of the building, each named after the nearest faculty member parking spot, and that Hewlett's favorite was "Terman's Route" because it was riskier and more challenging, the metaphor becomes complete.*

When rock climbing proved inadequate to burn off Hewlett's natural exuberance, he took to playing practical jokes. The goldfish in the drip trays was classic Bill Hewlett of the era. But that was only one example.

One joke, in fact, had a six-decade-long punch line. For years it had been assumed that there were no surviving photographs of Terman's laboratory during those years, a loss considering its historic importance. Then, in 2003, the Hewlett family librarian, Robert Boehm, came upon a set of negatives that, when developed, proved to be a series of photographs taken in Terman's lab—featuring Bill Hewlett and one of his classmates, Bob Sink, pretending to drink bottles of booze and progressively slumping to end up, in the final image, passed out on the floor. Besides the sight of a future legend clowning around like a modern college kid, the photo is also astonishing for the sheer primitiveness of the lab and its equipment.

Terman indulged these antics, and perhaps even admired them a bit. He was not entirely without humor—though it appeared only rarely in public and was exceedingly dry (once, years later, he gave a completely deadpan presentation before the Stanford trustees describing how the three-mile-long Linear Accelerator was being used by students to pump beer from a nearby roadhouse to the campus).[32] So Terman may even have enjoyed Hewlett, and appreciated his contribution to the morale of his fellow lab students.

While Bill Hewlett was appreciated for his humor and his dedication, no one assumed he had any great aptitude in electronics. Rather, he was just a very smart, friendly guy who was good with his hands. But that was about to change.

Course Correction

Terman's strategy for Bill Hewlett had been a good one. Bill had wanted to attend MIT for his master's degree, and Terman, knowing both Hewlett and MIT's more difficult bachelor's program in electrical engineering, had wisely wanted to spend an extra year getting the young man up to speed.

Hewlett got his acceptance, and at the end of the 1935 school year left Stanford for Boston. His charming good-bye letter to Terman happily survives as a glimpse of both Hewlett's youth and the relationship between teacher and student:

Dear Sir:

I am sorry that I was unable to see you before I left for the East. My application to MIT was accepted with the requirements that I take some Economics and obtain a reading knowledge of French and German.

I would like to tell you how much I enjoyed my year in the lab under your direction. It was for that express purpose that I took the first graduate year at Stanford. I hope that I shall enjoy my year at MIT as much.

I am going to stop at GE for a week or so with Dave. He is going to show me through and in this way I hope to get some idea of research and development and large scale production.

Of the three keys I am enclosing, only two belong to the lab, and I don't know which they are. The odd one is no use to me, so if it does not fit anything you may throw it away.

Sincerely,
William R. Hewlett[33]

It is a classic student letter to an admired (and influential) professor, probably one of many that Terman received that spring. It is also touching in Hewlett's appreciation of all that Terman has done for him, amusing in its tone-perfect representation of a disorganized grad student who has found leftover items as he packed, and resonant in its mention of Hewlett's first re-union with Packard. And note the formal salutation and signature: no "Dear Professor" nor "Bill Hewlett" in this relationship.

If Fred Terman hadn't been so organized and passionate a record-keeper, it is likely that he would have tossed the letter soon after he read it; and if Bill Hewlett hadn't become a business titan, it is very unlikely anyone would be reading it today.

But if that first letter is trivial, the second letter from Hewlett to Terman, sent soon after he arrived at MIT, is not. In fact, it must have made Terman's jaw drop. Even the language was more that of equals, as if Hewlett was starting to sense his own abilities:

Dear Dr. Terman:

Several weeks ago I bought your new book on Measurements and al-though I had read parts of it before I have found it very useful. There are several mistakes in it that I have found and although most of them are mistakes in printing, there is one that seems fundamental. [34]

Hewlett goes on to describe how, on page 164 of the text, Terman's illus-tration of a setup for measuring "G of a tube in a bridge" contains a funda-mental (and dumb, though Hewlett is too polite to say it) error.

Terman, grabbing his copy of the book and tearing through the pages, must have felt a whole range of emotions: annoyance that his text wasn't per-fect, worry that he might have made a fool of himself in front of his profes-sional peers, calculation on how best to make a correction (erratum insert? a new edition?), and, not least, both amazement and a new appreciation of the young man who had sent him the note. Of all people, it was Bill Hewlett who spotted the error—not Oliver, not Packard, not one of Terman's academic peers, but class cutup Bill Hewlett. And so, even as he was kicking himself for making such a foolish mistake, the professor was also likely patting himself on the back for his prescience in identifying real talent in that young man.

After confirming for himself, Terman dashed off a return note:

> Dear Bill:
>
> I enjoyed your letter very much and also wish to thank you for the errors that you have discovered in the measurements book.
>
> You are absolutely right with regard to the circuit. . . . It is a rather bad and embarrassing mistake to have.[35]

Clearly, Hewlett was becoming someone with whom Fred Terman would want to stay in touch. Years later, Fred would marvel how he almost missed spotting the potential of his student: "I was slow in realizing that Bill not only solved problems but looked beyond them for their implications. He could see that one good creative problem solved always led to two more unsolved."*

Junior Exec

Meanwhile, if Bill Hewlett was finally finding his way, Dave Packard was just trying to find his way home.

Desperate to escape the endless dreary evenings testing refrigerators, Packard quietly began exploring other departments at GE Schenectady, desperately searching for some job that would both interest and challenge him. He finally found one in the radio transmitter department, which was hiring testers for equipment destined for the U.S. Army. It wasn't much more interesting than refrigerators, but at least it was radios, and it was a change. Meanwhile, he kept looking.

Finally, after a few months of searching, Dave finally identified and landed the job he wanted: in the vacuum tube engineering department. An added bonus was that this department shared a building with the GE's main research department—which meant Packard could make some connections with some of the company's top scientists.

The job title may have seemed familiar, but the reality was a long way from the elegant little radio tubes Packard had seen Charlie Litton fabricate back in Redwood City. These tubes were monsters—giant mercury vapor rectifiers the size of gallon jugs—and dangerous too. Each contained a reservoir of liquid mercury that would vaporize when current passed through the tube. A pointed piece of silicon carbide was also mounted into the tube to act as a control element.

As long as the control element worked, the giant tube worked just fine. But when it failed, the pressure of the mercury vapor spiked—and the tube exploded like a grenade. For that reason, the testing unit was placed inside a metal-mesh shield to stop the flying glass splinters and shards. Meanwhile, the doors on opposite sides of the ground-floor lab were kept open during the tests because when a tube exploded the technicians had only an instant to run outside ahead of the expanding poisonous cloud of mercury vapor—returning only when the lab had been (apparently) aired out. Such was worker safety in 1935.

It wasn't until Packard took the job that he learned that, basically, *every* tube exploded. Yield rates were so low on GE's mercury vapor rectifiers that of the previous batch, every one had failed, and most had blown up. Dave was informed that his job was to make sure the next batch got through.[36]

In desperation, he set about to learn every possible way that a mercury vapor rectifier could fail. At the same time, he went and planted himself on the factory floor, following each tube through every step of the fabrication process to make sure there were no mistakes.

No one at the company had ever done that before. And the factory workers, pleased that someone from the lab was actually paying attention and listening, proceeded to open up to the tall young man. It didn't take Dave long to identify the problem: the factory workers, who were taking the rap for the low-quality output, were in fact "eager to do the job right." The problem was that the instructions being given them by the engineering department "were not adequate to ensure that every step would be done properly."[37]*

So Packard rolled up his sleeves and joined the men on the shop floor. Together, they revisited each step of the production process, looking for errors, the workers explaining the best way to do their job even as Packard rewrote the instructions from engineering. The result was that, of the next batch of twenty rectifiers, *every one* passed the final test.

It was the first indication that David Packard was not only a brilliant manager but an innovative one as well. Years later, when HP codified its leadership practice, called "Management by Walking Around"—and business theorists began to write books about it—Packard looked back and realized that it was during those weeks on the factory floor that he first practiced it: "That was a very important lesson for me—that personal communication was often necessary to back up written instructions."[38]

The death of the culture of the private office and the unapproachable boss would, in many ways, prove to be the most pervasive and influential of all HP social innovations. Once Dave Packard stepped out on the shop floor at GE, the vertical corporate world began to go flat. Even General Electric, which was more threatened by than appreciative of Packard's little broadside for workplace democracy, would eventually adopt his philosophy.

Bill Hewlett, meanwhile, was buried in classes at MIT. Terman's prediction was correct: the courses were a handful, and had Hewlett not spent that year in preparation it is unlikely he would have survived. Instead, because he was ready, he received some of the best training on the planet in topics such as network synthesis and analysis, which would prove to be crucial to the creation of HP's early products. The courses weren't so hard that Bill couldn't sneak away from Boston every so often and catch the train—"that shake, rattle and roll operation"[39]—up to Schenectady to see his college buddy Dave.

Packard at this point was sharing a rented house with a half dozen other bachelor engineers—including John Fluke, who would also go on to become an electronics tycoon (and an HP competitor), and John Cage, who would write a well-known textbook with Barney Oliver and help set up HP Ltd. in the United Kingdom.

None of the young engineers was making more than ninety dollars per month, so they decided to pool their resources, renting a large house and hiring a housekeeper. Considering that these were guys fresh out of fraternities, one can only pity that housekeeper. Worse, the men had filled the attic of the house with piles of defective electronic equipment liberated for a nominal fee from GE's Building 97, the company's junk pile. In their spare time, the men would go up to attic and work on the various instruments, most of them designed for huge electrical plants, to see if they could coax any use out of them.

The result, unbeknownst to the quiet neighborhood, was something out of a mad scientist's laboratory. Recalled Packard, "We had so much power in [one] transmitter that when you pressed the key, the lights in the whole house would light up—whether they were turned on or not."[40] Remarkably, most of these men, including Packard, managed to survive this eating and sleeping in a massive electrical field and go on to enjoy long lives.

During Bill and Dave's visits, the pair likely talked about their various experiences at work and at college, discussed once more their dream of starting a company together, and made plans for future outdoor trips. They even managed several times to get out to the woods and do some canoeing. It was probably also during one of those visits that Dave told Bill that he was still sweet on that girl, Lu, he'd dated back at Stanford—that they were in regular touch, and that neither distance nor time had diminished his feelings for her.

Dave Packard's first meeting with Lucile Salter had been a blind date during his senior year. Some of his friends had organized a trip to San Francisco to go dancing at the Mark Hopkins Hotel and, surprisingly, the dashing football player didn't have a date. He also was scheduled to work until early that evening in his dishwashing job in the kitchen at the Delta Gamma sorority. No problem, said one of his friends, I think I know a gal there that will probably be willing to go with you.

Packard wasn't prepared for what happened next: "There I was in the kitchen, immersed to my elbows in pots and pans, when Lucile strolled up to me and said, 'When do you want me?' "[41]

By the time the band played the last dance that night, Dave Packard was in love.

But for now, there wasn't much he could do about it. He was a continent away in a mediocre job in a company that hardly noticed him—and it was the only job he could find. To make matters worse, in June, Bill Hewlett graduated from MIT and headed back to California. Now Dave Packard's best friend and his girl were back home and he was stuck in Schenectady.

Fred Terman tried to help. Interestingly, he too was already thinking about a partnership of Hewlett and Packard. While Bill was still at MIT a small Philadelphia electronics company wrote to Terman expressing interest in possibly hiring some of his graduates. Terman's reply offers an insight into how he perceived the two young men:

> I would suggest the consideration of David Packard. Mr. Packard has been with the General Electric Company for one and a half years. He is a Stanford graduate, Phi Beta Kappa, a varsity football and baseball player, campus politician, etc. He is a big, attractive fellow with unusual energy, very brilliant in theory, and extremely competent in the laboratory. He has had considerable amateur experience in radio, has taken my course at Stanford and is now working in the research division of the General Electric Company and is taking the Advanced Course.
>
> Another possibility is a former Stanford student, William Hewlett, who did one year of graduate work with us and has just completed a second year at Massachusetts Tech . . . [he is] a good substantial young man with an excellent personality and social poise. His chief characteristic is tremendous energy. He always has to have several irons in the fire going simultaneously and whenever he is around things happen. Hewlett needs a little finishing from the commercial point of view but is going to go places wherever he is.[42]

Besides Terman's superb insight into the personalities of his two students, two other features of this letter are of interest. First, there is the elevation of

Bill Hewlett into Terman's "first team" of graduates. For the first time, in this letter he is now almost the equal of Dave Packard, so that when Terman sat down to recommend his best talent, these are the two names that came to mind. The second feature is that, for all of his understanding of the two men, Terman is now behind the curve: in the intervening year, their roles had largely reversed, and would stay that way for the rest of their lives.

Hewlett, whom Terman still sees as a high-energy young hustler with entrepreneurial tendencies, has become in the intervening months much more of a research scientist. Conversely, Packard, whom Terman remembers as a focused young scientist, has in the interim at GE discovered an aptitude for management.

This is an important shift in both men's lives. During their many years at HP, Packard would always be seen as the "outside" guy—public figure, diplomat, and industry statesman—while Hewlett was always the "inside" guy, the hardcore technologist and innovator who made sure HP always stayed on the cutting edge. And yet anyone who worked with Bill and Dave for any length of time understood that the two men could easily switch roles whenever they needed to—and on many occasions did. This was only possible—and it was a key factor in the success of Hewlett-Packard Co.—because both men had known both incarnations, the businessman and the scientist, early in their careers.

But in early 1936, Dave Packard's apprenticeship as a business manager wasn't looking very promising. The factory-floor guys loved him, but the guys upstairs didn't even know he existed.

It only got worse. That summer, with the Depression still raging, GE announced that it was cutting back work hours to save money. For Packard and some of his roommates, that meant even less pay—but at least they got off work at 3 p.m.

With his engineering career temporarily frustrated, Dave threw himself into the one other activity he loved: sports. He took up basketball again, and, not surprisingly given his background, soon joined a local professional team. Composed mostly of working men, the team practiced in the evenings, and on weekends toured the small towns of upper New York and southern New England playing against local teams. Packard recalled, "We made only a few dollars a week, not a princely sum, but still very useful in those economically depressed times. We played our last game of the season in New York City at the Thirty-fourth Street Armory. I don't remember much about the game except that our team lost and that Kate Smith, a popular singer, tossed out the ball to start the game."[43]

Even though he was never a man for irony, even Dave Packard must have noticed that, having abandoned a potential career in professional sports to pursue his dream of being an engineer, he was now being slowly driven away from engineering and back toward a career in professional sports.

That autumn the situation had only marginally improved at GE, so Packard and his roommates decided to spend their weekends hunting and hiking in Vermont and New Hampshire. When winter came they drove up-state to North Creek and took up the increasingly popular new sport of ski-ing. It was the era of long hickory skis and rigid bindings, and thus only for the brave of heart. Despite his huge size, Packard loved it and took to it like a natural. And when disaster finally did strike—on three occasions he skidded off a path into the surrounding woods—he was so strong, and in such good shape from basketball, that his skis snapped before his legs did.

But Dave Packard couldn't put up with this idyll forever. He was an ambi-tious and impatient young man who knew his potential, and who couldn't bear to wait much longer on the sidelines.

If he knew what Bill Hewlett was up to, Packard might not have been so envious. Now both a Stanford and an MIT graduate, he had confidently sent out his résumé—and gotten exactly one job offer: at Jensen Speaker Co. in Chicago, a job he probably could've landed just as easily two years before. So, in desperation, he wrote to Fred Terman. If Terman had any hesitation before about Bill Hewlett, it had evaporated after the letter six months before. He not only quickly found Bill a job, but one that moved him back to the lab at Stanford.

The contract was with a San Francisco doctor who had a novel design for a new electroencephalograph. As Terman planned, it was an almost perfect job for Hewlett, combining multiple elements from his life: San Francisco, Stanford, electronics, and medicine. Better yet, the project would grow to con-sume two years. Yet there is no surviving record of any finished product com-ing out of the contract. It is almost as if Terman planned it that way; a more cynical conclusion is that it was all a setup to get an unexpectedly brilliant student back to the lab. He wrote to Barney Oliver, then on a fellowship in Germany, "Hewlett has been developing communications techniques for medical research during the past year and has spent most of his time in our laboratory although the work is being done for a doctor in San Francisco."[44]

If he did set up Hewlett, Terman had a very good reason. Just two years before, Bell Telephone Laboratories, the most important fount of innovation in basic electronics for much of the twentieth century, announced some ma-jor breakthroughs in the design of "feedback circuits," devices that fed a small fraction of their output back to the input to enable them to respond to changing conditions. Terman was intrigued—here was a way to make instruments more accurate, responsive, and even adaptive—and immediately embarked on research into the subject.

By 1937, he had made himself a leading researcher in the field, even publishing a paper in the new *Electronics* magazine on "Feedback Amplifier Design." He had also begun assembling around him a team of students who could explore with him the implications of this new theory. As if an expectation of this plan, Terman had stayed in close contact with the best of his old students. Hewlett had come home. His wall-climbing partner Ed Ginzton (who would be one of Silicon Valley's most important, and least remembered, pioneers) was there as well. And Terman made certain that other grads—Barney Oliver, Ed Porter, the older graduate Noel Eldred, all men who would one day be HP senior executives—were constantly kept in the loop as well via letters and visits.

Fred Terman's genius was that he combined almost obsessive preparation and attention to detail with a wide-open opportunism. He operated as if he knew exactly where he was going, yet was willing to throw out every one of his plans if something better came along. This was something his best students learned from him—and it proved to be the perfect strategy for the fast-changing world of high tech.*

Only one person was missing from Terman's team: Dave Packard. And, as it happened, Terman had a confederate in bringing him home to Stanford: Lucile Salter. Dave was so anxious to see her that in August he used his vacation to drive all the way across the country. He was so broke that he took along a sleeping bag and slept on the side of the highway.

The visit only convinced Packard more that he needed to escape GE and get back to Stanford. His feelings for Lu had only grown stronger, and they had begun to talk about marriage. Terman was doing the most exciting electronics research in the country—and hinting he'd like Dave back. And, on a landmark day, he and Bill Hewlett held their first "official" business meeting. Recalled Packard:

> The minutes of the meeting, dated August 23, 1937, are headed "tentative organization plans and tentative work program for a proposed business venture." The product ideas we discussed included high-frequency receivers and medical equipment, and it was noted that "we should make every attempt to keep up on [the newly announced technology of] television." Our proposed name for the new company: The Engineering Service Company.[45]

If the high-sounding title of the minutes smacks too much of young men without a clue, playacting at real business, and if the name of the company is hilariously sober and prosaic, what also stands out is the ecumenical nature of their search for a product. What separates Hewlett and Packard from almost every high-tech entrepreneurial team that follows them over the next seventy years (and probably for many years yet to come) is that *they started their business before they knew what they were going to do.*

This is a critical difference. Bill and Dave were friends before they were partners. They had learned to trust each other in situations as different as a university classroom and a Rocky Mountain trail hike. They knew how each other thought, and realized they were in fundamental agreement on values, interests, and ambitions—to the point that, in later years, dealing with either man was as good as dealing with both. And though the myth that they never fought is not quite true, it is accurate enough to be astonishing—and that too wasn't the product of identical personalities (which they most certainly weren't) but common goals and a deep mutual understanding.

It is interesting to note that this process of friendship before partnership and business before products, rare as it is, is not so unusual among extremely successful companies: think Jobs and Wozniak at Apple, Gates and Allen at Microsoft, and Noyce and Moore at Intel. But even these famous partnerships, largely because of Hewlett and Packard themselves, lacked one last feature of the Bill and Dave partnership. Which was that Hewlett and Packard, mired in the Great Depression, weren't trying to get rich, but were just struggling to make jobs for themselves. As Packard wrote later, "We weren't interested in the idea of making money. Our idea was if you couldn't find a job, you'd make one for yourself." Those entrepreneurs that followed, in better times, always aimed much higher—in large part because of the sheer success of the Hewlett-Packard Company. Every high-tech entrepreneur after Bill and Dave looked over his or her shoulder at the two founding fathers.*

Bill and Dave didn't have that example to follow. All they had were the comparatively humble role models of Federal Telegraph and Charlie Litton. And if that tended to lower their expectations—that is, what if HP had had an HP to emulate?—it also liberated them. At the beginning there were no venture capitalists second-guessing their every decision, pushing them toward some future liquidation event; no trade magazines analyzing their every move and trying to scoop their new product announcements; and no headhunters raiding their shop for the best talent. Instead, it was just Bill and Dave—and if they were embarking into the unknown, at least they were piloting their own ship.

Unexpected Genius

There was one last surprise before the birth of Hewlett-Packard.

Fred Terman, fresh from the strong response to his *Electronics* magazine article, decided to write the most comprehensive article to date on feedback amplifiers and oscillators (that is, devices used to generate a controlled signal). To create the article, he combined some of his recent writings with some additional work by several of his students. Being Terman, when the article was finished in May 1938, he decided to put not only his own name on the byline, but also the three grad students who had contributed most to the content: R. R. Buss, F. C. Cahill, and William R. Hewlett.

Hewlett was ecstatic. The student who had just dropped by to take a few courses four years before was sharing authorship of a major research paper with one of the giants of the field. It was beginning to dawn upon Bill that he might even be a real research engineer himself.

He quickly sat down and wrote a letter to Packard that is a classic for the boundless excitement of youth. In it, Hewlett manages to stuff three wildly different topics that more properly should have been the subject of their own notes.[46]

First, he congratulates Packard on his impending nuptials (Dave had proposed to Lu a few weeks before, and the news had made its way across the Stanford campus to Bill) in a manner that manages to be both polite and impatient to get on to the important stuff. He even manages to misspell the bride's name:

> In the first place, my heartiest congratulations to both you and Lucille. Everybody knows that it is an idea[l] match. I saw Lucille just before she went east, and was she excited. She was showing her presents and parading around in the dress she was to be married in—happy as a clam at high tide.

Done with the cordialities, Bill now gets down to his "good news":

> The first thing is that I have got my name on a paper with Terman as one of the collaborators. . . . Terman actually did all the writing, we just did some of the experimental and theoretical work. Nevertheless, the paper will have our names on it.

Hewlett then embarks on several paragraphs of description of a design for "a new type of oscillator" that has no inductances. It is a pretty arcane discussion ("It may be seen that the resonant frequency is proportional to R and

1/C, whereas in the conventional oscillator the frequency is proportional to (the square root of) 1/C . . ."), but it concludes with a telling phrase: "We should be able to sell them at quite a low figure."

Then, after announcing that he will be giving a paper on the subject at the Pacific coast convention of the Institute of Radio Engineers, Hewlett again switches topics to say that he has enclosed a diagram for a six-watt amplifier, noting that an old classmate of theirs, John Kaar, who had set up a factory in Palo Alto, has offered to build them at a unit cost of $24 in lots of five or more. "Porter is now drumming up trade for this in [California's Central Valley]. Put one together and see how you like it."

Finally, after several pages, Hewlett's letter changes direction one last time—and now Bill drops a bombshell:

> There is one more important thing and that is the possibility of a job out here. It seems that there will be a job open here next year as a research assistant in the lab. The pay is very small, $500 for nine months at half time, on top of that you'll probably have to register for a few units and that will reduce the net to about $400. It however would be a guarantee of some salary plus whatever you could make on the side. You would have a lab to work in, and I would work down here with you. It might be just the thing. If you are interested in the slightest get in touch with Terman at once. . . . In all events, get in touch with him by airmail.

Illumination

Terman had finally found the money. Dave Packard was coming home to Stanford.

Terman was ecstatic. He wrote to Charlie Litton, "Dave Packard has accepted the assistantship in connection with the ultra-high-frequency tube investigation and will be with us beginning some time in September. I think he is the best qualified man that one could conceivably hope to find, so I am highly pleased."[47]

Meanwhile, while he waited for Packard, Bill Hewlett went into the lab and continued his experiment with oscillators. It was summer, so the lab was almost always empty except for Bill and graduate student Bob Sink. Together they struggled to solve the most intractable challenge to building oscillators: maintaining consistently accurate signals over a wide range of amplitude settings. The underlying problem was getting the resistance to vary with the signal to produce "linearity" in the output. No one had yet come up with an easy way to do it, so the resulting instruments tended to be either cheap and inaccurate, or expensive and moderately accurate.

Hewlett and Sink were intent on finding an answer. And on July 27, 1938, Bill came up with a solution so simple and elegant that it astonished Fred Terman, and so profound in its bridging of theory and application that it was received as a work of genius in the electronics world. Seventy years later, what Hewlett accomplished that July day remains one of the most clever bits of practical invention in technology history. And it can still bring a smile.

All Bill did was take a fifteen-watt light bulb, in its socket, and solder it into the oscillator. It sounds simple, but at that moment only Bill Hewlett could have thought of it. That's because only he—not Terman, not Litton, not Ed Porter—combined both a deep immersion in feedback theory and years of experience building amateur radios and electronic instruments.

What dawned on Hewlett was that he needed a resistor in the circuit that would vary its resistance with the oscillator itself. And, after all, wasn't a light bulb's filament just a resistor that burned off extra power as heat and light? In emplacing the light bulb, Hewlett had found a way to hit a moving target with an arrow that paced its every shift in speed.

The more Terman and the rest of the electronics world studied Hewlett's solution the more they were flabbergasted and delighted. It was the very embodiment of the most arcane feedback theory—and young Bill Hewlett had accomplished it with something found in a drawer in every kitchen in America. It seemed to open the curtains to a new world of low-cost, high-performance electronic instruments for the everyday engineer, and hinted in turn at something even bigger: consumer electronic products, a notion that until then had seemed far in the future.

Even Bob Sink, who was sitting at the lab table next to Hewlett that day, could scarcely believe his eyes. He dashed off a quick, and somewhat dazed, note to Terman:

> Bill Hewlett and I are the only ones working in the lab now. Bill finally eliminated the bugs from his oscillator. As you know, the cheif [sic] difficulty was in the amplitude control. He finally hit upon the scheme of using a fifteen cent light bulb in the negative feedback portion of his circuit. The result was unbeliveably [sic] remarkable. His total distortion is better than one fourth of one percent![48]

From that moment on, Bill Hewlett would be known as the technologist of the partnership. And Fred Terman would list him among the greatest engineers he had ever known, far greater even than himself. Wrote Terman's son after his death, "Mother said that Dad had always felt that as a technical innovator and inventor, he simply was not in the same class as the best he knew—Ed Ginzton, Bill Hewlett, Dave Packard, Russell Varian, and the like."[49]

Bill Hewlett had become one of Terman's "seven-foot jumpers."

Homecoming

Fred Terman presented his feedback paper at two Institute of Radio Engineers conventions that summer, and in November submitted it to the organization's scientific journal for publication. As usual with such publications, the approval process took a number of months. During the intervening period, the U.S. economy, which had been recovering slowly during the late 1930s, underwent what economists have described as a "second Depression" that would last until the run-up to World War II.

The engineering profession was not immune to this downturn, and the IRE, to reduce its budget, decided to cut back on the number of pages in its journal—which in turn meant cutting back on both the number and length of the research articles. Terman's paper—and Bill Hewlett's section in particular—was one of the targets of the cuts.

Terman fought back with every bit of influence he had, arguing that Hewlett's work on the "Oscillator with Resistance-Capacitance Timing" was of major importance. He prevailed, and in November 1939, Hewlett had his first published paper.

An astute entrepreneur, had he or she read that section of Terman's paper, might have spotted a very competitive product-in-the-making—and beaten Bill and Dave to market by months. Not only did Hewlett's schematics show the brilliant light bulb resistor, but also the use of "ganged" tuning condensers (like those found in ordinary radio receivers), which together presented the prospect of a powerful new instrument for generating frequency—sound—at a bargain price that any small company could afford.

Luckily for the two young men, nobody did notice—the world was too distracted with a Depression that refused to die, and a growing world war in Manchuria, Poland, and Ethiopia.

By the time the paper did appear, Dave Packard was home in Palo Alto. It hadn't been an easy trip. In the spring of 1938, Lu accepted his proposal of marriage. In August, she resigned her job as secretary to the registrar at Stanford and took the four-day train trip back to Schenectady. She took the trip east because Dave considered his position at GE, given the economy, so precarious that he didn't dare take more than one day off work to get married.

He and Lu were married on a Friday, spent their honeymoon over the weekend in Montreal, and Dave was back on the job Monday morning.

Bill's long letter arrived in Schenectady about the same time as Lu did, and with it Terman's godsend offer of a part-time job at the Stanford Radio Lab. The $500 stipend was less than half what Packard was making at GE, and now it would have to pay for two, but Dave wanted to go home and do work that mattered. Proving that he had made the right choice in a mate, Lu agreed wholeheartedly with Dave's decision.

Prudently, especially when there few jobs to be found anywhere, Packard didn't simply resign from GE, but instead (on Terman's advice) convinced his bosses to give him a one-year leave of absence. By leaving open the chance of his returning, he was able to not only leave with their blessings, but also retain a backup in case Palo Alto didn't turn out to be the triumphant return he hoped it would be. He and Lu packed up the car, not only with clothes, but some of Dave's most important tools—including a Sears and Roebuck drill press in the rumble seat—and headed west. In Packard's mind that drill press represented his commitment not to Stanford and his new job, but to what lay beyond that. As he proudly recalled, "It would be HP's first piece of equipment."*

The scientist Dave was to work with was an eccentric forty-one-year-old alum from William Hansen's physics department named Russell Varian. Russell also happened to be an authentic genius, one of the few in Silicon Valley history who actually deserved the title. The project itself, to build a unique new kind of vacuum tube, would prove one of the most important of the twentieth century. And, still working his network, Terman arranged for the project to be located not at Stanford, but at Charlie Litton's laboratory. It may not have paid much, but thanks to his old professor, Dave Packard's new job was the most promising in the electronics world.

For someone as supremely sane as David Packard, working for Russ Varian must have been an unforgettably exciting, and frustrating, experience. Like Packard, Varian was something of a legend on the Stanford campus—but for an entirely different reason.

Russ Varian was born in 1898 in the tiny central California town of Halcyon, where his parents ran the general store and post office. One of his two brothers, Sigurd, was three years younger, and was as handsome and quick as Russell was huge and slow. Like Hewlett, Russell likely suffered from dyslexia (and probably a host of other learning disabilities), but so severe that he had to memorize everything he learned—which meant that he didn't finish high school until he was twenty-one, at the same time as his brother.

As a teenager, it was Sigurd who was the star of the family. He had a natural aptitude for flying, and an absolute lack of fear. Because military airplanes were dumped on the market after the Armistice, Sigurd and Russell were able to secure (almost for nothing) and assemble surplus World War I biplanes still in their cases. The miracle of these years was that both boys survived a number of horrible crashes. "We smashed our planes all over the state of California," Sig recalled later.[50]

Not surprisingly, Sigurd went on to a dashing career: flying Pan American World Airways' new Mexico-to-Central America route. He also married the daughter of a British consul in Mexico.

Meanwhile, giant lumbering Russ Varian applied to, and to the amazement of everyone, got himself accepted to Stanford in 1919. Because the family was so poor, Russ decided to help by packing his backpack and hiking the 225 miles to Palo Alto. Upon his arrival, he wrote home to tell his folks he had made it—and that the entire trip had cost him just ten cents. While at Stanford, he learned the locations of all of the fruit- and nut-bearing trees on campus and was known to forage for his meals.

After graduation, Russ went to work for an oil company. Then, for four years, he worked in San Francisco helping Philo Farnsworth perfect the television tube. Finally, in 1935, he went home to Halcyon. There he was joined by both Sig and their baby brother, and the three Varian boys built their own private laboratory. The impetus for the project came from Sigurd. Having spent years flying over (and sometimes crashing into) dangerous jungles, he had become something of an expert on aircraft instrumentation. Moreover he was haunted by the news, just then emerging from the Spanish civil war, of German fighter planes strafing defenseless civilians in cities like Guernica.

Wasn't there a way, Sig asked his big brother, to build an instrument that could spot these planes long before they arrived, so that people could either fight back or hide? Maybe, said Russell. There's this new device called a "rhumbatron"—because the current moves very little at the top and bottom, but a lot in the middle—and it might be just what you're looking for. And I know just the guy to tell us about it.

Russ contacted his old classmate, Bill Hansen, who was the inventor of the rhumbatron (officially an "electromagnetic resonator") and now a distinguished professor of physics in their old school lab. Hansen agreed to come down to Halcyon, not least because he was a budding pilot and wanted some pointers from the great daredevil pilot.

As the three men talked, they slowly began to define a device that would sweep the sky with an invisible beam, and then recapture and project that beam as it echoed off any object out there. Russ and Hansen also agreed that this would take a very intense high-frequency wave—and there was no current vacuum tube out there that could handle it.

Okay, suggested Sigurd, then let's go up to Stanford and build our own. Russ would later say that he was "rather dubious" about the idea, but went along anyway. Hansen took the brothers first to the head of the physics department, Dr. Daniel Webster, who also turned out to be a budding pilot. He was so impressed by the idea (and perhaps by Sigurd) that he took it to the university president, Dr. Wilbur—who in turn agreed to make the brothers research assistants and give them $100 for the project. But, he added, the Varian brothers would have to work for free.

The two men agreed, and Russell went back to his old habit of foraging the campus fruit trees for food.

The work quickly divided up to match the skills of the three men. Sigurd, of course, was to build the device once the other two figured it out. Russell, meanwhile, with his incredibly powerful but inconsistent brain, was to employ what he called his "substitute for thinking"[51] to make breathtaking inductive leaps in developing the design, while Hansen, the professor, systematically filled in the resulting gaps with careful mathematics. It was high tech's first great design team.

As word got out that fall about what the three men were up to, the physics lab was regularly visited by both physics and engineering students—among them grad student Bill Hewlett—almost all coming to see the amazing Russ Varian at work.

The design was finished at the beginning of March 1936, and Russ and Hansen turned the project over to Sigurd. Now even more students came to the lab, many, like Hewlett, offering to help out where they could. The sight of Sig Varian, a figure out of a Hollywood movie, slowly building—and inventing as he went—the most sophisticated electronic device on the planet, was an image that stayed with Hewlett the rest of his life. It may have helped fuel his need to regularly test (against other HP execs) his own skill at building the latest HP product.

Even Fred Terman came by to watch, commenting that, "unlike his brother, who was rather clumsy with apparatus, Sigurd had unusual design and mechanical sense, and great skill with his hands."[52]

By now, the Varian brothers were the talk of the entire university. All of Stanford groaned when Russell told Sigurd to throw out the half-finished device because he and Hansen had come up with a better design, this one using two rhumbatrons in a vacuum. So infectious was the project that even Dr. Webster, the department head, showed up to suggest that the rhumbatrons should be shaped like doughnuts—toruses—for greater efficiency—a contribution that got his name on the patent and a lot of very large royalty checks in the years to come.*

And that wasn't Webster's only contribution. So well-known was the Varian brothers' project on campus that Webster was able to walk over to the classics department and ask Professor Herman Frankel to come up with a name for the device. Frankel suggest "klystron," a Greek verb meaning to "splash in waves." Thus the name: klystron tube.

By mid-August, Sigurd had the six-foot-tall prototype klystron emitting sufficient microwaves to create some flashing on its detector screen. On August 19, 1937, Sigurd came running out of the lab shouting, "It oscillates!" and grabbed Russell, Hansen, and anybody else he could find and dragged them in to see the klystron fill the screen with a matrix of flashes. Bill Hewlett saw it as well—as did, by fortunate chance, Dave Packard, as this was the week he was in town to visit Lu and hold the first business meeting with Bill.

The klystron tube, along with the digital computer and the integrated circuit, is one of the three most influential inventions of the electronic age. Though the least known and understood of the three, it is no less important than the others. Its most immediate application following its invention was as the heart of radar, arguably the technology that won the Second World War for the Allies. Sigurd's dream of building a device to protect citizens from airplane attack would be realized in just three short years during the London Blitz. And radar, of course, would go on to become the crucial infrastructural feature in the rise of international private and commercial airline service.

Modified as microwave transmitters, klystrons, big and small, sophisticated and crude, would find homes in everything from cellular telephony to home microwave ovens, setting off mini-revolutions in everything from communications to family life.

But in the end, the klystron's most important contribution to the sweep of history may prove to be in high-energy physics. Even as Russ and Sig were completing the prototype, Bill Hansen was already thinking ahead to grand machines that would place one powerful klystron after another along a tube stretching as much as two miles. Atomic particles would be fired down this tube, accelerated by each klystron in turn to near-light speeds, and smash into a metallic target, spinning off subatomic particles at the point of impact.

Hansen would die at his desk in 1949, at age thirty-nine, from lung failure and exhaustion, still struggling to make his vision of this "linear accelerator" real. It took another seventeen years, but in 1966 Stanford University unveiled the mile-long Stanford Linear Accelerator. It has proven not only to be one of the most important tools in our understanding of the subatomic world, but, coincidentally, was the birthplace of the personal computer.

But first, the klystron had to move from prototype to actual, buildable device. The Varian brothers had assumed that the first, and most enthusiastic, customer for the klystron would be the military. But an initial approach to the U.S. Navy was met with indifference.

Luckily, the commercial world proved more astute to the potential of the device. Representatives of Sperry Gyroscope in New York, upon learning of the klystron, quickly hopped a train to take a look. By the time they left Palo Alto with a contract, the Varian brothers had paying jobs, Stanford had a royalty agreement (ultimately making millions off what had been essentially the slave labor of the Varians), and Professors Hansen and Webster had contracts to work on the klystron in their spare time. The team also had some spending money to hire talented young engineers to assist Russell in advancing the klystron's technology. It was this money, handled by Fred Terman, that was used to bring Dave Packard back to Stanford.

Thus, the invention of the klystron proved to be a watershed moment, not only in the history of warfare, and in the story of the electronics revolution, but also at Stanford University. The easygoing college for the sons and daughters (and very few of the latter, as Leland Stanford's original decree of a four-to-one male/female student ratio was still in effect) had been transformed over the previous decade into a serious and important academic institution. Now, thanks to Fred Terman's Radio Lab and the klystron project, Stanford would forever after be a world center for engineering and business—and ultimately, for entrepreneurship.

For Hewlett and Packard, the klystron project would prove equally important. Both men had now seen, up close, what it took to invent an important new electronic product: the combination of technological prowess, market understanding, and manufacturing skill. In Russ Varian, Bill had been able to work beside a great scientist-engineer at the peak of his abilities. And, thanks to the Sperry Gyro contract, Dave had been able to come home to Palo Alto and, as he would soon discover, get a job as an assistant to the Varians, working out of the lab at Charlie Litton's shop—in other words, an apprenticeship in daily life at what was then one of the world's most successful electronics start-up companies.

In Great Company

There are no surviving photographs, so we can only guess what it was like to see these two brilliant giants, one young and handsome, the other middle-aged and heavy-featured, both destined to become the wealthiest of tycoons, working side by side on giant klystrons, as tall as they were, in the—to our eyes—shockingly primitive laboratory in Redwood City.

Packard's assignment was to help Russ figure out how to tweak ever higher frequencies out of the klystron's vacuum tube—which was why they were based at Litton Engineering, as Charlie Litton remained one of the best tube makers alive. Though his time there was comparatively brief, Packard's work on the klystron project provided the last lessons he would need before the birth of Hewlett-Packard. First, there was the opportunity, as Hewlett had enjoyed a few months before, of working with a true engineering genius— with all of the good and bad that entailed. Varian, with his clumsiness, his unsystematic work habits, and his willingness to risk wild creative leaps, must have been a nightmare at first for the graceful, systematic Packard. But he learned to work with, and even admire, Russ Varian—and in the process saw what it takes to handle and cultivate creativity. Russ's learning disabilities presented their own challenges—basically, he kept everything in his head— which must have made being his assistant particularly difficult, but Packard seems to have dealt with it in good humor—and compared to Varian, a mere dyslexic like Bill Hewlett must have seemed a snap.

Russ Varian wasn't the only person there to teach Dave Packard that engineering life was much more complicated than engineering theory. Charlie Litton himself was the prototype of software code writers three generations hence: he typically ate breakfast in the late afternoon, didn't show up at the office until evening, and then sometimes worked until dawn.

Litton's odd schedule actually worked to Packard's advantage, because it enabled him to take the classes required by his contract in the morning, work with Bill and study in the afternoon, and spend at least a little time with his new bride before heading up to Redwood City. Without Litton's work hours, Packard recalled, "I'm not sure I could have juggled all this work and study and still have had time for a home life."[53]

Charlie Litton had another lesson for Dave Packard: humility. In almost every situation in which he had ever found himself, from high school on, Dave had been the best in the room. He may not have been as smart as Barney Oliver, but he was a better student. He may not have been the best player on the Stanford football team, but he was likely the best all-around combination of player and student.

But with Charlie Litton, Packard ran into a character who somehow combined humility with the ability "to do everything better than anyone else."[54] Litton was the classic self-made, independent entrepreneur. That autumn, when swelling orders convinced him that the company needed a new plant, Litton didn't hire a contractor, but simply showed up one day with a bulldozer and did the foundation excavation himself. He even let Packard take some turns on the machine—a skill Dave proudly put to use years later in cutting the roads for his ranch.

What Charlie Litton offered Dave Packard was a glimpse of how to find happiness in success. Litton by then was a very rich man, as well as unequaled in his field. Yet he found his joy in living a comparatively simple life, without putting on airs, setting his own schedule, and never getting far from the craft work that he loved best. He was largely indifferent both to the trappings of success (he could be found sometimes tromping around the Sierras in a home-made four-wheel-drive truck—the first of its kind in the West) and the rules of "how things are done." In other words, Charlie Litton taught Dave Packard that he didn't have to always be Dave Packard—and Dave loved him for it. They would be close friends for the rest of Litton's life.*

One of the benefits (though it may not have seemed so at the time) of working at Litton Labs was that Charlie never got tired of talking: about life, about science and technology, and most of all, about business. Packard was al-ready, in preparation for the company to come, using his required units to take business law and management accounting, but Litton gave him real-life management—and, to Dave's surprise, Charlie was a conservative business-man. "As eccentric as he was, he knew you had to support your company and pay your bills."

In a rare effort at structure, Litton even organized some seminars at his office on subjects as far-ranging as quantum mechanics and business plan-ning. Invitees included Packard, some Stanford graduate students—and an engineer from Dalmo Victor, a radar antenna manufacturing company, whose extraordinary career had already included time as a fighter pilot in the Rus-sian civil war, a heroic escape from the Red Army, and seven years trapped in Shanghai trying to get passage to America. His name was Alexander Poniatoff, and he would soon take his initials, add an "-ex" for excellence, and name his new company (located just blocks from Litton Labs) Ampex, the pioneering company of both audio and video recording.

Charlie Litton was also a patriot, and that too would have a lifelong effect upon Packard.

One of Litton's inventions was an innovative new all-metal vacuum pump featuring low-vapor-pressure oil. Until then, standard vacuum pumps, like those used by Packard at GE, used mercury vapor—and they ran so hot that they had to be cooled by liquid oxygen. Needless to say, this made them in-credibly expensive to own and operate. Litton, in a classic example of how his mind worked, came up with a better solution by simply buying a particular commercial brand of motor oil and distilling it down to a highly purified, low-vapor-pressure extract.

In 1939, a group of scientists paid Charlie Litton a top-secret visit. He was not supposed to talk about the meeting, but being Charlie Litton, he told Packard all about it (probably over a beer in a Palo Alto saloon). It seems that the scientists were part of the Manhattan Project to build the first atomic bomb. Like most applied scientists in America, they knew all about Charlie Litton, his tubes, and his vacuum pump. So when the fission project discovered that it would need a huge volume of low-vapor-pressure oil, Litton was the only person they could think of to produce it.

Charlie didn't hesitate for an instant in taking on the job. It was, after all, both an interesting technical challenge and a service to his country. And his solution was, once again, classic Charlie Litton: he went and bought a huge redwood water tank (in abundance in the agricultural Santa Clara Valley), spent a few weeks assembling it, filled it with his distilling equipment to keep it from the public eye, then ordered railroad cars filled with the right motor oil. The Manhattan Project got its crucial low-vapor-pressure oil.

It was in this environment of fiercely independent entrepreneurship and brilliant seat-of-the-pants engineering that Bill Hewlett and Dave Packard set out to build their company.

They already had their corporate headquarters: even before Dave and Lu arrived from New York, Bill had scouted out available rooms and houses in the blocks of homes surrounding downtown Palo Alto. He found a perfect candidate on Addison Avenue, about six blocks from the "main street" of University Avenue: a thirty-year-old, two-story foursquare house with a porch at the front and a small storage shed and one-car garage in the back. Dave and Lu rented the lower floor from the elderly woman who lived on the second floor. Bill moved into the little shack—which was just big enough for a cot and a chair, and had no electricity. In the garage, which was to be the company headquarters, Dave unloaded the drill press from the car trunk, and he and Bill put up shelving and workbenches.

At some point the two men concluded that the original name for their company was just too insipid and forgettable. As was the custom of the time (as "-onics," "-el," and ".com" would be for tech companies in the decades to come), they decided to name it after themselves—just as Charlie Litton had done. To determine the order of the names, they flipped a coin. Needless to say, Hewlett won the coin toss, and Hewlett-Packard Company it became, as it would remain even after the trend became that of putting "Corp." on the name of publicly traded firms.

But the real point of the coin toss is not the result, but the very fact that it occurred. It shows that neither man was willing to put his ego first, and that both Bill and Dave were willing to accept the consequences of their agreements, no matter which of them benefited more.*

The next challenge, of course, was to figure out what the company would actually make. What is curious here is that, despite the fact that both Hewlett and Packard had spent the last eight years immersed in the world of electronic instruments and equipment, from Bill's work with oscillators to Dave's time at GE, to Varian's klystron and Litton's tubes, it never seemed to cross their minds to take their new business in that direction. Perhaps it was because Packard knew he wasn't an inventor, and Hewlett didn't believe he was—and so neither thought they could play on this ultra-competitive field. Or perhaps they thought that everything important had been invented in instruments, the market was mature, and that there was no space left for a newcomer. Or, charitably, it might be that they were among the first to recognize that the new generation of electronic instruments, building upon the now huge infrastructure of radio, was about to explode with a whole array of new consumer electronic products, especially television.

Though it would be nice to think they were that prescient, the initial businesses Bill and Dave tried to pursue suggest that in fact they were just a couple of young guys who figured they could use their engineering prowess to dazzle traditional companies with compelling new solutions—and make some money doing so.

Unfortunately, after a lot of discussion, neither could come up with a winning product idea. Instead, Hewlett and Packard did the next best thing: they used their own network of contacts—and prevailed upon Fred Terman, Charlie Litton, and others for their business connections as well—to drum up some contract work.

The result was a string of jobs notable only for their range, their singularity, and their lack of connection to anything the company did afterwards. For example, Bill and Dave were hired by a local bowling alley to design lane signaling equipment. Lick Observatory, whose domes still shine over the Santa Clara Valley from atop the region's highest mountain, contracted Bill and Dave for the synchronous motor drive for its telescope, then among the largest in the world.

For future generations, the most amusing failed business foray was into the design of a self-flushing toilet. Seventy years later, retired executive vice president Bill Terry would joke, "Every time I stood at a urinal I thought of Bill and Dave."[55]

Ed Porter, who had moved to Sacramento to work on some lucrative air-conditioning contracts, threw some bucks his old friends' way in exchange for controllers for his systems. Charlie Litton came through for Bill and Dave, letting them borrow his foundry to cast the aluminum parts for the air-conditioning controllers and use his engraving machine to engrave the names of the customer hotels on the front panels.

Oddest of all was the work the two men performed for T. I. Moseley, the founder of Dalmo Victor. Moseley was a combination of serious entrepreneur and maniacal promoter—the prototype for many Silicon Valley tycoons to come. He always had some crazy idea in the back of his mind, and when he learned from Terman that the two boys were available he quickly offered them work on one scheme after another.

One of these projects came to Moseley's mind after he noticed that almost every harmonica made in the world came from Germany. With Germany poised for war, it suddenly hit him that there was about to be a world shortage of harmonicas. The problem was that the Germans not only built all of the harmonicas, but they alone knew how to tune the reeds.

So, Moseley concluded, if he could just figure out how to tune the damn things, the actual building of the harmonicas would be a snap—and he would corner the world market. Build me a harmonica tuner, he told Bill and Dave.

As it happened, at that time there was only one electronic device in the world that had a chance of accurately tuning a harmonica—and it happened to be Hewlett's prototype of his audio oscillator. Moseley knew about it, and suggested the two men try using the device to build the tuner. Unfortunately, even Hewlett's oscillator wasn't precise enough for the job; otherwise HP might have gotten an earlier start with a lot better funding. Instead, in failing, Hewlett's invention found itself put on the back shelf in favor of other work.

Moseley, undaunted, had another harebrained scheme. This time he wanted Bill and Dave to design an exerciser that would use electric impulses to work muscles without any effort by the user. The idea didn't work any better then than it does today, and poor Mrs. Moseley had to suffer through one long Sunday afternoon having Bill Hewlett and Dave Packard attach electrodes to her leg, test various frequencies, and make her muscles twitch—all as her approving husband looked on.

Needless to say, neither invention for Moseley ever went into production. But they did help pay the bills, as did the other contracts. And that was important to the two men, especially Dave Packard, as he was largely living on Lu's small income as a secretary.

Looking back, Dave also concluded that, despite the wildly diverse natures of these contract projects, he and Bill learned some important things from the experience:

> The miscellaneous jobs made us more sure of ourselves and our skills. They also revealed something that we hadn't planned but that was of great benefit to our partnership—namely, that our abilities tended to be complementary. Bill was better trained in circuit technology, and I was better trained and more experienced in manufacturing processes. This combination of abilities was particularly useful in designing and manufacturing electronic products.[56]*

As 1938 closed, the two men could look back on the year with pride. They had landed some contracts and made some money. Not a lot of money, but enough to live on—and convince themselves that they could run a viable business. They had also learned a few things about themselves and each other. It was a measure of both their trust in each other and their doubts about the viability of their enterprise that Bill and Dave had yet to even formalize their business partnership. They resolved to do that by incorporating Hewlett-Packard Company at the beginning of the new year.

And as they toasted each other that New Year's Eve, the two men must have assured each other that 1939 would be a good year.

In fact, it was the year they would change the course of history.

Chapter Three:
That Damned Garage

In January 1939, Bill Hewlett and Dave Packard signed the papers and formally incorporated Hewlett-Packard Company.

Bill agreed, as part of the deal, to advance some money to the company to purchase some components and tools. Packard contributed the equipment he'd brought home from General Electric.

Although it was hardly an act without consequence, it doesn't seem to have been noted with any great importance by the two men. Packard, writing a half century later for *The Scientist* magazine, could only remember that "Bill and I signed our partnership agreement either shortly before or shortly after January 1, 1939."[1] It's likely they simply went to a lawyer's or notary's office one day after Packard's classes and signed the partnership agreement before Dave had to take off for Litton Labs. Hewlett, for his part, probably just went home to the garage.

Seventy years on, it is hard to separate the HP garage of myth from the one of reality. Over the course of the twentieth century, the little Addison Avenue garage came, at least at first, to represent the touchingly humble beginnings of a great American company.

But by the 1980s, when high technology was ascendant in the world economy and a number of other powerful companies (such as Apple and Fairchild) had also been born in "garages" ranging from real garages to cheap storefronts, the Packard garage, as the very first, became the cynosure for the world of tech entrepreneurship, seat-of-the-pants engineering, and tough, pragmatic business leadership.

A trillion-dollar industry and the largest employer in the developed world is an awful lot to place upon an old, uninsulated wooden structure of less than two hundred square feet at the end of a dirt driveway in a quiet residential neighborhood. But bigger myths have rested upon far thinner reeds.

The reality of the Packard garage—even now after the spiders have scurried away, after every board has been lovingly restored, and after the government has guaranteed that it will probably survive long after all of the other houses on the street have been demolished—is far simpler: Bill and Dave used it because it was cheap and expedient, and they walked away from it the instant they could afford something better.

That, of course, doesn't take away the importance of the Addison Avenue garage for the rest of us. It *is* the birthplace of the electronics age, and, in a world of multibillion-dollar corporations with magnificent and giant office buildings scattered all over the planet, it can be immensely moving to stand in that little garage, with its thin walls and crude workbenches, its boxes of vacuum tubes and oil cans, and realize that the modern world of computers, medical monitors, the Internet, cell phones, robots—all of it—begins *right here.*

That said, it is also important not to forget an anecdote told by David Kirby, HP's longtime PR director, about a visit to the garage with Dave Packard in 1989:

> They [had] declared the garage a state landmark and had a little ceremony. I drove Packard over there and as we were walking up the driveway he turned to me and said, "You know, this is the first time I've been back here in fifty years."
>
> That was Dave Packard. He never understood what all the fuss was about. For him, it was always just a garage: and he was glad to get out of it. What he cared about, even when he was an old man, was the future. What mattered to him was what was next.[2]*

After the ceremony, Dave joined Bill for a reception at HP to celebrate the occasion. One former HP employee had a vivid memory of that event:

> It so happened that I was behind Dave Packard in the line where the food and drinks were being served. I took the opportunity to congratulate him on the naming of the garage as an historic monument. He put his hand in the small of my back ushering me ahead of him in line and leaned over to reply in a low voice: "I am tired of that damn garage."[3]

While Packard was working for Russ Varian at Litton Labs, Hewlett had spent most of 1938 perfecting the design for his audio oscillator and researching the design of other new instruments. With Terman touring around giving speeches about negative feedback, the interest in Bill's innovative design was beginning to grow. And with Terman's article, with its section about Hewlett's work, heading toward publication, Bill decided that he needed to build a real working model of the instrument. Packard offered to help.

Their effort to get a working production model completed was given added impetus late in the year, when the little garage received a particularly important visitor. Harold Buttner had been one of Fred Terman's earliest students. These days, Buttner was the vice president of research and development at International Telephone and Telegraph. Terman convinced him to take a look at Hewlett's audio oscillator.

Buttner was impressed. So much so that he offered Bill and Dave $500—about as much as ITT was paying for a single oscillator in those days—for the foreign patent rights to the device. He even offered to provide the legal help to get the two young men the U.S. patent on the instrument.

Bill and Dave fairly reeled from the visit. Not only did the payment represent a tenth of their annual income to date, but more important, it suddenly suggested to the two that maybe, even while they were searching for their first good product, they might already be sitting on it.

So they decided to give Bill's design a market test. In November, they finished construction of their first audio oscillator and Hewlett took it up to an IRE conference in Portland, Oregon. Packard recalled, "The response was positive enough that we decided to make a run for it."[4]

By Christmas, they had built a model with a professional-looking case, and "I clearly recall having this unit sitting on the mantel above the fireplace. There we took pictures of it, produced a two-page sales brochure, typed by Lu, that we sent to a list of about twenty-five potential customers provided by Fred Terman."[5]

As Bill and Dave planned it, recipients of the brochure would believe that they were dealing with an established company. For that reason, they designated the new instrument as the "200A," because that number sounded like just the latest in a long line of products from a mature enterprise, not something from a pair of twenty-five-year-olds working out of a garage. The price the two decided upon was even more arbitrary: the 200A audio oscillator was listed at $54.40, a number chosen entirely because it amusingly reminded Bill and Dave of the historic phrase "54'40" or Fight!" that was used in the 1844 campaign to set the U.S.-Canadian border in the Northwest.

Though the story of the pricing has become part of the HP myth, less remembered is how foolish that decision was: $54.40 was well below what it cost the pair to build the 200A, meaning that they would lose money on every sale. It was not a propitious start for two future titans of American business. In fact, what saved them in the end was that competing products to the 200A, like the oscillators being sold by General Radio, were going for as much as ten times that price. That enabled Bill and Dave to scramble and reset the price higher, while still offering a bargain.

Not surprisingly, given the initial price, the brochure not only generated several orders, but some of the envelopes came back with checks stuffed into them. That convinced the two men that they had a real business on their hands and to finally incorporate. Later, by the time they discovered their pricing error, they were already too far under way to turn back. Hewlett-Packard Co. was now a real enterprise. At the end of January 1939, Bill Hewlett carefully drew up the schematic for the 200A and hired a San Francisco attorney to file a patent for it. By the time the patent was awarded (No. 2,268,872) three years later, it arrived to a very different world: Bill Hewlett had gone off to war.

For now, there were orders to fill—and given the foolish pricing Bill and Dave had settled upon, there was now no room for anything but the cheapest possible production. For that reason, the two men decided to buy the cabinets for the 200A but make their own panels out of sheets of aluminum they sawed and drilled. Then, once they'd spray-painted the panels, Dave would take them into the house and use Lu's oven to bake on the enamel. Packard would recall that during this period the food cooked in that oven always had a slight chemical taste.

Next came the assembly of the guts of the oscillator—board, tubes, transformer, and Hewlett's little light bulb—and their installation into the cabinet. Then Dave would take the box up to Litton Labs and use Charlie's engraver to engrave all of the front-panel markings.

This last was not an automatic process: rather, because of variations in the components of each instrument, Packard would first go up to Litton's place and engrave all of the designations, scratching through the paint on the front panel. Then he would go back to the garage to calibrate the instrument, marking the dial with a pencil, then back up to Litton's to engrave the final calibrations. Luckily, Charlie Litton was always there to lend a hand—and no doubt at some point told his young friend that this was no way to run a business.

In doing so, Litton taught Dave Packard one last lesson. Looking back, Packard would say, "He never saw us as competitors but always as compatriots."[6] That lesson was also reinforced by an unlikely source. Fred Terman called one day to say that he had a visitor who would like to come over to the garage and introduce himself. It was Melville Eastham, the founder of General Radio. Uncharacteristically, Terman brought the industry titan—and Hewlett-Packard's greatest potential competitor—over to Addison Avenue and left him alone with Bill and Dave for several hours. Afterwards, Eastham told Fred how much he had enjoyed visiting such fine young men; Bill and Dave, for their part, told Terman that Eastham had been very helpful, even giving them some pointers about running a successful business.[7]

The challenge now, with an underpriced but popular product, was to keep the fledgling Hewlett-Packard alive. Enter the most unlikely of corporate saviors: Walt Disney.

Dave Packard was always anxious to debunk the standard myth, one of the best-known in the story of electronics, that Hewlett-Packard would have gone out of business had it not been for the fortuitous sale of a bunch of HP audio oscillators to the Walt Disney Co., and that without these HP instruments Disney would never have made the landmark film *Fantasia*.

In truth, to quote Packard, "with or without the Disney sale, Bill and I were determined to move ahead with our company."[8] But that begs the question: *could* Hewlett-Packard have lasted much longer with only a handful of orders and an unprofitable product?

The genesis of the Disney sale was that Portland conference in November 1938 that Bill Hewlett attended with his prototype audio oscillator. One of the people at the event to whom he showed the instrument was Bud Hawkins, the chief sound engineer at Walt Disney Studios. Disney, flush from the success of its great, pioneering long-format animated films *Snow White* and *Pinocchio*, was now about to push the envelope of content, animation, and sound with *Fantasia*. In preparation for the project, Hawkins was upgrading his equipment, including the test instruments.

Hawkins was impressed by the performance stats for the Hewlett device, but what sealed the deal for him was the price Bill quoted to him: less than $100—one-fourth what Hawkins would have to pay for comparable General Radio oscillators. For the future of HP, Hewlett was lucky that he gave the higher estimate and not the final price.

He was doubly lucky that Hawkins came back to Hewlett-Packard and asked for some modifications to the original design. This enabled Bill and Dave to escape the legacy of their widely circulated brochure by announcing a slightly improved follow-up product, the HP model 200B—still a steal, but actually profitable at $71.50. Bud Hawkins ordered eight, which were used in the audio production of *Fantasia*, notably in helping the team achieve the trick, in the "Flight of the Bumblebee" sequence, of making the sound of the bee seem to come out of the screen and buzz around the theater.

Meanwhile, the profits from the Disney contract helped keep the fledgling Palo Alto Company alive. Recalled Packard, "We very quickly learned that we could raise the price [if] it was a good value and that was a lesson that was very important because it made it possible for us to finance the company as we went along."[9] HP—wags would later say the initials stood for "highest priced"—would never make that mistake again.*

Less remarked, but far more vital to the long-term success of Hewlett-Packard Co., was an encounter with another Los Angeles industry veteran. Norm Neely was a manufacturers' rep for radio and sound recording equipment whose beat included most of Southern California, especially the entertainment industry.

Like Hawkins, Neely was on the lookout for new products that he could sell to his customers. Hearing about the two Stanford boys with their innovative, low-cost audio oscillator, he thought there might be an opportunity there. So, sight unseen, Neely invited Bill Hewlett to come down to Los Angeles and speak to the local Radio Engineers Club, a group Neely had joined primarily to hunt for customers.

It was the most important letter Neely ever wrote in his life, and before it was over, fifty years later, he was a very rich man. But the evening started out as a disaster. The club president, as Hewlett remembered, "got up and gave me a very flowery introduction . . . that he'd known me for years and 'Now, I'd like to introduce my friend *Bill Packard!*' "

Fortunately, Hewlett found the whole thing hilarious—and in Norm Neely an ambitious and hardworking salesman Hewlett-Packard could work with. Neely, for his part, quickly followed that meeting with a trip up to Palo Alto. If he was shocked by the sight of the humble little garage, he managed to keep a straight face—and before he left, he and the two founders had, in Packard's words, "reached a verbal agreement and sealed it with a handshake. That was the way we were to conduct our business with Norm for the next fifty years."[10]

Before he left, Neely gave the two men one piece of advice: dump the contract business and focus on manufacturing products. You can't serve two masters or run two different kinds of businesses.*

There may have been self-interest in that advice, but there was also wisdom. The world was changing fast around them. Hitler had invaded Poland and Czechoslovakia, Russia had invaded Finland, Rudolf Heydrich had ordered all Jews in Warsaw into the city's ghetto, the Japanese were consolidating their control of China, and the Manhattan Project was under way.

Had Hewlett-Packard remained mostly a contract manufacturer, it might have prospered during the war to come, but disappeared soon after, a footnote like Federal Radio in the now delayed story of the electronics revolution, in a Santa Clara Valley that never became Silicon Valley. Instead, because they trusted the advice of a man they hardly knew, Bill and Dave dedicated their young company exclusively to product manufacture and, at the probable cost of some defense work during the war, positioned themselves for great success.

It was Neely's marketing and selling to the Hollywood and the Southern California aerospace industry that would create much of HP's early revenues. At first independently, and later inside HP, Neely would build the company's first powerhouse regional sales force—the prototype for HP field sales ever after.

Neely's efforts, and the increased revenues for HP that came from it, enabled Bill and Dave to take an important step: hiring their first employee. His name was Harvey Zieber, and he joined the pair as an assistant—the only HP employee besides the founders who could claim to have actually worked in the garage.

As 1939, that remarkable "World of Tomorrow" year in science and technology, ended, the rookie Hewlett-Packard Company had much to celebrate as well. Having started almost from scratch, and survived its first business crisis, the company had managed to produce two distinct products, made a customer out of one of the world's hottest companies—and earned $5,369 in sales.

Better yet, in spite of everything, Hewlett-Packard had managed to turn a profit of $1,653, with $500 cash on hand, zero liabilities, and an in-box full of orders. In other words, even in a year when half of its business was pickup contract work, when it had dangerously underpriced its only product, and when it had needed to purchase its start-up equipment, Hewlett-Packard had still managed to earn a pretax profit of *25 percent*. Few of the thousands of electronics start-up companies to follow over the next half century would manage to even turn a profit in their first year, and among those that did, most could only dream of margins that high.

HP now had products, a business strategy, a distribution and sales network, and enough cash on hand to grow the company without assuming debt. It had been a year of lessons. Bill and Dave were now convinced not only that they could build a real company, but that they could do so by financing their own growth—and thus never again leave the company financially vulnerable. Miraculously, they did just that for the rest of their careers, making HP one of the most fiscally conservative, and financially secure, large corporations of the century.

Lu & Flo

Bill Hewlett had more to celebrate in 1939 than just acclaim for his invention and the success of his new company. Despite the many demands of school and the fledgling company, he still found time to court and marry the tall and elegant Flora Lamson.

Bill had known Flo since childhood, though they had only recently been reacquainted. She was a Berkeley girl, born and raised, and when the time came for college, she applied to and was accepted at UC Berkeley. In an era when entire universities, much less science departments, were mostly male provinces, Flora Lamson chose biochemistry as her major.

She must have been quite a sight in the Cal biochem lab: a five-foot-seven blonde with a taste for elegant clothes that would characterize her for the rest of her life. Flora was not only pretty and smart, but her interests also tended toward art and literature, and religion (in later years she would found a library at the Graduate Theological Union and serve as a trustee of the San Francisco Theological Seminary). In that regard, she was very much like Hewlett's mother—though Flora was much more private—and it is likely the young woman easily passed muster with the Hewlett family matriarch.

She and Bill first met as youngsters, as the Hewlett and Lamson families regularly vacationed at the same camp in the Sierras. But the families lost touch during the difficult years that followed.

Whether Bill much noticed the younger Flora isn't recorded. But Flora noticed the older boy with his big grin and his mischievous ways. After she graduated from Cal in 1935 and by chance became reacquainted with Louise on a Sierra Club outing, she probably couldn't help but hear about him and his accomplishments at Stanford. Louise, for her part, being a protective sister and seeing her brother alone and, worse, living on a cot in a shack behind the Packard house, was resolved to find him a wife.

As the story was told later, Louise finally called her brother and asked, "Do you remember Flora Lamson?"

"Sure," said Hewlett. "Back when we were kids."

"That's right," said Louise. "Well, she's grown up now. And you need to ask her out."

Bill Hewlett would one day face down entire governments, but he was not going to fight his sister. He agreed to take out little Flora once, if only to humor Louise. But Louise, after all, was the sister of a man who would one day be famous for his judgment in people—she knew what she was doing with these two. Bill and Flora hit it off so well on that first date that it seemed almost preordained that they would marry.

Not everyone agreed with that destiny: almost to a person, the members of Flora's sorority tried to talk her out of the marriage, saying that Bill's plan to go into business for himself would only lead to poverty, unhappiness and possibly even starvation. They would remain married until Flora's early death in 1977. The marriage produced five children, their births almost evenly spaced over the next dozen years: Eleanor Louise (born 1942), Walter Berry (born 1944), James Sterry (born 1947), William Albion (born 1949) and Mary Joan (born 1951). It is a measure of the quiet strength of Flora Hewlett's personality that of the five kids, none followed their father into the corporate life. Rather, they chose a career like that of their grandfather (William Albion Hewlett, like his namesake, is a doctor) or followed their mother into low-profile, arts-related careers. Only Walter, a well-known software designer, followed his father into high technology.

There is a casual photo of the young couple, taken in 1938 and probably at a party at Cal, that shows Bill in jeans, shirt, and suspenders, standing beside Flora, who wears dungarees, white blouse, and kerchief elegantly tied around her collar. They look relaxed and comfortable in each other's company. And Bill has the smile of a happy man.

A second photo, taken a year later on their honeymoon in the Grand Tetons, is no less charming: Bill, wearing a khaki shirt and slacks, stands with his left shoulder just behind Flora's right. She is more formally dressed, with a skirt, blouse, and short jacket that has on its lapel a pin in the shape of a large bunch of grapes. It is obvious from their poses that Flora has grabbed another tourist and asked him to take a photo of the newlyweds. Flora faces the photograph head-on, her shoulders back, smiling but with the slightest touch of concern that the stranger work the camera right.

Bill, meanwhile, embarrassed by all of this attention, has shoved his hands in his pockets and ducked his chin in a way that says he doesn't quite approve of all of this. Still, he can't hide that he is very proud of his new bride. The sad and lonely teenager has become a contented and successful adult and husband.

Looking back on their long and happy marriage, son Walter Hewlett would conclude that one important reason for its success was his mother's education. His father, Walter would say, was a man of few words, and when he did talk, he liked to speak on technical topics. Because Flora had an understanding of technology few women possessed in those days—indeed, her children believed Flora had a scientific mind on a par with their father—the two could communicate on the same level.

Just as important, Flora had good instincts. She usually knew what her inarticulate husband wanted long before he could verbalize it. She used this skill (as the photo suggests) to "run interference" for Bill in difficult situations, all despite being an introverted person herself. As the photo also suggests, Bill Hewlett admired these traits in his new wife. And he continued to for the many years they spent together.[11]

Gauging the contribution of spouses to the careers of successful men and women can usually never be more than speculation. But it is interesting to note that not only did Bill and Dave enjoy lifelong marriages, but that their first great year in business corresponded to the first year of their marriages. We know of Lucile's obvious contribution to the early Hewlett-Packard, from her bookkeeping and marketing to her donation of the Addison Avenue kitchen oven. Flo Hewlett's participation is less visible, but certainly the very act of enabling Bill to move out of the shed into her Palo Alto house brought a new structure (and much-improved living conditions) to his daily life.

It may go deeper than that. Hewlett-Packard Co. became famous as the most "family-oriented" of large corporations. And the famous "HP Way" business philosophy has been compared to that of a highly functional family in which each member has a role to play and is trusted to fulfill that role responsibly. There is no question that for both Bill and Dave, their notion of family begins with Flora and Lucile.

———

There is an often-told story about the early days of Bill and Dave in the Addison Avenue garage. It is that Terman and others could quickly gauge how the new company was doing merely by driving by the Packard place and peeking down the driveway. If the car was in the garage, business was slow; if the car was parked outside, then orders had come in and the pair were hard at work.

If the story is indeed true, by fall 1939, the car was always outside. Business was booming and the two men were starting to run out of room for parts, manufacturing, and inventory storage. In advising Hewlett and Packard to focus on products, Norm Neely had added one more piece of advice: don't stick to one model, or even to a single market segment, but diversify the product family as quickly as possible.

Hewlett-Packard now had the 200A and 200B audio oscillators, and the two men were busily investigating the commercial potential of other audio frequency products that Bill had developed the previous year with students at Stanford. There was enough there to convince the two men that HP's immediate future would involve a full-on assault on the audio frequency measurement business—and that meant, as Packard said, "we would be in direct competition with the General Radio Company."[12]*

Keep in mind that General Radio in 1939 was the world's leading manufacturer of test and measurement instruments. The very idea of taking on the company in one of its key markets was ambitious enough, but to do so from a cramped, unheated garage on a neighborhood street thousands of miles from the main customer base was, even Bill and Dave knew, utterly insane. HP not only had to think like a real company, it now had to act like one—and look like one as well.

For that reason, in the fall of 1939 the two men scouted for and finally found a real headquarters/factory building, a small structure, tucked behind Tinker Bell's Fix-It Shop, the general repair workshop of John "Tinker" Bell. It was located just a mile southeast of the Stanford campus at the intersection of the founding, and still primary, road down the peninsula, El Camino Real, and a barely used cross street, Page Mill Road, an old logging road that ran up into the nearby hills. They packed up their tools, test equipment, and a few parts, and, with Harvey Zieber, moved the ten blocks to the Tinker Bell building.

John Minck, an executive in HP's Microwave division, and later an informal company historian, moved into the neighborhood a decade later. He never forgot the gritty industrial area—what would one day be Ground Zero of Silicon Valley:

> I remember it well because there was a concrete-mixing plant at [a nearby] intersection. At midnight the Southern Pacific railroad would deliver rail cars full of sand and gravel and cement to the plant. As the switch engine shuttled the cars around, the Page Mill street crossing gates would come down for about 30 minutes, with the crossing bells loudly sounding. With a brand new baby, that didn't help her sleep, or ours.[13]

Though the facility was small, it was nevertheless big enough for Hewlett and Packard to set up a small office in the front and, in the large back room, a combination paint shop, machine shop, and assembly and test area. After the garage, the new facility seemed immense. Recalled Packard, "It seemed as if we had all the space we would ever need."[14]

It was, in fact, smaller than the lobbies of most HP facilities to come.

In retrospect, for both Hewlett and Packard, it was in this little building (now long since demolished) where they really learned about how business worked. Their experiences there would be the template for generations of high-tech entrepreneurs to come—making big plans and dreaming even bigger thoughts—even as they had to do every odd job around the place, from answering the phone to cleaning the toilet. Recalled Packard:

> In those early days Bill and I had to be versatile. We had to tackle almost everything ourselves—from inventing and building products to pricing, packaging, and shipping them, from dealing with customers and sales representatives to keeping the books, from writing the ads to sweeping up at the end of the day. Many of the things I learned in this process were invaluable, and not available in business schools.[15]*

That wasn't all of it. As anyone who watches weather reports knows, the Bay Area may have near-perfect weather, but the cost is that most of the rain falls within a couple of months each winter—and as the Santa Clara Valley is one vast alluvial plain striped with ancient, and now largely hidden, streams, whole regions of it are prone to flooding.

Unfortunately, one of those floodplains happened to be just outside the door of HP's new building. On several occasions, Bill and Dave had to stack sandbags in front of the front door to keep the flood from running down Page Mill Road and right through their offices.

The two men were also taught a little humility when it came to the practical application of their engineering skills. They may have been brilliant students and terrific product designers, but they weren't Charlie Litton, or even "Tinker" Bell next door. Learning that fact didn't come easy for either Bill or Dave, and on one occasion their overestimation of their tinkering skills almost proved disastrous.

It had to do with a new oven. When the pair first moved to their new building, they still carried the newly painted parts back to Addison Avenue to cure in the Packards' oven. Eventually, even Lu ran out of patience, and told the two men that she wanted her kitchen back exclusively for actual cooking.

Instead of contracting out the work, Bill and Dave decided to build their own paint drier. And, to save even more money, they decided to build the oven out of a good, cheap, insulated box: a used refrigerator. Unfortunately, neither knew much about refrigeration—and Ed Porter, who did, was in Sacramento, so he wasn't there to warn them. Thus, even as they were rewiring the refrigerator, neither noticed that its insulation was made out of flammable kapok, the stuff in life vests.

When the rebuilt refrigerator/oven was first fired up, it worked perfectly, and the two men patted each other on the back and reminded themselves what great engineers they were. In fact, the oven worked so well that Bill and Dave took to putting another load of panels in before they left in the evening and letting the oven run all night.

The reader can guess what happened next. Luckily—and those were the days when even El Camino Real was empty by midnight—the driver of a passing car happened to notice flames flickering in the windows from inside the HP plant, and he called the fire department. The burning oven was put out before it destroyed the building, and HP in the process.

That wasn't their only beginners' mistake. Hewlett on one occasion started up Packard's old drill press without removing the key from the chuck—sending the key hurtling, fortunately not into Hewlett, but through the plateglass storefront. Then, after replacing the window, the two men noticed that the building had no privacy; every passerby seemed to stop and peer in. So Bill and Dave decided to paint the windows black for privacy—which worked fine until the first hot day, when the absorbed sunlight cracked every pane.

Luckily, new orders for the 300B were continuing to pour in—enough that the two men could not only cover the cost of glass replacement, but contract out some of the work to craftsmen with more practical experience than their own. One of these was a carpenter and cabinetmaker named Al Spears. In keeping with the style of the time, once HP began to market premium instruments it was expected they would feature wooden cabinets—typically walnut, but Bill and Dave told Spears to go with oak for durability, cost, and appearance.

Before long, however, especially for their high-frequency products, Hewlett and Packard decided to switch to sheet-metal cabinets. For that work, they went to a neighbor on Addison Avenue, a crusty old guy named Ernie Schiller, who had his own small custom metal shop. Ernie was so gruff that often when Bill or Dave would stop by—even after HP had become his sole client—Schiller would act as if he didn't want to see them. Still, he remained HP's cabinetmaker until he retired, and when the HP work grew to be too much for one man, Bill and Dave sent over an HP employee to help him.

Lessons in Loyalty

Ernie Schiller is the most minor of players in the story of Bill Hewlett and Dave Packard. And yet he symbolizes something profound and crucial to the long-term success of the Hewlett-Packard Company:

For Hewlett and Packard, the twenties, their childhood, was the decade of curiosity and risk-taking. The thirties were the years in which they apprenticed to great mentors, including Fred Terman and Charlie Litton, as well as listened to and followed the advice of people like Norm Neely, Melville Eastham, and Russ Varian.

For Bill and Dave, the forties would be the decade of loyalty. They had already learned to be loyal to each other—a fidelity that would soon be tested by a world war. Now they would learn to show that same loyalty to others. It is easy to be loyal to your employer and to your mentors, especially if they are good people. It is far more difficult to be loyal to people who need you more than you need them. By the end of this new decade, Hewlett and Packard would, for the first time, be men of importance, wealth, and power—and their loyalty to the friends they had surpassed, and the people whose livelihoods now depended upon them, would regularly be tested.*

That they passed this test, and did so with both graciousness and dignity—even to difficult men like Ernie Schiller—was at least as important as the Addison Avenue garage in the creation of the myth of Bill and Dave and the philosophy of the HP Way. One comes away from reading the Hewlett and Packard story with the sense that they *never* left anyone behind. The many people whose lives prospered because Bill and Dave returned their loyalty stand as proof that sometimes, even in the unforgiving world of business, there can sometimes be justice.*

————————

Loyalty came in many forms to Bill and Dave in the 1940s.

In early 1940, ITT, having just won a major contract for the development of an electronic aircraft landing system, put out a request for bids on two components for that system: one a variable-frequency oscillator, and the other a crystal-controlled, fixed-frequency oscillator. General Radio jumped on the first deal, but experience told the big company to stay away from the second.

Hewlett-Packard lacked that experience and naively took on the second job. It wasn't long before Bill and Dave realized that they were in trouble: that there weren't enough hours in the day to get the project completed on time. Though they had begun hiring employees—over the next two years they would bring on board a secretary, Helen Perry, to finally relieve Lu Packard of the secretarial and bookkeeping work; a machinist named Dick Arms; Harvey Zieber's brother Glenn; two technicians named Harold Hance and Brunton Bauer; and Bill Girdner, a mechanic—Bill and Dave realized to their dismay that, though the company was now fully staffed with builders, it was woefully short of designers. They had failed to look beyond Hewlett's original design to the day when the young company might have a wide product family.

So the two men quickly went out and began hiring the best available talent they could find, recruiting top engineers from the nearby veteran short-wave radio maker, Heintz and Kaufman, where Dave had interviewed for work when he was still a Stanford senior. That job interview had been handled by a young Heintz and Kaufman engineer named Noel Eldred. As Packard would remember, "and fortunately as it turned out they didn't have a job [for me] . . . because I might have just stayed there."[16]

Packard had been impressed by Eldred, so, over the next two years, when he went looking for talent at Heintz and Kaufman, he knew whom to contact first. Eldred took the job—as did, among others, a test engineer named Bill Doolittle. Eldred and Doolittle would prove crucial to the long-term success of HP, and both would eventually serve as HP vice presidents.

Thanks to the added talent, and an immense amount of hard work, HP finally managed to build the fixed-frequency oscillator for ITT. But the young company had paid heavily for the effort: the employees were exhausted, other deliveries were late, and worst of all, as the days passed and no ITT check arrived, the two founders realized they were within a week of not making payroll. Finally, a desperate Dave Packard called Harold Buttner at ITT and explained the situation. Buttner immediately wired the funds.

Bill and Dave never forgot that gesture, made especially gracious by the fact that it came from the busy CEO of a big corporation who literally had to override his own staff procedures. It colored Hewlett-Packard's own dealings with small vendors in the years to come. And when Buttner retired from ITT, Packard immediately called him and asked him to sit on the Hewlett-Packard board. Buttner accepted and proved an important source of industry contacts when HP began its first era of spectacular growth in the 1950s.*

They had been saved, but the close call had shaken both Bill and Dave. Being children of the Great Depression, they had built their little company entirely as a pay-as-you-go enterprise. All growth was to come from profits, not debt. But the ITT episode had taught them the dangers of poor cash flow; that a company could go out of business even with an in-box full of new orders. And that in turn meant they had to learn the differences between short- and long-term debt, and the advantages and disadvantages of each.*

In the end, Dave Packard resolved to establish a line of credit for the company at the Bank of Italy (now Bank of America), founded in nearby San Jose, the largest bank in California, and famous for being the friend of the little guy. He applied for a loan of $500, an amount he and Bill deemed sufficient to tide the company over if it got stuck again.

B of A, as was its procedure, sent a loan officer over to the Tinker Bell building to check out the company and its facilities. Recalled Packard, "He apparently wasn't very impressed, for the bank agreed to give us a loan only if we would sign over to it our accounts receivable."[17]

Packard refused. Instead, he drove over to the little neighborhood bank, Palo Alto National, and introduced himself directly to the bank's president, Jud Crary. Crary, it turned out, was a huge Stanford fan who remembered well Dave Packard's glory days on the gridiron and the track. Packard explained about his new company, its current financials, and its need for credit. How much? asked Crary. Five hundred dollars, Packard replied. Crary nodded, pulled out a notepad, wrote out a promissory note for that amount, and asked Dave to sign it. Then he escorted Packard to the other side of the bank, and there drafted for him a deposit slip for $500.

Once again, trust given—and trust returned. Out of loyalty, Hewlett-Packard continued to do business with Palo Alto National for years—and when the company grew too big for the little bank, exceeding its legal financial limits, HP still maintained the relationship by moving to National's associate bank, Wells Fargo.[18]*

That $500 loan proved to be worth tens of millions of dollars for those two banks. And the story doesn't end there, because when HP shifted its banking to Wells Fargo the bank shrewdly sent a retired engineer out to HP's headquarters to meet with Packard and gauge the company's financial plans. Recalled Packard, "I spent a full afternoon with him and I have remembered ever since some advice he gave me. He said that more businesses die from in-digestion than starvation. I have observed the truth of that advice many times since then."[19]

These stories suggest a culture in the San Francisco Bay Area before World War II characterized by an extraordinary willingness to share resources, tal-ent, and experience among its players. No doubt all of these companies were deeply competitive, even with one another. And yet—perhaps because the in-dustry was so new, because the population of technologists was so small and interdependent (everyone seemed to be orbiting around Fred Terman and his lab), or perhaps because of the isolation of the West Coast electronics industry—there was a degree of camaraderie that didn't exist among the giant electronics firms of the East Coast, or for that matter in the Bay Area itself in the Silicon Valley that would soon emerge.

It is interesting then to speculate that the Hewlett-Packard culture, the legendary "HP Way," was at its heart like a fragment of a lost world kept alive in a glass case, the enlightened (and obviously successful) business environ-ment in which Bill and Dave had founded their company—that Hewlett and Packard were brilliant preservers of the past, at least the best of that past, rather than corporate revolutionaries.

This in no way takes away from the two men as business and organiza-tional innovators—on the contrary, they alone had the courage and genius to actually make the old work in a new era and within a giant company. But it of-fers a different perspective on their achievement. It means that they weren't gambling their company on some radically new management idea, but rather fighting to preserve something they had already seen work. And their greatest accomplishment as managers was to figure out how to elucidate what had once been taken for granted, and do so before it disappeared.*

Thus, it was Bill and Dave who held fast to a fixed place—where a hand-shake sealed a deal, a man was as good as his word, you built friendship and business relationships that lasted a lifetime, and you knew and trusted every person who worked for you—while the world around them moved on. It must have been surpassingly difficult to hold to what they believed, even as the wildest, most aggressive community on the planet grew up around them, and largely because of them. But Bill and Dave knew they were right, and as much as any business leaders ever, they had the courage of their convictions. In time, after the world had changed so completely that the HP culture went from looking anachronistic to appearing revolutionary, others began to won-der if Bill and Dave might have been right all along.

A Product Family

Norm Neely hadn't only told Bill and Dave to get out of custom work and stick to standardized products. He also told them—in a message seconded by another new company distributor, Midwest radio tycoon Al Crosley—that they needed to expand their product line.

The HP 200A had been a great first product, and the 200B actually made money. But a company with multiple product lines enjoyed a number of advantages, including greater brand recognition, greater strategic flexibility, more customer loyalty, and less vulnerability to attacks from competitors. It also went without saying that Neely had a greater chance of getting through the door of a potential customer if he had a number of different products to sell.*

Once again, Bill and Dave listened. Moreover, after the nightmare of the ITT contract, the prospect of designing and building a product actually within their expertise must have been appealing indeed. Nevertheless, they shrewdly chose not to stray far from their original products, but instead designed devices that were related to, even dovetailed with, the company's existing catalog. The result was what would now be known as a "suite" of products—and in the years to come, HP would use this accretionary strategy to slowly take over the workbenches of America's electrical engineers.

Like IBM with computing products a decade later, each sale of an HP instrument to an engineer helped to sell the one that followed. That, accompanied by the high quality of the HP products, began to create a purchasing process among thousands of engineers in which the first, and safest, choice was Hewlett-Packard. Eventually, even when HP didn't have the best version (as was the case with oscilloscopes), it still usually got the benefit of the doubt from its immense customer "family." As was said about IBM, "No one ever got fired for buying Big Blue," so it was with HP for the next forty years.

Hewlett-Packard's first new product after the two oscillators was the model 320 distortion analyzer. This was followed by a harmonic wave analyzer, the model 300A, designed by Hewlett. Then, having staked out this new turf, Bill and Dave revisited their original line and upgraded it with an oscillator that featured a gain control (the model 205A).

On this product, once again—and essentially for the last time—Bill Hewlett displayed his amazing gift for clever design. Until the model 205A, most oscillators with gain sets were low-power systems in which an attenuator (a device that reduced the amplitude of the signal) was mounted past the transformer in the circuitry.

Hewlett instead put attenuators in front of the transformer. It was a small design change that in turn caused the little company a lot of trouble to get it to work. But when it finally did, Hewlett-Packard Company found itself with one of the best higher-power (up to five watts) audio sources on the market. This alone would have earned the company a lot of sales in the years to come. But with the war, the demand for audio sources for low-wattage radio transmitters skyrocketed—and with it the demand for the 205A. It would become perhaps the most successful single product of HP's first decade.

Bill and Dave then followed up that landmark product with one last instrument to round out the 200 family: the model 210A square wave generator, which would prove especially useful to "clock" digital circuits as they began to emerge a decade in the future.

————

Nineteen forty would be a signal year for Hewlett-Packard Co.—and Bill and Dave—for a number of reasons, not all of them product related.

That November, Dave and Lucile had their first child, David Woodley Packard. He would be followed by three daughters, Nancy, Susan, and Julie, born in 1943, 1946, and 1953, respectively. To cope with this growing family, the Packards moved several times during those years. The first of these moves, from the Addison house, was to a larger home in south Palo Alto, across a vacant lot from Tinker Bell's Fix-It Shop.

With the birth of her first child, Lucile resigned from her job at Stanford University. At the same time, her responsibilities at Hewlett-Packard were greatly reduced, thanks to the hiring of Helen Perry, HP's first secretary. Nevertheless, Lu still managed to put in a few hours each week at the company helping to interview prospective new employees, and at home with the baby, helping with company paperwork.

In June of that year, HP gave five dollars to local charities. It was the first official act of philanthropy by the company and its founders, all three of which would in time create some of the largest foundations in the world. What makes this small donation important is that it occurred so early in the company's history. Many large firms around the world donate enormous sums to worthy individuals and to nonprofit organizations. But typically, especially in Silicon Valley, this corporate philanthropy begins after the firm has achieved some real measure of success, often after it has gone public and needs both the tax break and the good publicity. HP's first donation occurred just eighteen months after the partnership was founded, when it had a grand total of five employees. HP became a good corporate citizen even before it was a corporation, likely even before it was listed in the phone book.

Also that year, Bill and Dave, in a casual decision that would have a monumental impact upon American business, decided that every HP employee should participate in the company's success. Toward that end, they announced a production bonus—that is, if the company exceeded its production goals, and thus increased its profits, the employees would get a piece of those profits. The two founders had seen this program work at General Radio, but there it had only been for engineers; Bill and Dave decided to extend it to all HP employees. What seemed mere common decency to Bill and Dave was in fact the birth of corporate profit sharing, one of the most important sources of wealth distribution in the modern economy.*

And that was just the beginning, because that December Bill and Dave stunned the staff by handing out five-dollar Christmas bonuses for everyone. It was a practice begun with just three employees that would continue even when HP had 30,000 employees.

Hewlett-Packard finished 1940 with total revenues of $34,396, a staff of five full-time employees, four products in its catalog, expanded quarters in the Tinker Bell building, and a new baby. The electronics industry was growing rapidly, demand for new products was accelerating, and little HP, just two years old, already was developing a reputation for innovative, high-quality, and affordable instruments. It must have looked like nothing could get in the way of the company's success in 1941 and beyond.

But the world had other plans.

Calls to Duty

Whatever plans Hewlett and Packard had made for their company and for their own lives in 1941 and beyond were tossed aside that spring. The world was at war. The German army had overrun most of Europe, bombed England in preparation for an invasion, and then shifted to attack Russia. Closer to home in California, the Japanese were fighting the British in Southeast Asia, had annexed half of China, and tensions were building to the breaking point between Washington and Tokyo over Japanese aggression and the resulting American oil embargo of Japan. Warships regularly called now in San Francisco before steaming out through the Golden Gate en route to Hawaii.

Even as Bill and Dave had been handing out bonus checks to employees the previous Christmas, Hitler was giving orders for the invasion of Russia, the British army was locked in battle with the Italian army in North Africa, and London was facing the worst of the Blitz.

War was coming to the United States. It was inevitable; the only question now was when. The U.S. military, understaffed and underequipped, was desperately playing catch-up before conflict erupted. In September 1940, President Roosevelt reinstituted the draft and Dave Packard registered. Bill Hewlett was a different matter: thanks to ROTC at Stanford, he already held a commission in the Army Reserve. For him, it was just a matter of time—and in the spring of 1941 the call came. He was ordered to Washington to join Army Aviation Ordnance, ordnance (munitions) being the engineering side of the army in those days. But even Hewlett, who like Packard was intensely patriotic, recognized that this was a waste of his talents, and that he could make a better contribution to the war effort: "By that time I was pretty well established in electronics and it didn't make much sense."[19]

Dave Packard had a solution. A year before, when HP had just been starting, he and the company's new East Coast sales rep, David Burlingame, had called on the Army Signal Corps laboratories in Fort Monmouth, New Jersey, in hopes of landing a contract. They hadn't succeeded, but Dave had met a Colonel Colton, who ran the labs. So Packard made a call. Colton not only remembered him, but thanks to Burlingame's regular visits had been tracking HP's work. He quickly agreed that Hewlett would better serve his country from Palo Alto coming up with new instruments—and prepared orders to transfer Hewlett under his command. From there he could be quickly designated as an "essential employee" and sent home.

So far, so good. But then the plan hit a snag. Though Bill arrived at Monmouth in July, he wasn't released until September. Recalled Hewlett, "The reason that didn't happen before was that we were just a partnership, and the government didn't recognize that a partnership could be like a corporation except under a different title."[20]

Had Hewlett left HP at that moment, the company would have been in serious trouble. Instead, his three-month absence served as a warning. The two founders now realized that Bill's presence at Palo Alto was now temporary, and if the company was going to survive the impending transition, it would have to restructure, scramble to hire new engineering talent, and prepare for its own war.

Then came Pearl Harbor. Within weeks, Hewlett was called up again, this time as an officer with the Army Signal Corps. He would serve at that post for the duration of the war, only visiting Hewlett-Packard a couple times, and was rarely in contact with his business partner. He would not return for nearly five years.

Hewlett-Packard finished 1941 with revenues of $106,458—nearly triple those of the year before. It also now had six full-time employees, but was hiring fast. It had to. Within two years, those annual revenues would jump to nearly $1 million. And at war's end in 1945, HP would employ two hundred people. The company Bill Hewlett returned to in 1945 looked nothing like the one he'd left just five years before.

Partners Apart

Though the professional careers of Bill Hewlett and Dave Packard are so similar as to seem interchangeable, during the war years they lived very different lives. And if the two men ever exhibited envy for each other's experiences, this interval was the cause.

For Bill Hewlett, like many men who have been in uniform but never seen combat, his army years were, with a few exceptions, a long boring sidetrack in what was otherwise an exciting career. It frustrated him knowing that he could make a far greater contribution to the war effort back at the Tinker Bell building. And during the few visits he did make to Palo Alto, it was obvious that Packard was accomplishing extraordinary things with the company— and without him. Dave was proving that he could run HP by himself if he needed to, something Bill could never be sure of about himself.

But if the war years were frustrating for Hewlett, they were far worse for Dave Packard. At a time when it seemed that every able-bodied man in America was in uniform, when 4Fs and other men in civilian clothes were seen as shirkers, David Packard, a physical giant, a former Stanford three-letter man, could still be seen around town in a suit, looking increasingly prosperous from war contracts. And to protest that he was doing "essential" war work was a waste of time: only a handful of people in Palo Alto had a clue what the company did.

Thirty years later, this envy would finally find an outlet when Washington again came calling—this time for Dave Packard. And the behavior of the two men then, seemingly inexplicable at the time, could best be understood by what had happened three decades before.

Bill Hewlett's call to return to the army came from the man who had let him go the first time, Colonel Colton, and Bill would work for him for most of the war in the office of the Chief Signal Officer in Washington. It was a staff position, primarily involving the introduction of new products from industry into the military.

Hewlett quickly learned that military life, onerous perhaps for corporate types, was frustratingly easy for a high-tech entrepreneur:

I remember going to Washington, and not being used to [only] working twelve hours a day. . . . I would stay working until 8:00 at night—until they finally said, "Oh no, we have to close the safe, so you can't work after 6:00." It was a shock. Here [we] were, in the middle of a war, and you're trying to do things—and just for convenience's sake you're told that you have to leave at 6 p.m. I'm sure my wife was pleased, but still.[21]

The job really only became interesting as the war ended. Hewlett was transferred to the command of a General Wharton, who ran a special staff in the Signal Corps. The details of this new assignment only became clear when Hewlett and the team were transferred to the Philippines, ostensibly to continue introducing new commercial products. When Japan surrendered, Hewlett suddenly found himself part of a secret team formed by Koral T. Compton, a legendary MIT physics professor in the Fred Terman mold.

According to Hewlett, the team's assignment was "to go into Japan before they could destroy technical evidence and try to find out what they'd been doing."[22] What that meant in practice was that "we interviewed all the people we could to find out what science had been going on in Japan. I think partially it was to find out what they had been doing with the atom bomb, but we weren't told that."[23]

It proved to be an unforgettable experience—and one that Hewlett, in his typical manner, would turn to an immense business advantage. Among the scientists Hewlett interviewed was a man named Hidetsugu Yagi, who arrived formally dressed in a cutaway coat and striped pants. Yagi turned out to be the director of all of Japan's civilian research and development, the empire's Vannevar Bush. He was also a famous scientist, the world's leading expert on antennas—his reflector antennas are still used today on many televisions. They were also used, in terrible irony, in the altitude-sensitive fuses of the atomic bombs dropped on Japan. Yagi had made his own contribution to the new forms of terror: he was also the scientist responsible for the incendiary balloons that Japan developed to float across the Pacific and attack the United States.

Yagi was a very frustrated man, because the military didn't want him doing anything, and he found himself being used [mostly] as a propaganda device. For instance, the government announced they were developing death rays, so he had to develop a death ray, although he knew you couldn't do it. . . .

But he also told us where all of the technical information lay and whom we ought to talk to in the military. So he was really quite helpful.[24]

Yagi's experiences, and his willingness to turn on his former bosses, was a warning to Hewlett about the danger of disgruntled former employees.*

But Hewlett's tour of occupied Japan had an even bigger lesson to teach. The more he and the team traveled the country, the more disappointed they were by Japan's much-vaunted war machine.

> I remember I thought it was pretty primitive. The thing that impressed me was the lack of cooperation between the army and navy. There was a device . . . called IFF, which is "Identification of Friend or Foe," so you could tell by looking at radar whether you were looking at a friendly plane or an enemy plane. [But] the navy IFF did not work with the army IFF, so if the army plane flew over the navy ship [it] would get shot at. That just shows the degree of competition between these two groups. . . . It was a very fundamental problem.[25]

Seeing the literally fatal effects of incompatible technology standards on the Japanese military had an enduring impact on Bill Hewlett. In the years to come (and even to this day), Hewlett-Packard would play a leading role in establishing standards in the electronics industry—that is, finding a common ground of performance and compatibility on which highly aggressive tech companies can compete without tearing their industry apart or ruining the experience for customers with products that cannot be interconnected.*

Some of these standards committees sat for a decade or more before they reached a consensus. HP wasn't involved in these working committees for purely selfless reasons, of course—the story of the company has always been an interesting balancing act between good works and self-interest—but the mere fact that it stayed at the table for years, and accepted the compromises needed to reach a solution, is a measure of Bill and Dave's commitment to the process.

The most famous of these standards is the IEEE-488 interface bus, which began its life inside Hewlett-Packard as the HP Interface Bus (HP-IB). Offered to the entire industry in the late 1960s, and adopted in the mid-1970s, it became the underlying standard for linking together computers and their peripherals—and proved to be the crucial standard that made possible the personal computer revolution.

In December 1945, Lieutenant Colonel Bill Hewlett at last earned his honorable discharge and was demobilized. He returned home to Palo Alto not only with Flora, but with a new daughter and son. He was titularly the half-owner of a thriving business, though he wasn't sure just where or how he would fit in.

Balancing Act

If Hewlett was bored with his work most of the time during the war years, for Packard it was just the opposite: HP shuddered under an avalanche of defense contracts, and it took every ounce of energy and every bit of skill Dave had just to keep up.

Almost from the moment that Hewlett left for the army, Packard resolved that the best way he could serve the war effort was to give his all to helping the company meet its obligations, produce top-quality products, and make its deliveries on time. To do that, Packard said, "I recall moving a cot into the factory and sleeping there many nights."[26]

The contracts came in quickly after Pearl Harbor. Strictly speaking, HP was not a supplier directly to the military, but to the companies that manufactured weapons and infrastructure for the military. That meant Hewlett-Packard was typically called upon at the very beginning of the design process—and that in turn meant that contracts were already pouring into the little company even before Bill Hewlett left, and long before most of the U.S. military even saw combat.

Thus HP, already handicapped with the loss of half of its senior management, had to ramp up at lightning speed. Packard took to haunting the Palo Alto branch of the state employment office in search of talent. He took what he could get—mostly women and retired men—and was grateful to do so. And, as usual, he proved lucky in his hires. A retired army officer, "Cap" Stuart, hired to take over payroll, proved superb at the job. Recalled Packard, "He did a very thorough job and made sure that everything balanced down to the last penny."[27]

A retired mechanical engineer, Rufe Kingman, brought in to make precision bearings and gears for an antenna servo-motor contract, not only did a brilliant job, but in the process designed a machine to make plastic "cards" to hold the components. It proved so innovative and effective that HP used the process for years.

But the most important person to join HP during the war years was Noel Eldred, the engineer recruited out of Heintz and Kaufman. During those darkest moments at HP in 1942, when David Packard was sleeping on a cot in the office, fearful that he would never be able to keep up with the many orders rolling in and would let down himself, Bill, his employees, and his country, he must have felt very alone. After all, the dream of what would become Hewlett-Packard had begun with Bill Hewlett and Ed Porter sitting outside Fred Terman's Radio Lab. Then it had been three, when they were joined in the dream by Barney Oliver. Only then, thanks to his friendship with Bill, had Packard become part of the plan.

Now Ed Porter was gone—first to the air-conditioning job in Sacramento, then to Bowdoin College to grad school, and now, thanks to Hewlett's recommendation, he was working in the Bureau of Ships. Barney Oliver, who had graduated well after the others, was working at Bell Labs. And even Bill Hewlett, his business partner, was gone. Dave Packard, the last to join, was now the last left.

He couldn't do it himself. Nobody could. Between 1941 and 1942, HP's revenues *quintupled* to more than $500,000—and then would nearly double again in 1943. Staffing grew even faster, until the company was running two shifts per day. Adding to the challenge was the fact that most of the workers were either retirees or women, the former short on endurance and the latter short on job experience. Everyone, from the lowest-level assembler to the executives like Doolittle, stepped up to the task magnificently. But none more so than the "other Noel" (because "Ed" Porter was Noel as well), Noel Eldred.

During the war years, Eldred became, if not the surrogate for Hewlett, at least Dave Packard's most reliable operations officer. At first, when new product development was crucial, Eldred acted as HP's chief technologist. Later, when production of those products became all-important, he shifted over to running HP's manufacturing. At the end of the war, when HP was desperately trying to shift from the dwindling military market to industrial and commercial customers, Eldred jumped in and ran marketing. Packard would remember, "I liked to do things with a broad brush and he'd fill in all the details and it worked out fine."[28]

Having been tested on his leadership skills, Dave Packard next faced a test of his friendship.

In the beginning of the 1940s, ITT, under the direction of its founder, Sosthenes Behn, built one of the largest electronics factories in the world. The New Jersey plant was designed specifically to be the primary manufacturer of magnetrons for the Allied war effort. Like many decisions made by Behn, it was as much political maneuver as thoughtful business strategy. As Packard would recall, tartly, "It was laid out with wide aisles in the production area so that Behn could comfortably escort the big-brass visitors from Washington. It had only one problem: It couldn't even produce one good tube!"[29]

In desperation, Behn reached out to the one man in his entire multinational corporation who he believed could save him from this impending disaster: Charlie Litton. No doubt regretfully, Litton agreed.

Now Dave Packard had not only lost his partner, but his mentor.

As Litton headed east, he was passed by Jack Copeland, another ITT executive, going in the other direction. Copeland was assigned to take over Litton Labs and keep it going until Charlie could return. It would have been a daunting task for any technology entrepreneur—but, incredibly, Jack

Copeland was neither an entrepreneur nor even a technologist. He was lost at Litton Labs, and would likely kill the place within months.

What happened next is one of the greatest testaments to David Packard's loyalty and sense of honor. He could easily have ignored what was happening in Redwood City—after all, there was a war on, HP was being crushed under orders, and Dave himself could barely fulfill his own duties. And Charlie was gone. Instead, Packard contacted Copeland and offered to help in any way he could. His offer was happily accepted, adding more work to Packard's crowded schedule.*

Then, a year later, the unthinkable happened: a fire broke out at the labs and utterly destroyed Litton's machine shop. Without it, the company simply could not function. Once again, Packard came through: he offered to let Litton Labs use the HP machine shop during the night shift. "That fitted their schedule and enabled them to keep going until they could rebuild and re-equip their own plant."[30]

Litton Labs survived. Charlie would return to a thriving company (and a rebuilt machine shop). As Litton Industries, the labs would go on to become a billion-dollar corporation, and a vital defense contractor for the United States throughout the cold war.

A wife and baby at home—and now another on the way. Sleeping on a cot at the office. Dealing with two shifts of aged and inexperienced workers. Turning over his machine shop every night to strangers. The business and staff growing so fast that the entire company would soon have to pack up and move to larger facilities. And a business partner who was lucky to stop by the plant every six months—just long enough to enjoy a celebratory dinner and get an update on the status of the company—before shipping out to some distant spot on the globe. It is little wonder that in late 1942 and early 1943 David Packard was a man close to cracking.

He had always been perfect—and almost perfectly unflappable. He had always made it look easy. But not this time. Maintaining your integrity and upholding your standards isn't hard when times are good; it is infinitely harder when times are tough, especially (as Silicon Valley has seen many times since) when part of the problem is that business is *too* good.

At times like those, even a calm man, given the right goad, can explode. And that moment came for Packard just a few months after Bill left. It was a moment so singular in Dave Packard's long career that he never forgot it. He even chose to tell it, undoubtedly in a more restrained manner than it actually occurred, in *The HP Way*:

> One day early in the war, I came to the office to find two men from the lo-
> cal Renegotiation Board waiting to see me. Renegotiation was a proce-

dure established by the federal government to prevent companies from making excessive profits from their war efforts. It was a good program under which the government tried to allow a reasonable profit for good performance.

Bill and I had decided we were going to reinvest our profits and not resort to long-term borrowing. I felt strongly about this issue, and we found we were able to finance 100 percent growth per year by reinvesting our profits.

After some discussion with the members of the board, they seemed to be impressed with what we were doing, but said they had a limit of 12 percent of profit they could allow on equity.[31]

At this point, an exhausted Dave Packard snapped. It took everything he had to remain even remotely cordial:

I pointed out that our business had been doubling every year and that it would continue to do so for several years. I also told them that I had kept my salary at a lower level than it should have been because I did not think it was fair for my salary to be higher than Bill's army salary.

Moreover, I pointed out that we had controlled our costs to the extent that the government could not get better products from anyone else at a lower price. For these reasons I would not accept 12 percent on equity.

To have a towering young man with a booming voice in your face (especially if they remembered him making bone-crunching blocks) must have been an intimidating experience. And, like good bureaucrats, the two men from the Renegotiation Board reacted by doing what bureaucrats do best: they kicked the problem upstairs. Concluded Packard, "They said I would have to take my case to Washington. I did so and worked out an agreement with the government that gave our company virtually everything we asked for."

Packard called their bluff—and won. It is often forgotten now, after the rule has been regularly compromised by their successors, that during Bill and Dave's tenure at the top of Hewlett-Packard Co., healthy profits were sacrosanct. It is not for nothing that even in the company's famously enlightened list of corporate objectives, "Profit" comes first.

Again and again, Bill and Dave dropped beloved company products, even abandoned entire businesses, if they failed to produce an adequate profit. That point of view was expounded for the first time to that frightened pair from the Renegotiation Board, and it would prove essential to the company's unmatched success in the years to come.

Eye of the Storm

One of the most interesting attributes of Dave Packard during the war years is that, despite being crushed by work and the stress of hurried deliveries and an inexperienced staff, he still managed to stand by his core principles. He showed that in the episode with Litton Labs, as well as in the fight with the government over profits. His refusal to take as a salary a penny more than Bill Hewlett was making in the army showed that he was unwilling to take advantage of either his country or his business partner.*

But perhaps the most remarkable trait that Packard sustained during this period was his willingness to take huge risks. A typical executive, even a die-hard entrepreneur, when faced with a business growing fivefold every year, wouldn't even consider launching into a whole new market, but would instead work to consolidate current gains.

But that wasn't David Packard—he wasn't in business to get rich, but to build a successful company. And that meant he had to look beyond the immediate challenges, overwhelming as they were, to the long-term growth of his firm. Even while the fate of the world was still undecided, he was already looking to the direction HP would take in the postwar world.

Much of HP's business during the war years came from the U.S. Naval Research Laboratory. It was among the most progressive and inventive of the government's technical operations and a major customer of HP's off-the-shelf instruments. As Hewlett-Packard was always looking for business, it wasn't long before the company's sales and technical people began asking if there might be any other instruments the lab could use.

The most positive response came from a section head named Dr. Andy Haeff. Haeff and his team had designed a prototype microwave signal generator and they were in search of a reliable manufacturer. Though HP didn't have a clue how to build these devices, and was suffering from a seriously overburdened machine shop, Packard took the contract anyway. As he recalled, "We really were a little overly ambitious because when we got back we didn't have any of the tools needed."[32] In the end, the machinists did their usual miracle, a new engineer named Norm Shrock stepped up to direct the project, and the NRL got its signal generators on time.

Haeff was more than impressed. He gave HP a few more small contracts just to make sure the first project wasn't a fluke—and when the company again delivered on budget, on time, he was prepared to make an offer. Would Hewlett-Packard, Haeff asked, be willing to work on a top-secret project that might make a major contribution to the war effort? Packard quickly agreed.

The project was code-named "Leopard," and it proved to be an extraordinarily sophisticated technology for the era: an electronic countermeasures device that, in theory, would make a ship appear on radar as if it were somewhere else. To accomplish this, HP needed to design a system that used its own oscillators (Bill's other, absentee, contribution to the war effort) in a device that could pick up incoming enemy radar signals, synchronize on them, and then, by generating a new signal, "bounce" the pulses back after a delay or bury them—thus either changing the apparent location of the ship, or rendering it nearly invisible.

The components themselves, in all of which HP now had experience, proved to be the easy part. The challenge came with the design of the antennas and the servo motors needed to control them; the sending and receiving antennas had a tendency to interfere with each other.

The contract called for HP to deliver a finished, fully tested system to the Naval Research Lab by mid-1945. The company made it, field-testing a pilot model for the NRL on Chesapeake Bay in February. But it came at enormous cost. The record suggests that Dave Packard may have slept on his cot at the factory for the entire duration of the project.

The Leopard contract was not just one of HP's largest contracts during World War II, but also likely the most important. It not only brought the company into the microwave business—right at the birth of the modern communications industry—but also made it one of that industry's leading players. For the next quarter century, HP would be the world's leading manufacturer of microwave signal generators.

The Leopard project also gave the company's engineers a first look at what at the time was called an "A Scope"—and to work with its designer, a brilliant engineer-entrepreneur named Howard Vollum. The A Scope would soon evolve into the oscilloscope, one of the most important of all electronic instruments. And Howard Vollum would soon start a company, Tektronix, to build them. Hewlett-Packard would make a fortune on its own oscilloscopes, but Tektronix would, maddeningly, be one of the few companies HP would never best.

With the Leopard project, Hewlett-Packard positioned itself for the postwar world and, given what was to come, likely ensured its survival. Dave Packard, at the most unlikely time, had taken a gigantic risk—and it had paid off handsomely.

Few celebrated high-tech entrepreneurs, before or since, have ever been that forward-looking, or that risk-embracing. For those later generations who saw only the aged business titan at the top of a giant multinational corporation, this is a very different image: young Dave Packard as the ultimate high-rolling tech entrepreneur.

Reassembly

With the war's end, Dave Packard took stock of himself and his company.

Hewlett-Packard Co. was now six years old—a fact that no doubt astonished Packard, his having been so immersed in work for the last three of those years. It had annual sales in excess of $1 million, more than two hundred employees, a large new headquarters facility in the Redwood Building, and a product line that had grown in four years from Bill Hewlett's original audio oscillator to a product catalog that included oscillators, microwave generators, audio signal generators (which turned out to be big sellers because of their use in the making of proximity fuses), wave analyzers, and distortion analyzers. The company also had an extensive network of government and commercial contacts, and a reputation for the highest quality—the last underscored in 1945 when HP became one of only three California companies to earn the prestigious Army-Navy "E" Award.

Packard knew that he had also put together a strong and highly adaptive management team, and that his factory floor was filled with talented and loyal craftsmen. Best of all, Bill Hewlett, the man whose skills best matched his own, and whose commitment to the success of the company was at least as great as Packard's, was finally coming home. Packard knew that it would take every bit of skill and experience both men had to get through the tough postwar years looming just ahead.

What is unlikely is that Dave Packard included in his mental audit of HP, precisely because it didn't fit into his (or anyone else's) thinking in those years, the intangible assets of the Hewlett-Packard Company. And for such a young company, these were considerable. HP already had—thanks to the war providing a national stage—a huge reputation for innovation, quality, and, best of all, fulfilling its contracts on time. Thanks to its willingness to work openly with other companies (even competitors) and to help out corporate friends in need, it had already developed a huge reservoir of goodwill. Because of that and despite their relative youth, Packard, and soon Hewlett, would be seen by their peers as industry leaders and trusted spokesmen.

But there was even more than that. The postwar slump wouldn't last forever. The technological advances in the military during the war signaled that a huge commercial, then consumer, electronics boom was waiting in the wings, and with it a race to recruit the very best talent, from scientists and engineers to marketers and manufacturers. Those companies that did the best job of attracting and keeping that talent would invent and build the best products—and in the end would win the race.

By 1945, by intention or not, Hewlett-Packard was already one of the best places to work in the world and, when it came to personnel management, easily the most innovative. Profit sharing and annual bonuses were just the start. In 1942, when one of their employees tragically contracted tuberculosis, Bill and Dave stepped in and supported the family financially. Then they took the extraordinary, yet characteristic, step of establishing a catastrophic health insurance plan for HP employees—a commonplace now, but a radical innovation at the time. To that, six years later in 1948, Hewlett-Packard added an insured pension plan for all company employees with more than five years' service.

And that too was only the start. During this era, it seems like every decision Hewlett and Packard made had a far-reaching impact on modern business, even their choice of buildings. When Bill and Dave decided to construct and move the company to the Redwood Building—which, like a survivor of a simpler and more primitive technological world, would stand on Page Mill Road almost to the dot-com era—the two founders consciously decided to keep the interior open and barnlike. That way, they figured, if business went bad they could always sell the place off as a grocery store.*

Obviously, that dark day never came. But the wide-open floor plan, which promoted communication between employees and democratized any hierarchies between labor and management, proved so effective that Bill and Dave retained it for all future company buildings, and it became the signature layout of the electronics industry. Indeed, what began on the floor of the Redwood Building became, in the form of open floor plans, dividers, and cubicles, the most visible feature of daily business life in late-twentieth-century America.

The crunch of contracts during wartime, the open floor plan of the Redwood Building, and the quality of talent that HP had been able to hire during the war and after also led Packard to develop two management techniques that would resonate right up to the present, and are likely to be studied and imitated for generations to come. Both were born in Dave's experiences at GE, were tested in the crucible of a young HP in wartime, and, in large part because they fit Bill Hewlett's personality even more than Dave Packard's, became institutionalized in HP's corporate culture.

The first of these, beloved by management theorists and authors in the 1980s, was "Management by Walking Around." This was the notion that a manager's job was not to sit in an office pushing papers and firing off memos, but to be out on the floor, talking with his or her people, looking for ways to help, resolving disagreements and disputes, supporting rather than dominating the staff.*

The second, called the "Open Door Policy," was unfortunately often confused with the simpler, and less effective, policy of the same name offered by a number of progressive companies of the era. The cruder "open door" of those firms typically meant that if an employee had a concern or complaint, he or she could take it to their superior at any time and get a hearing.*

Bill and Dave's Open Door Policy was much more inventive and powerful. It said that *any* employee of the company, if he or she had a concern or complaint, could immediately take it to their immediate supervisor, *and,* if the problem wasn't solved, they could take it to the next level above that supervisor—in theory all the way to the CEO or the chairman of the board. The only restriction (to keep every complaint from instantly being sent to the top) was that all possible remedies had to be exhausted at each level before it could move up the chain of command.

In practice, this rarely happened. But in theory, it could at any time, and that further cemented the feeling of a personal bond between HPers and the two founders. And indeed, forty years hence, it was just such a complaint, sent to Bill and Dave from the deepest recesses of the company, that arguably saved HP.

This kind of attitude came naturally to the two men, and even if it had not, the pressure cooker of daily business in the early 1940s would have forced them to it. Once instituted—by the late 1950s the aloof, detached manager was reviled rather than feared at HP—Management by Walking Around had the practical effect of turning the organizational chart upside down. In that inverted environment, when it worked right, the higher you were in HP management, the greater the number of people you reported *to.*

These countervailing forces of authority and responsibility, meeting each other across the HP org chart, had the effect of leveling the organization—to the point that even the entry-level hire or the janitor on the graveyard shift felt that he or she knew Bill and Dave personally, and that if they were unable to find remedy anywhere else in the company they could go directly to the founders. This wasn't just true in theory, but in practice. The history of Bill and Dave's HP is filled with employee anecdotes of precisely this kind, where the founders stepped in to help an employee far down the chain of command. Here is a classic of the type, from many years later:

> I met both of them when I was awarded the President's Club Award in 1988—an award given to 100 sales reps and managers from around the world. They were both standing in the reception line with then president John Young, congratulating all of the winners. I was one of 5 women, which was a great honor. Needless to say, Dave Packard shook my husband's hand and congratulated him. My husband said, "Oh no, it's not me, it's her." Then Dave said, "Well, it's very nice to have a young lady from the South here."

> Later on that evening, I was the first one up to receive my plaque from

Bill, Dave & John. In rehearsals we were told we would get our award, then turn around to have our picture made. [But] the four of us turned around, and there was no one there. So while someone ran off to get the photographer, I got the chance to talk one-on-one to them. They asked if they could get me anything, if they could ever help me, to let them know. I was almost speechless!

Several years later I was involved in a sexual harassment thing. HP had recently bought Apollo Computers and our area got a new Apollo boss. He didn't fit in. He came up to me once when I was on the phone and whispered in my ear as he massaged my shoulders, "I bet your husband doesn't do that as well as I do." Gag!

After I told personnel about it, he made it a point to try to destroy my professional reputation. He even took away my customers that I'd had forever and gave them to another sales rep, who was as slimy as he was. I found out that fake orders had been entered for the customers in order to get his numbers up. Then, when the orders were cancelled, he gave me back my customers, taking away money from my commissions. It was cheap and dirty.

I talked to my boss, but he was afraid of him. So I ended up just quitting the company because I couldn't take that crap anymore. I wrote Bill and Dave and told them what had happened. They both wrote me personal, hand-written letters apologizing for that behavior and assuring me that they would get to the bottom of it.

A few days later, they sent the corporate human relations director to my house to talk to me. He kept asking me what I wanted, and I said, "I want that man out of Bill & Dave's company before he does this to anyone else. He should not be an HP employee. He doesn't fit with the HP Way."

A few weeks later the man was fired.[33]

Note that this occurred when Hewlett-Packard had more than 80,000 employees in more than one hundred countries around the world. It was just such a note, from a secretary in that case, that led Bill and Dave to return to the daily operations of the company in the great final act of their professional career (see chapter 7).

Management by Walking Around wasn't the only corporate philosophy that arose at HP because of Bill's and Dave's experiences during the war and just after. This one was as subtle and complex and MBWA was simple and explicit. In fact, it never had even had a name—but it underscored what was to become famous as the HP Way, an overarching corporate attitude that was itself too ineffable and subtle for outsiders (and even at least one future HP CEO) to fully understand.

This second philosophy was, to put it simply, *trust*. Not merely integrity in the interactions between HP employees, though that was part of it. Not just the ability of customers, strategic partners, suppliers, distributors, and retailers to trust that HP would keep its word and deliver on its agreements— though that was part of it too.

No, it was even more profound, radical, and far-reaching than that. It was entrusting every single HP employee, from top to bottom, to do the work that they were assigned, to take responsibility for their actions, and to speak for and represent the company as if they were the owners (which they were) and the founders themselves.*

An anecdote from the early years of Hewlett-Packard, told and retold by generations of HPers, would come to symbolize the climate of trust that Bill and Dave cultivated—and furiously enforced—at the company.

There was a standing rule at HP that parts bins and storerooms were to be always left open. The genesis of that rule had, like many negative examples, come from David Packard's experiences at General Electric in Schenectady. While he was there, the GE plant was suffering from a perceived security crisis. Tools and instruments were disappearing left and right from the company's storage rooms. In reaction, GE clamped down, installing security guards and threatening serious punishments to the perpetrators.

The reality, as Packard well knew—after all, the attic he shared with his fellow GE engineers was filled with borrowed devices—was that most employees had simply taken the tools and instruments home to keep working on unfinished projects from their jobs. At worst, they were using them for hobbies that only enhanced their job skills.

Now, having criminalized what was in fact employee dedication to greater productivity, GE all but guaranteed that nobody would ever bring one of these borrowed items back—or ever again work on their own time. In fact, it was even worse than that: before long, angry employees were taking it as a challenge to see just how much they could sneak out of the storerooms under the eyes of the security guards. GE had managed to take a minor irritation and turn it into a major morale problem.

When it came time to build his own company, Packard remembered this debacle: "When HP got under way, the GE memories were still strong and I determined that our parts bins and storerooms would always be open. Sometimes not everyone gets the word, however, which accounts for an incident that occurred some years later."[34]

Packard was being charitable. The "incident" is one of the most cherished HP legends. No doubt some officious supervisor decided to assert his power by putting a padlock on the storeroom in his department. It was a big mistake, because one weekend Bill Hewlett wanted to do some work and stopped by that particular storeroom to pick up a microscope. When he found the door locked, he exploded, stormed off, and returned with a big pair of bolt cutters and snapped the padlock off. In the storeroom he left a signed note stating that the door was *never* to be locked again.

One can imagine the supervisor arriving on Monday morning, seeing the open door and the split padlock and angrily demanding to know who has violated his edict—then reading in stunned silence the note from William R. Hewlett as his subordinates smother grins behind him.*

———————

There is every reason to believe that this attitude of trusting workmates completely came easily to Bill Hewlett, who was the classic gruff character with a heart of gold. Whether or not it came naturally to Dave Packard is unknowable. But there is no question that it was reinforced by his life experiences to that point. In football at Stanford he had learned the power of a team that worked together and trusted one another to step up and make the play. At GE he had seen just the opposite, an operation filled with talent that had rendered itself utterly dysfunctional—to the point of having exactly zero net productivity when it came to fabricating rectifier tubes—because it was rent with distrust and contempt between the engineering staff and the factory floor.

HP during the war years had only deepened Dave Packard's appreciation of the power of trust in creating a successful enterprise. Buried in work, perpetually understaffed, and lacking sufficient management assistance, he had no choice but to entrust his employees with inordinate amounts of responsibility—literally placing the fate of the firm in their hands—and pray that they would come through. In the end, the employees not only did all that was asked of them, they turned HP into one of the highest-quality manufacturers in the United States—a fact that even the federal government publicly recognized. They answered Packard's unprecedented trust with superhuman performance, and his loyalty with their own.

Packard, true to his personality, learned that lesson better than anyone.

One and Only Time

If the 1940s were the years of loyalty at HP, it wasn't only because Bill and Dave learned the importance of not only taking care of each other and their employees, but also that they came to appreciate that this loyalty extended to their teachers, their community, and their nation—and even to the most un-likely people, like their competitors. Ultimately, they learned that the real test of loyalty might demand taking trust to terrifying heights.

But even that might not have been enough to convince the duo to main-tain this philosophy, at all costs, even when Hewlett-Packard had grown to a giant multinational corporation. That kind of commitment required a nega-tive lesson, a betrayal of trust that haunted Bill and Dave for the rest of their careers—and made them privately swear never to repeat that experience again.

Hewlett and Packard had anticipated that the end of war would cause a slump in the demand for electronics instruments—after all, the military and its defense contractors had represented a huge market with an insatiable de-mand for the newest and the best. But if the demands of wartime had driven technology to unprecedented heights, there was no equivalent need—yet—in the commercial or industrial worlds. On the contrary, after four years of ra-tioning, repurposing of production to military goods, and the transfer of the best technical minds into uniform, any advances for tech in the everyday world were likely in reverse.

Thus, what was expected to be a downturn with demobilization turned into a rout. Hewlett-Packard's business, which Bill and Dave hoped might be protected by the company's now diverse product line, collapsed. In 1945, company revenues had been nearly $1.6 million. In 1946, they were half that.

The only good news in all of this was that HP's labor force was already beginning to drift away, as many of the women workers, with husbands com-ing home, abandoned their years as Rosie the Riveter to go back to being housewives.

But even that wasn't enough. In the end, Bill and Dave faced the bitter pill of layoffs. Before they were done, HP's staff of two hundred had been cut to eighty. This was the hidden cost of loyalty: companies that hired and fired employees with impunity never suffered the pangs of conscience during ma-jor layoffs. But Dave Packard especially knew what these people had done for the company, what they had sacrificed, and how much he depended upon them. This era was one he rarely discussed, other than to say, "It was a tough dip. But we kept going even so."[35]

So traumatic was the experience for both men that for the next thirty years—their entire tenure directing the daily operations of the company—Hewlett-Packard never again had a mass layoff. In an industry characterized by endless cycles of overhiring and brutal cutbacks, Hewlett-Packard was the shining exception. HP was actually willing to forgo extra hiring during good times, thus risking the loss of added revenues, to keep from having to mass fire employees during the bad.*

Even in the darkest days of 1973–74, when the end of both the Vietnam War and the Apollo space program triggered a recession that devastated the entire electronics and aerospace industries, Bill and Dave found an inventive way to navigate their company through without firing a soul. Their success at saving employees during those years stood as a perpetual rebuke to almost every other high-tech company.

This is not to say that Hewlett and Packard suffered from the weakness, found in even some great entrepreneurs, of being unable to fire bad or unsuitable employees. The long-standing joke that the only way to get fired at HP was to shoot your boss—and that even then you'd get a second chance—wasn't really true.

Bill and Dave learned that lesson early, and painfully. Recalled Hewlett:

> One of the most difficult steps that I can remember occurred a few years after we started the company. This was when we had to release our production manager. We finally had to face the fact that, despite everything we had done to improve our management skills, he was not doing the job that needed to be done. Although he was a good friend, it simply came down to a question of his job or the jobs of all of the other employees.
>
> The impact of that decision is still with us, and in subsequent years has led us to make every effort to find an appropriate niche for a loyal employee. Interestingly enough, we have had a good success through the years in relocating such employees within the company.[36]

The heart of this relocation program was the notion that a loyal, hard-working employee shouldn't be punished for being put in a position beyond his or her ability. On the contrary, that is the fault of the supervisor for not paying attention, or not understanding that employee's abilities. The under-performing employee was given the chance to look elsewhere in the company, or take a demotion, without being stigmatized.*

Improper, or illegal, behavior was another matter. That was indeed a firing offense, an insult to a company synonymous with corporate integrity, and the resulting dismissal was supported all the way to the top of the company.

Most problematic were those employees who, for personality reasons, or sheer incompetence, just didn't work out at HP. Toward these benighted individuals, Hewlett-Packard showed a deep humanity.

This attitude even reached beyond the walls of the company. John Minck recalled an encounter with Hewlett in the mid-1960s during a management meeting at Rickey's, a local restaurant. It was a period when both HP and its chief competitor in oscilloscopes, Tektronix, had both concluded for business reasons that they no longer needed independent sales representatives.

Tektronix had simply fired its independent reps. HP, which shared many of the same reps, decided instead to buy them out. Eleven of the thirteen reps took HP up on its offer—a very expensive proposition.

Confused by the decision, Minck approached Hewlett:

I asked him why HP had spent something like $10–15 million for this move. I noted to Bill that Tektronix hadn't spent a penny, but simply released their reps, one at a time, over a couple of years to smooth the transition, and set up their own company sales offices.

His answer was, "Goddamnit, Minck, you just don't understand the situation. These reps are all personal friends. For a decade, we did business with them, on a handshake. We owe them most of our success, in building both the industry and our company, and there was no way we were going to just fire them one at a time."[37]

Baby Boom

In 1947, demand finally bottomed out in the electronics industry and began to once again rise. America's warriors had come home and were now building businesses, filling corporate offices, and rushing through a quick college degree on the GI Bill. Their wives were giving birth to the baby boom, the largest demographic bulge in human history. Together, in the appliances and entertainment devices—radio, television, stereos—they purchased, this new generation propelled the second great boom in consumer electronics.

At the same time, the United States was itself rebuilding. After the double hit of the Depression and then the Second World War, America's physical plant was woefully out of date. The promise of rural electrification, a national highway system, and pervasive telephony would at last be realized.

Meanwhile, three other new factors—two of them products of the war, the third sitting in a laboratory awaiting war's end and the time to be perfected—were also emerging on the scene, all of them promising to redefine both electronics and the postwar world.

The first of these, as already noted, was microwave, born out of the Varians' klystron and radar, but rapidly moving into the world of wireless telecommunications.

The second was information processing. The first modern computers had been created during the war in Germany, Great Britain, and the United States to compute complex artillery trajectories and to decode enemy secret messages. Now, though the potential market would be famously underestimated (one prediction was for a total U.S. demand of ten computers), it was increasingly apparent that computers could be useful in managing corporate financial records and preparing sophisticated statistical analysis.

As huge as each of these technologies would one day be, they would still be surpassed by the third: the transistor, arguably the greatest invention of the twentieth century. Before the war, two Bell Labs researchers, John Bardeen and Walter Brattain, had seen a compelling demonstration of how an insulator, silicon, with the presence of certain impurities, could not only conduct a strong current, but even be switched on and off with a small, intersecting second current. But before they could investigate further, war-related projects took them away. They returned to the pursuit after the war, and with the advice of another Bell Lab researcher, William Shockley, one of the greatest scientific minds of the century (and future HP neighbor), they perfected that switch into a tiny, solid-state "gate," the transistor.

The miracle of the transistor was that it replaced the fragile, hot, power-consuming, and comparatively slow vacuum tube with a tiny, fast, solid-state device that was constructed from the most elemental natural materials: silicon, oxygen, and copper. The impact of the transistor on the electronics industry was both complete and far-reaching—for on the one hand, within a decade it had replaced the vacuum tubes in almost every existing instrument, rendering them smaller, more powerful, and sturdier. At the same time, the transistor made possible several new generations of fundamentally new electronics products and instruments, which in turn made electronics the hottest new industry of the 1950s.

These products and this immense new infrastructure would all be designed upon, manufactured with, and tested in operation by electronic instruments, themselves transformed by some of these new inventions. There may have been no better time to build a great technology company, if you could manage to stay on top of the growing, but ever-shifting, wave. IBM did it in computers, General Electric (remarkably) did it in consumer electronics, and Ampex in video and audio recording. And in electronic instruments, though giant competitors such as General Radio seemed to rule the field, in fact no company was better positioned to dominate than little Hewlett-Packard of Palo Alto, California.

The question was whether HP could survive long enough to do so.

One thing is certain about Hewlett-Packard Co. during the difficult years right after World War II: the two founders, whatever their doubts about the company's chances of survival in the near term, never stopped building the company for long-term success. Thus, even as they were being forced by slumping orders to lay off many of their manufacturing workers, they were still actively recruiting the small cohort of scientists and executives they believed could lead HP into its next era.

The source of much of this talent was their old friend and mentor, Fred Terman.

At the beginning of the war, Fred had been called east by his old friend (and occasional rival) Vannevar Bush. Bush, the archetype of the scientist-politician, had been named FDR's science adviser, and been assigned to give the U.S. leadership in defense technology. To that end, he first established a Radiation Laboratory at MIT. Then, noticing that it mostly recruited scientists and engineers from the East Coast, he vowed that the next such program, the comparatively larger Radio Research Laboratory at Harvard University, would be run by a West Coaster who could draw from that talent pool.

There was only one real candidate for the job: Fred Terman. Terman was better known as a theoretician than a practical scientist, but he did have an unequaled talent for identifying great young engineering talent—and it wasn't long before the Radio Lab was filled with some of the brightest talent still available, and was in regular contact with those (like Hewlett and Packard) who weren't.

There is a wonderful symmetry between some of the work that came out of the Harvard Radio Lab and Terman's work at Stanford before the war, and nowhere more so than in the use Terman and his team made of Bill Hewlett's HP model 200A audio oscillator. The 200A was cheap and very reliable, which made it perfect for uses ranging from Morse code training (where it generated tones) to signal testing. There is even an official photo showing an HP 200A mounted on a shelf inside the cabin of an airplane cabin that was used for electronic countermeasures. The plane would fly over enemy territory and analyze the characteristics of incoming radar signals.

During the war, Hewlett visited the Harvard Radio Lab whenever he had the chance. And when peace arrived, he and Packard quickly moved to recruit talented lab members. As with HP's earlier engineering hires, many of these men—Ralph Lee, Bruce Wholey, Ray Demere, Howard Zeidler, George Kan, Horace Overacker, and Art Fong—would stay with the company for as long as a half century and reach senior management positions.

Of this group, the men who would run HP during its golden age, the most important was Art Fong—the nonagenarian former vice president who would shuffle through the restored Addison garage as the last surviving "founder." Fong's supreme importance was not due to his contributions to the company, though they were considerable (it was once estimated that he was responsible for more than $200 million in HP revenues), but because of who he was: the first Asian-American engineer in Silicon Valley history.

This part of the HP story is rarely told. But even in the largely segregated world of the late 1940s, HP was nondiscriminatory—and that attitude began at the top. As with many apparently radical moves by Bill and Dave, this was less a desire to change the world than simple common sense and decency: Hewlett-Packard in the postwar years could only afford to hire a small number of very talented people, and so it wanted the best, whatever their color.*

But seen in the context of a California where Japanese Americans were just returning home from wartime internment camps and Chinese Americans were largely isolated in metropolitan "Chinatowns," the hiring of Art Fong was a major victory for civil rights. Given the current demographics of Silicon Valley, one of the most ethnically diverse communities on earth, the decision to hire Art Fong was one of the most far-reaching that Hewlett and Packard ever made.

The second, potentially fatal, risk that Bill and Dave took during this first major recession in the company's history was to expand rather than contract their product catalog and the industries they served. Even as the market was drying up on some of their businesses, they were rushing to consolidate their position in other businesses, such as microwave instruments, that they believed would be the source of the industry's future growth.*

This was an incredibly gutsy move, especially when at the same time older, bigger—and presumably more experienced—companies such as General Radio were choosing to back away from markets such as microwave test equipment because they presented no immediate return on investment. Needless to say, executing this strategy stretched the already thin company nearly to the breaking point. HPers, old and new, assumed multiple duties, some discovering skills they never knew they had. For example, Noel Eldred, Packard's operations officer and manufacturing director during the war, transformed himself into a world-class marketing executive—a role he held at HP for the rest of his short life.

The biggest surprise, however, was Dave Packard himself. He had always been the golden boy—the perfect student, the perfect employee, and, increasingly now, the perfect employer. But no one had ever considered him a great engineer. There was no grad school epiphany, as there had been with Bill Hewlett's audio oscillator, when everyone suddenly stepped back and looked upon him with newfound respect.

But Packard still had a surprise left in him. And, during the desperate days after VJ Day, when HP was looking everywhere for that killer product that would keep the company alive, he sat down and quietly came close to doing just that: he designed the first of what would be five decades, and more than a dozen generations, of HP voltmeters. The HP model 400 AC voltmeter would stand as eternal proof that Bill Hewlett wasn't the only inventor-founder of Hewlett-Packard.

As proof of his versatility, at about the same time that he invented the model 400 voltmeter, Packard was in intense conversations with HP's top builder, Rufe Kingman, on how to deal with the main problem in microwave instruments: that of keeping their touchy components in the right configuration. Kingman was a classic HP hire of the era—an old-time mechanical engineer who, after a career in mining and working for the nearby Hendy Iron Works (later Westinghouse), had retired, only to be lured back to the challenge of working on new inventions at HP. Kingman had already devised a process that had reduced the company's fabrication time by more than 15 percent. Now he found himself sitting with the president of the company, plotting how to build reliable microwave instruments.

In the end, the answer came to Packard at an unexpected moment: "I remember one morning I was taking a shower and I thought of the idea of mounting those [components] on a frame . . . and setting the frame so that the top of the waveguide element that you want had an indexing point. Rufus worked out that design."[38]

Then, just at the moment when he proved that he too was a top-tier electronics inventor, Dave Packard turned his back on the lab and spent the rest of his career in the executive offices. It was as if, having convinced himself of his ability, he could now move on to his real destiny. He didn't even mention these accomplishments in his memoirs.

Over time, even the company forgot Packard's early contributions as an inventor and engineer. In the late 1980s, HP ran a series of television ads under the catchphrase "What If . . . ," one of which featured an engineer having a design brainstorm in the shower and rushing to the telephone to call the idea in to the office. Apparently no one left in the company knew that exactly the same thing had happened to the man whose name was on the titles at the end of the commercial.

Packard before the Elders

The most likely reason that Dave Packard left the lab was that his thoughts were now turning in a new direction, toward a vision of the company HP could become—and what it would take to get there.

As always, he discussed it with Bill. Though as usual there is no record of their conversations, it is obvious they reached a consensus, and once they did, they moved quickly.

The first step was turning the partnership into a real company. In August 18, 1947, Hewlett-Packard formally incorporated, with Dave Packard as president and Bill Hewlett as vice president. The ostensible reason for ending the partnership was that the legal reorganization as company conferred some added tax advantages. But the unsaid reason, as Packard later admitted, was that "it also provided more continuity to the business than a partnership could."[39] The war had obviously taught them that nothing, even the business partnership of two healthy young men, was forever.

During this era, HP began to make its presence known within the electronics industry, and not just for its quality products. The same year that the company incorporated, HP rolled into the IRE show in New York City—the leading industry gathering in the country—not like a company trying to survive, but one in a hurry to move forward. HP now had a catalog of thirty-six products to sell—still small compared to the giants, but remarkable for a young company all but written off for dead a couple of years before—and dazzled the crowd.

But that was only the start. Packard had now reached that level of credibility in the industry where he was being invited to give keynote speeches and presentations. Just that opportunity presented itself at the IRE, and Dave took advantage of the moment: before the assembled crowd, he announced that "HP's future appears very promising." It was a bold thing to say in front of your peers during the worst recession they had ever known. But Packard wasn't making idle predictions: he had seen the recent sales numbers and knew that Hewlett-Packard had at last turned the corner.

That year, 1947, HP's revenues had climbed back to $851,287, up nearly 50 percent from the bottom of the postwar crash. And the company was hiring as well, and not just a few top-flight engineers: by the end of the year, employment would reach 111.

But the next year was the real breakout. In 1948, HP's revenues nearly *tripled* to $2.2 million, its employment to 128. The industry upturn had finally begun, and by taking the huge risks of the preceding years, Hewlett-Packard was now in position to benefit most from this turnaround. Bill and Dave would never again have to design their buildings with a fallback use—like a supermarket—in mind.

The new products were now coming fast: a second generation of voltmeters that could measure very high frequencies never before possible; a frequency counter that, thanks to Al Bagley's decision to add a second gate circuit, was able to count as many as 10 million cycles per second, fifty times as fast as anything currently on the market; and the first of the company's microwave instruments.

One might imagine that just staying on top of this explosive growth would have occupied every second of Bill's and Dave's workdays. But, as seen over and over during the half century of their careers, the two men's greatest strength was their willingness to do the right thing at the absolute worst time. It was almost like a perverse test of both their integrity and their endurance—and it proved on numerous occasions to be their biggest competitive advantage.*

Thus it was in 1948, when most other executives faced with runaway growth simply tried to hold on for the ride, that Hewlett and Packard chose to experiment with HP's personnel policies: this was the year when the company instituted its insured pension plan.

It was also the year that both Bill and Dave decided to involve themselves more deeply in their community and their industry. This was the first manifestation of their mutual and deeply held belief that HP must be a good corporate citizen. It was a laudable philosophy—and a profoundly influential one, given that HP would eventually set the standard in this area for the entire high-tech world—but it is hard to imagine a worse time for the two men to come to such a decision.

For Packard's part, he would run for, and be elected to, the Palo Alto School Board, a position he would hold for the next eight years—still dealing with questions about the number of teacher parking spaces at local elementary schools long after he had become a global figure.

Bill Hewlett took a different path, once again on the advice of his old mentor, Fred Terman. Terman's tenure as head of the Harvard Radio Lab had been one of both singular achievement and considerable grief. The lab had produced hundreds of inventions and, in the form of electronic countermeasures, made an enormous contribution to saving the lives of U.S. airmen and sailors.

But Terman was a teacher, not a CEO, and running the lab, which by war's end had grown to more than two hundred scientists, was not his shining hour as an administrator. It didn't help that the Harvard Brahmins he reported to condescended to this rough-hewn westerner. Terman tried to manage the entire place without emplacing sufficient middle management, and it nearly crushed him; so much that even some of the people who worked with him thought him a decade older than his real age.

Terman returned to Palo Alto in 1946, six months after Hewlett. The job of dean of engineering at Stanford was waiting for him. He was even short-listed to be the next president of Stanford—a job that he vigorously fought against. In the end, the presidency went to Wallace "Wally" Sterling, former head of the Huntington Library and well-known radio personality during the war. Sterling proved to be an able administrator, a big thinker, and best of all for the future of Hewlett-Packard and Silicon Valley, a huge supporter of Fred

Terman and his dreams. The two men became close friends, and in 1955 Sterling would appoint Terman as his provost ("Never have I worked so harmoniously with an extremely able colleague," Sterling would say of Terman)[40] and together they would take Stanford into its greatest era.

Over the next few years, as Terman began to build his department and journey around the country looking for talent, he would sometimes join his old students, Bill and Dave. Recalled Hewlett:

> Dave and I used to go back fairly regularly to New York. We usually traveled by train, because I didn't like air travel, and Terman very often was along. So we had a lot of chances to talk with Terman and see what he thought. It was very interesting because he had very clear ideas about what needed to be done in the field of engineering education.
>
> He pointed out that schools of engineering had very much gone into the how-to-do-it side rather than the theoretical side. [At the same time] large companies like Bell Labs, GE, and RCA, had set up their own schools of advanced study to teach theory . . . that this had all gotten turned around.[41]

One of Terman's ideas was that too many young engineers, anxious to earn a living, were getting jobs right out of college and and not going on for their master's degrees. He proposed a co-op model, by which engineers could work at a company such as HP half-time and attend Stanford the other half. To make the idea even more palatable to companies and students, the courses could even take place at the firm, rather than on campus.

This would prove to be the genesis of HP and Stanford's Honors Cooperative Program, one of the most influential graduate continuing education programs ever devised, a model for universities and corporations around the world, and a huge source of talent for Hewlett-Packard. As Hewlett noted in 1984, "The eastern universities looked down on this—but now they're realizing it's a hell of a deal."[42]

Another Terman idea was to make use of the thousands of acres of unused land owned—and paid taxes on—by Stanford University. A notion was growing in his mind that somehow this open space might be turned into a new kind of industrial park, filled with high-technology companies—perhaps even those run by his former students—in a uniquely symbiotic relationship with the university.

This idea, perhaps Terman's greatest, would take a decade to be realized.

In the meantime, he had one more idea that could be acted upon immediately: put some of his former students and contacts into positions of importance in the electronics industry. Recalled Hewlett, "Terman said, 'Bill you ought to run for director-at-large of the IRE. You spend quite a bit of money on advertising your name. People [now] know it.' I ran against Lloyd Burtner, who was a very good scientist—and by gosh, [Terman] was right, and I won!"[43]

Hewlett served in the leadership of the Institute of Radio Engineers for a number of years, in the process cementing HP's position as a dominant player—and standard-setter—in the industry. In 1954, he even became the president of the IRE. The college kid who wasn't sure he wanted to study electronics was now, at forty-one, one of the acknowledged leaders of the high-tech industry.

Packard among the Elders

As Hewlett-Packard Co. approached its tenth anniversary, a traditional milestone for taking stock, all the experiences of the previous decade began to come together in the minds of the two founders. The garage, the sudden ramp-up to wartime, the hard postwar crash and layoffs, the inventive new personnel programs, the gathering of management talent, and now, most recently, the turnaround—all seemed like pieces of a larger lesson.

So too did the many relationships—between the founders, their friends, their mentors, their industry peers, and their competitors—that had defined the founding and the early years of HP.

But perhaps most of all, Bill and Dave, from their experiences not only at their own company, but at General Electric, in the military, and even as far back as Terman's lab and the Stanford football team, had come to appreciate the power of a team in which each person was given the freedom to use their own skills and judgment to choose the best path toward a common goal. They understood even more that in electronics, especially, where rapid innovation was crucial to corporate survival, these empowered "families" of employees, under enlightened managers, could perpetually produce near-miracles of invention, quality, and adaptability.*

As yet they had no term for this new business philosophy—that would take yet another decade. For now it was just the "HP way of doing business." Bill and Dave didn't even know if it would still work when they scaled up from the little company in the Redwood Building to the giant corporation they intended HP to become.

But they were willing to give it a try. Bill and Dave were risk-takers after all—otherwise they wouldn't have made it this far. They were pragmatists too: and the evidence so far suggested that this new model could outrace any existing business model they had yet faced, just as their instruments consistently surpassed the competition.

Most of all, Bill Hewlett and Dave Packard were ambitious. They wanted to win. They wanted to beat their competitors and build a great company. And they wanted to become great men.

They knew they could compete with anyone on the playing field of high technology. But *this,* this new way of doing business, was something else entirely. It not only offered a path to success that few other companies would dare follow, but it was a natural fit to their own personalities—indeed, it had arisen organically out of Bill and Dave's daily business interactions with HP employees.

Best of all, this new way of doing business was responsible, honorable, and, in Bill Hewlett's term, *humane.* They had gone into business together simply to earn a living; now the prospect before them was to become wealthy and powerful men. From the beginning they had tried to do the right thing for each other, for their employees, and for everyone else with whom they did business. They didn't want to surrender that integrity now just for a little more market share, even for a lot more personal wealth. And, being good engineers, they believed they were close to a solution that would assure them both honor and honors. The more they thought about it, the more this new way of doing business seemed the only way to go.

It was just these thoughts that were on Dave Packard's mind when, in 1948, he was invited to attend a gathering of corporate CEOs and senior executives from a number of different U.S. industries and organizations. Eventually the conversation came around to corporate responsibility. Packard recalled, "We began talking about whether businesses had responsibilities beyond making a profit for their shareholders."

Packard watched, stunned, as one executive after another expressed his opinion that profits were a company's *only* responsibility. "Looking back, I suppose I shouldn't have been surprised. During the early decades of the twentieth century, profit was the businessman's sole objective. Labor was a commodity that could be bought and sold on the market."

Finally, Packard could take no more. He rose to his full height, surveyed the room, and told the assembled worthies that he completely disagreed with their position. He told them they wrong, "that we had important responsibilities to our employees, to our customers, to our suppliers and to the welfare of society at large."[44] And he admonished them to look beyond mere profit to their larger civic responsibilities.*

It was an incredible, historic moment, the turning point between one era and its successor. In a career of many milestones and accomplishments, this was perhaps David Packard's most shining moment.

The reaction of the other CEOs? Laughter.

Not the howls of ridicule, but the knowing and indulgent chuckles of jaded old men toward the naïve idealism of a callow young man. The boy will learn, they told each other, give him time.

In fact, it was *their* time that was running out. Thirty-six-year-old Dave Packard had stood before the captains of American industry and given them fair warning. Now he was going to pull the entire edifice of traditional business down around their heads. When the new decade was over, and HP was a $50 million company celebrating its twentieth anniversary, nearly every company represented in the room that day would have adopted the business philosophy pronounced by David Packard in that electrifying moment—or they would be fading away.

Having launched the future, Bill and Dave now set out to live there.

Chapter Four:
The HP Way

Between 1950 and 1960, Hewlett-Packard Company grew from $2 million in annual revenues to $61 million—a thirtyfold increase in just ten years. At the same time, the company's employment rolls jumped from 146 to more than 3,000, and the number of HP products from seventy to nearly five hundred.

It was one of the fastest ramp-ups in American business history to date—and if it was exceeded in later years by other high-tech companies, such as Google, eBay, and Microsoft, it should be remembered that those later firms had the benefit of HP's example to follow. Hewlett-Packard, by comparison, had to traverse with this kind of explosive growth with few markers along the path ahead.

Moreover, many of these later meteoric companies—Apple, Sun Microsystems, Wang, and Silicon Graphics being the most obvious—reacted to this kind of growth trajectory by essentially coming apart. They cratered, or meandered around lost for years, or they simply lost their edge. Hewlett-Packard, by comparison, followed the fifties with an even more amazing sixties, in which, now a giant corporation, it still managed to grow sixfold—and remained arguably more organized and more competitive than ever.

How Bill and Dave, and the growing coterie of men (and a few women) who filled the upper- and middle-management ranks of Hewlett-Packard during these years, pulled off this extraordinary achievement has been studied by business schools and other companies ever since.

A definitive answer may never be found—even HPers who were there at the time are undecided about exactly what happened, in part because they were so busy in the trenches that they had little time to survey the overall scene. And no doubt part of the answer lies in the human heart, in the subtle interactions between the personalities and perceptions of the thousands of employees who made Hewlett-Packard in the 1950s perhaps the greatest company there has ever been.

But we do have a precise record of the events of that decade, of the decisions made by Bill and Dave and their lieutenants, and the memories (if incomplete) of the people who were there.

Finally, we have Hewlett's reminiscences and Packard's own memoirs of those years, and, as we have seen, the experiences and values that drove them to make the decisions they did. The past is indeed another country, and the United States of the 1950s—triumphant, fearful, confident, and ambitious—only grows more alien and astounding by the year. But by putting all of these diverse pieces together we can begin to puzzle out just what Bill and Dave did, and just how Hewlett-Packard groped its way forward during the decade that made it the ideal of all companies to come.

The Valley of Heart's Delight

The biggest factor underlying HP's extraordinary growth in the 1950s was, of course, the economy itself. After twenty years of being constrained by the Great Depression and redirected by the Second World War, the United States finally broke out in the 1950s. It was propelled by the Korean War, the reconstruction of war-battered Europe, and the return of international trade.

But most of all, it was driven by a population of returning GIs anxious to get on with their lives, women ready to go home from war work and start families, and the unprecedented demographic bulge—the baby boom—they created together. The modern consumer culture was born in those years, and as Americans rushed out to buy appliances, televisions, and radios, they set off a secondary boom in the tools and instruments needed to create and test them.

As the decade progressed, other powerful economic forces also came to bear: the cold war, Sputnik and the space race, audio and video recording, the arrival of mainframe computers in the workplace, even the interstate highway system. One after another, they nudged the U.S. economy to ever-higher levels, quickly making the United States the wealthiest nation the world had ever known. The American people responded by consuming more, demanding ever more sophisticated products, and ultimately enjoying a standard of living their grandparents could only have dreamed of.

A second factor working in Hewlett-Packard's favor was the migration of America's population, powered by the automobile and the new highway system, south to the Sunbelt and, more importantly, west to California. Hundreds of thousands of GIs and sailors passed through the ports of San Francisco, Long Beach, and San Diego and, remembering the beautiful weather and the good times they had there, swore that if they survived, they'd return and make a new start. They arrived throughout the late forties and early fifties, GI Bill degrees in electronics or aeronautical engineering in their pockets, new wives on their arms, babies on the way, and ready to make up for lost time.

The result was that companies such as Hewlett-Packard had their pick of some of the best young engineers of the new generation—and HP in particular was a talent magnet precisely for the graduate co-op program with Stanford that the big East Coast companies (and universities) had dismissed.

There were secondary benefits to this population shift as well. Two other Santa Clara Valley boys made good—the Lockheed brothers had set up shop before the war in Burbank and built themselves an aviation empire. As the space age loomed, they decided it was time to get into missiles and other high-altitude hardware. The brothers looked north to their old hometown and saw Stanford, Hewlett-Packard, and a burgeoning population of young, technically trained workers and professionals—and decided to go home.

The arrival, in the mid-1950s, of Lockheed Missile and Space Corp., followed by the thousands of employees who would quickly make it the Valley's largest employer, started the transformation of the Valley from an agricultural to the world's first high-tech community. Those thousands of families also formed a suburban infrastructure, drawing retail business, building schools and junior colleges, and attracting homebuilders like the innovative Joseph Eichler, and ultimately creating safe and shiny new neighborhoods that were a further attraction to talented technologists everywhere.

One of those drawn to the Valley was the man widely acknowledged as the most brilliant American scientist of the age, William Shockley. Having walked out of Bell Labs in hopes of getting rich, Shockley looked at all of the ferment out west and decided to go home to California.

He set up shop in 1955 in Mountain View, geographically halfway between HP in Palo Alto and Sunnyvale, where Lockheed Missile and Space Corp. would open its doors a year later. He called the company Shockley Transistor and put out the word that he wanted to hire the most brilliant young solid-state physicists and electrical engineers in the country. He hired eight of them; they arrived just in time to help him celebrate his new Nobel Prize for Physics. Shockley's presence in the Valley, and his promise to build the world's most advanced transistors, cemented the area's image as the new capital of high technology.

There was one other company also making its name in the Bay Area. Ampex had been founded in 1944 by Alexander Poniatoff, that former Russian fighter pilot who had joined Packard in the seminars at Charlie Litton's offices before the war. Ampex had started out fast building small electric motors for the military, but in the postwar recession it found itself facing bankruptcy if it didn't find a new business, and fast.

But Poniatoff was a survivor. He jumped on a new technology, liberated from German laboratories, that other companies had deemed impractical. It was called a magnetophone, and it could record images or sound on specially prepared magnetic tape. The name didn't stick, but the technology did—and before long, thanks to its existing expertise in small motor drives, Ampex was the world's leading manufacturer of video and audio recording equipment.

As fast as Hewlett-Packard Company grew in the 1950s, there were periods when Ampex grew even faster—to the point where that company became synonymous with the go-go growth of technology companies during that era. Its modernist buildings and huge sign beside Bayshore Freeway in Redwood City, not far from Litton's old lab, became iconic, the very emblem of America's technical prowess.

Thus there were in the Bay Area alone three other companies besides Hewlett-Packard—Lockheed, Shockley Transistor, and Ampex—that were well-positioned to take advantage of the boom in electronics in the 1950s. To this list can be added two more with familiar names: Litton Industries and Varian Technology Corp., the latter now in the business of commercializing Russell and Sigurd's klystron tube.

And, indeed, every one of these firms enjoyed spectacular growth in the fifties, and some well into the sixties. Yet of all these remarkable companies, only HP emerged on the far side stronger and healthier than when it entered.

Shockley Transistor only lasted a few months, as the founder proved so tyrannical, paranoid, and impossible to work with that the "Traitorous Eight" finally gave up, found money elsewhere, and quit. The scientist who led the money search, Eugene Kleiner, and the man who found him the investment capital, Arthur Rock, would go on to create the Silicon Valley venture capital industry, while another two of the "'traitors," Robert Noyce and Gordon Moore, would build that new firm—Fairchild Semiconductor—into a company of legend, then go on to found Intel Corporation.

Lockheed Missile and Space, like its parent company, found itself trapped in the boom-bust cycle of the military aerospace industry and shook itself to pieces through one round of layoffs after another—culminating in a devastating bust in the early 1970s that seemed to put half the men in the Santa Clara Valley on the unemployment rolls. LMSC would never be the same again. Much the same thing happened to Litton Industries, especially when the death of the charismatic Charlie Litton stripped the company of its strong center.

Varian survives to this day, but as a quiet Silicon Valley backwater company. In 1950, it made what seemed like a prudent decision to focus almost exclusively on its klystron business. To that end, it sold off its microwave waveguide business. It was a mistake that was only apparent in retrospect, as it began a process of narrowing Varian's business at the very moment when it should have been expanding it—dooming the firm to steady but uninteresting growth and a long, slow twilight.

The buyer of Varian's waveguide business? Hewlett-Packard.

Most tragic of all was the fate of Ampex. It managed to roar out of the 1950s with IBM as the hottest growth stock on Wall Street. It essentially owned all sound and television recording in the world—and might still yet had it made intelligent business decisions.

Instead, a kind of collective madness seemed to descend upon the company. Poniatoff's wife held her horticultural society meetings in the corporate cafeteria, while Poniatoff himself became increasingly eccentric—he started wearing baseball caps, only driving white cars, and eating only raw foods in the hope of living forever. Meanwhile the company, which for years had never make a mistake, suddenly couldn't do anything right.

In the arrogant belief that a backward economy would never become a serious competitive threat, Ampex licensed the jewels of its intellectual property to Japanese corporations—only to have them turn around and flood the U.S. market with medium-quality, but low-priced, cassette audio and video recorders. Ampex tried to fight back with its own consumer products, but in the words of an ex-employee, "It only knew how to do things well and costly." The company lost tens of millions of dollars.

The final straw came after Poniatoff's death, when it was discovered that the company's books had been "cooked," that millions in leased items had in fact been recorded as sales. The stock collapsed, the company suffered a major shareholder suit, and Ampex faded away. Today only the famous sign, like the Packard garage an historic site, remains to draw quizzical looks from passersby.

So, the real question is: why, of all of these companies, each of them ideally positioned to dominate their industries in a time of unprecedented economic expansion, did Hewlett-Packard alone thrive *and* endure?

The answer seems to lie in a series of momentous decisions Bill Hewlett and Dave Packard made throughout the 1950s, dealing not only with the business itself, or even the products and technologies, but with the culture of HP. Between 1950 and 1957, Hewlett-Packard embarked on the most important run of innovative employee initiatives ever attempted by any corporation before or since—and in the process changed the quality of daily work life for hundreds of millions of people around the world.

The 1940s was the decade in which Bill and Dave took the loyalty they had to each other and mapped it outward in ever-increasing circles to the larger world. This new decade—reflecting perhaps the changes in their own lives—was one in which Bill and Dave grew that loyalty into something much deeper: into a family. Packard would later remark, with amazement, "I remember thinking and making the comment that most of the best friends I had were working here in the company."

And once it was a family, those ties grew ever deeper and stronger with time and experience, until Hewlett-Packard, at its best, was the most emotionally complete work experience of any major public corporation, ever. This was the HP Way at its full flowering: a fabric of rules, experiences, myths and legends, relationships, and rituals as complex as any real family—and just as difficult to describe to an outsider.*

Old Friends and New Family

After the war, Bill and Dave made two special, and final, hires to their core executive team. Both carried particular resonance as they also closed the circle on the beginnings of the company.

One of these hires was the man who might have been the "P" in HP. Noel "Ed" Porter, Hewlett's childhood friend and the classmate of both men. During the war, after Bill had helped Ed obtain a position at the Bureau of Ships, the two men had stayed in touch, and after the war Hewlett regularly tried to recruit his old friend. But Porter had always gone his own way, working as an applications engineer for an air-conditioning business before the war. Finally, with demobilization, Hewlett convinced Porter to join HP as its director of manufacturing, filling the gap left by Noel Eldred when he shifted over to marketing. Porter's arrival led Hewlett to joke that HP was the only company with "two Noels" in charge.

The second hire was Barney Oliver, who arrived in 1952. Oliver, the smartest classmate Bill and Dave ever knew, graduated from Stanford and went on to Cal Tech to earn his doctorate. When the war came, he was hired by Bell Labs—working in the same facility as his intellectual equal, Bill Shockley—where he spent the duration. Whenever Bill Hewlett was in New York City on work with the Signal Corps he would also swing through nearby Murray Hill, New Jersey, to visit his old classmate.

(It is important to note the extraordinary degree to which Bill and Dave maintained their personal networks during these years. They seemed to have lost track of no one they thought they might one day hire at HP.)*

Convincing Oliver to join a struggling little company back in Palo Alto took years. It seemed that every time Bill and Dave had their young friend ready to pack his bags, Bell Labs came up with some exciting new project to keep him in New Jersey. In the end, the partners finally recruited Oliver not through his head but his heart. Recalled Hewlett, "His mother was a widow and lived down near Santa Cruz, and we played on all of the heartstrings we could."[1]

HP now had its genius in the lab.

Historian Edward Sharpe would write, "The addition of Barney Oliver completed the formula for [HP's] success. Hewlett-Packard's basic organization went like this: Eldred in charge of sales, Porter in charge of production, Barney in charge of R&D, and [Frank] Cavier in charge of finance. This basic structure, [complete] by 1952, was to remain intact for many years to come."[2]

"Those were the four people," said Hewlett, "three of whom were Stanford graduates trained under Terman."

The continuity of this senior management team was crucial to the development of the HP family. Had the first line of management come and gone quickly as it does in many modern high-tech companies, Hewlett-Packard likely would never have enjoyed the stability and continuity it needed to underpin its complex corporate culture. As it was, Bill and Dave ensured the cohesiveness of this top team by hiring not only proven talent, but friends. These were men whose character they knew, whom they had known in good times and bad for years—and in the case of Ed Porter and Bill Hewlett, since childhood.*

These were ties that, once made, would never be broken merely by a better job offer—as if, during this decade, there was a better job to be found anywhere in American industry. Interestingly, of this group of four, all would spend the rest of their careers at HP. They would stay at the company until either death (Eldred and Porter) or retirement after more than thirty years' service (Cavier and Oliver) took them away—an amazing accomplishment in what would soon be Silicon Valley, the most frenzied and disloyal business community to be found.

But, unlike many companies, the "family" didn't stop on executive row, but reached out to include every person in the organization. In 1950, Lucile Packard, no doubt spurred by the sudden domestication of postwar America, began a tradition of buying a wedding gift for every employee who married, and a blanket for every employee family having a child. The practice survived the entire decade, until HP had thousands of employees and hundreds of new babies each year.

Company picnics, a common feature of business life during this era, had been a regular practice ever since the Redwood Building days. Packard, in *The HP Way*, recalled:

> Bill and I considered picnics an important part of the HP Way, and in the early days we had an annual picnic in the Palo Alto area for all of our people and their families. It was a big event, one largely planned and carried out by our employees themselves. The menu consisted of New York steaks, hamburgers, Mexican beans or frijoles, green salad, garlic bread, and beer.
>
> The company bought the food and beer. It became customary for the machine shop people to barbeque the steaks and burgers, with other departments responsible for other parts of the menu. Bill and I and other senior executives served the food, giving us the opportunity to meet all of the employees and their families.[3]*

With the exception, perhaps, of having senior executives and the founders as servers, this is a basic description of most corporate annual picnics of the era. But then, with HP at last on a firm financial footing, Bill and Dave decided to take the experience to a whole new level.

In 1955, HP bought a parcel of land an hour's drive up into the Santa Cruz Mountains above Palo Alto. It was called Little Basin, and to get a sense of its size, one need only know that Big Basin was one of the Bay Area's largest state parks. With Packard helping run the tractor and Hewlett helping on the saw, HP employees cleared part of the parcel to create an open recreation area capable of holding two thousand people at one time. The rest of the redwood forest was left untouched and made available to HP employees and the families for overnight camping.

It is hard to fully measure the impact of Little Basin on the collective morale and memories of generations of HPers. The annual picnic was always jammed, with employees' cars not only filling the parking lot but lining the entrance road for a half mile. Inside, one might see Dave Packard standing tall in a cowboy hat chatting happily with an old janitor or a group of PhDs from the lab, or have Bill Hewlett, in an apron and chef's toque, a turning fork in his hand, ask, "How do you like your steak?"

For many families, Little Basin was a beloved place to camp on weekends—and very often the most vivid memory many children had of their parents' work life. It was part of the added value—like the stock options and the annual bonus—that made working at Hewlett-Packard different from anyplace else—and yet another reason to stay with the company even in the face of better offers elsewhere.

The goodwill created by Little Basin survived even Bill and Dave. During the difficult Carly Fiorina years of 2002–2003, when HP stock was falling, sales were flat, and the new management was indulging in one round of lay-offs after another, there were still hundreds of surviving employees who stayed loyal to the company because one of their parents had worked at HP and had taken them as children to Little Basin. They had fallen in love with that Hewlett-Packard, had joined that company to relive that experience, and now, even as the company seemed to be turning on them, still poignantly hung on in the belief that someday the HP of Bill and Dave and happy days in Little Basin would one day again return.

But that was a half century into the future. In the mid 1950s, HP's picnics were still a novel concept. They were also wildly popular. As Hewlett-Packard grew, in typical manner, Bill and Dave decided that the experience should be available to all company employees, wherever they were. Recalled Packard, "In Colorado we bought some land in the Rockies next to Estes Park, and in Massachusetts on the seashore. In Scotland we bought a small lake, featuring good fishing (and possible sightings of the Loch Ness monster) and in Southern Germany we bought land suitable for skiing."[4]

In the era of William Whyte's *The Organization Man*, of the lonely corporate climber, and the faceless company conformist alienated from himself and his family, Hewlett-Packard offered a real alternative: the Family Man.

It is interesting to speculate that one source of Bill and Dave's evolving attitude toward HP's employees and business partners was their own maturing personal lives. Thus the company they founded just out of college was largely built upon the teacher-student relationship they had enjoyed with Fred Terman. After the war, as they moved out into the larger world and experienced the early years of their marriages, the two men reoriented the HP culture around their partnership, their friendships, and their sense of loyalty to others.

Now, as men approaching middle age, both with marriages more than a decade old, and nine children between them, they began to map their understanding of the dynamics of family life onto the equally large corporation they had created.

It was not a coincidence then that just two years after HP bought Little Basin, Bill and Dave together bought a ranch in the hills of southern Santa Clara Valley. Packard wrote:

> Bill and I had been deer hunting at a place named San Felipe just south of San Francisco Bay. We liked the area, so when the land was offered for sale we decided to begin a ranching partnership. It was a family participation arrangement from the first. Most of the Hewlett and Packard children learned to swim in the pool at San Felipe. The children [also] rode horses

through the hills and learned about the pleasures and problems of cattle ranching.[5]

The San Felipe ranch purchase was also one of the first examples of the partners beginning to feel the power of their new wealth—and, tellingly, it wasn't used for flashy, public display, but to purchase a working ranch. As the two men grew wealthier, they added to San Felipe with the purchase of an adjoining old Mexican land grant spread, Los Huecos, thus creating a vast holding that stretched for miles along the ridgeline above the southern end of the Santa Clara Valley. They later also purchased a second large ranch in the Central Valley—thereby making the two men among the largest landowners in the state of California—as well as a large ranch in Idaho.

The HP ranch at San Felipe would host many off-site meetings for HP managers and other events, but ultimately it was a retreat for the two families. It was a place where Bill and Dave, the two outdoorsmen usually trapped in white shirts and thin ties, could escape from the politics and pressure of daily corporate life; where they could perpetually recreate the places and experiences that had first made them friends and business partners. Packard recalled, "Another benefit from ranching was my friendship with Bill Hewlett. By running the ranches together—as well as the company—Bill and I developed a unique understanding of each other. This harmony has served us well every single day of running HP."[6]*

It was during these getaways—far more than while working together at HP—that Bill and Dave truly took the measure of each other, saw each other's strengths and weaknesses, and learned to anticipate how the other would react to almost any situation. Surrounded by their families in the big cabin, or out hunting together in the woods, the two men, different as they were in almost every way, learned to think each other's thoughts.

Hewlett remembered, "It got to be a joke. People are like children: when they don't get the answer they want from one person, they move on to the next person, and they very quickly found that independent of each other [Dave and I] came up with the same answer. Dave and I worked together for so long that we really felt very much alike."[7]*

According to Packard, "Every season we'd round up the cattle from the range and drive them to the corral. Along the way, we'd come to a gate; the trick was to get them through the gate and not stampede them. I found, after much trial and error, that applying steady gentle pressure from the rear worked best. Eventually, one would decide to pass through the gate; the rest would soon follow. Press them too hard, and they'd panic, scattering in all directions. Slack off entirely, and they'd just head back to their old grazing spots. This insight was useful throughout my entire management career."[8]

Beer and Bonuses

Little Basin was only one of a series of inventive new programs devised or approved by Bill and Dave in the early years of the 1950s 1960s to strengthen the HP family. The Christmas bonus had now become an annual tradition, with Dave taking the stage at the Christmas party and handing out the checks to each employee in turn. These moments, like the serving of the food at the summer picnic, were ways in which Bill and Dave maintained direct personal contact with each company employee—and it is a testament to their relatively prodigious memories that they managed to know every HPer on sight, and by name, well into the fifties, even after the company's employment passed 1,000.*

(An interesting side note is that the tradition of Packard handing out bonus checks to employees didn't end because it became too big, but because, in the words of unofficial HP historian John Minck, "too many employees were arriving home long after the party, drunk, and with a good chunk of their paycheck gone."[9] Still, a form of holiday celebration did survive until the end of Hewlett's and Packard's time at HP: the company would shut down at noon on Christmas Eve, and by early afternoon restaurants and bars along El Camino Real in Palo Alto would be crowded with employees. Bill and Dave would split up and try to visit all of these groups before evening. It is a company legend that on one of these Christmas Eve afternoons, a couple of drunken HP executives decided to drive up to the Packard home, where they were graciously entertained by Lucile Packard and the kids until they sobered up and excused themselves.)

Profit sharing too was a regular event at Hewlett-Packard, with Bill or Dave twice each year (after the second and fourth quarters) taking to the company loudspeaker to announce the percentage upon which each employee's paycheck would be multiplied. Even into the late 1970s, long after Christmas bonuses had been moved to the department level, one of the two founders would still pick up the microphone and announce to tens of thousands of employees in company plants across the planet the bonus percentage—to nods, cheers, and pumped fists.

Two other HP employee traditions, these gustatory, came into practice during this era as well. One was the coffee break—a legacy of the Redwood Building days, when a small army of working women would leave their worktables and walk down to the end of the room for refreshment and perhaps a cookie.

A decade later, the HP coffee break had become institutionalized as an important part of the workday, a moment when employees—from assemblers in the manufacturing area to scientists in the laboratory to the senior managers in the executive offices—would, at the sound of a bell, leave what they were doing (sometimes even business calls) and walk over to one of the scores of coffee stations set up throughout the company to get a drink, eat a doughnut or a piece of fruit, and, most of all, get together and talk for ten minutes until the bell rang again.

It was also, as always with Bill and Dave, a combination of kindness and business calculation. Says historian John Minck:

> Twice a day [at 10 a.m. and 3 p.m.], the chimes would ring and everyone would leave their desks or production people their stools, and drift to the end of the production line, where there were coffee pots and large trays of donuts, or some days, Danish rolls. I recall that some production line donut and Danish trays were set over the top of several soldering irons, set up with variable power transformers to heat them up without burning them.
>
> Those breaks were all company furnished and used to amaze customers [whom] we were touring through the plants. . . . At my previous job in Albuquerque, not only did we employees have to buy our own coffee and donuts, but as it turned out, we chose to walk about 20 minutes each way to the cafeteria. . . .
>
> One summer we hired a young business intern, who we assigned a study . . . to determine the real cost-effectiveness of having company-paid coffee breaks . . . Not surprisingly, the study showed the costs to have a very high payoff factor.[10]

The coffee break was the most humble of HP traditions, but in terms of overall impact (the high-calorie food selection aside) it may have been one of the most important. In a world of increasingly anonymous and isolated work, the HP coffee break each day struck a blow for community. Office mates stood and talked about their families, the latest joke making the rounds, the status of their projects, last night's football game. Employees and bosses met on equal footing, and receptionists and switchboard operators talked with vice presidents.*

Most remarkably, so uniform was the process throughout the entire corporation that HPers visiting from one continent fit right in during coffee break at another. And if an employee was visiting another plant, wherever they were at 10 a.m. when the bell rang, they were invited to stop at the nearest coffee table—which sometimes meant that an intern passing through the executive offices delivering a memo might find himself being asked by Bill Hewlett if he took cream and sugar in his coffee.[11]

The cost of all of this food (the doughnuts were suspended in the 1980s for health reasons) and drink eventually ran into the hundreds of thousands of dollars each year. The value to the company, in terms of enhanced communication, morale building, and "family," was easily many times that.

————

In early 2000, construction workers, building the Agilent headquarters on the site of the original Hewlett-Packard Redwood Building, unearthed a dirty old brown box that, when opened, was found to contain a case of Lucky Lager beer, circa 1940.

There were several theories as to why a case of unopened beer would have been buried at the former Hewlett-Packard building site—the most likely being that it was some sort of joke time capsule—but whatever the reason, the old case was a reminder that the oldest and most enduring of HP's traditions was, in fact, the Friday afternoon beer bust.

The beer bust likely began during the war as a way to let the employees, exhausted after a week of long hours and high quotas, blow off some steam. In a world of rationing, children who needed watching in the evenings, tight budgets, and limited entertainment, a glass of beer and some crackers and cheese at the end of the shift on Friday must have been a welcome benefit.

After the war, as the company grew, the Friday afternoon beer bust was seen as yet another way of leveling the hierarchies within the company. It was also a chance, like the coffee break but on a larger scale, for employees to mingle and talk. There was an unsaid agenda as well, which was to let Bill and Dave and their executive team talk directly to every company employee without the filter of a supervisor or manager.

By the 1950s, the beer bust had become a hallowed company tradition, not only at headquarters but in all of HP's sales offices as well. Nobody took this further than Norm Neely at his sales offices in California, Arizona, and New Mexico. Neely's headquarters in North Hollywood, located on the site of the treaty signing that ended the Mexican War in California—the Campo de Cahuenga—featured a well-stocked bar of the same name.

> Neely built most of his district offices, around California, Arizona and New Mexico, in the Spanish mission style, with tile roofs, graceful outdoor corridors, etc. And almost all of them had a stylish bar room, usually called the Cahuenga Room, which opened for special occasions during the day, but would always be opened at the end of every work day. Visitors were always pleased to take a period of relaxation in the bar.[12]

Whenever Bill or Dave visited a Neely office (or any of the other HP sales offices) it was not unusual for them, at the end of the workday, to step behind the counter and serve as bartender for everyone else present.

As important as the Friday afternoon beer bust was to the HP culture, one of its concomitant effects would prove far more influential to the world business culture. The beer bust, as it became ritualized, led to the idea of Friday being a "Blue Sky Day," in which employees were allowed to dress casually, asked to use their time on the job to open their minds to new ideas and new inventions, and then, as a thank-you for their contributions, join Bill and Dave at the end of the day for the beer bust.*

Whether Blue Sky Days actually added to HP's innovativeness is unknown. But the practice of wearing casual clothes on Fridays quickly became standard practice at the company—and, thanks to visitors who saw the practice, and employees who left to start their own firms, casual Friday soon became de rigueur throughout Silicon Valley and other high-tech enclaves where HP had an office or plant.

As the next generation of workers entered the high-tech world, including HP, in the sixties and seventies, they looked at their elders in their white shirts and ties and asked why casual Friday couldn't be every day. By the early 1980s, at places such as Apple and Atari, casual dress itself became the dress code—setting off a revolution in business dress throughout the high-tech community that continues to this day.

Today, in a new millennium, the young code writer or department manager in Bangalore or Budapest or Burlingame, dressed in jeans and T-shirt, probably has no idea that his or her mode of dress on the job has its roots during World War II in a small wooden factory in Palo Alto, California.

The Spirit of Invention

As seismic as these cultural innovations would ultimately prove to be, at the time they were merely seen, inside and outside HP, as some nice added benefits for company employees—and yet another reason to work there.

What *was* being noticed about HP, especially by competitors, was the sheer pace of invention taking place at the company. Year in and year out, Hewlett-Packard seemed to be introducing new products—even inventing whole new categories—faster than even its biggest competitors. The company averaged twenty product introductions per year during this era, an astonishing figure, given that in 1951, for example, HP had just 215 employees.

Many of those products were upgrades of existing HP offerings. But some were true milestones. None was more so than the HP model 524A high-speed frequency counter.

The two men running HP's families of audio frequency and microwave instruments were Bruce Wholey and Horace Overacker, both among the group of engineers hired just after the war, and now running major portions of the company. Looking to expand their product offerings, the two men decided to look into nuclear counters: instruments, such as Geiger counters, that would measure the rate of radioactive decomposition. They assigned two of their best engineers to the task.

In end, after developing some prototypes, the pursuit of nuclear counters was abandoned as financially impractical. But in the process, the company did identify an unmet need for a different kind of counter, one that would measure the frequency of a radio signal. There were already instruments on the market that could perform this measurement, but they were painfully slow—taking as long as ten minutes to make a single measurement of a high-frequency signal.

Al Bagley, another member of the early HP engineering team, took one of the prototype nuclear counters, which had been designed to measure particles at an unprecedented 10 million counts per second, added a second electronic gate—and found he had created a frequency counter that could measure 10 million cycles per second. This was fifty times the performance of the then best frequency counter on the market, which had a top limit of just 200,000 cycles per second. In practice, this meant that, instead of the usual ten minutes, the HP 524A could precisely measure a signal in just one or two *seconds.*

The resulting device, the HP 524A, was a bombshell, a classic case of a revolutionary product appearing on the scene just as a giant market needs it. In this case, the market was commercial radio. Local radio stations were facing new Federal Communications Commission regulations regarding the stability of their signal frequencies. Without efficient measurement instruments, some stations' signals would wander and interfere with adjoining stations on the dial. In response to complaints, the FCC mandated a very small average drift for radio stations over the course of a day.

Radio stations throughout the United States were in a panic as they realized that there was no way—at ten minutes per test—that they could possibly stay on top of their frequency drift to the precision needed. And then, like a miracle, the HP 524A high-speed frequency counter was announced. It offered stations the prospect of measuring their signal almost continuously, in what today is called "real time." Hundreds quickly put in their orders to HP, creating almost overnight a major new business for the company, and, over the next thirty years, putting millions of dollars in Hewlett-Packard's coffers.

In 1952, not long after he arrived at HP, R&D director Barney Oliver sat down and pondered the company's founding invention, the HP model 200A audio oscillator. It had, of course, been invented by Barney's old schoolmate, Bill Hewlett, and already held a mythical place in the company's short history.

In the intervening thirteen years, the HP 200A had sold thousands of units and was a commonly seen instrument in laboratories all over the world. Bill's original version had an upper frequency limit of just 20 KHz (20,000 cycles); that had been improved to about 50 KHz with the upgraded version, the 200B, after the war. But there development had stopped, as the circuitry had begun to produce so much noise that it impeded itself.

The best engineers at Hewlett-Packard had studied the problem and been stumped. Oliver merely looked at the circuitry—for the first time, in fact—and decided that a new, more balanced circuit configuration would solve the problem. He tried it, and the upper frequency limit of this new version—eventually named the HP 200CD—jumped twelve-fold to 600 KHz. Bill Hewlett's audio oscillator was given twenty more years of working life. And if anyone at HP had any doubts about the reputed genius of the new R&D director, they quickly evaporated.

But the spectacular growth of the company during this era doesn't tell the entire story. Bill and Dave also made some very large business mistakes during these years—a reminder that these were still young men, in a young company, without the wisdom yet to refrain from taking some dangerous risks.

One of the most notorious of these was the Electronic Lettuce Thinner. From the earliest days of the company, Bill and Dave had used Paul Flehr as their patent attorney. Flehr's signature, in fact, appears on the original 200A audio oscillator patent.

It was Flehr who introduced Hewlett and Packard to another of his clients, Leo Marihart, a lettuce farmer in the Salinas Valley. Marihart had been working, without success, to develop a device that could automatically thin lettuce and other row crops.

Bill and Dave, unfortunately, loved the idea. They were growing concerned that HP's product line, though large and growing, was insufficiently diversified. Electronic agricultural equipment, they concluded, might be just the thing.

It wasn't. And after considerable time and expense—both of which might have been used more productively elsewhere—Hewlett and Packard finally abandoned the project. The two men convinced themselves that the idea was just ahead of its time, and that someday they would return to it. Needless to say, they never did. But the experience taught them the importance of sticking with their core competence, which, for now, was test and measurement instruments.*

A second story from this era, one which often stuns later Hewlett-Packard employees, who knew HP only as the paragon of honest business deals, is the story of the company's model 410A AC/DC voltmeter. There is a story that can never be fully confirmed, but is generally believed by older HPers, that when the 410A was introduced at the 1950 IRE trade show it was, in fact, a fake. The voltmeter displayed had a battery and a knob to set the meter position, but otherwise had no internal circuitry.

It was one of the earliest, and most shocking examples of the "vaporware" that bedevils the electronics industry to this day. And only Dave Packard—and perhaps Bill Hewlett—could have signed off on this deceit. Perhaps, as Minck argues, "Packard had decided that it was important in a recession time to get orders first and finish the production engineering later."[13]

Maybe, but that is no different from the rationale used by generations of hardware, and especially software, makers, many of whom never deliver on their promises. Hewlett-Packard did indeed manufacturer and deliver the 410A, and it proved the beginning of yet another major business for the company. But it was a risky move, suggestive of a company still desperate enough to cut corners to survive. And it likely haunted Bill and Dave, because not only did HP never again try to introduce an unfinished product, but its formal policy of refusing to do just that became a hallmark of the company's sterling reputation. Had any HP product manager done in 1960 or 1970 what Bill and Dave did with the 410A in 1950, they would have been fired on the spot.*

The New Athens

Fred Terman had been talking about creating an industrial park on Stanford's unused acreage as far back as those train trips with Hewlett and Packard just after the war. In the years that followed, he regularly suggested both to Bill and Dave, and to Russell Varian at Varian Associates (he sat on the boards of both companies), that they should consider building their future headquarter buildings on Stanford land.

But that unused land, about 9,000 acres, wasn't available. Not yet. Proposals for its use ranged from turning it into a natural refuge for biological research to building a new town of 44,000 citizens that would support the university with property taxes.

Terman had his own vision. Though he had happily hiked the hills around Stanford for most of his life, he was still willing to give up that world—at least part of it—to create what he saw as the most beautiful and progressive of industrial parks. Terman was convinced that if he could continue to keep nearby the companies created by his past students, and add to them the firms likely to be founded by future Stanford grads, he could earn huge rental revenues for the university. But just as important, he also believed that such a park would establish a powerful synergy between companies and campus that would make the Stanford community hugely competitive on the world scene.

In a marvelous example of the teacher beginning to learn from his students, Terman's model for the ideal company for his industrial park was, as he later admitted, Hewlett-Packard:

> I had come to the conclusion that there were important advantages in locating high-technology companies near a university—that by being close together we could benefit each other in a variety of ways. In this the Hewlett-Packard Company was my model. Their first product was the result of a thesis, and during their first year or two in business they were in and out of the Stanford Communication Laboratory almost every day. Today they hire our graduates and employ our faculty people as consultants, while we make it possible for HP engineers to obtain advanced degrees at Stanford by enrolling in courses that are made conveniently available.[14]

In pursuit of this vision, Terman got himself appointed in 1951, to Stanford's Land and Building Development Committee. There, as one alternative after another for the use of the land was shot down by various interest groups, he pushed on. By early 1954, his proposal was the last left standing, mostly because it seemed the least draconian: it proposed to expand the campus to include areas for radio research (such as satellite dishes) and William Hansen's proposed linear accelerator, leave pristine the vast tracts of land in the high hills west of campus, and, importantly, open up 579 acres in the rolling pastures and low hills to the south, by invitation only, to industry.

Approval for the Terman plan came, fortuitously, at about the same time as Terman's promotion to provost, putting him in the perfect position to quickly implement his own idea. A significant contribution to the program came from Terman's neighbor in Palo Alto, Alf Brandin. Brandin, like Packard, had once been a Stanford football player, but these days he was the university's business manager. And a particularly enlightened one as well: it was Brandin who set the remarkable, and unprecedented, architectural standards for the new Stanford Industrial Park. According to Terman's biographer C. Stewart Gillmor:

> Maintaining absolute architectural control, Brandin required facilities to be designed with deep landscaped setbacks, parking screened from view by trees and shrubs, no heating or smoke stacks, and especially lawns that flowed from property to property with no fences, "one long sweep of

lawn," as one of Brandin's staff later described it. "This came to be known as the 'Brandin Theory on Lawns.' "[15]

The Terman-Brandin team worked exceedingly well. Brandin was able to set such high standards simply because Terman was so efficient at using his network of contacts throughout the electronics industry. Both HP and Varian quickly signed on, as did Lockheed Research Laboratories, General Electric Microwaves (which spun off Watkins-Johnson, which also moved into the park), and Beckman Laboratories (which, ironically, now included the gutted Shockley Semiconductors). Other nontech companies, such as publisher Houghton Mifflin, moved in as well.

It wasn't long before Brandin was turning down applications to the park, accepting only those firms with the greatest potential to benefit the university. As for Terman, his reputation soared, especially among the general public—not so much for being a great professor, but for having created the most beautiful business district on the planet. As building after building, plant after plant, rose on the land beside Stanford, hugging the contours of the green hills, missing the usual smokestacks and naked parking lots, horses and cows grazing on the green strips between them, it became evident that Stanford Industrial Park—like its biggest resident, Hewlett-Packard—represented a revolutionary way of doing business, a radical new vision of quality of life at work. A half century later it remains that shining ideal. A report from 1984 notes, "Driving through the Park, one can admire Terman's vision. It is all there, the smokeless factories of glass and steel nestled in green hills, magnificent homes tucked away in glens, horses grazing in meadows, ancient gnarled oak trees. It is indeed the New Athens, with each company an intellectual Academy, each president a Scientist King."[16]

Architects and urban planners hailed the park, workers everywhere dreamed of working there, and corporate tenants boasted to recruits of being there. In 1960, when French president Charles de Gaulle visited California, he specifically asked to see two places: Disneyland and the Stanford Industrial Park.

The first company to move into the park was Varian Associates, locating its headquarters at the base of the hill, just up from El Camino Real, on Hansen Way, touchingly named after their late friend and teacher (Bill and Dave weren't the only entrepreneurs in the neighborhood who honored their mentors.)

Hewlett-Packard, which owned fifty acres on the hilltop above Varian, broke ground in 1956, and began manufacturing in its first building in the Stanford Industrial Park the next year. The entire corporate headquarters wasn't completed until 1960, by which time 1501 Page Mill Road—the old logging trail now a busy boulevard—had more than eight acres of manufacturing and office space under one roof. HP's new headquarters building, low and wide, with a sawtooth roof and stretching across the top of a green hill, backdropped by the ultramarine silhouette of the Coastal Range, quickly became a Valley icon.

HP's headquarters building reflected the company it housed. The space-age entrance on the mountainside, featuring a cantilevered portico, was surrounded by trees and berms that hid the employee parking area. The other side, facing the Valley below, was a vast curtain of glass, offering employees both a spectacular view of the southern part of the San Francisco Bay and ever-changing natural light. The sawtooth roof served the same purpose, its exposed glass face drawing sunlight to create a pleasant interior environment. The buildings were also air-conditioned—rare for the era in Northern California—and the floor space wide open.

Only Bill and Dave had private offices, and those were used mostly for meeting dignitaries. Their doors were always open, symbolically and literally. Everyone else, right up to senior vice presidents, shared the floor with all of the other employees. The message was unmistakable: if bosses really were "managing by wandering around" they would have no need for hermetic offices. Indeed, the challenge for many employees at HP over the years was not in getting to see the boss, but in finding him.

The huge rooms at HP's new headquarters were parceled up only by dividers. There were no doorways, rarely even glass windows atop the dividers. It was thus possible to stand at one end of the huge room and see just about everyone in the company arrayed out before you across several hundred thousand square feet of sunlit expanse.

A half century later, after comics like *Dilbert* and satirical films like *Office Space* have rendered the working world of cubicles as a kind of organizational hell, in which employees hide behind carpeted walls trying not to be noticed, and "prairie dog" up at the slightest sound, it is hard to remember just how revolutionary this kind of workspace was in the mid-1950s. Then, offices and factory floors were divided into two layouts: private offices, usually for management; and vast, open floors featuring ranks and rows of desks and not a moment of privacy—and that, of course, was the province of the workers.

What HP offered instead was a middle ground: privacy in a public place. The layout of headquarters was the visual analog of the HP culture—and it, in turn, reinforced that culture every hour of every day.

That Bill and Dave understood this is evidenced by the fact that soon after the opening of the headquarters, this layout became standard for all Hewlett-Packard buildings. By the 1970s, it was possible to walk into HP facilities all around the world and, even if the company logo had not been in evidence, it would still have been instantly obvious you were in a Hewlett-Packard building.

This corporate culture, because it was the heart of the HP Way, stood its ground when it encountered resistance from a local culture. As a case in point, in the 1960s, John Brown, co-director of Yokogawa Hewlett-Packard in Japan, announced YHP's first company picnic. Though Brown had sent out notices months in advance that the picnic was a family activity, on the day of the event only men from the company showed up. Recounted Minck:

> Brown was furious, because the value of getting employees' families into the mix was crucial. So the next year, he was extremely vocal in stating that there would be no excuses. It was causing such a cultural divide that an employee committee was sent in to see him, to try to persuade him that Japanese custom didn't permit wives and children to join men in company affairs.
>
> So [Brown] had to make it a direct order, with serious consequences if not followed. That worked, because his employees observed direct orders, and considered [those orders] to be more important than their learned culture that excluded their wives and kids. Needless to say, future picnics were highly successful, and the cultures "intermarried."[17]*

Tackling Tek

By the mid-1950s, Hewlett-Packard was on a tear. In 1954, one of the most successful years in its history, the company introduced a series of important products, including wave tube analyzers for microwave applications, a new (model 400D) voltmeter, two frequency counters, and a decade counter (a device that counts electric pulses).

The financials were equally impressive. That year, HP's revenues reached $15 million, and employment jumped to more than 750. With nearly a hundred products in its catalog, and twenty more being added each year—as well as a worldwide reputation for high performance and even higher quality—Hewlett-Packard was the hottest young tech company on earth. And that, not surprisingly, also made the company cocky.[18]

Bill and Dave were not boastful men, but they were ambitious—and enormously proud of the company they had built. They believed they had a team of scientists, engineers, and marketers who could take on any competitor, large or small, and win. And there was one tech instrument business they coveted—oscilloscopes, devices that graphically present electronic signals as waves on a cathode-ray display.

The leading supplier of oscilloscopes was a company called Tektronix in Beaverton, Oregon. Tektronix had been founded by Howard Vollum, the brilliant scientist-entrepreneur Dave had met during the war while working on the Leopard project. Indeed, the Tek oscilloscope was an evolved version of the "A Scope" Vollum had shown Packard at the time.

Tektronix oscilloscopes were exquisitely built and highly reliable, thanks to little details like their carefully dressed wiring harnesses and isolated component mountings. Oscilloscopes were also rapidly becoming the test instrument of choice for electronics engineers, and as the Tektronix name had become synonymous with this technology, few engineers even thought about buying anything else.

For Bill and Dave, Tektronix's ownership of the oscilloscope business was a growing annoyance—a fact made especially ironic considering that it was Bill and Dave who had advised Vollum at the founding of Tektronix, and even introduced him to Norm Neely, who became Tek's West Coast distributor. Hewlett and Packard saw scopes as a natural extension to HP's current product lines, and a linchpin to their long-term goal of providing a complete test and measurement solution to engineers everywhere. They resolved to take Tektronix on and steal its business with superior products, better prices, and unmatched service.

In this ambition they were goaded on by their own sales reps. During this era, Hewlett-Packard shared many of its sales representatives with other companies, including future competitors. This was because the reps were not only independent contractors, but also because they wanted to offer customers complete product packages across all technologies. Thus, many reps sold HP voltmeters, counters, and other devices *and* Tektronix oscilloscopes.

But then, starting in the mid-1950s, Tektronix began to systematically fire those reps and replace them with in-house salespeople (as noted earlier, HP eventually did the same, but hired the reps instead). For their part, the reps suddenly found themselves without an oscilloscope supplier to round out their offerings. So they begged HP to enter the business.

Needless to say, the calls landed on an HP already contemplating just such a move, and in 1954 Bill and Dave initiated a new product development program in scopes. Development took two years, and in 1956, HP introduced its first two oscilloscopes as the opening salvo in what would become a forty-year battle with Tektronix. One of these scopes, the model 130A, was a beautiful low-frequency oscilloscope perfectly targeted at a niche where Tek had no competitive offering.

But the main weapon in HP's attack was the model 150A, a 10 MHz model targeted at the very heart of Tektronix's business. It offered a few real innovations, like a better display, but most of its differences from its Tek counterparts were obvious (and not very compelling) attempts just to be different.

But worse, the model 150A was a dog. It suffered terrible reliability problems, and HP wasn't prepared to deal with overwhelming demand by furious customers for immediate service. Hewlett recalled, "We came out with this fancy scope and the thing was just incredibly unreliable . . . we had to replace all of those scopes."[19]

Tektronix oscilloscopes, by comparison, were not only designed for reliability, but Vollum expected his field people to be repairmen first, salesmen second. Every one was trained to align the company's products. Vollum even required his salespeople to carry a screwdriver with them on calls, just to fine-tune any Tektronix scopes they found on-site.

To challenge an industry standard, it is not enough to be just as good— you have to be *much* better. And the HP 150A wasn't even close. Existing Tektronix users found no reason to switch and new users were quickly warned to stick with the proven brand.

For the first time in its history, Hewlett-Packard stumbled with a new product strategy. The humiliation sent a shock wave through the company. Convinced it was a temporary setback, Bill and Dave, with the support of their senior executives, decided to redouble their efforts and assault the market again. And again.

But they were up against an entrenched competitor, focused on a single business, with a culture of quality and innovation as robust as their own. For the next four decades, HP and Tektronix slugged it out in the oscilloscope business. HP enjoyed some victories at the low end of the business, but they were soon matched there by comparable Tek offerings. HP even tried to leverage its position by going into the business of building its own cathode-ray tube displays.

But try as it might, Hewlett-Packard never managed to capture more than 15 percent of the oscilloscope market. As this would become a billion-dollar business, that meant the company still enjoyed huge revenues even from its minority share. But it was always playing catch-up to a better competitor—an experience HP, accustomed to being the leader, could never really stomach. Packard said later, "In retrospect we should have gotten into the oscilloscope business much earlier than we did."[20]

The Tektronix experience grated no one more than Bill Hewlett and Dave Packard. And, in typical manner, they found a way to convert their frustration into a business lesson. Never again, they concluded, would the company attack an established market or competitor unless HP could offer a decisive contribution—usually technological—over what was already there, no matter how lucrative the potential payoff.*

This was just one more chapter in a growing collection of lessons about doing business that Bill and Dave were compiling in the back of their minds. They would soon put them all together into a coherent vision of how a great company should be run.

Public Exposure

In 1957, Hewlett-Packard Company went public. Its initial public offering of stock took place on November 6 at $16 per share.

Coming out of an era (1995–2000) in which companies with little sales, no profits, few employees, and little more than a storefront office went public to great fanfare and stratospheric valuations (and died just as quickly a few months later), it is important to remember the world of HP's IPO. In 1957, the New York Stock Exchange listed about nine hundred publicly traded companies (compared with six thousand today on the NYSE and NASDAQ), and the Dow Jones stood at 435. In the entire state of California, there were fewer than a dozen publicly traded companies, none of them in electronics.

Interestingly, Hewlett-Packard and Walt Disney Co., two firms with historical links, went public the same month—as if heralding the arrival of a new generation of companies, and of the Pacific coast as the next great region for growth in the U.S. economy.

Going public was only part of what Packard would describe as "a watershed year for HP"[21]—and for him and Bill. The company entered the year with 900 employees and $20 million in sales, and finished with nearly 1,800 employees and $28 million in sales. Its older buildings at Page Mill Road and El Camino Real, now numbering four including the Redwood Building, were full. In September, the first building of the new headquarters on the hill opened—and was quickly filled. A second building, a new laboratory, opened in October, and ground was broken for four more buildings on the site.

It was obvious to everyone, even the growing number of cars driving past on Page Mill Road, that Hewlett-Packard was undergoing a profound transformation. Nobody appreciated this fact more than Bill Hewlett and Dave Packard. They knew that to continue growing at its current rate into the indefinite future, the company would have to restructure itself, look to new and distant locations for expansion, and even consider a strategy of acquiring other, much different companies.

Great executives worry most when times are good—and even while the rest of the company was celebrating HP's incredible success and the prospect of real fortune at the stock offering, Hewlett and Packard met privately almost every day trying to chart out the path ahead. Hewlett said, "We were concerned about the company growing and the fact that we were afraid we'd lose the personal touch we felt was so important."[22]

One place where the two men saw enormous opportunities for growth was Europe. The Treaty of Rome, the precursor to the Common Market, had been signed that year, and Hewlett (in part, perhaps, influenced by his teenage tour) was convinced that it presented a unique business opportunity for the company. After trips to three countries, and visits with officials, bankers, and executives there, he came home more enthusiastic than ever: Europe had a burgeoning electronic products industry in the form of Siemens, Philips, and others, but not a comparable instruments industry.

He quickly set up a task force of Doolittle, Demere, and attorney Nate Finch to investigate how and where Hewlett-Packard could set up operations in Europe. By the time of the HP IPO, the team was already settling on Geneva, Switzerland, as the site of the first HP European office—eventually European headquarters. It opened in April 1959, followed soon after (July 1959) by a West German sales office, and (in September) by a small instrument assembly plant near Stuttgart.

Thus, within two years after making the decision to look *at* the European market, HP became one of the largest U.S. electronics presences *in* Europe. It was a pattern of decisiveness that HP would repeat in Japan and China. Moreover, it is interesting to note that HP chose to extend its manufacturing operations halfway around the world even before it expanded its operations within the United States—it became a global corporation even before it became a continental one.*

Meanwhile, this pending geographic extension of the company's operations convinced Bill and Dave even more that HP risked being led astray—or worse, torn apart—by its own success. Hewlett recalled, "We were growing from a very small technical company where only Packard and I owned the stock into a publicly owned company with a very different appearance." What was needed, they had decided in late 1956, was for the two of them to gather a group of senior HP executives, get away to someplace far from the distractions of daily work, and discuss how to keep the unique Hewlett-Packard culture alive in a time of explosive change.

Rethinking the Company

The retreat was held in early 1957 in the wine country town of Sonoma, seventy miles north of San Francisco, at the Sonoma Mission Inn—"a summer place in winter," as Hewlett would later describe it. About twenty HP employees attended. Packard wrote in *The HP Way*:

> Bill Hewlett and I decided to have the meeting for at least three reasons.
>
> First, we thought it was a good idea to get our key managers together at least once a year to discuss policies and problems, to exchange views, and to make plans for the future.
>
> Second, there were now more than 1,200 people in the company, making it increasingly difficult for Bill and me to know everyone well and to have a personal knowledge of everything that was going on. So we felt it essential that despite HP's growth, we try to maintain a small-company atmosphere and to have our key managers thoroughly familiar with our management style and objectives.
>
> The third reason we had the meeting was to present to the group for their review and study a set of corporate objectives that I had previously drafted and discussed with Bill.[23]

Because this meeting was so important to the future not only of Hewlett-Packard, but of modern business everywhere, it is worthwhile to take a closer look at the proceedings and Bill and Dave's goals for it.

To begin, there was the matter of precedent—and indeed, the Sonoma retreat served as the prototype of annual executive off-site meetings that would continue throughout the rest of Hewlett's and Packard's tenure at the company, and beyond. It was also the template for a growing number of group, divisional, and departmental meetings that would come to characterize the HP annual planning process.

The second item on the agenda was the matter of how HP was to deal with its rapid growth and the strains that growth was putting upon management. Hewlett recalled, "Out of this came the concept that what we probably should do is divisionalize. We had [nearly] 1,500 people at that point and we thought it was too big. By dividing up into two or three small units, we might be able to keep that personal touch."[24]

Other large corporations had decentralized into a division-based structure. Indeed, the idea of independent operating divisions, as devised by Alfred P. Sloan at General Motors in the 1920s, was one of the most popular management fads of the era. But, almost universally, this restructuring was done for product line or marketing reasons. Companies got too big and unwieldy for senior management to control directly, or their products became too diverse to manufacture or market in a unitary way, and managers concluded that the best solution was to create separate, self-contained operating units working under an umbrella of corporate governance.

Unquestionably, these were motivating factors as well for the Sonoma group to conclude that HP needed to move from a monolithic, centralized organization to a decentralized, divisional one. In fact, it was generally agreed that anytime in the future a division reached the current size of HP Co.—that is, fifteen hundred employees—it would divide once again.

But note the fundamental difference: the primary reason for this move was cultural—the men who ran Hewlett-Packard, especially the founders, were deeply concerned about retaining the company's innovative, and already well-established, "Way" of doing business. Once again, HP was choosing to approach its business challenges backwards, giving priority to family over financials.*

But the very choice of moving to a divisional organization, the group knew, meant stressing that culture to a degree it had never known before. The question then facing the Sonoma group was: how do you turn Hewlett-Packard into something entirely different, while still remaining fundamentally the same?

Those months of conversation had produced an idea that posed considerable risk, but just might work: a set of corporate objectives that would serve Hewlett-Packard as a kind of Constitution to the body politic of the "HP Way" culture. Packard remarked, "While we were thinking about how a company like this should be managed, I kept getting back to one concept: If we could simply get everybody to agree on what our objectives were and to understand what we were trying to do, then we could turn everybody loose, and they would move along in a common direction."[25]

Hewlett said, "I think we were the first people to initiate this program known as Management by Objective."[26] But hardly the last: after the success of the HP model, thousands of companies around the world over the next half century prepared their own lists of corporate objectives, most in the form of that most vapid of corporate instruments, the "mission statement." Almost every one failed, most because they were quickly forgotten, others because they were used for the wrong purposes—typically as a way to control employees rather than empower them.

What made Hewlett-Packard the first—and the best—example of Management by Objective?

Because, once again, Bill and Dave approached the problem from the opposite side. Whereas most companies that imitated the HP model looked upon corporate objectives as a way to keep their employees locked into the specific targets set by the firm, Hewlett and Packard did just the reverse. They set out to keep HP management from interfering with the natural desire of employees to do their jobs well, to advance the interests of the company, and to do so within the common value system they shared with other company employees.*

Interestingly, it was Hewlett who used a football analogy to describe Management by Objective: "We just basically said that if managers know what kinds of decisions are wanted, they are best able to make those decisions from their level rather than from above. So what you need to give them are some guidelines of what's expected and let them run with the ball."[27]

It was for this reason, as James Madison did in drafting the U.S. Constitution, that Bill and Dave intentionally, in Hewlett's words, made those objectives "very broad in nature." The idea was never to straitjacket any employee with responsibilities and goals that were too specific and too rigid to deal with an ever-changing and unpredictable world. That in turn meant setting very general corporate goals at the top, then enforcing a process by which each layer of management pushed as much decision-making and responsibility down the organizational chart as possible in order to leave the greatest possible freedom of action to those below. Thus, in the perfect scenario HP's Management by Objective would always place decision-making in the hands of the one person most experienced and best positioned to make the right choice— whether that person was a senior vice president in Palo Alto or the guy on the loading dock in Boeblingen, Germany.

In practice, what this meant was that, at HP, unlike almost everywhere else, managers gained power and authority by giving up control and responsibility. They had to *trust* the judgment and wisdom of the people who worked for them.

Needless to say, this didn't come easy to many people. Most men and women go into management to gain greater control over their careers, *not* to put themselves at the mercy of their subordinates' decisions. That's why the Hewlett-Packard culture of "family" was so critical. Successful families are built upon trust, on the assumption that every other member is working toward the common good.

At Hewlett-Packard every employee could see that this trust began at the top. Bill and Dave, after all, regularly let the other make even major decisions for the both of them. Bill Hewlett went off to war knowing that he could trust Dave Packard to represent him during one of the most critical periods of the company's history. A decade hence, Packard would do the same thing, going off to Washington and entrusting Hewlett not only with his company, but with his fortune.

Now, at the Sonoma retreat, Bill and Dave set another example by dividing up their company and entrusting the leadership of the individual parts to their senior lieutenants. The assumption—severely enforced by the two founders—was that these new division managers would in turn entrust their own lieutenants with similar authority. And so on down the line.

That was the first step in Bill and Dave's plan. The second was to create just the right number of corporate objectives, with just the right vagueness, that would encompass and provide guidelines for all corporate decisions—yet get out of the way of the people having to make those decisions.

The result, officially the product of consensus, but no doubt carefully guided by Bill and Dave, was a masterpiece of compression—and the model for generations of companies to come. There were originally five objectives. The sixth and seventh, *Organization* and *Citizenship,* though implicit in the original list, were added in the mid-sixties in the interest of clarity. Here is the first complete set of HP Corporate Objectives, circa 1966:

1. *Profit:* To recognize that profit is the best single measure of our contributions to society and the ultimate source of our corporate strength. We should attempt to achieve the maximum possible profit consistent with our other objectives.

2. *Customers:* To strive for continued improvement in the quality, usefulness, and value of the products and services we offer our customers.

3. *Field of Interest:* To concentrate our efforts, continually seeking new opportunities for growth but limiting our involvement to fields in which we have capability and can make a contribution.

4. *Growth:* To emphasize growth as a measure of strength and a requirement for survival.

5. *Employees:* To provide employment opportunities for HP people that include the opportunity to share in the company's success, which they help make possible. To provide for them job security based on performance, and to provide the opportunity for personal satisfaction that comes from a sense of accomplishment in their work.

6. *Organization:* To maintain an organizational environment that fosters individual motivation, initiative and creativity, and a wide latitude of freedom in working toward established objectives and goals.

7. *Citizenship:* To meet the obligations of good citizenship by making contributions to the community and to the institutions in our society which generate the environment in which we operate.*

Almost every one of these words resonates with the history of Hewlett-Packard and the acquired wisdom of its founders.

For example, No. 3, *Field of Interest*, is the embodiment of the lessons learned by the company in its ill-fated venture into agricultural products and its frustrating experiences competing with Tektronix in oscilloscopes. The *Employees* section is a distillation of the company's profit-sharing and stock-option programs, as well as Bill and Dave's deeply held antipathy to mass lay-offs. And *Citizenship* hides within it not only HP's growing charitable work, but Hewlett's and Packard's own sizable commitments to public service: Hewlett at the time of the Sonoma retreat was president of the IEEE (the Institute of Electrical and Electronics Engineers, formed in 1963 from the merger of the Institute of Radio Engineers and the American Institute of Electrical Engineers), and, since 1953, at Fred Terman's behest, Packard had been serving as a trustee of Stanford University, and within a year would be appointed chairman of Stanford's board.

Note as well the order of the HP Objectives, which is not arbitrary. For example, *Profit* comes first. This is a reminder that Hewlett-Packard, before and after everything else, is a for-profit business—and all other good things accrue from those profits. It says that the HP Way is not a social experiment, but rather a sober calculation that employee empowerment, a positive workplace environment, shared success, and a commitment to continuous innovation is the best recipe for a healthy, competitive, and profitable company.

This primacy of profits rebuts any notion that HP was merely a family business that got very, very lucky. On the contrary, it underscores the reality that Hewlett and Packard were tough, ambitious businessmen. They weren't lucky tyros, like many of the dot-commers of the late 1990s, who all but tripped over their billions—and lost them just as quickly. It took Bill and Dave three decades to earn their great fortunes, and they did so systematically, against ruthless competition, using pragmatic business practices and a realistic vision of the future.

The positioning of *Profit* is also a reminder that, as radical as the HP Way was, it was merely revolutionary, not utopian. That Bill and Dave demanded of themselves, and other HPers, that they trust one another and work together to achieve common objectives was hugely difficult, but not impossible. Many firms that attempted to imitate the HP model tried to show they were even more progressive by embarking on initiatives that ultimately failed because they crossed the line of human nature. A classic case was Apple Computer's attempt, in the early 1980s, to remove what it perceived as an organizational stigma by giving secretaries the new title of "area associates"—a plan that was quickly abandoned when it became more an occasion for derision than social engineering.*

The positioning of *Customers* is also interesting. At HP, the trite motivational phrase "the customer always comes first" finally has an answer: no, it comes second—right after profits. Note as well that nowhere is the equally tiresome word "satisfaction." HP realistically assumes that it can never really know something as complex, subjective, and ultimately metaphysical as what it takes to satisfy another human being. What the company *does* know is that if it can continuously improve the quality, usefulness, and value of its products, those customers will come back and buy more. And that is enough.

Next, *Growth*. Notice that it has two essential points. First, that a company must continue to grow in order to survive. This may be contrary to more organic theories about business equilibrium, but Hewlett and Packard were pragmatic enough to know that, in electronics at least, a company that stopped growing quickly lost its best people to companies that still were growing—and soon died. That's the meaning of the second point: "growth as a measure of corporate health and strength." Did that mean Hewlett-Packard could theoretically keep growing forever? Perhaps not, but it would as long as Bill and Dave were there.

Employees. As already noted, here there is the implicit commitment from Bill and Dave that HPers will not only enjoy the sense of security that comes from not having to worry about being laid off when times are bad, but also the thrill of knowing that they will enjoy a piece of the company's success when times are good. But note that here, unlike in the *Customers* objective, the word "satisfaction" actually does appear. It arises from two sources: opportunity and a sense of accomplishment. It is a glimpse into the founders' own attitudes about work and career. For HPers, it is a two-edged sword: if these are the factors that satisfy them about work, then they are in the right place. If not—and it wasn't for many Silicon Valley entrepreneurs who craved independence and control of their own lives—HP was absolutely the wrong place to be.

The *Organization* objective is, ultimately, a reminder of the underlying trust factor in the HP Way. The phrase "wide latitude of freedom in working toward established objectives and goals" is something of a tautology, as it refers back to the Objectives as well; nevertheless, its point is clear: everyone in the organization is to be allowed enough room to make their own path to their goals.

Finally, *Citizenship*. The call to good citizenship, especially of the corporate variety, is one of the most overused—and underaccomplished—goals in

American business. It is also a popular PR fig leaf for just the opposite corporate behavior. But notice the singular phrasing of this HP Objective: at Hewlett-Packard, good citizenship is an *obligation.* You make *contributions* to your community. Most interesting of all is the final phrase. It is entirely pragmatic, a kind of cultural quid pro quo: HP and HP employees are obliged to contribute to those institutions in society that create the conditions for Hewlett-Packard to survive and thrive. This is a very practical, sober, and transactional view of citizenship. Once again, it harkens back to those other founders and their rationalism, rather than some transcendental notion of moral duty and social justice.

The HP Way, Packard's memoir, written at the end of his career, is a gold mine for Dave's take on the major events in his (and Hewlett's) career. But it can also be a frustrating book because Packard can be so judicious in his phrasing and so reserved in his emotions that it can be hard to find the living, breathing man behind the words. (And Packard was the more eloquent of the pair: Hewlett's written memories exist only in rare interviews and speeches.)

And yet there is in *The HP Way* one moment when David Packard's words take on a passion that makes them rise almost to the level of poetry. It is when he talks about how those HP Objectives underscore the larger culture—the family—of Hewlett-Packard:

> Any organization, any group of people who have worked together for some time, develops a philosophy, a set of values, a series of traditions and customs. These are, in total, unique to the organization. So it is with Hewlett-Packard. We have a set of values—deeply held beliefs that guide us in meeting our objectives, in working with one another, and in dealing with customers, shareholders, and others. Our corporate objectives are built upon these values. The objectives serve as a day-to-day guide for decision making. To help us meet our objectives, we employ various plans and practices. It is the combination of these elements—our values, corporate objectives, plans and practices—that forms the HP Way.[28]*

From these words, it is apparent that, as much as anyone who founded a great institution in the twentieth century, Dave Packard and Bill Hewlett saw HP not just as buildings, intellectual property, and inventory, but as people as well. It is also clear that, beginning that last day of the Sonoma retreat, the two men began to treat Hewlett-Packard as not only their company, but as owned by everyone who wore an HP name badge.

(Bill and Dave would continue these annual off-site executive meetings for their rest of their tenures at HP. An annual highlight was a raucous skit, usually devised by Bagley, van Bronkhorst and corporate attorney Jean Chouinard, and typically at the expense of Bill and Dave.

One such skit was so outrageous that Kirby felt obliged to warn Packard, "This is pretty tough on you guys."

Tellingly, Packard replied, "The tougher the better.")

Moving Out

The decentralization of Hewlett-Packard not only enabled the company to better deal with the strains of rapid growth, but also to look beyond its current geographic, and even institutional, confines.

With a system for divisional management established, and a structure to preserve the HP Way now in place, there was no longer a reason why the company needed to confine itself to Palo Alto. The Santa Clara Valley was growing rapidly, becoming a mecca for engineers, but it was also increasingly apparent that the competition for those professionals was going to be fierce. Meanwhile, as Bill, and especially the Coloradoan Dave, knew, there were a number of excellent graduate electrical engineering programs at universities around the country, producing thousands of alumni who dreamed of staying just where they were.

There were other factors at work as well. For example, in a way rarely understood by East Coast companies, being based in California severely handicapped HP's ability to sell into Europe, then the world's second most important electronics market. The time difference interfered with communications, and shipping costs—either east by train to the Atlantic coast, then via ship to Europe, or west via ship 15,000 miles through the Suez Canal—were prohibitive.

The test and measurement industry was also maturing. Hewlett-Packard wasn't the only instrument company born in World War II—Tektronix being a case in point—that had survived and thrived. Now the rapid economic expansion of the 1950s, driven by all of the forces already mentioned—the Korean and cold wars, the baby boom explosion in demand for consumer electronics, the semiconductor revolution—plus a new one, the space race (Sputnik had been launched in October 1957), had seeded the landscape for a new generation of instrument companies, each seeking out, as HP had done, hot new niche markets where they could grow.

In many of these new markets, such as medical devices and analytical instruments (such as gas chromatographs, which could quickly detect the chemical components of a sample), Hewlett-Packard had no experience, and might forever play catch-up as it was doing, to its dismay, in oscilloscopes. In others, young companies were experimenting with the use of transistors and other solid-state devices. There was simply no way that Hewlett-Packard could assign enough talent to become a player in all of these new businesses—thus increasing the likelihood that one of the markets it missed would explode, creating a major future competitor.

Then there was the matter of customers. The fact that an instrument company like Hewlett-Packard could be one of the largest electronics companies in California only underscored the fact that while the West Coast was increasingly a hotbed for new electronics start-ups, the big tech customers were back east. Disney and the big aerospace companies aside, Bill and Dave had largely built the company on big eastern customers. If the company was going to continue to grow, it would need more of a presence there as well.

It wasn't as if expanding into other locations and new markets was a new idea for Bill and Dave. On the contrary, they had after all experimented with agricultural equipment a decade earlier. They had also bought the microwave division of Varian Associates. And, by the time of the Sonoma meeting, Hewlett had already been to Europe and begun setting up sales offices there.

But now the two men for the first time agreed that the environment was right to bust HP out of the Stanford Industrial Park and into the bigger world. Crucial to this change of attitude was not just the structural innovations that had come out of Sonoma, but the changed financial picture of the company. According to Packard, "By the late 1950s, the need for diversification was clear. We were becoming the largest supplier in most of the major segments of the electronic instrumentation business. But these segments, in total, were growing at only 6 percent per year, whereas we had been growing, out of profits, at 22 percent. Obviously, that kind of growth could not continue without diversification."[29]

Before continuing, it is important to note here an essential part of Hewlett's and Packard's personalities: realism. Like many great business leaders, and unlike most failed executives, Bill and Dave were ruthlessly realistic about their company, in good times or bad. No matter what the press releases, or the media, or even their own hearts said, they knew that the numbers didn't lie.*

Unlike, say, the legions of dot-com executives, or the management teams at legendary corporate meltdowns from Lockheed to Eastern Airlines to Enron, they never deluded themselves that the market would keep growing forever, or that somehow they would just "turn things around." Whatever personal affection they had for other people in their private lives or at the office, Bill and Dave both prided themselves on being unsentimental when it came to making business decisions. Whether it came to walking away from the Addison garage or from some product line that had helped build the company, they never hesitated to pull the plug, walk away, and never look back.

Not surprisingly then, in 1958, when Hewlett and Packard looked at HP's growth curve versus the industry's, they knew they would have to quickly diversify, expand, and acquire. That belief had been growing for some time, thus the Sonoma meeting. But there was one other sticking point, where the needs of the future had collided with the basic principles that had been formed in their past: debt.

Hewlett's and Packard's aversion to long-term debt, which to outsiders seemed to border on the pathological, was in fact (as was often the case with the two men) less due to any moral objection to borrowing money than a practical one. It was more than just the lesson Packard had learned watching his father deal with bankrupt companies during the Depression. It was also the realization that once a company assumed debt, it had to serve two masters: customers *and* lenders. And the demands of the two were not always congruent. Once they diverged, a company lost its ability to maneuver, to innovate, and to take risks. It often found itself choosing short-term profits (to service the debt) over long-term customer relationships. And that was the road to disaster.*

That's why, from day they first walked into the Addison garage, Hewlett-Packard had always financed its growth on profits alone. By the late 1950s such an attitude was looking, even to some of their lieutenants, as both anachronistic and limiting HP's potential for growth. But the two founders were firm. Packard recalled:

> I know that in some industries, particularly those requiring large capital investments, the pay-as-you-go approach just isn't feasible. I also know that it has become popular throughout the industry to meet capital needs by leveraging profits with equity financing and long-term borrowing. The advocates of this approach say you can make your profits go further by leveraging them. That may be, but at HP it was our firm policy to pay as we go and not to incur substantial debt.[30]

But how then to square this fiscal conservatism with the needs of an expanding company growing faster than any of the markets in which it operated? The answer, like almost all things HP, was found in a synthesis of business, finance, and people.

The business solution arose from an interesting dialectic between Management by Objective and the company's new decentralized organization. Rather than acquiring other businesses willy-nilly based solely upon their potential business prospects, HP once again worked backwards: if, in pursuit of its objectives, a division of the company determined that the company needed to enter a new market, and that HP did not have the resources or the time to enter that market and immediately "make a contribution" with innovative and superior products, that desire moved up through the organization to the top. If that evaluation was accepted, only then would HP look at potential targets for acquisition—once again using the same criteria of contribution.

Next came the financing. As a debt-free company, the scenario of borrowing to make the acquisition was always off the table. That left cash, of which Hewlett-Packard, despite reinvesting as much as 10 percent of its profits back into research and development (which eventually became the electronics industry standard), usually had in abundance during those years.

But successful young companies don't always come cheap—and that led HP to implement a second source of capital—the equity markets. When Bill and Dave decided to take Hewlett-Packard public it wasn't solely to enable company employees to share in the ownership of the company; it was also to have available the shares they might need to purchase other companies. Said Packard, "It is often more practical to acquire a company by an exchange of stock than by outright purchase."[31]

The best part was that for HP, stock was comparatively cheap, while to the firm being acquired it was the chance to jump on board a rocketing stock with the prospects of even greater heights.

Corporate acquisitions through a combination of cash and stock wasn't new, not even in the electronics industry. Charlie Litton, for one, was building an empire from mergers and acquisitions. But Bill and Dave brought something new to the process, one that smart companies of the future would attempt to duplicate: they didn't simply take over other firms, putting the Hewlett-Packard logo over the door; they completely absorbed into the Hewlett-Packard culture the firms they acquired. The day a company was bought by HP it was expected to operate by the HP Way, in all of its facets.*

With those expectations also came rewards: profit sharing, stock, employee empowerment, picnics, coffee breaks—all of the things that made HP's culture so singular and enviable. And that was the critical factor in Bill and Dave's acquisition strategy: the people.

Whatever company Hewlett-Packard targeted for acquisition, it was almost always the case that the opportunities, the work environment, and the company culture were vastly superior to anything the executives and employees at the target firm currently enjoyed. Unlike many later, more predatory, high-tech giants, such as Oracle, Hewlett-Packard never made an unfriendly acquisition, nor set off a bidding war, nor instigated a shareholder revolt. During the Hewlett and Packard era, it never had to. So successful was HP, and so legendary its reputation for corporate munificence, that most company boards were happy to be bought, most management teams saw the acquisition as a positive career move, and most employees were likely thrilled.

This was Hewlett-Packard's secret weapon. Negotiations always go easier when the other party is rushing toward you rather than running away.

As would be typical with HP under Bill and Dave, while the procedures, processes, and corporate structures might take a while to prepare, once they were in place the company moved quickly. HP made its first corporate acquisition in 1958, of the F. L. Moseley Company of Pasadena, California.

Moseley was a scientist who, in the 1920s, grew frustrated with the tedious task of marking out data points on X–Y graph paper. He came up with a design for an electric printer that moved along two axes and marked designated positions. In 1951, working out of yet another California garage, Moseley incorporated his company and began to sell a line of "Autograf X–Y plotters" that were soon beloved by researchers and statisticians everywhere. He also quickly earned a reputation for being an enlightened boss.

Thus Moseley's firm encompassed innovative products, a small but successful company, and a happy staff—along with the belief by Bill and Dave that HP had the resources Moseley needed to reach the full potential of the technology. Best of all, it offered to Hewlett-Packard not only an important new product family, but a new business direction—into information output devices for the laboratory.

The deal, for an undisclosed amount in cash and stock, was completed in October 1958. Within a few years, the Hewlett-Packard Moseley division was moved to San Diego, where, indistinguishable in look or culture from the rest of the company, it spent three decades producing the world's best X–Y plotters, some of them the size of billiard tables and used in the design of everything from semiconductor chips to skyscrapers, and to map the landscapes of other planets.

But that was just the beginning, because the same technology that enabled data points to be plotted automatically on a sheet of paper could, when souped up with digital intelligence, plot the thousands of points that made up a page of type, or even a color photograph. Thus, in the 1990s, the comparatively cheap acquisition of a little Pasadena company became the foundation of Hewlett-Packard's printer family, a multibillion-dollar industry in which it dominated the world market.

A year later, in 1959, HP became a global company when it opened its manufacturing plant in Boeblingen, West Germany, to go with its sales office in Geneva. Within months, Hewlett-Packard was one of the largest electronics manufacturers in Europe—and U.S. visitors to the factory were astonished to find that, other than the German signs and the better beer on Fridays, the plant was almost indistinguishable from its counterpart in Palo Alto. The employees even talked about "Die HP Way."

A year after that, in 1960, HP opened its first new U.S. plant outside of the Bay Area—in Loveland, Colorado, north of Denver. HP Loveland would eventually become the home of the company's desktop calculators, which would ultimately transform Hewlett-Packard, first in pocket calculators and then in personal computers.

With these three expansions, HP became, in turn, a conglomerate, a national firm, and a global business. It was the end of one era and the beginning of another. And yet for all of the changes the company had undergone—and the many more it was about to experience—it still remained, thanks to its culture, largely the same.

At the time, this continuity, mostly because there was no visible change, went largely unremarked. But in retrospect, now that we have seen hundreds of companies stumble and lose their way in the face of rapid growth, HP's run-up during the 1950s was one of the most phenomenal corporate expansions in modern business history.

The High "Way" and the Low Way

By the end of the 1950s what had been a collection of practices and attitudes at Hewlett-Packard had coalesced into the HP Way. And with it had come a distinct HP corporate personality.

That personality was not for everyone. For example, a number of people would bail out of their companies when those enterprises were purchased by Hewlett-Packard. These were typically people who were happy in the old company because it fit their personalities or because they saw a clear advancement path ahead. They were discomfited by the prospect of joining a giant corporation with a way of doing business so different from what they knew and so highly evolved that it seemed at best counterintuitive, and at worst incoherent. For them, no amount of reward in terms of position, salary, or benefits was enough.*

There were also thousands of people, mostly in what would be known in another ten years as "Silicon Valley," who found Hewlett-Packard to be an alien culture for entirely different reasons.

There was, as observers remarked, almost a topographical split in the Valley's culture. Up on Page Mill Hill, in the elysian Stanford Industrial Park, Hewlett-Packard embodied enlightened management, a harmonious workplace, quality products, and gentlemanly competition. But for many people, especially entrepreneurial personalities who wanted control over their own lives and careers, who dreamed of building their own companies and becoming tycoons, and who relished a good, winner-take-all fight, the real excitement lay among the companies of the plain.

These individuals—and they were legion—found their home on the floor of the Valley, alongside the descendants of Shockley Labs. The most important and famous of these was Fairchild Semiconductor in Mountain View, created by the "Traitorous Eight" after they walked out on Shockley.

Fairchild was a company of legend—perhaps the most extraordinary collection of business talent ever assembled in a start-up company. If Fairchild had a corporate culture, it could only be described as volatility incarnate. If Hewlett-Packard had grown older, with Bill and Dave now in their late forties, and their vice presidents just a few years younger, Fairchild Semiconductor was by comparison a company of post-adolescents. Bob Noyce and Gordon Moore, the "old" men running the operation, were barely in their thirties.

Not surprisingly, Fairchild Semiconductor was a company-as-frat-house: brilliant young engineers and marketers working long days, and partying long nights. New hires were often recruited by drunken salespeople or Fairchilders misrepresenting their job titles. One early company sales meeting featured scotch and brownies set out on a board stretched across two sawhorses. The Fairchildren, as they would one day be called, stole each other's women, crashed cars, chopped down trees out front of the plant, and started lifelong feuds and friendships. And somehow, in the middle of it all, they also managed to invent the integrated circuit, the defining product of the late twentieth century, and in the process helped to create the modern world.

Though Noyce and Moore were actually quite similar to Hewlett and Packard in personality (and Noyce in particular was a good friend of Bill and Dave), they came from a different generation and inhabited a different world.

The semiconductor industry, as it emerged in the late 1950s and exploded onto the world scene over the next two decades, was the Wild West. Companies stole technology, customers, and employees from each other, squabbled in endless lawsuits, and hired and fired thousands of their workers with the quadrennial cycle of chip demand. It was a high-risk game, and it was thrilling. And if it produced a lot of walking wounded, it also offered unimaginable rewards.

Except for the commitment to perpetual technological innovation, Silicon Valley and its culture was almost the perfect antithesis of Hewlett-Packard and the HP Way, the yin to HP's yang. It was a place for the young, the reckless, and the unrooted, even as Hewlett-Packard was older, more careful, and family.

Ironically, modern Silicon Valley was created precisely because Fairchild Semiconductor lacked the very structures that Bill and Dave had implemented to make HP more cohesive. In particular, Fairchild Camera and Instrument, the New Jersey parent company of the Mountain View firm, categorically refused to let Fairchild Semiconductor employees share in the enormous profits they were creating, or even be awarded company stock.

As a result, within the decade, Fairchild Semiconductor would begin to bleed talent from every doorway. Within a few years, this diaspora of Fairchildren and grandchildren would found more than several hundred companies, most of them on the Valley floor, so many chip companies that the journalist Don Hoeffler would byline a series of articles on the area he called "Silicon" Valley, and the name would stick.

The first generation of these Silicon Valley companies, nearly all of them semiconductor manufacturers—Intel, Advanced Micro Devices, Intersil, National Semiconductor, Zilog—would all, to different degrees, carry with them the germ of the Fairchild culture. Their perspective on competition, work environment, employment, even on time itself, was fundamentally different from Hewlett-Packard—indeed, they often operated in counterpoint to the older firm.

For the second generation of Valley companies, thousands of firms crowded into concrete tilt-up buildings, often being born, peaking, and dying in a matter of months, the vast army of workers migrating from one hot company to the next. Hewlett-Packard, the shining company on the hill, began to seem as distant and as exotic as the old castle above to the citizens of the new city below.

Here, at the historical heart of supercharged, double-dealing, wildcatting, card-sharping Silicon Valley was a company of Little League coaches and den mothers, Mormons and Republicans. Even more extraordinary, this low-keyed, often self-effacing company continued year after year growing at a breathtaking pace—without the usual sideshow of table-pounding executives, trade secret thievery, employee-raiding and price-slashing. Inside the beautiful buildings and quiet offices, things were being accomplished—almost [from nothing] for all of the visible work being done. Bill and Dave had found a key to greatness, and the rest of Silicon Valley looked on in awe.[32]

But not yet in envy. That would come later, as Silicon Valleyites grew older and wiser.

For Hewlett-Packard—and perhaps for Bill and Dave, though they never publicly commented on it—the fact that many people would choose not to join, or even stay a part of, the HP family came as a shock. The hidden danger of the HP Way, as would become more apparent as the years passed, was that it tended toward the hermetic, to isolate itself from the nastier, more ruthless business world beyond its walls. The threat that would always face Hewlett-Packard Co. from this point on was not that it didn't understand the new zeitgeist emerging on the Valley floor, but that it didn't feel it needed to.

HP was a happy family—rich, healthy, growing fast, and proud of its achievements. It believed it was the best company on earth—and by the end of the 1950s it very nearly was. But that family still had to live in the bigger world, and that world was changing fast.

A new order was emerging—not just in Silicon Valley, but everywhere. The sixties were coming, the biggest cultural crisis in America in a century. And before the decade was over, Hewlett-Packard—and Bill and Dave—would be seen as both hidebound and progressive, reactionaries and revolutionaries, both out of date and the greatest company on earth.

An Army of Owners

As the fifties drew to a close, Bill and Dave had one more surprise—one final "family" innovation for the decade that would, in time, prove the most influential and important of all. This is especially ironic because it was also the first such employee program that the two men got wrong.

By 1959, HP stock had been publicly traded for more than a year, and the company was preparing its application for that great valedictory of success in America, listing on the New York Stock Exchange. It was at this point that Hewlett and Packard announced the creation of an employee stock purchase plan. The HP stock purchase plan enabled employees to apply a percentage of their salaries to the purchase of HP stock at a discounted price, with the company picking up the rest of the tab.[33]

The announcement not only electrified the ranks at Hewlett-Packard, but caught the attention of the rest of the business world. In essence, it was free money: as an HPer you merely had to designate at the end of each quarter what percentage of your salary (up to 6 percent of your base earnings) would go to the purchase of company shares. Those shares, in turn, were sold at a discount from market price—sometimes by as much as 25 percent—and HP paid the difference.[34]

Not surprisingly, HP employees as a group quickly became among the largest shareholders in Hewlett-Packard stock. And if workers at other companies didn't already envy their counterparts at HP, they certainly did now.

Meanwhile, Bill and Dave looked to the larger public like the most benevolent of bosses.

One of the least-noticed aspects of Hewlett's and Packard's managerial genius was their ability to hide shrewd business strategy inside of benevolent employee programs, and enlightened employee benefits within smart business programs—often at the same time.*

The HP employee stock purchase program was a classic example of just this kind of maneuver. By transferring HP stock to employees at a bargain price, Bill and Dave simultaneously rewarded HPers for the company's success, further empowered them (this time on the shareholder side) according to the dictates of the HP Way, and increased the likelihood of their retention in the face of growing employment lures from the outside. At the same time, Bill and Dave were also keeping large volumes of stock out of the hands of institutional investors, who might use their holdings to leverage unwanted changes in the company—something far less likely to happen with thousands of employees voting small portfolios of shares. Having so much company stock in the hands of HP employees ultimately meant that Bill and Dave could better resist any pressure from Wall Street to substitute short-term gains for long-term success.*

But strategically, the most important advantage Hewlett and Packard recognized in the stock purchase program was that it was a powerful engine for cash creation. What the employees saw was a chance to buy stock and make some money; what HP saw was millions of dollars of salary overhead being reinvested in the company. For a company that was almost pathologically averse to long-term debt, this represented a huge source of investment, one that only grew as the years passed and the employee rolls grew. The stock purchase plan, Packard would say later, "has provided us with significant amounts of cash to help finance our growth."[35]

Keep in mind, this was 1959, at a time when Fairchild Semiconductor was just being founded, and its young management had not yet begun to feel the pinch of being left out of their own success. In fact, the realization that a night janitor had more chance of getting HP stock than the general manager of Fairchild Semiconductor did in getting shares of FC&I surely grated—and within a decade would cause enough friction to set off an explosion.

If indeed it can be argued that the history of Silicon Valley and modern high tech is really a story of stock ownership—especially the use of stock options to lure talent to risky new start-ups—then it all begins with Hewlett-Packard and its munificent (and clever) methods of transferring stock ownership to its employees. The fact that the American people, by any measure, are the largest owners of common stock in the world—and thus, as

workers, have the greatest democratic commitment to their own economy—
also has its beginnings in these HP corporate initiatives.

But if the Hewlett-Packard stock purchase plan helped to change the
world, it also proved to be a small disaster for the company. Bill and Dave had
assumed that, this being a great family, HPers would be as prudent with their
money as Hewlett and Packard had always been. They were in for a rude
awakening. Recalled Packard:

> In setting up the stock purchase plan we made one important mistake.
> We did not require our employees who bought HP stock at a preferential
> price to keep it. There is a long-standing truth about wage and salary
> levels—no matter what the pay, the employee thinks he or she needs
> about 10 percent more. We found that many of our people who partici-
> pated in this preferential stock purchase plan sold their stock right away.
> Even our employees at high levels had standing orders to sell their stock
> as soon as they received it.[36]

Packard is being judicious in his phrasing here, sagely noting that even
wealthy people budget beyond their means, but you can sense that he is
speaking through clenched teeth at the memory. In truth, Hewlett and
Packard were furious—especially at the realization that even some of their
own senior executives were flipping their stock. It might have been forgivable
for some entry-level salary worker trying to pay for a mortgage and his kids'
braces to turn this little company discount into an extra payday—but for men
already making a small fortune, to then cynically build a second fortune on
what they knew was an employee retention tool was, to the two founders, beyond the pale. (No one dared to ask what young Dave Packard would have
done had General Electric offered the same plan.)

This was, in Bill's and Dave's minds, a violation of the trust that underlay
the HP Way. And perhaps it was. But it was also the first indication of a growing, and irrevocable, gap between the founders and the men and women who
worked for them. Hewlett and Packard as the major shareholders of a large
and growing company had already been wealthy men before the IPO. But
putting a price on their shares had shown them to be not only hugely wealthy,
but made those fortunes liquid. They never again had to worry about putting
their hands on any amount of money they needed. That wasn't true for the
people who worked for them.

Hewlett and Packard were already legendary in their commitment to
understanding the lives of their employees, of sharing their successes and failures. But the demands placed on the leaders of a global corporation, and the

benefits and responsibilities of being multimillionaires, were a long way from those of meeting a quota on the assembly line or paying off a $100 Visa bill. And that gap, the two men realized, could only widen in the years to come, especially if their dreams for the company came true.*

It was a sobering realization: Hewlett and Packard could never again be fully of Hewlett-Packard, the company they had built from scratch, and that bore their names. The new divisional structure of the company only accelerated that process. The two men would have to discover new roles and a new relationship to the company. They would have to accept the fact that the corporate culture they had created, and of which they were deeply proud, would henceforth have to allow two exceptions. In a company where everyone was equal, Bill and Dave needed to be more equal than others—if only to enforce the rules of that culture and keep it from going astray.

Being set above the rest is a role that would appeal to most senior executives. That is, after all, the goal of most business careers. But that wasn't why Hewlett and Packard created HP, and it was not a change they welcomed. But as the decade ended, like all of the other changes taking place with the company, it was a task the two of them had to face. They would have to learn when and how to intervene in the company's operations.*

That is just what the two men did when they decided to violate the HP tradition of trust and stepped in to rewrite the stock purchase program to include a vesting period. They knew it was the right thing to do—and that there was little chance of their employees imposing that discipline on themselves. If HP truly was a family, this was a moment when Dad had to lay down the law.

A quarter century later, Packard would look back with pride on the decision, saying, "That situation has been corrected, but it is ironic that many of our employees who held on to their stock and sold it when they retired often had gains of more than a million dollars."[37]

In fact, one can make an even bigger claim for the wisdom of Bill and Dave's intervention and the new rule they imposed by fiat: for all of the high-rolling going on in the rest of Silicon Valley, with the millions in stock options being tossed about in hiring incentives and the fortunes made and lost on paper, the odds of an average worker becoming rich in the course of a high-tech career were likely greater at dull old Hewlett-Packard than anywhere else in town.

But knowing when to intervene was only half of it. The far more difficult challenge facing Bill and Dave was knowing when to keep their hands off the company's operations. For two men accustomed to being intimately involved in every aspect of Hewlett-Packard's business, this self-imposed detachment would take enormous discipline and self-restraint.

Bill Hewlett and Dave Packard had already successfully negotiated the transition from entrepreneurs to business executives—a jump that even some great company founders had failed to make. And Bill and Dave had made it look easy. But, as the scores who had failed before them (and the hundreds who would fail after them) would prove, this next step—from management to leadership—was far, far more difficult.

If that wasn't enough, the two men would have to make this leap during one of the worst cultural crises in American history: the sixties. The baby boomers were coming—bright, iconoclastic, and rebellious. And Bill and Dave were two middle-aged men who, for all of their own maverick behavior over the previous decades, now seemed to epitomize the old establishment.

The HP family, like every other American family, was about to be stressed like never before. And Hewlett and Packard, even as they were learning their new roles, would have to figure out how to lead their company through to sanctuary on the other side.

Chapter Five:
Community

Buried in a distant corner of the Internet, on a Web site run by a radical leftist organization based in San Francisco, is a blog entry entitled "A Day in the Life of Employee 85,292" by an author named Jay Clemens.

As one might expect from an agitprop group that began as the "Union of Concerned Commies," the essay is resentful, anticapitalist, and bitter. What is less expected is that this rant, apparently based upon the author's work experiences in the late 1990s, is targeted at, of all places, Hewlett-Packard Co.

In it, the author describes his first days on the job at the HP Instrument Division in Santa Clara:

> I was sent to a big introduction to the company, to "see the garage" as they say. It was a four-hour media extravaganza with a talk by some VIP, a slideshow, and a big presentation by personnel on "The HP Way." The garage was the highlight of the slide show, the garage being the place where Bill Hewlett and Dave Packard built their first instrument, an oscillator for the Walt Disney production of "Fantasia." I was fully indoctrinated by the end of these four hours and found myself becoming an android for Bill and Dave.
>
> I kept trying not to think about the time when Dave Packard was Undersecretary of Defense for Nixon during the Vietnam War and a group of us lit fire to the hotel he was speaking at. The flames were licking around the hotel and we could actually see Packard and his buddies at the top of the hotel. We all chanted "Pig Nixon, you're never gonna kill us all" as we blocked the arrival of fire trucks. It took several squads of riot cops to break us loose and send us scattering into the balmy Palo Alto night.[1]

What is astonishing about this essay is not the predictable attitude of its author, nor even the hint of self-delusion (he seems more impressed by the orientation video than he is prepared to admit), but the very fact that it has been written at all. What has happened to Hewlett-Packard Company in the intervening forty years since the 1950s that would take it from the family-centered enterprise led by two benevolent and beloved founders to a firm that would employ this angry anarchist who despises his employer and looks back fondly on the time he tried to kill David Packard?

The answer is a long one, but most of this traverse takes place during that great and controversial decade of inflection in U.S. history, the 1960s. Like almost every other institution in American society, in those years Hewlett-Packard would be changed forever. And so would its founders.

HP entered the 1960s as a company with $50 million in annual revenues, 3,000 employees, a reputation for innovative products and personnel policies, and taking its first steps as both a national and international corporation. It left the decade as a $330 million global giant, with 16,000 employees, and the most admired company on earth—but also embroiled in the political and generational conflicts taking placing just beyond its walls.

In between, the company would fight to extend both its business model into new territories and often forbidding cultures, and its products into altogether new markets—including the biggest technology market of all. And it would have to make these changes even as it struggled to adapt to a new generation of workers—the baby boomers—who represented not just the largest demographic group in history, but one that challenged almost every assumption upon which the business world was based.

To do that, Bill Hewlett and Dave Packard would have to expand the notion of the HP "family" into something larger that incorporated not just the employees of Hewlett-Packard and their families, but also those institutions—vendors, customers, governments, universities, even average citizens—that shared its values and its vision of the future. In the 1960s, the HP family metamorphosed into the HP community, and on more than one occasion that community had to be defended from the outside forces that threatened its survival. In the process, HP and its two founders for the first time found themselves making blood enemies.

As if this weren't enough, in the midst of all of this tumult, Bill and Dave also had to fundamentally change themselves. They were middle-aged men now. They had first been entrepreneurs, then business executives. Now they were going to have to make the dangerous, and largely (in high tech) unprecedented transformation of becoming leaders: of their company, of their industry, and even of their country. They would have to learn—as history has shown, a profoundly difficult task for entrepreneurs—when to delegate and when to intervene, when to make history and when to let it take its course.

Like everyone else in the 1960s, they were entering uncharted waters. Unlike almost everyone else, they held the fate of thousands of other people in their hands. In a volatile age, where the rules seemed to change by the day, Hewlett and Packard had very little room for error.

Looking East and West

The 1960s began for Hewlett-Packard about the way the 1950s had ended, only pitched even higher. It was a time for milestones, and their celebration. In 1960, the company passed $50 million in annual sales and five hundred products in its catalog. A year later, it raced past five hundred employees, and in 1962 broke the $100 million sales barrier. Nineteen sixty-two was also the year the company was first listed in the *Fortune* magazine list of the 500 largest U.S. companies, entering the list at number 460.

Two years later, in 1964, there were more than 7,000 HP employees on hand to help the firm celebrate its twenty-fifth anniversary. A few of them joined in the celebrations from HP's first joint venture, Yokogawa Hewlett-Packard, in Tokyo, Japan.

In the midst of all of this, HP also had its official coming-out party in the U.S. economy: on Saint Patrick's Day, March 17, 1961, Hewlett-Packard was officially listed on the Big Board of the New York Stock Exchange (as well as the Pacific Stock Exchange). Bill and Dave were in attendance—though it was a close call.

As remains the custom today, the chairman of the NYSE invited HP's executives to be on the floor of the exchange as HP's symbol went up on the Big Board. Bill, Dave, and several other HP executives flew back to Manhattan the night before, stayed at the Essex House on Central Park South, and got up early the next morning to head downtown to Wall Street.

It says something about David Packard—perhaps that, twenty years later, he still equated New York with his days as a poor young engineer at GE—but instead of grabbing a cab (or as a modern CEO would do, hiring a limousine), Packard led his crew to the nearest subway station. As he later recalled in *The HP Way*:

> Unfortunately, I wasn't much of a subway navigator; after much debate, we made the wrong connection at Times Square. We arrived on Wall Street several minutes late and were immediately ushered into a huge corner office and greeted by the chairman of the exchange, Keith Funston. He chuckled when I explained that we'd gotten lost on the subway. I don't think that he could fathom that we would take the subway to such an important event.

No doubt. And Funston would have been even more surprised if he'd been told that one day this company with the two founders who didn't have the sense to call a cab would someday become one of the thirty Dow Jones leading industrial stocks.

To America's financial czar, Hewlett-Packard may have appeared small town—but it was now anything but. Even as the HWP symbol was appearing on the board, the company was in the midst of one of the smartest business moves in its history.

By the early 1960s, driven by the universal desire of its population to restore the prosperity it lost during the war, and armed with some important technology licenses from naive U.S. manufacturers such as Ampex, the Japanese electronics industry was beginning to become a force on the world market. It wasn't yet a serious competitor to the U.S. electronics industry, but an astute observer like Bill Hewlett could see the future. Japan itself was also becoming a major market for electronics, as the younger generation began to exhibit a love for consumer electronics unmatched anywhere on the planet— and needed the tools to build them.

Yokogawa Electric Works had been founded in the 1920s out of an electric meter research institute in Tokyo. By the 1960s it was not only a major Japanese industrial instrument maker, but was already a veteran of agreements with U.S. companies, having signed a technical assistance deal with Foxboro Co., the Massachusetts industrial equipment maker. It was now looking for a U.S. high-tech partner to advance its research and, with luck, develop some new instruments for the Japanese market.

Bill Hewlett, meanwhile, as he had with the European Common Market five years before, saw an emerging opportunity, and didn't hesitate to make his move. He remembered the brilliant scientists he'd met in Japan at the end of the war. Plus, he'd already been proven right on his European decision, as international sales now amounted to 16 percent of HP's business. Japan was the future, he decided, and HP needed to be there.

But there was one big obstacle in his way, one that would become a major source of contention between U.S. tech companies and their Japanese counterparts in years to come: the Japanese home market, thanks to both government restrictions and impenetrable trading networks among domestic firms, was all but closed to outsiders.

But there was one loophole into this walled economy—and both HP and Yokogawa found it: a joint venture. Yokogawa Hewlett-Packard, YHP (later HP Japan), was formally announced by the two companies in 1963, at a time when most U.S. companies still looked upon "Made in Japan" as the epitome of cheap schlock. Dave Packard led the negotiations—and after seeing the comparatively inferior manufacturing and management quality of his counterpart, insisted that HP lead the new venture. Yokogawa agreed, and the deal was signed.

YHP would prove to be a major factor in Hewlett-Packard's continuing success—and in unlikely ways. Though the operation was always a successful manufacturer of, in turn, printed circuit boards, medical and analytical equipment, and computers, YHP's greatest contribution was as a portal. It gave Hewlett-Packard a beachhead in the Japanese market that few other U.S. technology companies could duplicate, especially after the competition in tech between the two countries heated up and Japan all but walled itself off to outside competitors. Because Bill Hewlett was so prescient, HP went through the Japan-U.S. technology war of the early 1980s not only unscathed, but calmly did business inside both camps.

But the biggest effect of the YHP portal came from the other direction—from inside Japan.

The two apostles of "total quality," Joseph Juran and W. Edwards Deming, all but ignored in their own country, had found a ready audience in Japan in the 1950s and 1960s. But Yokogawa had not yet joined this crusade, and so HP had little idea of the extraordinary gains being made by other Japanese firms during this era. On the contrary, Packard had seen just the opposite—a fact underscored in the first few years after the deal, when at the annual HP division managers' meeting the YHP director consistently presented quality (product failure and warranty cost) numbers at about the average for the rest of the company.

It wasn't until the late 1960s that Bill and Dave realized something miraculous—and all but unreported—was going on in Japanese industry. At a company event, the two men were cornered by an ambitious (and fearless) young YHP manager named Kenzo Sasaoka. Packard recalled:

> He said, "Why don't you let me run YHP? You send an American manager to us to oversee our work. We spend a lot of time—in fact, wasted a lot of time—talking to him, and if something goes wrong, he's the fellow we blame. We really think you can do better."
>
> So we said, "Okay, you go ahead—you run the operation and we'll see how it goes."[2]*

Before continuing, it is important to take a second look at what happened during that encounter. A young manager from a company division on the other side of the world—and thus only occasionally visited by senior management—buttonholes the two founders at a company event and asks them to let him run the division. Even assuming that Packard truncated a longer process—vetting Mr. Sasaoka more closely, investigating his claims about the American management of YHP—what happened next is still almost incredible. It suggests two things: first, that even in a global company, now with ten thousand employees, the two founders were still keeping close track of the most promising employees well down the organizational chart; and second, that, at least in this case, the legendary Hewlett and Packard ability to really *listen* to their employees seems true.

And, once again, Bill's and Dave's judgment about people and their abilities was validated. After just a year under Kenzo Sasaoka's leadership—and his implementation of Japan's new culture of total quality manufacturing—YHP turned into a benchmark for quality at Hewlett-Packard. Even Packard, who expected good things, was taken aback: "Here is an example of what YHP was able to do. We had been making printed circuit boards in various parts of the company. Our best failure rates were about four in a thousand. We thought that was fairly good. . . . Our Japanese unit, on the other hand, came in with a failure rate on its printed circuit boards of only *ten per million.* That's four hundred times better than anything we had been able to do."[3] YHP would in time win that most prestigious and contested of all quality awards in Japan, the Deming Prize.

This quantum leap in quality galvanized the rest of Hewlett-Packard, and by the early 1970s it would be one of the first U.S. companies to make a philosophical commitment to total quality. Just as important, the lesson of YHP, and the struggle of the rest of the company to match its high standards, made the rest of HP quality-obsessed—and unsympathetic to its vendors and strategic partners whose quality fell short.

That's why, in 1980, Hewlett-Packard dropped a bomb on the U.S. semiconductor industry by going public with the results of its own research, which showed the quality of Japanese chips to be far superior to their U.S. counterparts. It was the single most humiliating moment in the history of the U.S. semiconductor industry, and HP was accused of everything short of treason. But it was also the beginning of the turnaround, and eventual triumph, of American chip makers—and the restoration of U.S. leadership in electronics.

All of that because Bill Hewlett decided to take HP into Japan ten years before any of his competitors even thought of it.

Geography as Destiny

Hewlett-Packard's first domestic expansion, into Loveland, Colorado, proved to be just as unusual—and ultimately just as important to tech history.

Thanks to a shortage of meeting notes, the reason that Loveland was chosen over other sites is a bit obscure. It is known that Dave Packard, recognizing the need for the company to diversify geographically, was attracted by the idea of opening a plant in his home state, near one of the major universities and its engineering school. Pueblo lacked that attribute, so in 1960 Packard sent HPer Stan Selby to the northern part of the state to check out opportunities around Boulder, which offered, beside spectacular scenery, both the University of Colorado (for recruitment) and the National Bureau of Standards (a customer).

Meanwhile, two small-town businessmen in Loveland, a town twenty miles north of Boulder, heard that Selby was in the area conducting a search. Paul Rice was president of Loveland First National Bank and Bob Hipps was an appliance dealer—and both had big dreams for their little town.

However, they had never even heard of Hewlett-Packard, so before they approached Selby, they first had to determine if HP was a legitimate entrepreneur. Thus assured, they invited Selby to Loveland. Anyone who has visited both Boulder and Loveland knows that Rice and Hipps must have made one hell of a good case for their town. Certainly Selby was impressed, because he in turn invited the two men, plus a representative from the governor's office, to come to Palo Alto and make their case in front of Bill and Dave.

Bill and Dave had come out of the Sonoma meeting with a newly organized company essentially structured into four product groups—frequency and time, microwave, audio and video, and oscilloscopes—each with one or more manufacturing divisions. There was also HP headquarters, which provided executive management, personnel, finance, and other corporate functions—and, most important for this part of the story, corporate research and development, which was run by Barney Oliver.

Individual product groups, and some divisions, employed their own R&D managers, but those individuals also reported to Oliver. This was designed to keep diverse company operations from conducting overlapping research or creating redundant products. But it was also a leftover from the days when all of HP shared a single facility in Palo Alto—as well as a function of Barney Oliver's personality.

But the creation of the Loveland division in 1962 made this centralized R&D structure increasingly untenable. Loveland was originally chartered to manufacture voltmeters and power supplies that were designed in California.

But it wasn't long before the Colorado division began to conduct its own research.

One reason was practicality. According to desktop calculator historian Steve Leibson:

> With geographic dispersion, HP's centralized R&D structure started to unravel. It became much harder for the R&D engineers in Palo Alto to learn about manufacturing issues arising at a remote location and they could not easily benefit from the knowledge manufacturing engineers were developing when ironing out design problems and manufacturing-process bugs. As it grew from both internal organic growth and by acquisition, HP developed a more decentralized R&D structure. Each HP division became more independent of Palo Alto by starting and nurturing its own R&D lab.[4]

No doubt, divisional pride and a sense of independence also played a part. After all, the Loveland R&D operation started as early as 1961, months before the real plant opened. The R&D lab was housed in a Quonset hut that grew so hot in the Colorado summer months that a sprinkler system was installed to spray water over the curved roof. The lab also shared the building with the transformer manufacturing line.

It may have been small, but the Loveland R&D set the precedent for other divisions that followed, including a second Colorado facility a few miles south of Denver in Colorado Springs, which was established in 1962. By 1966, it had become obvious to Hewlett, Packard, and Barney Oliver that as the divisions began to assume more control over the research and development in their own product lines, HP corporate R&D was free to pursue new technologies and products. The result was a reorganization of Oliver's Palo Alto operation into HP Labs.

Freed to pursue its interests, HP Labs embarked on its most creative and fruitful era. Oliver and his team had been watching the convergence of two major high-tech trends. One was semiconductors. Over at Fairchild, Noyce, Moore, and Jean Hoerni had found a way to "print" arrays of transistors on flat sheets of specially prepared silicon. The result was the integrated circuit (IC), the computer chip. Even better, this lithographic printing process was amazingly scalable, offering the prospect (it seemed at the time) of putting scores, even hundreds, of transistors on a single chip.

Fairchild, Motorola, and a number of established corporations such as IBM were already racing to stuff more and more transistors per chip— and the resulting exponential improvements in miniaturization led Gordon Moore, in 1965, to first formulate what would become known as Moore's law, the fabled doubling of chip performance every 18 to 24 months. Moore's law would prove to be the defining rule not only of the advance of the tech world, but the metronome of modern life.

HP was cognizant of Intel's work and of Moore's law, but it had long resisted incorporating integrated circuit technology—instead of tubes and transistors—into its instruments because, in Hewlett's words, "We just didn't trust it."[5] The quality of the early chips was just too low for them to be put into HP's instruments, with their reputation for high reliability.

The second trend was computation. Computers had been around since World War II, when they had been used for artillery trajectories (ENIAC) or codebreaking (Alan Turing's Bombes). After the war, in spite of the now notorious prediction that the world market for computers would never amount to more than a few dozen machines, companies such as IBM, Burroughs, and Univac set out to develop ever more advanced computers for industry. Their competition was the greatest technology business story of the 1950s.

But these early "mainframe" computers were behemoths, the size of rooms, costing millions of dollars, and requiring an army of technicians to service them and feed them raw data from great "batches" of punched cards or giant spools of magnetic tape.

These giant mainframes were primitive by today's standards—indeed, they had a fraction of the processing power of a single cell phone—but for their time they were miracles of efficiency. Every major corporation, including Hewlett-Packard, owned several, typically used for payroll, accounting, and research.

The increasing pervasiveness of these computers in universities, government agencies, and corporations began to change the nature of work for engineers and scientists. Increasingly, they saw the output of laboratory instruments as raw data for computer processing, not as results in themselves—and that the incorporation of computer technology in their work could increase accuracy manyfold. But that also created frustration, because the ever-growing mountain of raw data had to queue up to be dealt with in batches by the computer—which in turn set off one of the great business feuds of the age: between engineers and the computer technicians in the IT department.

What engineers wanted, and what they told Hewlett-Packard they needed, was a new generation of laboratory instruments that could do their own processing—or, better yet, talk directly to the big computer. The term that would eventually attach to this new capability was that they wanted their lab instruments to be "smart."

It is worth a closer look at how HP learned of this need from its customers. The most salient fact is that this information gathering took place across the company. In sales, Noel Eldred had long fostered a culture of customer advocacy. Recalled Packard:

> [Eldred] wanted our sales engineers to take the customer's side in any disputes with the company. "We don't want you blindly agreeing with us," he'd tell them. "We want you to stick up for the customer. After all, we're not selling hardware; we're selling solutions to customer problems." Noel stressed the importance of customer feedback in helping us design and develop products aimed at real customer needs.[6]

Thus, when customers began talking about changes that would require the reinvention of almost every product in the HP catalog, the sales engineers didn't defend the status quo or assume such a transformation was impossible, but argued their clients' case to their own company.

Meanwhile, Bill and Dave had begun looking for large-scale solutions. They knew that most of the interesting work in the field was taking place along Route 128 outside Boston. So Packard set out to visit the computer companies and, if the opportunity presented itself, discuss the possibility of at least a joint venture and, most likely, an acquisition.

In his tour, Dave focused particularly on two companies: Digital Equipment Corp. and Wang Laboratories.

DEC was hard at work developing what would become one of the most influential "mini" architectures in computing history, the PDP-11 Packard saw the work and was very impressed (as would be Intel in a few years, when it used the PDP-11 as the model for the circuitry of the microprocessor chip). He even went so far as to enter into negotiations to buy DEC. Unfortunately—especially given the minicomputer war that would be fought by HP and DEC throughout the 1970s—the deal fell through.

So Bill and Dave did the next best thing: they set Oliver and his team to work on coming up with a Hewlett-Packard minicomputer, one that took the best of DEC's architectural innovations, but that also incorporated those features that best answered the needs of HP's engineer customers.

Packard's reaction to his visit to Wang Labs was just the opposite. There, An Wang and his people were developing what could be described as an electronic calculator (the difference being that, at least in those days, computers processed data via user-configurable programs, while calculators performed fixed arithmetic operations on numbers). Packard was intrigued, but not sufficiently impressed, and concluded that the calculator was not a product technology that HP wanted to pursue.

So even as the calculator idea was abandoned (only temporarily, it would prove), HP's initiative in computers raced forward. Thanks to the maverick actions of the Loveland research lab, HP's corporate R&D department was increasingly free to take on special projects—and none at the moment was more special that devising an HP computer strategy.

Two company engineers, Kay Magleby and Paul Stoft, had began to experiment with the design of an HP computer. Packard recalled, "They presented me with a vision of a system of HP computers automating HP instruments that were connected with our printers and plotters. I began to get excited about the prospect of an HP computer."[7]

Packard loved the idea because it so perfectly fit his and Bill's emerging business philosophy, which was to extract the maximum benefit not only out of individual products, but out of their interconnection. In this new strategy, computers were not simply data processing machines, but the glue that turned discrete laboratory instruments into test and measurement networks. That, in the classic HP fork, sold not just computers, but even more of the company's instruments.*

As seductive as that vision was, it would prove to be far more difficult to realize in actuality. As would occur with other many other popular new technologies that followed, the minicomputer industry was taking off so quickly that it was already becoming a networking Tower of Babel. One company's computers typically could not talk to another's, nor one brand of instruments interconnect with a different one. Meanwhile, customers were too prudent to bet the store on a sole-source provider of everything in the laboratory—even if it was HP. Besides, IBM, the world's greatest computer company, was already rumored to be preparing a major move into the market, and as the saying went at the time, "No one ever got fired for buying Big Blue."

Still, shrewdly, Hewlett and Packard refused to give up on that vision. And if the computing world refused to establish a common interconnection standard, HP would create one of its own. The company immediately set to work developing a common protocol by which instruments and controlling computers could talk to one another over short linking cables; to use the technical term, "bus."

The result, introduced by Hewlett-Packard in the early 1970s, was called the HP Interface Bus, or HP-IB. It proved hugely successful—so much so that with the support of HP's representation on the standards committee, the IEEE adopted it as the standard interfacing protocol for the entire computer/peripheral/instrument world. And IEEE-488 didn't end there. By 1978, an improved version became the standard for connecting not only instruments, but peripherals such as printers and disk drives, to all kinds of computers, including those for general-purpose applications. A decade later, further enhanced, and now known as GP-IB (General Purpose Interface Bus), the protocol was extended to all kinds of programmable devices, from laptop computers to video game players.

By then, what started as HP's internal interconnection scheme had also been adopted by other standards agencies throughout the world, including the American National Standards Institute (ANSI) and the International Electrotechnical Commission (IEC). Today, what was HP-IB is now the global standard for connecting digital products—and, as with many things, Dave Packard's dream came true not only for Hewlett-Packard but for the world.*

Rough and Tumble

In the short term, there was still the matter of what to do with HP's new computer, the model 2116A, introduced in 1966 and priced between $25,000 and $60,000 depending upon the configuration. The 2116A was a good computer, but hardly better than its DEC counterpart, and it certainly didn't enjoy the latter's name recognition. It had every reason to be a noble failure, yet another HP product that sold well to the company's core base of engineers and scientists, but no further.

And then came a surprise. Orders began to pour in from the most unlikely place. It wasn't long before HP was selling more 2116s as stand-alone minicomputers than as controllers in lab environments.

The founders were pleased, but astonished, as was HP sales. Only with time did the company finally realize what had happened, and what had been the HP 2116's hidden appeal: quality. That pursuit of high quality, a legacy of a quarter century in the instrument business, had been part of the HP computer project from the beginning, sown there by Bill Hewlett:

> I remember telling these guys, "Look, we're not in the computer business; we're in the data reduction business." We very carefully stuck to that area. Now, that had a secondary advantage that we hadn't appreciated at the time: our instruments had to pass Class B specs for shock, vibration, and so on, and we made them that way because we wanted them to work well. So it was natural to make the computers pass those [same] standards.
>
> Well, most of the computers at that time were "hothouse" devices [i.e., they needed very protective operating environments]—and suddenly, we found our computers out on Texas towers [oil derricks], which was a very hostile environment, simply because they were more reliable.[8]

The first 2116A had, in fact, been sold to the Woods Hole Oceanographic Institute, and placed aboard a research vessel. There, in the most difficult operating environment—continuous motion, salt air, and inconsistent power supply—it worked flawlessly for a decade. It was the first of many examples of customers using the computer in the most demanding situations.

In one respect, the company responded quickly to this discovery. When further customer research determined that many of the stand-alone 2116s were being used in time-sharing activities thanks to their high reliability, HP set up its own time-share applications unit to serve them.

But when it came to fully committing the company long-term to this huge prospective market, Hewlett-Packard hesitated. And that hesitation began at the very top. As Packard admitted later, "we were slow to get the message."9*

Yet HP made this misstep for all of the right reasons. The matter revolved around the next generation of minicomputers and how Hewlett-Packard would approach it. The model 2116, as the last two digits suggest, was a 16-bit computer—that is, its data was formatted into 16-bit "words." That had been part of the appeal of the 2116 when it was introduced, as it was an early entry in the industry-wide shift from 8 bits to 16 bits.

Inside HP, at the newly formed computer division in Cupertino, California, it was obvious that, as Moore's law predicted, a new generation of 32-bit minicomputers—twice as fast, able to access much more memory, and capable of far more sophisticated applications—would arrive sometime in the early 1970s. And it was just as apparent to the R&D people in Cupertino and at HP Labs that Hewlett-Packard Co., if it put its heart and money into a major initiative, could be the first company out with a 32-bit machine—and perhaps capture a lion's share of the market.

There was an even a project, code-named Omega, started by the Cupertino division just to chase that dream. By the end of the decade, there was even a prototype Omega computer running in the Cupertino labs.

Then, shockingly, Bill and Dave pulled the plug on the project. They had been following it from the beginning, and despite their attraction to the idea, the reality of Omega and what it represented had become a subject of increasing concern. Packard still felt the need to justify the decision twenty-five years later in *The HP Way:* "It clearly represented a departure from HP's basic principles. It was expensive. We would have to take on debt to fund it, and rather than building on existing HP strengths, the project required expertise and capabilities we did not have at the time, such as an electronic data-processing center, large-business processing applications, twenty-four-hour service, plus leasing and sales operations."10

And that was just part of it. Packard also admitted to worrying about the marketing expense of going toe-to-toe with IBM itself, as Omega was so powerful that it would reach beyond minicomputers and actually compete with the bottom of Big Blue's mainframe business. He even quoted Bill Hewlett's standard advice about taking on large, entrenched competitors: "Don't try to take a fortified hill, especially if the army on top is bigger than your own." And IBM had the biggest army in tech.

The decision, as Packard later admitted, "was difficult and controversial."[11] That was an understatement. It was the first time that Bill and Dave had ever allowed a major new product development project to go this far, and then killed it.*

The announcement, delivered by division general manager (and later HP director) Tom Perkins, landed with a sickening thud on HP Cupertino, a young division just beginning to grow confident of its abilities, and excited about the prospect of capturing leadership of its corner of the computing world. And now, in an instant, all of those hopes had been dashed.

For many, it seemed a betrayal, a violation of the trust in people that was supposed to be at the heart of the HP Way. It seemed as if Bill and Dave had suddenly lost their courage in the face of IBM—and had reacted by intervening, brutally and arbitrarily, into the most exciting and important new product program in the company.

For some of the most talented young people in HP's computer operations, that decision, and the way it was made, were simply unbearable. In fact, the head of the Omega project quit the company in frustration. A number of HPers in Cupertino took to wearing black armbands for their now dead dream.

But Omega wasn't dead. Apparently there was a small coterie of people at the division who refused to give up on the project and secretly maintained an ongoing skunk works to perfect Omega—all apparently without Palo Alto's knowledge. Whether this secrecy was real is a matter for speculation. The way Packard casually describes this clandestine project in his memoir suggests that he may have known about it all along.

What is known is that somewhere along the way the secret team, conscious of Bill and Dave's concerns, continued pursuing the project—and when they were ready, they presented it to their bosses. Those managers in turn, impressed by some of the design features of this revised computer, decided to scale back Omega to a 16-bit minicomputer with a simpler operating system, rename it "Alpha," and present it to corporate.*

When Alpha was sprung on an ostensibly surprised Dave Packard, he expressed his satisfaction with the revamped product and gave it the green light to continue development.

The result, introduced in 1972 (and, as will be shown, several times thereafter), was the HP model 3000 computer, a general-purpose computer designed to take on all of the real-time (as opposed to batch) processing needs of small and medium-sized business. The HP 3000 became (in terms of total revenues) probably the most successful product in Hewlett-Packard history—and one of the most popular computers of all time. The model 3000, in its many variants, would live on in the HP catalog for thirty-one years, nearly as long as the audio oscillator. Wrote this author on ABCNews.com at its retirement, "[The HP 3000] ranks with the IBM 360, the DEC VAX, and the Apple II as one of the greatest computers ever made . . . [and] the cornerstone of HP's entry into the mainstream computer business, which in time would lead the company into PCs and printers—and turn HP from a $500 million company into a $50 billion one."[12]

There are a number of important insights into Bill Hewlett and Dave Packard that can be taken away from the 2116A/3000 episode at HP. The first is that the two men were utterly unsentimental about the business they were in: they knew that computers represented a significant departure from Hewlett-Packard's historic product offerings, and were willing to make the leap.

That said, they were only willing to enter this new business if they could do so without violating the core philosophies of the firm, notably those of making a real contribution, of not assuming long-term debt, and of not directly attacking well-defended markets. Thus their embrace of the 2116A, which had the added advantage of creating synergistic effects among HP's existing products, and their initial resistance to the HP 3000. And if their decision to initially kill the model 3000 seems both autocratic and in violation of the HP Way, it should be remembered that central to that business philosophy was the idea that decisions should be made by the people closest to the problem: since a major corporate move into the business computer market to take on the biggest electronics company on the planet was in fact a decision that put all of HP at risk, the CEO and chairman reserved that decision for themselves.

As for the charge that Bill and Dave showed a lack of courage in not jumping on the 3000 immediately and challenging IBM, it should be enough to note that both men were willing to accept the calumny of their own beloved employee "family," even the loss of some key personnel, to defend their decision not to violate the company's business standards. And, it should be added, that four years later, when the time was right—and IBM was even bigger—they went for it with every resource in HP's business arsenal. History showed it to be an inspired choice.

Meanwhile, during those intervening years, the two founders never showed their hand. Did they know about the secret skunk works? Probably. Did they have a hand in making sure those computer division managers opted for a more realistic final version of the model 3000? Very likely. Did they take credit for having stage-managed the whole thing? Never.

Listening to Outsiders

Hewlett-Packard's entry into a second new market during the 1960s offers another glimpse at the way Bill and Dave were evolving their management techniques to match the changing nature of their company.

The Loveland division's decision to conduct its own R&D, and thus free HP Labs to explore emerging technologies, resulted not only in HP's entry into computers, but also calculators. Even more than computers, arithmetic calculators had a very long history, predating electronics by centuries. Their roots lay in ancient mechanical devices, such as the abacus, and, beginning in the seventeenth century with John Napier's discovery of a logarithmic equation to perform multiplication and division, the slide rule. By the early twentieth century, mechanical adding machines were a common desk tool and the heart of accounting and statistics. By the 1950s, these machines were not only electrified, but capable of very sophisticated mathematical calculations. They seemed a natural target for the improvements in speed, power, and miniaturization made possible by the transistor and the integrated circuit.

But was it a job for Hewlett-Packard to take on? Dave Packard had thought perhaps so, but his visit to Wang Labs had convinced him otherwise.

Yet just a few months later he not only changed his mind, but embraced the idea of an HP calculator with even greater fervor than he had the computer. Why? Because Packard finally saw a version of the technology that fit the company's criteria for innovation, contribution, and integration with current HP products. What makes this story especially compelling is that it came from a most unlikely source. HP had almost always invented its own products—and when it didn't, it acquired those products and their underlying technologies, patents, and so on as part of a corporate acquisition.

But in the case of HP's entry into calculators, one of the most momentous decisions in its history, the idea literally walked in through the door—twice.

In 1965, just as HP Labs was embarking on the 2116A project, Barney Oliver was visited, independently, by two inventors over the course of as many weeks. The two men, who had never met each other, in fact embodied the absolute leading edge of the two great movements in the automated computation world.

Malcolm McMillan was a Los Angeles physicist and mathematician who had come across the innovative work of an aerospace engineer named Jack

Volder. In 1956, Volder had published an internal Convair report (published in two formal reports to the IRE three years later) describing how to use binary numbers in a process of repeated shifts and adds to perform amazingly complex trigonometric and other calculations.

McMillan realized that this "algorithm," called CORDIC, which had originally been created for use in the world's first supersonic bomber, the B-58 Hustler, could be used as the brains of a new kind of calculator for scientific applications. He contacted Volder, convinced him to team up, and together they built the prototype of the world's first scientific calculator. Then McMillan hit the road to find a buyer.

Given his background, it wasn't surprising that McMillan eventually arrived at Hewlett-Packard, where, in June 1965, he made a presentation of his product, code-named "Athena," to Barney Oliver and Paul Stoft (the latter back from his work on the 2116A). As Oliver described his meeting with McMillan, "He and the other guy [Volder] had developed a calculator which could perform transcendental operations, transcendental functions, and he brought this big kluge with him. It was a box about the size of two beehives. They finally got it working and computed a tangent and other trig functions for us. It took over a second to do this."[13]

Oliver may have been disappointed with McMillan and Volder's hardware, but he instantly recognized that the CORDIC algorithm was a major breakthrough. So he decided to show just enough interest to keep the pair talking to HP, but not enough to let them any closer than arm's reach. Meanwhile, he hoped to find a hardware solution somewhere.

Within days, in an amazing bit of serendipity, that solution walked into his office.

Tom Osborne was a singular individual, a classic Silicon Valley personality. A young Berkeley grad, he was working at a typewriter/office equipment company, SCM, that was already a major manufacturer of old-fashioned rotary mechanical calculators under the Smith-Corona brand. SCM knew that if it was going to stay competitive it would need to get into electronic calculators. It licensed just such a technology from consultant (and former Manhattan Project physicist) Stanley P. Frankel—and then hired Tom Osborne to evaluate the idea, then make it real.

It wasn't long before Osborne hit what seemed an insurmountable obstacle: Frankel's design required a lot of diodes, and to cut costs, SCM wanted to use "off-spec" diodes, which cost a nickel, rather than higher quality, full-performance versions that cost a quarter. Osborne knew it wouldn't work: SCM's plan would either produce a machine that didn't work at all, or would be painfully slow.

But he couldn't convince his superiors. "I was a junior employee and totally unable to convince them that there was a better way to design things," he recalled.[14] Finally, he could stand no more: he refused to continue working on the project: "In the fall of 1963 I told them that I could no longer help them produce a calculator that, in my opinion, was doomed to failure (it was, and it did). I offered to design a machine for them at no cost if they would give me lab space. Later, if they liked what they saw, they could pay me for the time I had spent in the design and construction.[15]

SCM turned him down, saying it didn't conform to company policy. Then the company turned around and threatened to sue him if he didn't turn over all of his research into the alternative calculator design, as well as the calculator prototype itself. When Osborne replied that there was no prototype, the SCM lawyers refused to believe him, determining that no one could be so confident as to make such a "can't lose" offer to a major corporation without having already built one. Exasperated, Osborne hired his own lawyer and ran the company off.

(SCM did in fact go on and build its calculator with the off-spec diodes. Introduced in 1966, it was a disaster. Oliver himself dismissed it as "a miserable machine. It took forever to do anything.")[16]

Tom Osborne began 1964 "unemployed, miffed, but well armed with good design techniques."[17] With his wife supporting him, he set out to finally build the calculator that had existed only in his imagination. From the start, he planned to build a prototype that was "going to be about 100 times faster, take about one tenth of the power, be about a third of the size and weight of the then-existing calculators, and have a floating point arithmetic unit that produced 10 significant digits of accuracy."[18] In other words, he planned to build the first true electronic calculator.

Shrewdly, he also decided to divide the prototype into two connected boxes—one with a keyboard and display that would show the anticipated size of the finished calculator, the other containing the real processor guts of the calculator. This enabled him, unlike McMillan, to show the actual anticipated size of the finished product—and not scare prospective customers into thinking the machine would be huge.

It took him most of the year to build the prototype, all the time wishing he had just such a calculator to help him design it. He finished on December 24, 1964.

Finally, on Christmas Eve afternoon in 1964 the calculator was totally functional. I remember the overwhelming realization that sitting in front of me on a red card table in the corner of our bedroom/workshop, sat more computing power per unit volume than had ever existed on this planet. I felt more like the discoverer of the object before me than its creator. I thought of things to come. If I could do this alone in my tiny apartment, then there were some big changes in store for the world.[19]

Mounting the components it into two handmade balsa-wood boxes, Osborne finished by spray-painting everything with Cadillac green automotive paint. Then, with his "Green Machine" in hand, he set out to find a buyer.

He soon discovered the nightmare of being a lone inventor trying to show a new product to a major corporation. Some flatly refused to talk with him. Others demanded he sign a nondisclosure agreement so onerous that he could only conclude they were preparing to legally defend themselves after they stole his idea.

There were times when Osborne's sales tour devolved into farce:

> The IBM people were not slowed down a bit by their inability to find [my] apartment's slightly hidden entry. They climbed the fire escape and knocked on the fire exit window. I opened it and they entered by climbing over the hi-fi set which partially blocked their entry. Through it all they retained their composure.[20]

The only good thing to come out of that meeting was that henceforth Osborne adopted IBM's nondisclosure agreement as his own.

Before he was done, Tom Osborne pitched to and was turned down by thirty companies—including Hewlett-Packard. A few had even passed on the calculator but offered Osborne himself a job—and he returned the favor by turning them down. The absolute nadir came in a series of meetings with Friden Corp., then the world's leader in calculators, and the reason SCM had been rushing to get into electronic calculators. Friden initially showed enormous interest in his calculator, but as negotiations went on, Osborne grew increasingly suspicious of the company's motives. Finally, he nixed the deal— only to learn later that Friden had planned to buy his technology and kill it to get rid of any competition to its current line.

It was a weary, frustrated, and much wiser Tom Osborne ("I was about at my rope's end") who, in June 1965, finally decided to take a break after six miserable months pitching his invention, and gave himself a vacation.

At precisely that moment, across the Bay in Palo Alto, Tony Lukes, an HP engineer, was talking with Paul Stoft about the meeting with McMillan and Volder. They've got something there, Stoft told him, at least in the software. But the hardware is a mess. We can't even consider taking it on without a better box to put it in.

A light went on in Lukes's head. He told Stoft about a guy he used to work with at SCM, a terrific design guy, who he heard was working on a calculator project of his own.

Bring him in, said Stoft, and let's see what he's got.

But when Lukes called, he only got Osborne's answering machine. Eventually the two men connected, and Tom Osborne at last found himself inside Hewlett-Packard, in Paul Stoft's office, giving yet one more demonstration of the Green Machine. Stoft quietly watched the presentation for a few minutes, then asked if Osborne minded if they could be joined by Barney Oliver, the head of the lab. Sure, said Osborne.

Oliver in turn watched the presentation and, like Stoft before him, realized that he was seeing the future: Tom Osborne's Green Machine, the best calculator hardware design yet devised, running McMillan and Volder's CORDIC algorithm. There would be nothing on the planet to match—and likely nothing even being developed close to it. And the two company scientists knew that HP's customers would love it.

Recounts historian Steve Leibson, "How did Oliver and Stoft know? They used the same marketing technique that served HP well from its founding in 1939 to about 1990: next-bench market research. Briefly, next-bench market research means taking an idea to the engineer at the next bench. If he (all HP engineers were 'he' back then) liked it, then it was sure to succeed."[21]

Oliver had only one question: could Osborne redesign his device to run CORDIC? "Yes," replied Osborne, not knowing what Oliver was talking about, but convinced he could do anything with his design.

Oliver then took Osborne down the hall and showed him a prototype printed circuit board for a new kind of onboard computer memory for microcode called read-only memory (ROM). The Green Machine only used simple diode-based logic. Could the calculator be redesigned using this? Osborne hesitated, not because he didn't think he could do it, but because he wasn't sure that HP Labs could really scale the ROM up the fifty times needed to drive his calculator. "Yes," he finally said, praying that he was right.

Great, said Oliver. He inquired if Osborne could return the next day and meet with Bill and Dave. "Bill and Dave who?" Osborne asked.

The meeting the next day was memorable. Nothing like it had occurred with the previous companies. It appeared to me that while other companies were looking for a weakness that might preclude them from success, HP was looking for the opportunity that might lead to a success.*

We discussed the project's good points, its weak points, and the risks involved to both parties. We agreed to give it a try for six weeks during which I would explain my design processes to HP's engineers and perform a total evaluation of the project. The meeting was about over when Mr. Packard said, "Oh Tom, we won't take the project without you coming along with it." I said, "You can't have it without me."

In those few words it was clear to me that one of my main tasks was to transfer the information that existed only in my mind into the minds of the people with whom I would be working for a couple of years. It was also clear that I was among people who were open minded and trained to advance the state of the art.[22]

At the end of the meeting, Hewlett asked if he could take the Green Machine home for a few days and play with it. Osborne agreed, but when he returned to HP to pick up the machine and get to work, he was met by a sheepish and apologetic Bill Hewlett. It seemed that Bill had been so excited playing with the calculator that he had somehow managed to poke his thumb right through the balsa-wood box. Worse, he was afraid that he'd burned out all of the circuitry by accidentally plugging in the power supply backwards—which appeared to have shorted out the Green Machine.

Luckily, Tom Osborne had prepared for just such an eventuality by installing a protective power diode. It saved the calculator. Relieved, Hewlett welcomed Osborne to HP, and they agreed upon a brief four- to six-week evaluation period to work with McMillan (now a company consultant) and HPer Dave Cochran to see if the Green Machine could be turned into a real, CORDIC-equipped product. Osborne recalled:

At the end of the six-week evaluation process, Al Smith of HP's legal department dropped by and gave me a check which meant that the project was a go. I was excited. The check was nice, but the opportunity to do the project was everything I had hoped for. At that time, I decided that if the project was to get into serious trouble, I would be the first one to know, and I would immediately tell Barney that we should cancel the project. The HP people had placed a great deal of faith and trust in me and I was not going to misuse it.[23]

Tom Osborne, it seems, was already part of the HP Way. He would never be a Hewlett-Packard employee ("He had a kind of free spirit about him," recalled Oliver) but would remain connected with the company for more than a decade as a consultant or contractor. His very presence at HP—an increasingly legendary figure who would come and go at the company according to when he was needed or when inspiration struck—was something new for Hewlett-Packard.*

The First Desktop Revolution

The product that emerged from the marriage of the Green Machine and CORDIC was the Hewlett-Packard model 9100A desktop calculator. The prototype, built at the same time and alongside the 2116A computer at HP Labs, took just over a year to complete.

It was a masterpiece of design discipline. Oliver would later describe the creation of the HP 9100A as "exothermic," thereby comparing it to a chemical reaction in which various components mixed together spontaneously produce heat and light. What he meant was that the 9100A project brought together the lab's in-house experts in logic circuits, minicomputer core memory, software, firmware, displays, and industrial design. And presiding over it all was the nonemployee Tom Osborne.

Some of the most important players in the project had no real experience in what they were assigned to do. Thus, Dave Cochran, who had just finished work on an HP digital voltmeter, found himself in a meeting about the calculator, listening to Barney Oliver talk about developing the right algorithms for the calculator to compute efficiently. "What's an algorithm?" Cochran asked—and Oliver immediately gave him the job of devising them. Cochran quickly embarked on a months-long research project—including learning how to program a computer—before he could even get started on his new assignment. He recalled, "Up until at least the 1980s, HP believed that any engineer it hired could undertake just about any engineering project: analog design, digital design, IC design, software programming, production engineering, component design, etc. After all, Bill Hewlett was an engineer's engineer and the same was expected of all HP's engineers."[24]

Cochran's experience wasn't unique. In fact, the engineer eventually assigned to manage the 9100A project, Dick Monnier, had most recently been a project director in oscilloscopes, and he had almost no experience with computers.

But it all worked, not least because Tom Osborne's long months working in his apartment had given him not only an unequaled expertise in calculator function, but the kind of supreme adaptability that comes from building sophisticated electronics with Elmer's glue, balsa wood, and automotive paint. Over and over through that year, whenever the project hit a wall in circuit design or architecture, he somehow—and to the astonishment of others on the project—came up with a solution.

The most famous of these was Osborne's decision to use a most unlikely form of memory in the calculator. In those days, any integrated circuits you could trust were too expensive for use in anything but rockets and aircraft, and those you could afford for everyday use were too unreliable. For that reason, HP decided to build the guts of the 9100 from standard diodes and other discrete semiconductor devices and stacked, custom-made printed circuit boards. But, as Osborne laid out this circuitry, he realized that the 9100A just didn't have enough read-only memory.

His solution was to create a memory 'rope': a braid of wires linking together an array of tiny doughnut-shaped magnets (the "core" in old-fashioned mainframe computer core memory) threaded through the limited space that remained in the box. It was this kind of practical engineering genius that made Osborne a legend inside HP even before the 9100A was completed.

All the while, watching over the 9100A project like a nervous father, was Bill Hewlett. Perhaps in part because he had almost destroyed the Green Machine, and because he was, in Leibson's words, something of "an engineering aesthete," but most of all because he wanted HP to create the biggest possible splash in the calculator market, Hewlett ordered for the 9100A an absolutely top-notch package: sleek and space-age, it was so distinctive for the time that the 9100A would eventually find a home as a prop in a number of movies. (It would also be echoed in the design of the iconic Apple II.)

Practical as always, Hewlett also made another demand of the 9100A: calling a meeting in his office, he had the team gather around his walnut desk. Pulling out the standard typing stand built into the desk, he told the team that he wanted the new calculator to not only fit on the stand, but also be small enough to be folded away with it just like a typewriter. If the 9100A really was to be an office tool, as well as a lab tool, Hewlett told them, it would have to fit into the office world. Writes Leibson, "It was a little ironic that the form factor of this extremely complex and advanced piece of electronic computing equipment was to be determined by an old piece of office furniture . . . a 19th century piece of equipment."[25]*

But Hewlett was right. One revolution at a time. If the assembled team suppressed a collective gulp, they also now knew exactly what was expected of them. And if they set to work with serious doubts whether they could accomplish everything expected of the 9100A, they also had the enthusiasm of engineers working at the very limits of the known tech world. Recalled Osborne, "For the next two years I spent some long hours keeping the various aspects of the HP 9100 project on course. I was barely able to stay ahead of the alligators on my tail."[26]

The prototype of the 9100A was at last finished in early 1967. In the end, it was everything HP wanted in its first calculator: a beautiful design, breakthrough technology, and performance that far outdistanced anything else on the market. The 9100A didn't just make a contribution, as required by the HP Way, but fundamentally changed an entire industry—arguably creating a brand-new one. Calculators would never be seen the same way again; almost overnight, they went from being simple arithmetic tools to powerful computational engines. And in a world still ruled by slide rules, the HP 9100A literally changed, in both labs and offices, the very notion of what constituted precision in measurement.

But there was still one small matter: would it fit in Bill Hewlett's desk?

Luckily, Hewlett was out of town. So the team carefully lugged the prototype calculator over to his office—tellingly, how many other CEOs would allow employees to wander around his office while he was gone?—and set it on the desk's typewriter stand.

It fit. The team silently cheered.

Now the acid test: they slowly folded the stand into the opening in the desk. There was a dull clunk as the top of the 9100A smacked into the top of the opening. The team gasped: it didn't fit. Now what?

What happened next offers an interesting glimpse into not only the ingenuity but also the generally unappreciated humor and iconoclasm that also characterized Hewlett-Packard during this era.

The team quickly agreed upon a solution, and one of them ran off to retrieve one of the carpenters from downstairs in the company shop. He soon arrived with his tools, and under the instruction of the team widened the opening in the desk by about an eighth of an inch, then carefully cleaned up the evidence.

According to Dave Cochran, Hewlett never noticed the subterfuge. But other team members weren't convinced; they believed that Hewlett immediately spotted the work done to his desk and, amused, never said a word.*

The first public unveiling of the 9100A was to be at the March 1968 IEEE Electro show in New York. By then, the team had built five prototypes and planned to set them up in a hotel suite (standard procedure for new products not yet ready for market) to show off to select visitors, such as large customers, distributors, and even competitors.

One of those competitors invited, out of professional courtesy, was An Wang, the already legendary CEO of Wang Laboratories, the company Dave Packard had long ago visited and concluded that calculators weren't in HP's future. Now HP had a calculator that it believed put in the shade anything in the Wang catalog.

But not long before Wang was schedule to arrive, Barney Oliver did one last quick check-over of the five machines. As he opened the lid of one to check on the components inside, his tie, full of static electricity from having walked across the suite's carpet, accidentally brushed across the 9100A's logic board, shorted out the circuitry—and instantly killed the prototype.

Hewlett quickly ordered the dead calculator taken away and hidden, the four surviving machines were rearranged, and the team pretended that nothing had happened. When Wang at last arrived, Hewlett immediately led him to a 9100A and had Oliver and Osborne demonstrate to him how the machine worked.

Wang watched the demonstration in stunned silence. Then he shook the men's hands and took his leave. At the door, he turned to Hewlett and said, "You have a good machine. We had better get busy."

It was a moment of triumph. In just two years Hewlett-Packard had come out of nowhere, entering one of the most innovative and hotly contested new businesses in high tech, and had produced an initial product so superior to anything on the market or under development that it had left one of the current industry leaders in a state of barely concealed panic. The HP 9100A was about to make Hewlett-Packard Co. a fortune.

(Thirty years later, *Wired* magazine noted that an October 4, 1968, ad for the $4,900 "Hewlett-Packard 9100A personal computer" was the very first recorded use of that term. It seems that the 9100A not only kicked off the scientific calculator revolution, but, in language at least, the personal computer age as well.)

The others may have been ready to go out and celebrate. But not Bill Hewlett. In one of the defining moments of his career, he was already looking ahead. Wang, to save his company, would now move heaven and earth to catch HP. So would Friden. HP had won today, but it would be a brief victory if the company didn't keep moving.*

Hewlett turned to Osborne and pointed at the row of shiny new calculators. "I think the next machine should be a tenth the cost, a tenth the size, and be ten times faster than the HP 9100."

Tom Osborne was at least as shocked as An Wang had been. At that moment he was the world's leading expert on electronic calculators. He had just built the greatest calculator in the world. And now, at the moment when he should have been savoring his achievement, he'd been given instead a new assignment—one that he knew in his heart was technically impossible.

Four years later, with the help of some fortuitous technology breakthroughs, Osborne built that calculator. It would be the most famous product in Hewlett-Packard history.

In the Chips

The third in this troika of new businesses for Hewlett-Packard in the 1960s was semiconductors. With all of the attention given to HP computers and calculators, the fact that HP was both a pioneer and a major player in semiconductors is often overlooked. Founded in 1960, HP's semiconductor operations were only a few years younger than Fairchild's, and a decade older than most of Silicon Valley's chip companies. HP was also regularly one of the ten top chip makers on earth, though that detail was typically buried in the company's overall financials.

One reason for the near-invisibility of HP's chip business was that it was so different from the rest of what was emerging in Silicon Valley. It wasn't brutally competitive, or particularly entrepreneurial, or even filled with outrageous characters. That in part was due to the fact that HP's semiconductor business was almost entirely dedicated to producing components for other HP products. Moreover, at the beginning, as with calculators, HP didn't see much opportunity in chips. Recalled Hewlett:

> Shockley was a genius, but very difficult. He attracted a bunch of star people, but he wasn't a manager, and his thing quickly fell to pieces. They were the seed that started the semiconductor business here. This was not of any great interest to us. We didn't perhaps get into it as quickly as we should have, but nonetheless it began to grow around us. Then at some point we decided we needed to get into that business.
>
> . . . That's how we got into the semiconductor business. Our objective was not to be selling semiconductor products, but using specialized semiconductor products to make our own products better. That's a different twist, and we followed that. We now have a lot of our own proprietary products and make them in several spots, which is quite unusual. Usually you make them in one spot. We have a small semiconductor operation we sell to outside—but the bulk of them are really for our own use.[27]

But if HP's semiconductor operation didn't draw much public attention, it certainly was in the minds of others in the field—not just for the components it made, but for the philosophy under which it operated. In an industry best-known for being brilliant but ruthless, computer chips at Hewlett-Packard still bore the stamp of the HP Way.

Even the origins of this business, officially called HP Associates, was uniquely Hewlett-Packard. And it is telling that the best recounting of that birth was made by one of Bill and Dave's peers.

Dr. Lester Hogan was already a tech legend for the invention, early in his career, of the gyrator, a fundamental device in microwave communications. Shockley himself had dubbed it "amazing." Hogan had gone from Bell Labs to Harvard to huge success running Motorola's chip business to, at last, the presidency of Fairchild following the departure of Bob Noyce.

Hogan had been hugely successful wherever he'd worked, and as one of the leaders of the semiconductor industry he had known every major figure in his industry—and their flaws. It is interesting then, in his retirement, when asked about Hewlett and Packard, that Hogan chose to tell the story of the founding of HP Associates almost a half century before.

It remains one of the best stories about Bill and Dave and the HP Way. It is also a valuable glimpse into how the two men were seen by one of their few industry peers. Here it is in full:

> Jack Melchor left Sylvania in 1956 with three other engineers and founded a company that was very successful. He left the company in 1960 [and] subsequently sold the stock. Don't know how much he made, but he made a few millions.
>
> He went to Dave Packard in 1960 and convinced Dave that he [Packard] had to be in the semiconductor business. Integrated circuits had just been introduced, but obviously they were going to get bigger and more complex and—be it ten years or twenty years away—eventually you would not be able to build a unique state-of-the-art piece of equipment unless you had people who could design and even build unique chips. That's because the chip finally becomes the whole thing; you just put a box with some buttons on it around the chip and that's it.
>
> Dave had enough foresight to recognize this. He was impressed with Jack and he made him president of a new venture called Hewlett-Packard Associates, in which Hewlett-Packard owned like 50 percent and Jack and the principals he was going to attract to the firm would also own roughly 50 percent. Hewlett-Packard had an option to buy 100 percent—the other 50 percent—five years later and the contract stated that the price would be based upon the [current] sales of Hewlett-Packard, as well as the profits. It would also be based upon the contributions that Hewlett-Packard Associates made to the rest of HP by building unique products that made the company's equipment substantially better than competitors.
>
> Now, that last is the subjective part of the contract. So when you come to the day of establishing the price, [that's where] it gets hazy.
>
> So [five years later], on a Friday night, Dave Packard called in the principals and said, "I guess you fellows know that Monday morning I can buy you out. I have an option to buy and I'm going to exercise that option. So, I want you fellows to go home over the weekend and figure out what you think a fair price is."
>
> Well, they not only did that, they [created] a forty page flip-chart presentation to justify the price. And the flip-chart presentation consisted of: "Here is the lowest possible price you can offer, which gives us no credit

for contributions. . . . Now, this is the highest, if you were very generous and gave us all kinds of credit for all of these immeasurable contributions. We feel that [the latter] is a top-level price and we think that it is probably too greedy. We think that some place in-between the two would be proper."

As with all things like this, you end up with an average and say "That's fair."

So, they walked into Dave Packard's office on Monday morning with this forty page flip-chart presentation—and Dave saw that it was awfully thick. He said, "Hey, what's this?" And they said, "This is our presentation."

And Packard said, "What do you need a presentation for? I just need a price."

"Well, this is to justify the price."

"Ohhh, I see," said Packard. "But look: I don't want to have to listen to your entire presentation. How's this? Let me make my offer—and if you don't like it, I'll listen."

Then he offered them 20 percent *above* their high-ball price![28]*

Melchor went on to become one of Silicon Valley's most famous venture capitalists, investing in more than one hundred start-up companies, even advising the British government on developing a venture capital industry in the United Kingdom. Through it all, he was known for his maverick, high-risk investments—many of which paid off handsomely (ROLM, 3Com, the Learning Company). It is interesting to speculate just how much Melchor learned at that Monday morning meeting with Dave Packard. Certainly, he went in carrying a formal presentation—and came out the most unconventional of venture capitalists.

Acquiring Directions

HP, from the beginning, had always been a closed company. Its culture, with its unique patterns of responsibility, trust, and interdependence, enforced a rather hermetic attitude (too much so, some observers complained) toward outsiders. There were HPers, and then there was everybody else.

But that changed in the 1960s. The rise of new divisions outside Palo Alto, as seen in the relationship between the Loveland division and HP Labs, began to turn the company's perspective away from Page Mill Hill. So did Boeblingen, Germany, and the new European sales office in Geneva, which forced the company to see itself for the first time as a truly global organization.

As the decade continued, this process of expansion continued apace. In a process of pairing that soon became standard procedure for the company, Palo Alto was joined by a new home for the computer division in nearby Cupertino, not far from where young Steve Jobs and Steve Wozniak were attending junior high school. Loveland also got a twin, in a new manufacturing plant in Fort Collins, Colorado. Meanwhile, the instrument business expanded with the addition of yet another Colorado plant, this one south of Denver, closer to Packard's childhood home in Colorado Springs.

But expansion wasn't the only way Hewlett-Packard grew in the 1960s: the company also embarked on the most active era of acquisition in its history. As always, each buyout was voluntary, and each was chosen as a way to bring HP quickly into an important new instrument business.

Thus, in 1961, Hewlett-Packard bought Sanborn Company in Waltham, Massachusetts, a maker of medical electronics. HP Waltham would become the company's first East Coast division, and its products—including fetal monitors and nurses' stations—would fill hospitals around the world and become among the best-known of HP product lines.

Four years later, twinning once again, HP purchased a second East Coast company, F&M Scientific Corporation, in Avondale, Pennsylvania. F&M was a highly respected maker of analytical instruments. HP's acquisition put F&M's operation into overdrive—and soon HP's gas chromatographs and mass spectrometers were a staple of forensic labs and pollution control authorities.

The newly acquired companies, some with hundreds of employees (Sanborn had nearly a thousand), had to be assimilated quickly into HP. Before, when Hewlett-Packard was still geographically centralized, educating new hires in the HP Way had occurred organically. So deeply did the everyday work experience reinforce the corporate culture that it typically took only a few weeks for a new hire to become a true HPer.

But by the mid-sixties, as the company reached a dozen operating divisions, it was becoming obvious that the old, casual way of dealing with new employees, especially when they arrived by hundreds at a time, had become unworkable. The simple analogy of HP to a family, which had worked so well in the 1950s, was becoming less tenable when Hewlett-Packard was a divisionalized, multinational corporation with, by 1966, more than 10,000 employees. The days of Dave handing out Christmas bonus checks in person to every employee were gone. So was Lucile Packard giving blankets to newborns. And though it was still possible to see Bill or Dave, or sometimes both, at divisional summer picnics, even that ritual was becoming hard to maintain.

Indeed, Hewlett and Packard were struggling so hard to maintain a presence at the company's increasingly far-flung operations, and spending so much time in transit, that a joke went around HP Palo Alto, to wit: What's the difference between God and Dave Packard? God is everywhere, while Dave Packard is everywhere but at HP.

The changes taking place within the traditional HP family were only part of the matter. The presence of Tom Osborne, a contractor, playing such a critical role in the fate of the company—as well as the joint venture in Japan with Yokogawa—showed the company moving into new business relationships vastly different from those it had known in the past.

Bill and Dave saw this coming as early as the late 1950s. In the same year that the two men called for the divisionalization of the company, as well as the formal adoption of the company's Corporate Objectives, they also ordered the creation of a corporate personnel department. The fact that this move didn't occur until 1957, eighteen years after the company was founded, is astonishing. The fact that the institution of HR at Hewlett-Packard finally did take place shows the increasing concern of the two founders that they were losing their ability to personally deal with the growing legions of HP employees.

By the early 1960s the two men were obviously formulating a new vision of the company, one that had evolved from "family" to something closer to "community," encompassing not just HPers but all of those—contractors, suppliers, vendors, distributors, retailers, even customers—who touched, or were touched by, the HP Way.

For most of the decade, even as the company was expanding at a dizzying pace, hiring thousands of new employees and introducing hundreds of new products, the two men devoted much of their attention to spinning out of the implications of this new notion of HP as a community—and their own roles within it.

Only in this light does one of their most decisive, and unusual, moves during this era become explicable. This was Bill and Dave's decision to acquire all of HP's long-independent regional sales operations. As noted earlier, in the mid-sixties, competitor Tektronix fired all of its independent reps and created its own internal sales operation. Hewlett-Packard chose to honor its commitments and hire its reps instead.

But the question remains: why did HP shut down its outside sales operations at all? One standard explanation is that, for competitive reasons, it imitated Tektronix's decision. But that not only seems uncharacteristic of Hewlett-Packard, but also unlikely, given that Tektronix only competed with the company in just one—oscilloscopes—of dozens of markets HP was now in. Besides, any sales reps the two companies shared were now HP's by default.

The best explanation may be that this was yet another case of an "HP fork," after the move in chess that positions you to capture a piece in more than one direction. That is, with every important strategic business decision Bill and Dave always seemed to have, though often hidden, a cultural strategy as well—and vice versa.

Buying the independent sales representatives is a classic example. Certainly it made good business sense at this point in HP's development to bring sales in-house and erase some of their 15 percent commissions. But, at the same time, if Bill and Dave were going to build a real HP community, with a common corporate culture, the sales reps, the biggest renegades in the company's larger sphere of relationships, had to be brought under control lest they undermine the new HP community.

And no doubt some of these operations would have done just that if left on their own. Salespeople are always corporate mavericks, and in the hard-drinking, fast-living, and high-paying world of tech in the early sixties, this was particularly the case. At hot new companies, such as Fairchild, this behavior regularly crossed the line into criminality. Among some of HP's sales reps, it often wasn't much better.

Especially notorious was the annual IEEE convention in New York City. Unlike today, when there are scores of trade shows covering almost every niche in electronics, throughout the 1950s and into the 1960s, IEEE was the only game in town—a Consumer Electronics Show, Semicon, and Comdex rolled into one—the one time each year when every supplier, manufacturer, and customer in the digital world met in one spot. It was the single week each year toward which most companies targeted their big product introductions, and salespeople were unleashed to make as many deals as they could, no matter what it took and no matter what they had to promise.

Needless to say, with each year the event became more chaotic, beginning with the bribes paid to Teamsters to get exhibits into the New York Coliseum, to the hookers and booze used to close crucial deals. Hewlett-Packard would rent almost the entire Essex House hotel, including the ballroom, for its annual sales meeting, and most of its independent sales firms would take rooms there as well. The booze flowed continuously in the downstairs Bombay Bicycle Club bar.

Tiny Yewell, whose firm represented HP in Boston and New England, was one of the wildest of the independent-operation owners. He became notorious for the initiation rite he inflicted on his newly hired reps. According to historian John Minck:

> All of his managers and senior personnel would gather in Tiny's hotel suite on an upper floor of the Essex House. Previous to the trip, the fledgling engineer would have been told that he would get a call at a particular

time, and to come up to Tiny's suite for a drink and informal talk. One can only imagine the worry that engineer might have when he finally got that call.

[Then,] with the whole senior group sitting around the room, and the new man knocking at the door, Tiny would tell him the door was unlocked and to come in. Imagine his surprise, and the delight of the audience, when the engineer opened the door to find a naked woman greeting him.[29]

In the male-dominated business world of the 1950s, these activities, taking place just beyond the edges of the HP family, were tolerated, and even appreciated. But they were not acceptable in the newly emerging world of modern business, with its growing role for women. It especially could not be allowed in the new HP community. When the sales reps were acquired by the company, these "rites" were immediately ordered stopped (no doubt to the dismay of many of the newly anointed HP sales professionals. Said Minck, "They had no place in a professional company, and probably not even in the old independent organizations."[30]★

This notion of a corporate community extended outward to include not only HP's outlying divisions, but the civic communities in which they operated. Here, ironically, is where Hewlett and Packard faced some of their biggest challenges. Already described in these pages is the resistance by the male employees at Yokogawa HP to the idea of bringing their wives and children to the company picnics. At Boeblingen, the paradoxical challenge was enforcing independent thinking and entrepreneurial attitudes.

But not all of the problems dealt with conflicts with the cultures in other nations. In the end, Loveland proved to be one of the thorniest personnel challenges the company ever faced: the arrival from cosmopolitan California of well-educated and well-paid young engineers created more than a little chaos in what had been largely a ranching town. And when these new arrivals started stealing girlfriends and wives, driving up real estate prices, and increasingly dominating local politics, there was a backlash. In the local newspaper, at city council meetings, and in the everyday conversations at coffee shops and high school football games, HP was blamed for most of the community's problems.

The bad blood lasted for more than a decade—long enough to convince Bill and Dave that future HP divisions needed to be emplaced in communities with an existing university and a more affluent population. That is why HP divisions of the 1970s were located in Boise, Idaho; Corvallis, Oregon (near OSU); and Santa Rosa, Sacramento, Santa Clara, and San Jose, California. It was an admission that the HP corporate community wouldn't work in every civic community—and thus, for the first time, the HP Way encountered a limit on its influence.

Sending a Message

It was this growing recognition of the limitations of its business model that led Hewlett-Packard to create the most unique advertisement in Silicon Valley history.

As with personnel, advertising and public relations at Hewlett-Packard were essentially improvised as needed up through the 1950s. Advertising, as noted, actually predated the company's first product, but as late as 1960 all company ads for every HP division were created by marketing VP Noel Eldred in conjunction with a succession of advertising agencies, ultimately finding a favorite account executive named Dick Garvin and following him through a succession of agencies. Together the two men would devise the ads for every product line at Hewlett-Packard, as well as corporate ads.

Public relations consisted mostly of the company putting out announcements of its new products and the trade press asking for interviews with, or comments from, the two founders. What little mainstream press coverage there was typically was handled the same way.

This marketing communications strategy had both strengths and limitations—the latter coming to dominate by the 1960s. The advantage in advertising was that Hewlett-Packard spoke with one voice—and all of its ad campaigns were consistent and internally congruent. It helped that Garvin was something of an advertising genius, whose campaign ideas—notably the "Small Wonder" series of ads for HP's microwave component products—were milestones in the world of tech, and models for many of the great campaigns (Intel Inside, the early Apple ads) to come.

But the problems with this methodology were manifold. For one thing, the sheer number of different products HP was producing by the beginning of the decade inevitably led to a queuing up of product managers anxiously waiting for corporate to design and place their ads. Worse, the process, in violation of the spirit of the HP Way, moved decision-making *away* from the people most in the position to make correct decisions—division marketing managers—and put it in the hands of a senior executive and a contractor who often knew little about the product, its customers, or the best media venues. And that in turn meant mistakes in copy, style, and placement. Recalled HP historian Minck, "[Eldred and the ad agencies] never asked many questions of those of us out in the product groups—I was an application engineer with the microwave lab—and we would usually find out about a new ad on our own product when it appeared in print. The process always contained the elements of disaster, because there were often errors of specs and message."[31]

By the early sixties, this process was becoming untenable. It couldn't keep up with demand; it was beginning to make dangerous mistakes in a business where precision was everything and the stakes were getting higher by the year; it lacked sufficient flexibility to deal with a company that was in a dozen different businesses; and ultimately it undermined the corporate culture. The stress of keeping up this pace was playing on the two managers as well: Garvin was turning into a serious alcoholic, often stopping at a local Palo Alto bar after dropping off his latest ad mock-ups, while Eldred's health began a swift decline.

It was clearly time for a shake-up. But before the old, handmade and idiosyncratic method of doing advertising disappeared at Hewlett-Packard, Eldred and Garvin produced one last great campaign.

Even today it has the power to astonish—perhaps more than it did then. Created in 1962, it featured a black-and-white photograph of an engineer in white shirt and dark tie, surrounded by electronic instruments and, with an intense look of concentration, staring forward and slightly to his right, apparently at the screen of an oscilloscope. The headline read:

Want a little more experience before you start a business of your own?

The body copy, above the Hewlett-Packard logo, read:

Hewlett-Packard may be the perfect proving grounds for you. One word of warning: You may never want to leave!

As an R&D engineer at Hewlett-Packard you'll be encouraged not only to develop ideas for marketable products, but given every opportunity to follow your concepts through research and development, pilot runs, manufacturing and finally even into marketing. You will be totally involved in every area of a business enterprise, gaining experience both as an engineer and entrepreneur.[32]

Visually, an unremarkable, quarter-page corporate ad. But the message—by then Silicon Valley companies were already beginning to sue each other and their own ex-employees for jumping employers or for leaving to start their own firms. Entrepreneurs who just a few years before had quit their employers to start a new company now turned around and sued their new employees for leaving. Even the normally dignified Gordon Moore, ignoring his own career history, publicly denounced "vulture" capitalists for stealing some of Intel's best engineers.

By the 1980s, suing and countersuing over lost employees had become a standard part of Valley business life. Secret meetings, second sets of non-employer-related lab notes, complicated employee contracts and noncompetition clauses—by the end of the century, exiting companies to start your own firm (and keeping you from doing so) had become an art form in high tech.

And yet there was Hewlett-Packard, at the very beginning of the era, placing a recruitment ad that *invited* potential employees to join the company even as they schemed how to quit. That offered to let them not only advance their technical talents, but also offered to teach them the other skills—manufacturing, management, marketing—they would need to start their own companies. And that was so secure in the quality of its corporate culture that it was willing to bet that, in the end, these entrepreneurial souls would choose to stay.*

No company in Silicon Valley history, before or since, has had the courage to duplicate this HP advertisement. And none likely ever will. It is sui generis, a testament to the supreme self-confidence of Hewlett-Packard in the early 1960s.

It would never be quite this self-assured again. But the philosophy exemplified by that one ad would stay with HP for the duration of Bill's and Dave's time with the firm. It was this attitude toward entrepreneurship, combined with the HP Way and the company's standing rule that employees would suffer no consequences for leaving the company and then returning (indeed, it was seen as a way of gaining more worldly experience), that increasingly made HP the heart of Silicon Valley, yet not *of* Silicon Valley.

It is this attitude as well that made Hewlett-Packard, perhaps even as much as Fairchild Semiconductor (and for entirely the opposite reason), the greatest seeder of the Silicon Valley start-up boom—and thus of the entire electronics revolution. If the tragedy was that so many tried to duplicate the HP Way, only to fail, the wonder was that a few of the great ones—Applied Materials and Tandem Computer among them—largely succeeded. The fact that most of the rest of them—Apple, Cisco, Sun, eBay, Google, Intel, and Yahoo!—implemented at least part of HP's cultural model likely saved Silicon Valley from its own excesses. It is a long leap in time but a short jump in attitude from Dave Packard handing out bonus checks at the Redwood Building in 1946 to the employees sitting with their dogs and bicycles in their offices at Google sixty years later.

————

The 1962 ad was the last great achievement of the old marketing communications operations at Hewlett-Packard. By the mid-1960s, Hewlett and Packard had agreed that it was time to create larger and more specialized operations—public relations and advertising/marketing communications—that would be more responsive to the divisions and to the marketplace. Tapped to direct "marcom" was the brilliant and imperious Russ Berg, late of *Scientific American* magazine. Berg's manner, combined with a standing "good taste review" committee that vetted all division-created ads for false claims, bad taste, and inaccuracy, enforced a consistency of style and content on HP advertising equal to that of his predecessor, with a lot more scope and speed. Hewlett-Packard ads would never again be as remarkable as those under Garvin and Eldred, but they would be a lot more numerous—and accurate.

Berg's department also standardized the "look" of HP advertising: simple fonts, elementary colors (mostly HP blue), and a lot of white space—a style that would later be adopted and taken to legendary heights by Apple Computer. His department also created a second technical magazine (the first was the *HP Journal*, founded in 1949), called *Measure*, that would become the voice of HP's engineers and scientists to the larger technical community.

Dave Kirby, a local PR agency executive who had worked for years with HP, was tapped to become the company's PR director. Kirby was the antithesis of Berg: hunched over his typewriter, chain-smoking cigarettes, his tie askew and sleeves rolled up, he was a throwback to another era of journalism.

Kirby was also a wonderful, and simple, prose stylist, and he quickly became Dave Packard's editor (Packard wrote most of his own speeches), a position he held for the rest of his career and beyond. It was Kirby who found the "voice" of Packard—simple, plainspoken, using few adjectives and adverbs, eschewing exclamatory phrases and self-congratulation, and honoring competitors—that would become the official style of the company itself during this era.

Kirby's second important contribution was to build the first great corporate public relations department in high tech. Silicon Valley already had two outstanding PR executives, Regis McKenna (National Semiconductor, later Intel and Apple) and Fred Hoar (Fairchild). But Kirby's influence was ultimately more sweeping, if less known. An indifferent manager, he was a superb recruiter, and one of his first acts was to raid the dying Ampex of its key PR talent, one of the few remaining bright spots at that troubled firm.

This core team, with the addition of several retired newspaper reporters, became the most innovative corporate publicity operation in tech, inventing a number of techniques—press tours, application/feature stories, customized press releases, and so on—that are now standard tools in the field. More important, HP corporate PR set certain professional standards—no leaks, no preintroduction of products that weren't ready to ship or that had not yet been priced, no negative comments about competitors, no unproven specifications—that brought the HP Way (at least temporarily) to the PR profession.

In the Family Way

Just as the rest of the corporate world was beginning to implement HP's cultural innovations, such as profit-sharing and stock-purchase plans, some of them now in place for a quarter century at the company, Hewlett-Packard announced what would be the best-known of its employee benefits: "flex-time."

The notion first appeared in 1967, interestingly, at the HP plant in Boeblingen, Germany—showing not only how fully integrated the international divisions had become to the company, but also how completely the employees at those divisions had internalized the HP Way. "Flex-time," as HP implemented it throughout the company five years later, allowed employees to arrive early or late to work—typically 6:30 a.m. to 9:30 a.m.—as long as they worked a full day afterwards.

In other words, come to work at 6:30 a.m. and take off at 3:30 p.m. if your work is done. Roll in at 9 and plan to stay until at least 5 p.m.

If the 1960s was HP's decade of community, then there was no better example of this commitment than flex-time, as it recognized not only that its employees were fully rounded human beings (HP in the 1940s) and members of families (HP in 1950s), but also members of a larger community, who had larger commitments within that community.

More than all of the billions in donations made by Bill and Dave and by Hewlett-Packard itself over the course of a half century, it was flex-time that most fulfilled the HP Corporate Objective of *Community*. By enabling employees around the world to individually adjust their own work schedules to best fit their larger lives, HP unleashed millions of hours of volunteer time into the communities where it operated. The result was uncounted Little League teams, Girl Scout troops, PTAs, and United Way campaigns led or manned by HP volunteers taking advantage of flex-time.

Once again, as with every Hewlett-Packard employee initiative, flex-time was a lot more subtle and complex than it appeared at first glance. It too also featured the HP "fork" in that, though it appeared to be strictly for the benefit of employees, it also had a hidden business component.

With closer inspection, many of these other features become clear. For example, flex-time was really just flexible on the edges. That is, only the first and last three hours of the workday—the time when employee arrivals and departures are variable anyway—are in play. The core six hours, between 9:30 and 3:30, when most office productivity occurs, are still fixed. Moreover, the nature of everyday office life naturally drew most people to the center; that is, most HPers still went to work from about 8:30 to 4:30—and given the expanding work hours of life in Silicon Valley, many stayed until 6 p.m. or later.

But that isn't what counted: what really mattered to HP employees (and the millions of other workers who looked upon them with envy) was merely the fact that flex-time was *there;* that the company assumed their loyalty without demanding it, and trusted them to make the right choices in balancing their personal lives and their careers. Humans are creatures of habit, so most HPers found the schedule that best fit their needs—typically the standard 8:30 to 4:30—and stuck with it. Thus, on any given workday, probably 90 percent of Hewlett-Packard employees were in the office at the same time, probably about the same percentage as most corporations.

But it was on the rare days—the morning after a late night, an early departure to beat the holiday rush, a child's afternoon soccer game—when HP flex-time showed its value. And it was on those days when HPers silently thanked Bill and Dave, and their loyalty grew just a little deeper.*

The rest of the world may have overlooked many of HP's earlier employee innovations, but flex-time was too simple, and too obvious in its benefits, to miss. The story took on a life of its own: every couple of years, well into the late 1970s, the world press would erupt in a spasm of interest about flex-time at HP. Feature stories would be written, camera crews would show up from some corner of the world, and the wire services would light up briefly. Eventually, the story would die down—only to erupt again a few years later.

Ultimately, flex-time would prove to be the single most popular nonproduct story in Hewlett-Packard history. It was also the last great *positive* employee innovation during the Bill and Dave era (which also meant, unfortunately, the last in the company's history). The 1970s would prove to be a much different decade, one in which Bill and Dave would be devoted not to enhancing their employees' jobs, but defending them.

Racing Against the Clock

Beyond all of these organizational and cultural stratagems, Hewlett-Packard in the 1960s remained one of—and perhaps was *the*—most innovative companies in high technology.

For now at least, HP's forays into computers and calculators were little more than a sideshow. The company's bread-and-butter businesses remained test and measurement instruments, microwave, and, thanks to acquisitions, medical and analytical instruments. By the end of the decade, HP had a catalog of almost a thousand products, nearly all of them from the older product lines.

Several of these new products were of major—and in the case of one, historic—importance. In 1963, for example, HP introduced the model 5100A frequency analyzer. It was the single most complex HP product to date—indeed one of the most sophisticated instruments of the age—and it pointed toward a new direction for the company.

The 5100A was essentially a collection of several established HP instruments, all linked to work together in such applications as automatic tests for manufacturing companies and, more famously, for communication with Apollo mooncraft.

Beyond putting HP in the thick of the space program (HP instruments were already, in fact, used in laboratories all over NASA), the 5100A also put the tech world on notice that product *integration*—not coincidentally the decade's theme of "community" applied to HP's technical side—would be the future of Hewlett-Packard.

In many ways this was inevitable. The rise of semiconductor devices, interface technology, and onboard computation was increasingly making it possible for instruments not only to share information, but process it as well. Combined with the right software, it was obvious that these new "systems" would soon be able to take over much of the testing and measurement work themselves, running through a battery of tasks far faster and more accurately than any human operator could tell them to.

What delighted customers and frightened competitors about the 5100A was that it not only showed HP was leading the way in this systems strategy, but that, thanks to its wide product line, HP would likely get there faster and more efficiently than anyone else.

And that is exactly what HP then proceeded to do. The 5100A was followed by a series of HP systems products—notably vector and scalar network analyzers—that stunned the instrument industry and transformed the world of electronics manufacturing and testing. For example, the model 8410 network analyzer, introduced in 1967, transformed the business of component design and test. A year later, the HP 8540A Automatic Network Analyzer—a big two-cabinet system that essentially bolted the new HP 2100A minicomputer to the 8410—did the same thing for the testing of both microwave chips and commercial communication satellites.

The technology may have been arcane, but the business strategy was clear: HP was using its leadership, or near-leadership, across a broad range of businesses, to create complex systems that rendered obsolete entire traditional instrument industries. With the exception of a few superb companies that could leverage their special expertise in a single business—such as Tektronix in oscilloscopes—few instrument companies could withstand this onslaught. By the end of the 1960s, Hewlett-Packard dominated entire regions of the instrument world.*

It was the perfect moment to be in that position. The late 1960s would prove to be the most famous technological confluence in history. A number of different forces were at play: the Vietnam and cold wars—wars always being a time of major technological leaps and quick application; NASA's race to the moon with the Apollo mission; a communication revolution (the music industry, FM radio) driven by demand from teenaged baby boomers; the centrality of television in modern life (color broadcasting, commercial video recording, UHF); minicomputers and desktop calculators; and sophisticated new logic and memory semiconductor chips.

They were all to converge in that technological annus mirabilis, 1969, which saw the birth of the microprocessor, the Internet, and the first man to walk on the moon. Hewlett-Packard would play a part in all of them.

———

The historic product for Hewlett-Packard in the 1960s was the model 5060A cesium-beam atomic clock. Interestingly, it remains the least known of the company's great products, perhaps because it is so utterly different from anything else in the HP inventory—yet it may have been HP's most basic elemental innovation, more so even than the company's semiconductor devices.[33]

Timing had been one of the great challenges in electronics ever since the Second World War. The war had seen the explosion of communication technologies, from wireline to wireless, cable to microwave, and, soon, to satellite. Every one of these communication protocols required exact synchronization of the signal between the transmitter and the receiver. The more precise this synchronization the more accurate the transmission, and thus the greater the information that could be conveyed.

The earliest way to achieve this kind of synchronization was to send a signal from both the transmitter and receiver, and use a quartz-crystal oscillator (quartz being a very stable source of signal vibration) to "discipline" the two signals.

But there were two big problems with quartz oscillators. The first was that the oscillators themselves would begin to show frequency drift with age, temperature change, and environment. As a result, they had to be regularly recalibrated. This was accomplished in the United States through a collection of standard signals broadcast on radio out of Boulder, Colorado, by the U.S. National Bureau of Standards. And that clock in turn was calibrated using yet another, this one timed by astronomical readings, based at the U.S. Naval Observatory in Washington, D.C.

These superclocks, which timed every communication transmission in North America, were themselves only quartz oscillators, and subject to the same stresses as their commercial counterparts. So they were kept in the most controlled environments imaginable and monitored continuously.

But all of that didn't solve the second problem, which was that the demand from telecommunication, computing, defense, and space research for ever more precise timing was rapidly approaching the physical limits of the quartz crystals themselves.

Luckily, nature itself offered a solution. Certain elements resonated at astonishingly predictable rates at the atomic level, and if those resonances could be measured, it would be possible to create clocks accurate to mere seconds per century. By the end of the 1950s, the Bureau of Standards had installed just such a clock, but it was hugely expensive, complicated, and of questionable long-term reliability.

The technology proven, the next question was: would it be possible to build an affordable commercial atomic clock?

In 1962, Hewlett-Packard took on the challenge. The company already had a new division, based down the road from Palo Alto in Santa Clara, dedicated to time and frequency. Leading the design team was a famously personable scientist named Len Cutler (indeed, Cutler was so open to visits from customers and queries from his marketing department that it remains something of a miracle he ever got anything done).

It was Cutler who chose to use cesium as his elemental timer, and to synchronize it at a microwave frequency for maximum precision. And among the constraints he set for the finished product was that it had to be as small as a standard HP bench instrument, that it carry an onboard battery to keep the clock running when it was transferred from one electrical source to another, and that it be tough enough (like the 2116A computer to come) to function perfectly in the most extreme physical environments.

The model 5060A, introduced in 1964, was one of the biggest technological leapfrogs of all time—comparable to, say, the more celebrated Apple Macintosh twenty years later. Its accuracy, for the time, was breathtaking: less than one second of error in 3,000 years.

Then, just to make sure the world noticed, Hewlett-Packard put on an uncharacteristically flamboyant promotional stunt for the clock. Two HP engineers configured a pair of cesium clocks, booked first-class tickets on a commercial airliner, and (after making sure they could tap into the planes' power systems) flew from San Francisco first to the U.S. Naval Observatory in D.C., then on to the official world timekeeping laboratory in Neuchatel, Switzerland, where the two standard clocks were compared. The stunt made headlines around the world.

It wasn't long before the HP cesium clock was the de facto world standard. It remains so today; the descendants of the 5060A, now manufactured by Agilent, account for 80 percent of the world's standardized timekeeping. Few product families have ever owned a market so completely and for so long. HP cesium clocks were used for critical timing tasks in all subsequent NASA space missions, up through the space shuttle, for telecommunication, airplane collision avoidance systems, deep-space astronomical measurements, and hundreds of other applications.

But it was for one particular use that the cesium clock took Hewlett-Packard into a dangerous new world: the testing and fusing of nuclear weapons.

The success of Silicon Valley and the rest of the U.S. electronics industry had not been lost on the world. The seemingly infinite innovation of the industry, and the regular appearance of new and more powerful generations of chips, computers, and instruments, was giving the United States a distinct and growing advantage in economic development, productivity, and defense. At the same time, just how this magic was being pulled off—the complex web of interaction between Moore's law, entrepreneurship, established tech companies, and venture capital—was not easily explained.

Not surprisingly other nations, both friend and foe, saw this as potential threat and responded accordingly. Some, like Japan, Israel, and the nations of western Europe, set out to create their own high-tech industries, typically through government initiatives. But that was a long-term solution, with few guarantees of success. A more immediate opportunity was to gather intelligence on the newest technologies—either by buying and reverse-engineering them, or gathering intelligence on the ground in Silicon Valley.

As a result, beginning in the 1960s and continuing well into the 1980s (and perhaps even today), a number of countries conducted corporate espionage or set up "listening posts" in the Valley. The number, and the identity, of nations it was believed ran intelligence programs in Silicon Valley alone was quite astonishing: the Soviet Union, China, Taiwan, Japan, France, Germany, and Israel, among others.

Hewlett-Packard, as Silicon Valley's biggest company, and the world's leading manufacturer of the instruments used in the design and testing of other electronic devices, was an obvious target. But HP's cesium clock took the issue of security to a whole new level.

In the early 1980s, two reporters for the *San Jose Mercury-News*, while interviewing sources for a series on drug abuse in Silicon Valley, came across a young man in a San Jose halfway house recovering from a methamphetamine addiction. In the middle of the interview, as an aside, the young man mentioned that he had been a low-level clerk at Hewlett-Packard's Santa Clara division, working in the cesium clock group. As he described it, several men, with "foreign accents" he didn't recognize, approached him offering to pay for a copy of the blueprints for the latest atomic clock. For a few hundred dollars that he quickly burned up on speed, the young man sold out his nation's security to agents unknown.

The third new HP product family, though perhaps not as revolutionary as the first two, ultimately may have had the greater impact upon mankind.

In 1967, fittingly at the same time that it was enabling working mothers to schedule their time with their children though flex-time, HP's Boeblingen, Germany, division introduced a noninvasive fetal heart monitor. This device enabled obstetricians to track the heartbeat of babies during labor and delivery—and thus, for the first time, determine if the infant was experiencing dangerous stress and required immediate delivery via C-section.

The fetal heart monitor was emblematic of the great wave of new patient monitoring tools that HP began to sell starting in the 1960s. These ranged from simple heart monitoring tools to complex multiple-patient monitoring systems that became the heart of nurses' stations in hospital wards throughout the world. Indeed, so complete was HP's penetration of this market that it is likely that every reader of this book who has ever spent time in the hospital has been hooked up to an HP monitor, either in surgery or during recovery in the wards.

Medical monitoring devices were among the most ubiquitous, but least known, of HP's products. And their contribution to the company's revenues and bottom line were comparatively negligible—probably less than 10 percent of the company's $3 billion total sales in 1980 (HP never revealed division revenues). But, looking beyond traditional metrics, such as financials and intellectual property creation, to the thousands of infant, child, and adult lives saved through precise monitoring and early intervention, HP's medical devices were probably the company's most enduring contribution to mankind.

Combining its products into powerful systems—and crushing competitors in the process; becoming the timekeeper for the world—and ending up both deeply involved in nuclear warfare and the target of international espionage;

and inventing devices that save thousands of lives—and being vital to the fate of generations of newborns—the "community" Hewlett-Packard of the 1960s marched out into the bigger world only to discover that it was even more paradoxical, and ambivalent, than even the founders had imagined.

And it was only going to get worse. This was the late 1960s after all, and even as technology was reaching one of its apogees, the surrounding culture seemed to be heading in the other direction. The Vietnam War was approaching a crisis point with the Tet Offensive and the bombing of Cambodia, the utopian fantasy of Woodstock and Haight-Ashbury was turning into the darkness of Altamont and the Manson Family, and the assassinations of Robert Kennedy and Martin Luther King had led to riots, despair, and the sense that society itself was about to collapse.

America's youth, the biggest demographic bulge in the country's history, were in full revolt. And if their anticapitalist view of the world had any business heroes, it wasn't a thirty-year-old electronics giant full of middle-aged men with Ivy League haircuts, horn-rimmed glasses, white shirts, and skinny ties, no matter how enlightened that company might be. To the students beginning to march in antiwar protests on the Stanford campus a few blocks away, Bill Hewlett and Dave Packard were no longer the famous entrepreneurs they sought to emulate, but the very embodiment of the military-industrial power struggle that was the enemy of everything good and just in the world.

And in 1969, in a move that shocked HPers, but only confirmed the protesters' suspicions, Dave Packard made a decision that would change his reputation for a generation.

Fork in the Road

In 1969, Bill Hewlett was fifty-six years old, Dave Packard was fifty-seven. And though the garage myth was still new and spreading fast around the world, the two men were a long way from those budding young entrepreneurs in Terman's laboratory.

Terman himself was growing old. He had retired with great honors from his position as provost of Stanford University in September 1965. He and his wife, Sibyl, donated their campus home to the university to benefit the Terman Engineering Fund, and, after recovering from cataract surgery to both eyes, he devoted himself to preserving the history of the high-tech revolution, both with IEEE (where he mostly failed) and at Stanford, where, with the help of a $300,000 grant from Bill and Dave, he set up a research program in the subject at the Bancroft Library.

But Fred Terman's retirement was not a happy one. Sibyl, after a lifetime of heavy smoking, began to lose her health. She began to experience dizzy spells and chronic bronchitis, and though feisty as ever, increasingly had to give up her lifelong work in childhood literacy. Terman himself was beginning to exhibit moments of confusion—a shocking experience for a man famous for the acuity and precision of his mind. Though he still traveled extensively as a consultant and speaker—80,000 miles in the first few years of his retirement—the trips increasingly left him exhausted.

Beyond his family, the brightest thing in Fred Terman's life was his position as a director of Hewlett-Packard. In the summer of 1969, Sibyl's health rallied and she accompanied Fred to Europe on a tour with other HP directors of the company's facilities in Switzerland, Germany, Scotland, and England. It would be her last major trip.[34]

The friendship between Hewlett, Packard, and Terman is one of the most storied, and important, in American business history. But the focus of that story is almost always upon the early years, when the legendary professor served as teacher, mentor, and adviser to the two young entrepreneurs. Less often told is the story of the final years of that friendship, when the roles had reversed, and the two young men, now middle-aged and far more famous than their teacher, honored, protected, and indulged the old man.

Their actions during the last decade of Fred Terman's life say as much about Bill and Dave, and redound to their credit, as anything else important they did in their lives.

Time and the hard work of thirty years had taken other tolls as well. On November 30, 1970, Noel Eldred, HP's vice president of marketing, died suddenly at just sixty-two from a heart attack. His death, the first of Hewlett-Packard's original management team, stunned the company—but nowhere more so than in the executive offices in Palo Alto. After all, Eldred had been one of the company's first management hires during World War II, and after Hewlett had left for the army, Eldred had served as Packard's right-hand man, where he did a brilliant job running manufacturing in the most difficult conditions imaginable.

In many ways, Eldred had proven himself to be not only one of the most capable, but certainly the most versatile of Bill's and Dave's lieutenants. It was Eldred, after all, who after the war pieced together HP's sales force from a crazy quilt of different distributors. Then, in his last decade at the company, he had, as vice president of marketing, given Hewlett-Packard both the look and the voice that would define the company ever after. It could be said that in the first quarter century of the company, nobody, Bill and Dave excepted, did more for HP than Noel Eldred.

Now he was gone. And his death underscored to all of his peers that even success was a poor defense against the stresses of working in a fast-moving electronics company. It was also a reminder that the first generation of HPers, the men and women who had joined the company in the Redwood Building, were no longer young—indeed, many, including the two founders, were now within a decade of legal retirement.*

Succession wasn't the only question facing these senior HP executives. There was also the matter of dealing with the sheer size of the company. Between 1968 and 1969, HP grew to more than 15,000 employees, located in a dozen divisions in a half dozen countries, and was becoming increasingly unwieldy to manage in its current divisional structure. It was obvious that the company urgently needed to rethink its organization.

The watershed 1958 meeting had successfully *decentralized* Hewlett-Packard into product divisions. Then, in the early sixties, as some of these individual divisions grew to an unwieldy size—usually about fifteen hundred employees—they were divided up again, in that "twinning" manner unique to HP. Recalled Packard:

> At that point [1,500 employees], lines of communications were stretched to the limit, management becomes more difficult, and people begin to lose their identification with the products and their pride in what the division is doing. So, it became our policy, still observed today, to split off part of the division, giving it responsibility for an established, profitable product line and usually moving it to a new but nearby location.[35]

Packard called this process "local decentralization," and it offered a number of other, less obvious advantages beyond dealing with division at critical mass. For example, creating a new division a short distance (typically less than fifty miles) away meant that many employees of the older division were willing to jump to the new opportunity without the stresses of moving their families. Starting the new division with an existing and proven product line both reduced the risk of creating the new division, gave it a well-developed customer list, and kicked it off with a ready-made identity.*

There were other, more subtle, advantages as well. For one thing, HP had enough faith in its reputation that it could almost always assume that the community to which it planned to move was already envious of the advantages its neighbor was enjoying—and would roll out the red carpet to the new arrivals. The local politicians were likely the same as well, so there were few surprises. R&D labs could easily keep each other updated. And given the congruence of the product lines, both salespeople and customers could stop at both facilities in the course of a single visit.

The result was that, despite a proliferation of Hewlett-Packard divisions

in the years to come—by 1992, HP would have sixty-five product manufacturing divisions—they would all be clustered within only about a dozen states
and countries. This was a new kind of economy of scale, written not on a balance sheet but a map.

The efflorescence of divisions had one more very big advantage, one not
lost on ambitious young HP managers: more divisions meant more available
openings in the senior management positions of division general manager
and division marketing manager—stepping-stones in turn to Palo Alto. And,
as Hewlett-Packard almost always promoted from within, rather than recruiting talent from outside the company—it was better for morale, and it was assumed that only HPers really understood the HP Way—young, upwardly
mobile managers knew they had a good shot of landing one of these coveted
positions within a few years.

But the path wasn't entirely clear, because many of the senior division
titles were still held by company veterans who had been in place for a decade
or more. They were too experienced, and the company was too loyal to them,
for HP to simply move them out of the way (and HP was already legendary
for *never* firing an employee without severe, or more likely criminal, cause).
At the same time, there was no place for them in the superstructure of the
company.

Bill's and Dave's solution was once again the Hewlett-Packard fork. Even
as the rest of HP was still spinning out the implications of the decentralization of the company, by the mid-sixties the two founders were looking ahead
at what would be the inevitable emerging problem of coordinating too many
divisions in too many locations. In other words, even as they still spoke of the
value, underscored by the HP Way, of spreading out authority in the company, of driving leadership and responsibility down into the organization, Bill
and Dave were already plotting how to reverse that process—to recentralize
the company by adding another layer of management.*

They unveiled the new "group" organizational model in 1968. Recalled
Packard:

> With the number of operating divisions and their product lines steadily
> increasing, we gradually adopted a group structure. This involved com-
> bining, organizationally, divisions with related product lines and markets
> into a group headed by a group manager with a small staff. Each group
> was responsible for the coordination of divisional activities and the over-
> all operations and financial performance of its members.
>
> We had two objectives: to enable compatible units to work together
> more effectively on a day-to-day basis, and to begin to decentralize some
> top-management functions so that the new groups would be responsible

for some of the planning activities and other functions previously assigned to corporate vice-presidents.[36]

It is important to stop for a moment and look more closely at the manifold, and often far-reaching, implications of what seems, at first glance, to be a
comparatively simple corporate re-org.

For one thing, clustering like divisions together and putting them under a
dedicated group management added structure, like installing a truss beam, to
strengthen the company's increasingly extended organization. Moving the
most talented and experienced division managers up into these positions—
there would eventually be thirteen product groups—rewarded them for their
hard work immediately, rather than forcing them to wait years and compete
with their peers for the occasional openings at corporate. It also gave these senior managers a new challenge to motivate them.

Meanwhile, by keeping these group operations small, with minimal
staff, it forced the new group vice presidents to defer most decision-making
and delegate most responsibilities to the divisions, thereby reinforcing the
HP Way.

Human nature being what it is, the group VPs would eventually aggrandize more power—but that would in turn signal another round of decentralization. That too was not a problem: Hewlett-Packard, at least during the
years it was well-managed, grew accustomed to regularly passing through a
cycle of centralization/decentralization about once per decade.

Yet even as Bill and Dave circumscribed the authority of this new level of
senior management, they also rewarded it with added capabilities. In one of
the cleverest organizational decisions of their careers, the two men managed
to find a way to decentralize the company even as they were recentralizing it.*

This clever counterstroke came with their decision to strip HP corporate
of some of its operations and give them back to the divisions via the groups.
The new VPs were empowered to manage the financials, the long-term planning, and the daily operations of their groups. HP even reorganized its entire
sales force, breaking up its established and monolithic structure and assigning
salespeople exclusively to individual groups.

In other words, the new group VPs were all but given complete control of
independent enterprises, many the size of major corporations. Already thinking about succession, Bill and Dave had now created an internal training
ground for the future leaders of the company.

Meanwhile, the shift to a group organization, and the promotion upward
of a number of veteran executives to group vice president slots, opened the
door for the next generation to move into middle management. The timing
was perfect, as a new cohort of young managers was at that moment seasoned

and ready to move into divisional leadership. This so-called Class of 1957–58, for the years that many were hired, would ultimately lead Hewlett-Packard for two decades after the founders retired from daily management of the company. This group, which included, among others, Tom Perkins (later one of Silicon Valley's most important venture capitalists), Jim Treybig (founder of Tandem Computer), and Dean Morton (eventually HP executive vice president) had been part of a conscious effort at the time by Bill and Dave to recruit young MBAs and bring some new blood into company management. A decade later, they were ready to lead their own company divisions.

One member of this Class of '57–58 had moved up through the ranks of the company more quickly than any of his peers: John Young.

Young, a native of Idaho, had grown up in southern Oregon, graduated from Oregon State, and then joined the air force, where he worked as a researcher in the famous rocket sled test program. Leaving the USAF, Young earned his MBA from Stanford and worked as a summer intern in HP's corporate finance department. A few months later he joined the firm full-time.

Young's next decade at Hewlett-Packard offers a glimpse of the wide-ranging and eclectic career development path that HP devised for its best junior talent. Upon joining HP full-time, Young was transferred to corporate marketing, and from there was appointed regional sales manager in charge of HP's New York, New Jersey, and Philadelphia sales organizations. Recalled John Minck, who worked with Young at the time, "We used to joke that our titles should really be Regional Sales Clerk. Our lowly status was confirmed at quota-setting time because, when the [sales] Rep owners visited to negotiate for the next year, they would talk to John and me, for a time, then excuse themselves and go talk directly with Noel Eldred and Dave Packard to set the real sales quotas."[37]

Two years later, Ed van Bronkhorst, HP's chief financial officer, assigned Young to a research project determining the future of the company's relationship with those same reps. Young's report was the genesis of HP's ultimate decision to buy out its reps. Recalled Minck, "As one could imagine, such a project was fraught with political landmines. Each of the owners was a personal friend of Dave and Bill, each was fiercely independent, and no one could be sure whether they would [even] consider getting merged into the big corporation."[38]

But Young's plan worked brilliantly. In the end, eleven of the thirteen reps joined Hewlett-Packard. Young now had the eye of the two founders—and in 1962, when the company formally decentralized, he was appointed marketing manager for the Microwave division, one of the company's four new operating divisions. Two years later, when his boss, Bruce Wholey, was transferred to run the new Waltham medical division, Young was promoted to division general manager—the first of the new generation of HP managers to hold that title.

There, he more than lived up to Bill and Dave's expectations. Indeed, he became a corporate superstar. Minck, who reported directly to Young during this period, recounted:

> Dave and Bill were "intuitive" managers who grew into greatness by sheer common sense and humanity. John [by comparison] brought his value to HP in a well-organized approach to professional management. It was his establishment of the Microwave division's new-product creation process that made that division grow from about $22 million in 1964 to $75 million plus in 1969. The normal growth for HP Test & Measurement in those days averaged 15 percent per year, or doubling every 5 years. John more than *tripled* our sales revenues in 5 years.[39]

Not surprisingly, in 1969, when Hewlett and Packard embarked on the re-centralization of the company, John Young, alone among his age cohort, was promoted to group vice president—and was already being spoken of as Bill and Dave's heir apparent. Young himself set about assembling the brightest talent from the new generation—Paul Ely, Dick Hackborn, and Ned Barnholt among others—and made them his lieutenants. This so-called Microwave Mafia would ultimately run most of Hewlett-Packard.

The Ultimate Entrepreneurs

As the divisional, then group, layers of management moved into position at HP during the 1960s, the role of Bill and Dave in the company inevitably changed as well.

They were beginning now to enter uncharted territory. Only a few men in American business history had taken a company from the very first day of its founding all of the way through going public, onto the Fortune 500, and then into global competition. Most entrepreneurs, then and now, fall to the way-side long before this point, the victim of impatient boards, personality flaws, or their own unwillingness to change.

The history of Silicon Valley and the high-tech industry is filled with stories of brilliant entrepreneurs who founded great companies, then one day found themselves driven out of those firms because the maturing organizations could no longer deal with their mercurial, high-risk personalities. The most famous of these stories belongs to Al Shugart, who founded the disk

Bill at nine years
(HEWLETT FAMILY LIBRARY)

Dr. Albion Hewlett, the distinguished physician (with a touch of whimsy).
(HEWLETT FAMILY LIBRARY)

Lt. William R. Hewlett, U.S. Army. (HEWLETT FAMILY LIBRARY)

Bill Hewitt rappelling on Mt. Owen, California, 1930. (COURTESY OF HEWLETT-PACKARD COMPANY. REPRINTED WITH PERMISSION.)

Packard in 1934, playing end for Stanford University.
(COURTESY OF HEWLETT-PACKARD COMPANY. REPRINTED BY PERMISSION.)

Bill Hewlett and friend Bob Sink in a joke photograph. Recently discovered, it is the only known image of Terman's electronics lab. (HEWLETT FAMILY LIBRARY)

Bill and Flora Hewlett on their honeymoon in the Grand Tetons. (HEWLETT FAMILY LIBRARY)

Lucille Packard, leaving Schenectady for California, 1938. (COURTESY OF HEWLETT-PACKARD COMPANY. REPRINTED BY PERMISSION.)

The garage at 367 Addison Avenue, Palo Alto. (COURTESY OF HEWLETT-PACKARD COMPANY. REPRINTED BY PERMISSION.)

Lucille Packard's kitchen oven, used to bake early HP instrument panels, 1939. (COURTESY OF HEWLETT-PACKARD COMPANY. REPRINTED BY PERMISSION.)

HP's first product, the model 200-A audio Oscillator. (COURTESY OF HEWLETT-PACKARD COMPANY. REPRINTED BY PERMISSION.)

HP's first building, behind John "Tinker" Bell's workshop. (COURTESY OF HEWLETT-PACKARD COMPANY. REPRINTED BY PERMISSION.)

The HP Redwood Building in 1942. Note the "E" flag for excellence in wartime production. (COURTESY OF HEWLETT-PACKARD COMPANY. REPRINTED BY PERMISSION.)

HP's new corporate headquarters on Page Mill Road, 1954. (COURTESY OF HEWLETT-PACKARD COMPANY. REPRINTED BY PERMISSION.)

Hewlett, visiting Packard while on leave, 1944. (COURTESY OF HEWLETT-PACKARD COMPANY. REPRINTED BY PERMISSION.)

Company manufacturing line in 1946. Ed Porter is in the center left. (COUR-
TESY OF HEWLETT-PACKARD COMPANY. REPRINTED BY PERMISSION.)

Dave handing out bonus checks in 1947. *Left to right:* Lucille Packard,
Flora Hewlett, Bill, and Dave. (COURTESY OF HEWLETT-PACKARD COMPANY. REPRINTED BY
PERMISSION.)

Bill and Dave, late 1940s. (COURTESY OF HEWLETT-PACKARD COMPANY. REPRINTED BY PERMISSION.)

Hewlett and Packard with their mentor Professor Fred Terman, 1952. (COURTESY OF HEWLETT-PACKARD COMPANY. RE-PRINTED BY PERMISSION.)

Bill and Dave serving food at the 1952 HP company picnic. (COURTESY OF HEWLETT-PACKARD COMPANY. REPRINTED BY PERMISSION.)

Dave handing out profit-sharing checks. Christmas, 1954. (COURTESY OF HEWLETT-PACKARD COMPANY. REPRINTED BY PERMISSION.)

Dave Packard's memorial photo. (COURTESY OF HEWLETT-PACKARD COMPANY. REPRINTED BY PERMISSION.)

Bill and Dave at San Felipe Ranch, 1957. (COURTESY OF HEWLETT-PACKARD COMPANY. REPRINTED BY PERMISSION.)

Bill and Dave, 1961. (COURTESY OF HEWLETT-PACKARD COMPANY. REPRINTED BY PERMISSION.)

Coffee break, c. 1965. *Left to right:* Ralph Lee, Jack Petrak, Packard, Bruce Wholey, Jack Beckett. (COURTESY OF HEWLETT-PACKARD COMPANY. REPRINTED BY PERMISSION.)

U.S. Deputy Secretary of Defense, David Packard, 1969. (COURTESY OF HEWLETT-PACKARD COMPANY. REPRINTED BY PERMISSION.)

The HP-35 pocket scientific calculator, one of the great tech inventions.
(COURTESY OF HEWLETT-PACKARD COMPANY. REPRINTED BY PERMISSION.)

Rancher Dave, c. 1980.
(COURTESY OF HEWLETT-PACKARD COMPANY. REPRINTED BY PERMISSION.)

Bill and Dave with John Young, 1982.
(COURTESY OF HEWLETT-PACKARD COMPANY. REPRINTED BY PERMISSION.)

Bill and Dave with new chairman/C.E.O. Lew Platt, 1993. (COURTESY OF HEWLETT-PACKARD COMPANY. REPRINTED BY PERMISSION.)

Dave Packard at the Monterey Bay Aquarium Research Institute, 1994. (COURTESY OF HEWLETT-PACKARD COMPANY. REPRINTED BY PERMISSION.)

drive company Shugart Associates, which bore his name—only to be fired by its board of directors. For years he had to drive past that company's sign in Santa Clara, knowing that if he entered the lobby he'd be barred entry by a guard wearing a Shugart badge. Eventually Shugart founded another disk drive company, Seagate Technologies, in the mountains above Silicon Valley, growing the firm to more than $1 billion in annual revenues—only to be kicked out of that company as well.

Great entrepreneurship requires a very special personality. Though entrepreneurs perversely see themselves as risk-averse—that is, they see their securest career path as one in which they report to no one but themselves—to everyone else who works with them or for them, they are perceived as often dangerously adventurous. There is a monomania to entrepreneurs: they have a vision of who they want to be and what they want to create—and they are willing to do almost anything, including destroying themselves and their personal lives, to get there.

All of this makes entrepreneurs alternately charming and rude, heroic and foolish, the greatest creators in our culture but also among the most destructive people, magnanimous and vicious. Because they devise most of the great inventions, provide most of the new jobs, and create much of the new wealth, entrepreneurs are among the supreme phenomena of the modern world. And, because the United States, more than any other society, supports and honors the entrepreneur, it has become the most wealthy and adaptive economy in human history.

But entrepreneurs also embody the atavistic side of modern life. To take the risks they do, and to risk the humiliation of public failure, losing the wealth of others, and wasting people's careers (including their own), entrepreneurs also need to be utterly self-absorbed—to the point, in some notorious cases, of near-solipsism. For the entrepreneur engaged in the pursuit of a new product in a new company, ideas, people, and money are merely tools to be used and tossed away as needed. Great entrepreneurs turn simple business into a crusade, and with their guts, charisma, and obsession draw others along in their wake—everyone knowing that even if it ends up badly, as it often does, they will have had one of the greatest adventures of their lives.

Bill Hewlett and Dave Packard are justly recognized among the greatest entrepreneurs of all time. And, with equal justice, they are celebrated for finding a way to be both successful entrepreneurs and enlightened businessmen at the same time. History has shown that most employee-centered companies become good employers *after* they get through the hard slog of getting to the top, when they are rich and established and trying to keep employees and hold their market position, rather than when they are young and ruthless and fighting for survival.

A half century later, it remains mind-boggling that Hewlett and Packard implemented most of the important employee innovations of the age during a period when the company was still young, small, and at serious competitive risk.

But in the glow that surrounds this remarkable accomplishment, what is often forgotten is that Bill and Dave were still, beneath it all, driven entrepreneurs. They are honored for their sensitive leadership, but as even Hewlett and Packard were at pains to remind others in later years, no decision they made as executives at HP was done purely out of decency, goodwill, or benevolence. Bill and Dave, beyond everything, were tough, unsentimental men. They were, as one early employee would describe them, "tigers at heart."[40]

This was especially true after Hewlett-Packard went public: Bill and Dave were rock-hard businessmen; they knew their first duty was to the shareholders of the company. Thus, you can be certain that if, say, flex-time had proven to reduce employee productivity, Bill and Dave would have abandoned it in a heartbeat.

What makes the two men singular in the annals of entrepreneurs is that they tried flex-time (and all of the other innovations) at all. Most of all, that they instituted the HP Way, a business philosophy particularly antithetical to the entrepreneurial personality. Entrepreneurs also aren't known for being trusting souls; yet Bill and Dave built their entire careers on trusting others.

This suggests that Hewlett and Packard, despite their conservative and traditional demeanor compared to some of the wilder Silicon Valley entrepreneurs who followed, were in fact among the greatest risk-takers in modern business history. Having determined that cultural innovations were as important to the competitive success of their fledgling company as technological innovations, they unflinchingly implemented some of the most radical employee programs ever devised. Having determined that trust was the single most powerful tool in their business arsenal, they willingly turned over the fate of their enterprise, and thus their own reputations, to others. This was risk-taking of the highest possible order.*

That may explain *why* they did it, but it still doesn't explain *how* Bill and Dave managed to adopt policies so contrary to the normal business practices of entrepreneurs.

One answer, the one generally accepted by most observers of the company then and now, is that Hewlett and Packard *were* different. Being a generation older, they arrived at entrepreneuring down a different path from those who came after. The two men seemed to subscribe to that explanation as well, constantly explaining their contrary approach—the family atmosphere of the company, the resistance to layoffs, the unwillingness to take on debt—as being the result of having grown up during the Great Depression.

There is certainly some truth to that. Like that harsh era, Hewlett-Packard Co. seemed to encase conservative values within the most liberal practices, just as the two men managed to be staunch political conservatives while at the same time the most radical of corporate revolutionaries.

But a strong case can made for the reverse argument, which is that rather than being different from other entrepreneurs, they were in fact just like other entrepreneurs—only more so. That they were, in fact, *über*-entrepreneurs, men so focused on the success of their vision, and so fiercely competitive, that they were willing even to sublimate their own egos in pursuit of their goals.

A glimpse into this other side of Bill and Dave can be found in a memoir, entitled "Three Generations," by William Jarvis. Jarvis was HP employee number 300, hired in the early 1950s directly by Noel Eldred with the approval of Dave Packard. More importantly, Jarvis later left HP to embark on a very successful career of building his own companies (including Wiltron and the Jarvis Winery). Thus, unlike many of the men and women who watched Hewlett and Packard up close and on a daily basis, Jarvis saw them through the eyes of a fellow entrepreneur. And though he holds the two men in enormous respect, he is also unsparing about their ferociousness. The result is a refreshing, if somewhat disorienting, break from the usual mythologizing of the two men.

Here is Jarvis's story about Bill Hewlett, capturing the man's voice in a way no public pronouncement ever did:

> Pete Lacy and I read a technical paper from an English engineer, a fellow at Harwell (the English atomic energy establishment) who had built a primitive sampling instrument that worked. As luck would have it, Hewlett was traveling in Europe at that time. I called him and told him to stop by Harwell and see the instrument. He did and seeing is believing; he bought the product idea and from then on I had top priority for my new product.
>
> I got the team assigned and once we got a first prototype instrument put together, I showed it to Hewlett and let him know that for certain applications it would give us 1,000 times higher frequency coverage than Tektronix. He was beside himself. Tektronix was our big competitor at that time and Hewlett never shrank from competition. Hewlett's eyes lit up as he chuckled, "Tektronix will be like a she-bitch in heat. If she runs she'll get chased and if she stands still she'll get screwed."[41]

This is a long ways from the smiling, avuncular image of Bill Hewlett as benevolent teddy bear, and far closer to the kind of ruthless drive to win normally associated with the likes of Bill Gates. Now, here is Jarvis's story about David Packard:

> Hewlett-Packard's feeling about competitors further came to the fore when I left the company to start up my own firm. I did everything properly, including a generous notice. But after I was out the door with all good wishes from everyone, Packard casually passed the word: Either he's for us or he's against us, and it's obvious he's not for us.
>
> I expected a little more neutrality on Packard's part since I had made a small fortune for him in the marketing area and laid the groundwork for the most successful product line [high-frequency counters] he ever had. Over the years, as both our companies progressed, Packard never forgot that I was no longer for him and he played the role of a most aggressive competitor, no holds barred.[42]

This may not jibe with the standard image of David Packard the philanthropist-patrician, but it certainly does with Dave Packard the athlete. In Packard's world, whether at Stanford or HP, you shook hands before the game. Then, when the whistle blew, you pounded your competitor into the mud—then shook hands again when the clock ran out.

William Jarvis, as long as he worked at HP, was a member of the family. The day he quit he became a competitor and his years with Hewlett-Packard were instantly forgotten. What Jarvis doesn't mention, though he no doubt knew, was that were he ever to decide to come back to HP, he would be welcomed back as a prodigal son, his years with the company immediately reinstated on his pension.

Jarvis's story about his treatment after departing from HP also doesn't quite fit with the image of Hewlett-Packard as the company that (at least during the Bill and Dave era) never publicly spoke ill of the competition. But it certainly helps explain how a little California company could come out of nowhere, take on some of the biggest companies of the age—and beat them soundly. Taking on Hewlett-Packard of the Bill and Dave era was to reap a whirlwind: HP would out-innovate you, outsell you, outflank you with other, related products, outservice you, defeat you with superior quality, bring in a living legend or two to close the deal—and, if all else failed, even outprice you.

IBM survived this onslaught by being bigger, Tektronix (for a while) by being even more innovative and staying focused, and DEC by getting into the market first and setting the standard. But they all ran their businesses for two decades or more looking over their shoulders at Hewlett-Packard. As for most other competitors, their days were numbered the moment HP entered the market.

Raising the Bar

But that was Bill and Dave as entrepreneurs, a role they increasingly had to abandon in the 1960s as Hewlett-Packard matured and, through the various reorganizations, gained ever more layers of management. Now, in what has become one of their most admired moves, they had to reinvent themselves as professional business executives.*

It is important to note here that most true entrepreneurs simply *can't* turn themselves into businesspeople. The last fifty years of high-tech history have underscored what psychologists have discovered during the same period in their research, which is that entrepreneurs and CEOs of established companies not only have different personalities, they almost have *opposite* personality traits.

Whereas entrepreneurial personalities correlate closest to Peace Corps workers, bounty hunters, and other individuals who see themselves as alone in a dangerous world, constructing their own reality and making their own rules as they go, the typical corporate CEO is a social creature, working within the confines of rules and regulations, like a general, marshaling troops and resources to conquer and hold territory, making incremental gains that can be secured over time, and taking controlled risks that still preserve the health and integrity of the enterprise.

It is not surprising, then, that many successful entrepreneur-founders eventually find themselves unwanted strangers in their own companies, or that there is a particular breed of individual called a "serial entrepreneur" who has no interest in ever being part of an established company of their own creation, but immediately jumps ship from their last successful start-up to start a new one. One of the most famous of these serial entrepreneurs, Jean Hoerni, one of the original Shockley "Traitorous Eight," started at least a dozen companies—and never stayed around to be part of their eventual success or failure.

So difficult is this psychological transition from entrepreneur to businessperson that when Bill and Dave embarked on the process in the mid-1960s, you could count the number of comparable successes in all of American industry on a couple of hands: Henry Ford, David Sarnoff, Louis B. Mayer, Walt Disney, and a handful of others. Hundreds of others, including even the men who had taught the world of business to Hewlett and Packard, such as Charlie Litton and Alexander Poniatoff, had failed.

The years that followed would see a greater number of tech entrepreneurs manage to transform themselves into professional businessmen and -women—Noyce and Moore at Intel, Larry Ellison at Oracle, Scott McNeely at Sun, Bill Gates, Steve Jobs, Michael Dell, Jeff Bezos at Amazon. But with the exception, perhaps, of Gates and Dell, most of these individuals remained essentially entrepreneurs in mufti, their mercurial (and, in many cases, unpleasant) personalities unchanged, but now wrapped in layers of PR, professional management teams, and, often, partnered with a traditional executive who knew how to play the corporate game (as with Ellison and Ray Lang, Noyce and Moore with Andy Grove, and Jobs with Apple chairman Mike Markkula).

By comparison, Bill Hewlett and Dave Packard seemed to make the transition from entrepreneur to executive almost effortlessly. Indeed, the two men seemed to do it so easily that they set the bar higher for every successful tech entrepreneur who followed—henceforth, real success in places like Silicon Valley meant not just founding a company and getting rich, but learning how to manage it into middle age. It now meant becoming a business titan, not merely an entrepreneurial success.

Moreover, Hewlett and Packard didn't end up merely as entrepreneurs pretending to be real businesspeople, depending upon a small army of professionals behind the scenes to do the real work. Look for a hidden power player behind their thrones and you will be disappointed. Bill and Dave remained, without a serious hitch or major misstep, the chief executives of their company from the Addison garage to $3 billion in annual revenues, and from just the two of them to a company of 60,000 employees. They managed this passage so smoothly that it was hard even for the people who worked for them to remember them any other way than they were at the end, and the two men transformed themselves so completely that in the process they also positioned themselves for the *next* career step—the one that no one else has been able to follow.

————

How Hewlett and Packard did this at Hewlett-Packard has already been described: it was a decade-long process, in accordance with the HP Way, of delegating more and more of their traditional decision-making down through the chain of command—while at the same time extending this chain first through divisional decentralization, then group recentralization. Before this process was over, Bill and Dave had probably given up as much as 80 percent of their daily hands-on control of the company.

But what hasn't yet been explained is how the two men brilliantly replaced this *operational* management with an extraordinarily sophisticated kind of *symbolic* management.

The company had grown too big for Packard to personally hand out bonus checks to every employee, for Hewlett to hang out every day in every lab with HP engineers, and for both men to cook a steak for each HPer at every company picnic. The two founders now found themselves forced to find a different approach, one that created a simulacrum of the old personal touch within the new reality of a global corporation.

The solution they found was a novel one: Bill and Dave decided to play themselves.

Chief executives are always actors. They need to act confident, competent, and optimistic in even the worst of times. In fact, this is what often trips up entrepreneurs turned CEOs: they are too honest in their statements, too content in their eccentricities, and they forget that they no longer personify the company, but are now its measured, public voice. Entrepreneurs speak only for themselves, and they tend to say exactly what they think. CEOs speak for the company, and sublimate their own opinions to the needs of the company.

Hewlett and Packard, as the founders and leaders of a major public corporation, were already accustomed to this side of their jobs—and, given the numerous times they were quoted in the press, asked to sit on industry committees, and charmed stock market analysts, they were good at it. But beginning in the mid-1960s, as the nature of their jobs changed, the two men took their performances to another level, one they shared with few other corporate executives but with many famous leaders.

What enabled them to do it were those two seemingly contradictory sides of their entrepreneurial personalities. Being that they were unlike most entrepreneurs, the personas Hewlett and Packard created were not unlike the men themselves—just expanded, and with a conscious effort to create the stories and assemble the legends that would survive them. And being ultra-entrepreneurs, they were willing to live within the straitjackets of these myths, to the point of sublimating their true selves, because Bill and Dave knew the roles they were playing would help assure the survival and success of HP long after they were gone.*

The notion of Bill Hewlett and Dave Packard consciously playing simplified yet mythical versions of themselves, beginning in the mid-1960s and continuing for the rest of their lives, doesn't fit with the standard HP story of the two founders, in their goodness, performing acts of honor, decency, and humility that others happened to notice and passed down through the company's history in a great oral tradition. In truth, many of these acts were noted and written down soon after they occurred, if not by others then by Bill and

Dave themselves in speeches, articles, and, in Packard's case, *The HP Way*. They were also quickly standardized and used by HP public relations in press releases and in the new-employee orientation—where even the radical employee who began this chapter heard them and was, against his will, affected by them.

This is not to suggest anything cynical or fraudulent in Hewlett's and Packard's actions during these years. Nobody could behave in such a manner for so many years if this persona wasn't in fact an amplification of the real person underneath. There is no moment in the Bill and Dave story where the angel masks are stripped away to reveal devils beneath; no cynical PR ploy like John D. Rockefeller handing out dimes to schoolchildren.

On the contrary, the reason Bill and Dave's transition from entrepreneurs to corporate leaders to statesmen is so seamless is that the characters they adopted were so congruent to themselves. After all, the two men had been creating legends almost from the day they opened the garage door. The difference was that "Bill" and "Dave" were now the vehicles through which Bill and Dave told simple stories to convey what they really believed to millions of people throughout the world, both then and still today.*

That Bill and Dave might have been consummate corporate actors self-consciously working through their own scripts may grate with the official biographies, but it certainly fits with what we know about the intelligence, shrewdness, and competitiveness of the two men—and it helps explain why HP seems to have more edifying tales about its founders than any other company.

If Bill and Dave performed all of these acts spontaneously, and out of natural decency, they are great men. If they did them consciously, with an eye to creating enduring moral lessons for HP employees, they are not only great men but geniuses.

Family Legends

There are scores of Bill and Dave legends—though, tellingly, they almost all seem to fall into a handful of categories that correspond with the core tenets of the HP Way. Almost all seem to deal with earning a profit, taking risks with innovation, personal humility, a family of equals, and trust.

The reader has already encountered a number of these legends. They include, in chronological order, the humble garage and Lucile Packard's stove, the tenacity to fail numerous times before discovering the right product, the dangers in the arbitrary pricing of the 200A, the miraculous sale to Disney, the crucial loan from the local banker, the support for the employee with TB, Hewlett breaking open the locked storeroom, and any number of smaller acts that captured something essential about Bill and Dave, their humanity and their commitment to the essential themes of the HP Way.

This corpus of stories served as the counterpoint to the rigorous and carefully constructed list of HP Corporate Objectives. The stories were those Objectives played out in real life. They were also moral lessons disguised as company anecdote. And, though unplanned at this early stage, they were also a way to make the founders present and vivid when they weren't there—and, ultimately, when they were gone from this world. Future HP employees would always have before them the "best of Bill and Dave," as it were, while Hewlett and Packard's successors (and any other business executive) had a template always at hand for how to become great executives and even greater men and women—if they had the courage.

Though these larger implications were unknown to Hewlett and Packard when they performed these acts in the 1940s and 1950s, they certainly understood them by the end of that era. They only had to read the newspapers and magazine stories about the company, which inevitably recycled a half dozen of the legends.

Thus, by the time of the Sonoma meeting, when the two men moved up and away from the daily operations of the firm, there is the sense that Bill and Dave had a kind of epiphany, a realization that these older stories, and any new ones they could create during the rest of their time with the company, might well be their most enduring contribution to Hewlett-Packard; that if they could no longer deal directly with every little problem faced by their now giant company, they could still perform symbolic acts to instruct their employees on how to behave when the two of them weren't there. They would teach by example and, as the HP Way dictated, trust that their employees would use these lessons to make the right decisions.

This is leadership of the highest order, a kind of management by aesthetics more common to sovereigns and field marshals than corporate CEOs. And it is a dangerous tightrope to walk, because the message, once sent, can be construed in unpredictable ways. For that reason, the lessons must not only be carefully designed, but edited well in their first few retellings to make sure that the right conclusion is drawn.

A lot of this task fell upon people like PR director Dave Kirby and his staff, who crafted the received versions of many of these stories for employees and then made them available to the media. Kirby, even after his retirement, continued sculpting the stories while working with Dave Packard on Packard's *The HP Way*.

Several of the best-known Bill and Dave stories of this second era have already been discussed. For example, there is John Minck's story of HP's deci-sion to pull its independent sales agents into the company rather than firing and replacing them—a decision justified by Bill Hewlett as being the right thing to do. And there is Packard's stunning offer to buy HP Associates for a price greater than that team's dream figure.

In both cases, Hewlett and Packard seemed to be sending messages about integrity in business dealings, about honoring even unspoken contracts, and about paying a fair price to retain a good relationship, rather than gouging the other party.

————

Here is a story, from the more skeptical William Jarvis, that teaches a more pragmatic lesson about profits and pricing.

> While in marketing at HP I made a study (after hours on my own time) of the profitability and competitive position of [the company's] major prod-ucts. I put together a list of about ten major instruments whose prices could easily be raised about 10 percent without affecting their competi-tive position, and I made a second list of a half dozen instruments where the profit was excessive, 30 or 40 percent. I felt those products should be reduced in price before they attracted competition. I passed on this infor-mation through my boss, Noel Eldred, to Dave Packard.
>
> After a couple months of thinking about it he finally came back say-ing he approved all of the recommended price increases, but for now not to lower the prices as recommended on the second list. That old fox was right; we never did attract any competition on those overpriced [instruments].[43]

This lesson, which corresponds to the first HP Objective of *Profit*, is a re-minder that Hewlett-Packard was in the business of making the best possible profit on its products—which, at the high end, meant whatever the market would bear. There was more than a little truth to that joke (first made popular in the 1970s) about HP standing for "highest priced."

Just the opposite was true at the low end. As already seen with the Addison garage, Hewlett and Packard had little nostalgia about the past unless it in some way enhanced the future. That's why it is telling that there are no senti-mental stories about the retirement of the HP 200A, the company's founding product, in the 1950s: once demand fell off, and all profits were wrung out of the product line, Bill and Dave jettisoned it with barely a glance back. A generation later, the company would do the same with its most famous product, the HP-35 calculator. Had corporate publicist J. Peter Nelson not written, on his own initiative, a press release elegy of the device, its passing would have gone unremarked.*

In Defiance

The most famous Packard story of the era deals with the so-called "medal of defiance." Chuck House, who would spend nearly thirty years at HP, was at the time a product engineer at HP's Loveland division. There, in his words, "I built a large screen oscilloscope that could be used as a computer display. My bosses weren't all that wild about it, but they let me show it to Dave and Bill."

The two founders weren't impressed.

Recalled House, "Dave told my boss, 'When I come back next year I don't want to see this [product] in the lab.' "

But House believed in his new oscilloscope—so, despite Packard's warning, he continued to perfect it, turning the project into an unsanctioned skunk work to finish a working prototype. When he went to California on vacation, he took a prototype of the monitor with him—and met with universal interest among potential customers. That convinced him to ignore Packard's orders. House talked the division R&D manager into rushing the monitor into production.

Then the day of reckoning arrived:

When [Dave] came back a year later, the product was in production. He was incensed. He said, "I thought I said to *kill* this thing."

And I said, "No sir. What you said was that you didn't want to see it in the lab. And it's not. It's in production."

The market forecast was for 31 of these things [to be sold] over time. [Instead], we sold 17,000 of them. Most importantly, it was used for you and I to see Neil Armstrong's foot hit the moon.[44]

In all, Chuck House's renegade monitor brought $35 million in new revenues to the company. House recalled, "I wasn't trying to be defiant or obstreperous. I really just wanted a success for HP. It never occurred to me that it might cost me my job."[45]

In this case, Packard's business judgment had proven completely wrong. A bad manager might have fired House and rewritten official corporate history to take credit for being right all along. A good manager would have quietly rewarded House, even as he was being punished for insubordination, and then buried the real story as a threat to the credibility of the CEO.

Packard, by comparison, called a departmental meeting a couple of years later and very publicly awarded House with a newly created medal for "extraordinary contempt and defiance beyond the normal call of engineering duty." House would go on to become a senior HP executive.*

The Hewlett Way

For his part, as he began to remove himself from the day-to-day activities of HP, Bill Hewlett began to experiment with a series of new programs and techniques to keep himself in touch with the work being done in the trenches of the company.

One technique, as described by Jerry Porras, Stanford professor and author of the classic book *Built to Last* (which discussed HP, among other great companies), was that "Bill had a great reputation for walking into a junior engineer's office, putting his feet up on the desk and saying, 'Tell me what you're doing. Tell me what we should be doing.' "[46]

Hewlett expected the same curiosity from his lieutenants, the senior vice presidents of HP. One way he enforced this was the creation of what he called "communications luncheons." Senior HP executives were not only expected to regularly visit company divisions, but while there ask to have lunch with a group of fifteen or twenty employees. No supervisors were allowed. Further, the names of the luncheon attendees were publicly listed so that other employees could contact them and pass on their questions or complaints. Hewlett described the program in 1982, after several thousand HPers had participated in it:

> The format is very simple. After light conversation to break down the barriers, usually an employee will ask a question about something in the company that he does not understand or with which he is unhappy. This provides an opportunity to discuss company policy or company problems.
>
> Sometimes these items are trivial, sometimes the "word" has not gotten down, sometimes the problems are strictly personal and must be treated with great care so as not to interfere with the supervisory process.
>
> Sometimes you detect a pattern of problems—say, for example, inadequate supervisory training. Such problems can be dealt with on a

broad company-wide basis. And in any event you always learn more about how the company actually operates. Equally important, employees have a chance to hear firsthand what is happening in the company and what management is trying to do.[47]

In practice, these luncheons usually began formal, and somewhat strained. Then, as Hewlett noted, someone would finally ask the question that broke the ice. Then the floodgates would open—especially when the employees realized that the VP was much more nervous than they were. Typically, the luncheons ended not when the HPers ran out of questions (they almost never did), but when the exhausted executive looked at his watch and announced that he had needed to get back to the office.*

Note Hewlett's comment about the "word" not getting down from corporate to individual employees in the divisions. This would become an obsession with Bill in the years to come. As he phrased it in an essay he wrote entitled "The Human Side of Management":

The people at the top of an organization may have the best intentions in the world of how they want the organization to be run. But there are a lot of layers between the top and the bottom and, in transmitting them from layer to layer, sometimes ideas inadvertently become distorted.

It always amazes me at our communications lunches to find out how much some concepts had changed in the transmission process. Feedback such as this is necessary if you wish to determine what is really happening in the organization.[48]

Hence, not only the communications luncheons were created, but also the broad range of employee communications programs at HP, from division newsletters to company magazines (*Measure* for business, *HP Journal* for technology), and the founding in the early 1970s of a television studio near company headquarters to produce HP training and news videos.

But even that wasn't enough: Bill Hewlett needed to know that the messages were getting through on a regular basis to every office in his vast company. So he hired a major polling company, the International Survey Research Corporation, to regularly poll HP's U.S. employees to, in Hewlett's words:

1. Give employees a chance to express opinions about their workplace;

2. Provide the company with an opportunity to listen to concerns of the employees; and to respond to these concerns and ideas;

3. Compare HP with other large companies with regard to the attitudes of employees; and

4. Set a standard, or benchmark, for future surveys, possibly in other parts of the HP world.[49]

Other large companies were also experimenting with this kind of employee surveying, but few as assiduously, and none in high technology. But the crucial difference was what Hewlett-Packard did with the results. They weren't kept as privileged information by senior management to determine how better to deal with the rank and file. On the contrary: they were published and distributed, good news and bad, to every employee. It was yet another reminder to everyone at Hewlett-Packard that HP was family, and that were no secrets: family problems were brought out into the open to be solved.

Truth be told, there were very few negative results from the surveys during this era. Twenty years of continuous success, a strong stock price, perpetual expansion opening endless doors to promotion, and, no doubt, a fair amount of the Hawthorne effect—the psychological discovery that employee morale and productivity sometimes goes up merely from a lot of management attention in *any* form—all converged to make a company of happy employees.

No doubt those results were gratifying to Bill Hewlett; but his real interest was congruence between the attitudes of the employees out in the divisions, and what senior management assumed those attitudes to be. For Hewlett, it wasn't enough that information be effectively conveyed down through the organization, nor even knowledge; what he wanted was a common *understanding* moving in every direction within the company. Only then could the mutual trust at the heart of the HP Way be converted—as it had with Chuck House and the large-screen oscilloscope—into independent, even maverick, action in support of the company's larger objectives.*

It was in pursuit of that larger goal that Hewlett instituted another ritual at HP: the executive build-off. On a regular basis, usually when Bill and Dave were visiting one of the divisions for its annual review, Hewlett would gather some of his vice presidents and other company veterans and hold a race to see who could assemble one of that division's newest products.*

These were relatively rowdy affairs, old engineers proving they still had the chops, ridiculing each other, and giving no quarter even to the founders. But for all of the fun, Hewlett was making a serious point—one not lost on his VPs. It was that no matter how high up you went in HP, you still needed to understand how the company's products worked, to appreciate what daily work was like for your lowest-level subordinates on the manufacturing line, and be reminded that every one of those employees could do this job better than you.

Bottom Up

Bill Hewlett wasn't only obsessed with how understanding was conveyed down through the organization. With each year he seemed to become more and more focused on how new ideas were nurtured *upward* through the company.

It was more than just putting your feet up on some young engineer's desk and picking his brain (itself a variant of Management by Walking Around—once again showing how Bill and Dave inevitably hewed to company objectives and values). By the end of the sixties, Bill had developed a specific technique for dealing with new ideas. It was an outgrowth of his long-standing Open Door Policy, and was designed to provide the maximum support for company innovators, while at the same time enforcing a necessary discipline to the development process.

Even Dave Packard found Hewlett's technique so interesting, and admirable, that he chose to describe it in his memoirs:

> How do managers provide encouragement and help the inventor retain enthusiasm in the face of . . . disappointment?
>
> Many HP managers over the years have expressed admiration for the way Bill Hewlett handled these situations. One manager has called it Bill's "hat-wearing process." Upon first being approached by a creative inventor with unbridled enthusiasm for a new idea, Bill immediately put on a hat called "enthusiasm." He would listen, express excitement where appropriate and appreciation in general, while asking a few rather general and not too pointed questions.
>
> A few days later, he would get back to the inventor wearing a hat called "inquisition." This was the time for very pointed questions, a thorough probing of the idea, lots of give-and-take. Without a final decision, the session was adjourned.
>
> Shortly thereafter, Bill would put on his "decision" hat and meet once again with the inventor. With appropriate logic and sensitivity, judgment was rendered and a decision made about the idea. This process provided the inventor with a sense of satisfaction, even when the decision went against the project—a vitally important outcome for engendering continued enthusiasm and creativity.[50]*

The single greatest threat to established high-tech corporations is that they lose the innovativeness that made them successful in the first place. Through a fatal combination of stifling bureaucracy and rules, choked lines of communications, nostalgia for the products that built the company, and risk aversion to cannibalizing existing product lines to support unproven new ones, established companies tend to resist new ideas to preserve the status quo—right up to the moment when a radically new innovation from a younger and less risk-averse competitor pushes the older company to the brink of disaster.

This "innovator's dilemma" of staying competitive in a disruptive market even as one's company matures—most famously described in the business best-seller of that name—haunts every high-technology CEO. Few find a way out of this trap of success, hence the high turnover among leading electronics companies year after year.

Hewlett-Packard did escape this trap, at least during the stewardship of Bill and Dave, and for a number of years afterwards—and credit for that may largely be given to Bill Hewlett's growing emphasis on the flow of communications at the company in the 1960s. He was, in fact, dealing with the innovator's dilemma a quarter century before it was identified, and three decades before it was named.

Once again, this is an example of the two founders building upon their natural tendencies and personality traits to create larger, company-wide structures—and then, in the sixties, institutionalizing these structures through stories, subtle manipulation, and carefully crafted symbolic gestures.

In this case, the two traits were Packard's general indifference to sentiment, nostalgia, and worship of the past, and Hewlett's bottomless curiosity about new technology. In the case of the former, this attitude enabled HP to abandon products and product lines, no matter how historic or linked with the company's past greatness, the moment they dropped below sufficient profitability. Packard's public indifference to the fate of the Addison garage became the defining story/myth. The message was: if I don't care about the fate of the 200A and the garage, why are you clinging to a five-year-old oscilloscope design? Dave Packard was practicing "creative destruction" at HP long before the term was devised.

As for Hewlett, as seen, his curiosity about new technology led him to become personally involved in every major new product development at HP (from the early instruments to the desktop calculator—and, in the years to come, the pocket calculator), always careful to nudge projects along, establish goals, and provide a reality check, yet never intrude into the actual creative process.

This, in turn, as layers of management began to intercede between him and HP's R&D labs, led Hewlett to make those regular drop-in visits to pick the brains of young engineers, as well as to institute the executive build-offs to make sure both he and his lieutenants were always up to date.

This focus on communication culminated in Hewlett's "hat-wearing process." Where a few other tech CEOs of the era were consciously trying to nurture innovation in their maturing companies, Bill Hewlett may have been the first to formalize the technique. His process, tested and perfected over years with scores of young inventors, served as a template by which he could assure that his engineers could get a fast, fair, and complete hearing—and Bill Hewlett could circumvent the layers of filters between them.

The "hat-wearing process" would have its defining moment a decade hence when Steve Wozniak would bring the personal computer to Hewlett. It was one of the most extraordinary meetings in Silicon Valley history, one of the most controversial, and one of the least understood.

But Hewlett didn't stop with communication. Inevitably, his work with all of these engineers, among them (like Tom Osborne) the most talented inventors of their generation, led Bill to ponder the nature of creativity itself. This wasn't surprising: he, after all, had, against what seemed like all odds, himself enjoyed one of the most celebrated moments of creativity in the early years of electronics. No doubt he often wondered just what happened to him that day in Terman's lab.

This meditation would culminate twenty years later, and a half century after he himself received his own graduate diploma there, in Hewlett's 1986 graduation address at MIT.

Afterwards, a number of graduates would complain in the school paper that Hewlett's speech was rambling, too much an advertisement for Hewlett-Packard Co., and addressed only to the engineering graduates. All of which was true, given Hewlett's lack of natural eloquence, his deep identification with his company, and his engineer's heart.

But, reading his words now—with his telling reference to one of HP's most famous mavericks—it is apparent that Bill Hewlett was a business executive ahead of his time. He was already wrestling with what would be one of the greatest problems of the digital age. And when he is describing the creative process, his words are precise and lucid.

Note as well how Hewlett, apparently unconsciously, is also describing himself:

> How do you define creativity? According to Chuck House, who heads up our engineering productivity program, "Creativity is what screws up my engineering program." Unfortunately, there is much truth in that statement.

Thomas Edison is alleged to have remarked about his laboratory, "There ain't no rules around here. We're trying to accomplish something."

These two comments say a great deal about the creative process. It works best when it is not too structured, but it must, in the long run, be tamed, harnessed and hitched to the wagon of man's needs. . . .

It is very difficult to spot a creative individual just by looking at a résumé. It is clear, for example, that education is not a sine qua non for being creative. Psychologists can't even agree on how to measure this characteristic, let alone predict who will display it. Establishing an environment that fosters creativity and observing who flourishes is probably the best way of finding this elusive characteristic.

Successful innovators share many common traits. Creative people have an abiding curiosity and an insatiable desire to learn how and why things work. They take nothing for granted. They are interested in things around them and tend to stow away bits and pieces of information in their minds for future use. And they have a great ability to mobilize their thinking and experiences for use in solving a new problem.

Problems, however, are rarely solved on the spur of the moment. They must be organized and dissected, then key issues isolated and defined. A period of gestation then sets in, during which these issues are mulled over. You put them in your mind and consciously or unconsciously work at them at odd hours of the day or night—even at work. It is somewhat analogous to trying to place a name on the face of someone you've met before. Often the solution to the problem comes to you in much the same way you eventually recall the name.[51]

A decade later, when the rest of the technology business world caught up, and fostering innovation became the talk of the day, Bill Hewlett's speech was long forgotten—except for one paragraph, which would be the most widely anthologized quote by this plainspoken man:

Creativity is an area in which younger people have a tremendous advantage, since they have an endearing habit of always questioning past wisdom and authority. They say to themselves that there must be a better way. Ninety-nine times out of a hundred, they discover that the existing, traditional way is the best. But it is that one percent that counts. That is how progress is made.[52]*

Those who thought of Bill Hewlett as merely an old man, an anachronism of another time, and read that quote, must have been shocked at the radical attitude and youthful perspective of those words. But even they would have had no idea how much earning that wisdom had cost Bill Hewlett, and Dave Packard, in the late sixties and early seventies.

King David

There is a popular story told about David Packard from this era. Packard himself liked it so much—and no doubt also saw it as an important lesson for other HPers—that he repeated it in *The HP Way*. It is the Packard version of King Alfred and the cakes, the classic tale of the rich and powerful who are taught a lesson in humility:

> I recall a time, many years ago, when I was walking around a machine shop, accompanied by the shop's manager. We stopped briefly to watch a machinist making a polished plastic mold die. He had spent a long time polishing it and was taking a final cut at it. Without thinking, I reached down and wiped it with my finger.
>
> The machinist said, "Get your finger off my die!"
>
> The manager quickly asked him, "Do you know who this is?"
>
> To which the machinist replied, "I don't care!"
>
> He was right and I told him so. He had an important job and was proud of his work.[53]

This is a classic "Bill and Dave" story of the era, so perfect that it seems fake, yet verified by numerous observers. Yet even if the event itself was spontaneous, it is important to recognize that a number of elements to the story are calculated.

First of all, Hewlett and Packard had, by the time Dave walked into that machine shop, developed a culture at HP that treated the two founders as mere equals with everyone else in the firm, and as individuals who could be spoken to without unnecessary diplomacy by anyone in the firm.

Second, the fact that it occurred in the machine shop, with a crusty master machinist, is probably no coincidence either—one wonders if a meddling Packard would have gotten the same response from a young assembler on the manufacturing line in Colorado Springs, or a senior engineer in the R&D lab in Cupertino.

As for the event itself, there were some other crucial factors. Assuming that it actually occurred as claimed—and we can be pretty sure it did—the fact that Packard *apologized* to the machinist is less important than that such an apology was seen as *characteristic* of Dave Packard. Experience suggests that 50 percent or more of corporate CEOs in the same situation would likely apologize as well, as it is an almost unconscious response to being caught doing something wrong. Thus we can assume, putting the real executive jerks and monsters aside, that there are probably thousands of CEOs running companies today about whom a similar story can be told. So why Dave Packard?

One answer is that he earned it. After thirty years of revolutionary and benevolent management, he and Bill Hewlett were beginning to become the beneficiaries of a growing body of stories and anecdotes even beyond their conscious efforts to create them. But equally important, he and Bill had created a culture at Hewlett-Packard—a family environment, a sense of personal familiarity with the founders, a sophisticated formal and informal communications network—that identified these stories as they occurred and quickly disseminated them through HP offices around the world. They became the "heart" of the HP family, ever more cherished as the founders grew older and pulled away from the daily operations of the company.

Finally, none of this was lost on Packard (or Hewlett), nor for that matter, on Dave Kirby. Stories, such as that of the machine shop, would be recounted one last time for future HPers, in the pages of *The HP Way*, where they could be referenced long after Bill and Dave were gone.

So the question needs to be asked: did Hewlett and Packard plan all of these moments ahead of time, orchestrating them to their desired results? Most likely not, with a few exceptions. Frankly, they didn't have to: twenty-five years in business had taught them the power of the grand gesture at just the right moment—and when such a moment presented itself, they were not afraid to jump in and, even at the cost of humiliating themselves, turn an interesting moment into a legendary one.

The Price of Success

By the end of the 1960s, Bill Hewlett and Dave Packard were probably as gifted and competent as any top business executives in history. They had literally changed the world not only with the products they sold, but in the inspirational way they ran their company. And they had been amply rewarded for their efforts: HP was consistently voted one of (if not *the*) best-run companies on the planet, Bill and Dave recognized as the finest managers of their generation, and, not least, the two men had joined the ranks of the world's wealthiest private citizens.

But for all of their achievements, Hewlett and Packard were still men, and they were not immune from the stresses attendant to their kind of career paths. They were now in their late fifties, the time of midlife crises, when many men suddenly recognize their own failures and their own mortality. Add to this the fact that both men had children coming of age in the cultural and generational divide that defined the sixties—both men experienced varying degrees of estrangement (political, social, and personal) from their kids, none of whom, as noted, followed them into corporate life.

Add to this the almost unimaginable pressures of holding the fate of thousands of employees and their families in your hands—all of them at risk of you making a single wrong decision. And the stress involved in taking a company from a tiny garage to a giant multinational, publicly traded corporation with thousands of shareholders, all in the course of a single career, with few markers to help you to the next level. And, not least, there are the surreal pressures that come with great wealth: that combination of euphoria in knowing that you are unimaginably rich, and horror in the realization that every predator, terrorist, and kidnapper out there in the darkness knows it too.

The golden aura that surrounds Bill and Dave in the public's memory obscures the visible toll all of this pressure took on both men. Frankly, they wouldn't have been human had they endured it all unscathed; conversely, it is a miracle, and a testament to their characters, that they survived a process that would have (and has) broken other men and women of great talent and intelligence.

But though hidden, there are clues to a deeper story. For example, though myth suggests that through all of their years of partnership Bill and Dave never fought,[54] and almost never disagreed, Bill's son Walter Hewlett vividly remembers his father coming home one day furious, and roaring, "I am so damn mad at David Packard!"

Still, rather than diminish the nature of their friendship, this story almost seems the exception that proves the rule: have any two business partners *ever* worked together for fifty years and had only *one* verified argument?

Indeed, it may be impossible to ever fully explain the friendship between Bill Hewlett and Dave Packard. Even people who knew both men well, who worked with them for decades, admit they don't really understand it. Said Dave Kirby a decade after they were gone, "I'm still puzzled about the relationship between those two guys."

But there are other, darker stories as well. In particular, though it was generally known among the senior executives at HP, few HPers and almost no one outside the company ever knew about Dave Packard's weakness for women. It doesn't quite fit with Packard's image as the paragon of American business leadership, but it is probably not surprising that the handsome young giant and football star, and later the awesome corporate giant and billionaire, would enjoy the attention of many women—or that he would sometimes respond. It was, perhaps, his way of temporarily escaping the burden of being the always perfect David Packard.

Short and chunky of all of his life, and notably uxorious toward Flora, Bill Hewlett wasn't the object of as much of this type of attention, and apparently was immune to what there was. But the pressures on him as CEO, if anything, were even greater. He found his emotional outlets in equally surprising ways.

In the mid-1960s, suffering a classic midlife crisis, he went out and purchased a Porsche. Art Fong would remember terrifying rides with Hewlett up to San Francisco in the Porsche, racing along the then two-lane Highway 280, the car's tires barely touching the ground.

But this burst of uncharacteristic flamboyance didn't last long. It was soon replaced by a return to simplicity and humble living that, though it had little to do with Hewlett's own affluent childhood, seemed to be a way for him to escape the expectations of tycoonship. Almost despite himself, he managed to make this too the stuff of HP legend: the retreats to the ranch where he fished, cooked, played cards, and awoke the house each morning by playing an accordion.

HPer Marc Saunders bumped into Hewlett one day at a Menlo Park hardware store. As told by John Minck:

> He noticed Bill Hewlett by a counter of wood screws, [and] introduced himself, since they had once met at a management review. He asked if Bill was doing some home project for the day. Bill nodded yes, but in an impatient voice complained, "Isn't this ridiculous? I just need three wood screws, but the way these are packaged, I've got to buy 24 of them."
>
> This, at a time when Bill's wealth was about $1 billion.[55]

Like many busy businessmen, Hewlett during this period also seemed to sense that his time was short with his fast-growing children—and he seemed to redouble his efforts to spend more time with them. During the 1960s, the Hewlett and Packard families spent considerable time on the ranch, until it became almost a second home.

He had tried to instill a love of science and engineering into his own children when they were young. Walter Hewlett recalled "many a painful moment when he would try to explain circular functions to me. I was in second grade."[56] Having largely failed then, he would try again now with his grandchildren, teaching them how a compass worked, how Lake Tahoe got its shape, how the colors of the rainbow are created—without much more luck.[57]

He also indulged his love of tinkering by becoming the fix-it guy for every broken appliance and tool in his extended family, a notable example being the time he heated a metal rod over a stove and used it to fix the circuitry of his nephew's stereo—an unforgettable glimpse for the new generation of what it must have been like in the Addison garage.

But these were only the most visible manifestations of Bill Hewlett's response to the enormous emotional stress that wealth, fame, and responsibility placed upon him. One of the most curious anecdotes about him during these years comes from Ned Barnholt, then an HP middle manager, and later CEO and chairman of Agilent, the spin-off of HP's Instrument Group.

As Barnholt tells it, he and his wife were in Manhattan late one evening, taking a walk, when they saw a hunched, stocky figure in an overcoat and hat shuffling toward them. "At first, I thought it was a homeless guy, or a vagrant," Barnholt recalled. Then the man glanced up—and to Ned's amazement, it was Bill Hewlett.

He greeted the couple warmly, walked them to their hotel, and then, as the Barnholts watched in amazement, Bill Hewlett shuffled off into the night. "I've never quite figured that one out," says Barnholt. Perhaps, deep down in the gruff but sunny character of Bill Hewlett there was still the lonely boy, lost and without his father.[58]

L'Age d'Or

In 1969, high tech's great watershed year, Hewlett-Packard Co. was a $325 million firm, with 16,000 employees. It was the market leader in most segments of the test and measurement instrument industry, as well as in analytic devices, medical diagnostic devices, and desktop computers. Though it was still far behind companies such as IBM and Digital Equipment in the overall computer industry, it was quickly becoming a dominant player in computers for use in laboratories and in-field applications.

Meanwhile, surveys found that the company itself was seen as one of the best places to work in the United States, and in most of the other countries where it had plants. Its business culture, employee morale, and innovative benefits were the envy of working people everywhere, and increasingly imitated by their embarrassed bosses. And its two founders were increasingly recognized as the premier business executives in electronics, perhaps in all of American business.

It didn't just stop at the walls of Hewlett-Packard either. The powerful relationship between HP, its founders, and Stanford had helped to make that university a magnet for smart young scientists, business students, and entrepreneurs—and in turn, when they graduated, these ambitious young men and women fed the growing (and increasingly powerful) companies of Silicon Valley.

This was Hewlett-Packard's golden age. The company was now thirty years old, ancient by high-tech standards, but young for a firm that appeared destined to survive for generations. It was the most innovative company the world had ever seen, led by two men of deep competence and even deeper humanity, and its jagged roof glowed like a diadem over the rolling green hills of the now famous Stanford Industrial Park.

There had never been a company quite so wonderful as Hewlett-Packard in the 1960s, and few companies have ever been so well run. And there would never be a company like it again—not even Hewlett-Packard.

Bill and Dave had gone as far in their careers as any entrepreneurs ever had, from garage to global corporation. In the process, with their remarkable vision, they had managed to anticipate each swing and turn the company would go through as it grew—and the changes they would have to make in themselves to lead it.

In bold strokes, Bill and Dave had turned a wartime company full of Rosie the Riveters into a lean and aggressive start-up able to move surefooted through the shoals of postwar bust and boom; then into a fast-moving "family" company capable of outthinking and outmaneuvering any giant competitor it met; then into a decentralized multinational moving into new markets through a combination of in-house innovation and company acquisitions, all while extending its family outwards into a "community" of strategic partners, like-minded competitors, and loyal customers.

Beyond a few minor missteps, Hewlett-Packard, led by its two visionary founders, had yet to make a major strategic mistake. And there was no reason to think that the company ever would, at least not in the decade remaining in Bill and Dave's tenure at the top.

But even the best-laid business plans can go astray when they collide with the zeitgeist. And at those moments, even business visionaries can find themselves lost and confused. Bill and Dave may have had great plans for their company and American industry, but the society around them had entirely different plans.

This was 1969, after all. The United States was still reeling from the year before: two political assassinations, race riots and burned cities, and the seemingly hopeless Vietnam War. Now, this year would bring Woodstock, the symbolic zenith of the counterculture generation before the short, dark slide to Altamont and the Manson Family.

Inside the peaceable kingdom of Hewlett-Packard these massive social changes barely registered at first. Older employees worried about their teen-aged sons and the draft, sideburns grew longer (including on Dave Packard), mustaches appeared in the workplace for the first time, as did hair over the collar, the secretaries wore miniskirts, and (at least in the outlying divisions) the reign of the white short-sleeved shirt came to an end.

But outside the walls it was a different story. This was the San Francisco Bay Area, after all, the epicenter of the sixties revolution. In San Francisco, Haight-Ashbury and the Summer of Love had already peaked and scattered its attitudes and iconography around the world. A folk group that had begun as the Warlocks in the campus cottages just across Page Mill Road from HP had gone electric as the Grateful Dead and become the house band of the various Acid Tests, then Bill Graham's Fillmore Auditorium. On weekends, the children of the Santa Clara Valley—and thus of HPers—would head north to the city to listen to the Dead, drop LSD, and dream of a perfect world without war and capitalist corporations and earnest men in white shirts and skinny ties.

Stanford, of course, changed as well. The pastoral college of Bill and Dave's undergraduate years—its sandstone walls filled with rich frat boys with few ambitions beyond drinking and deflowering the local girls—was long gone. So too increasingly was the Stanford of the fifties that Fred Terman had helped to create: the up-and-coming "Harvard of the West," filled with ambi-tious and brilliant young men and women with dreams of rising out of the middle class into professional glory. Stanford's sandstone quad now was marred with antiwar posters, the commons in front of the bookstore marked by daily protests, and the windows of the dorm buildings plastered with North Vietnamese flags and peace symbols. Black power and Chicano sepa-ratist groups held pride of place on campus, and in the classrooms where Bill and Dave's class had once prepared itself for war, professors now proudly taught sedition.

It was a world that had grown to despise almost everything that Hewlett-Packard and its founders stood for. Who cared about flex-time when the revo-lution would bring and end to the slavery of work? And who needed stock options when the whole evil capitalist system was about to pulled down to its rotting foundation?

The most tragic irony of the story of Bill Hewlett and Dave Packard is that they had finally managed to build the ideal business model and the most en-lightened corporate culture—just at the moment when the world was least in-terested in knowing about them. At the very instant when HP was ready to take its vision out into the community, that community recoiled from it. The chance would never come again.*

Summons

During the holidays in December 1968, Bill and Dave were on a hunting trip at one of their newest ranches, this one in Merced, California. While they were there, a call came in to the ranch house.

It was for Dave, from Washington. Melvin Laird, the secretary of defense, was on the line.

Packard had met Mel Laird a decade before when Dave had been the newly elected president of the Stanford board. At that time, Stanford had joined with Harvard and Yale in making the argument in Washington that certain private U.S. universities should be considered "bell cows"—that is, the leaders that other schools followed. As president of the Stanford board, Packard had joined with his counterparts at the other two universities (including Yale's Juan Trippe, president of Pan-American World Airways) and made their presentation before the Health, Education and Welfare and Labor Subcommittee of the House Committee on Appropriations—a group that included, among others, Congressman Mel Laird of Wisconsin.

The presentation had been successful, and the committee voted to authorize a 15 percent overhead allowance on federal research contracts to the "bell cow" universities. Laird, meanwhile, like almost everyone else who ever met David Packard, came away deeply impressed by the man.

In the mid-sixties, in one of his last acts as Stanford board president, Packard attended a meeting in New York of the Council of Foundations. There he gave a speech that, while characteristic of his management of HP, was so shocking in the world of nonprofit foundations that it even made the newspapers.

Once again, the topic was the "bell cow" universities. But this time, even though he was the president of the board of trustees of one of those schools, Packard turned against them. As the Vietnam War had heated up, it was precisely these top schools that had led the drive to kick military ROTC programs off their campuses and, in Packard's words, "in some cases supporting activities that I thought were not in the universities' best interests."[59]

In his speech, Packard called on America's corporations to *increase* their financial support to America's universities to ensure the continued creation of new scientists, engineers, and managers, as well as new technologies and inventions. But having said that, Packard went on to suggest that this support be *targeted* toward those schools and departments working to improve the country, not to tear it down.

"Many university people took exception to this," Packard would write later.[60] That's putting it mildly: the speech in fact created a storm of controversy. And this was in the mid-sixties, before the real anarchy hit America's college campuses.

It was also Packard's first real public statement of his personal politics. Until then Hewlett-Packard Co., like most postwar companies—especially those on the West Coast—had largely ignored politics. Few even considered hiring lobbyists; rather, when an important bill or regulation came up, they would contact their local congressman, or, rarely, present congressional testimony themselves. The attitude in Silicon Valley, well into the 1970s, was that if you ignored Washington, Washington might ignore you—and that was the best possible scenario for entrepreneurship.

Moreover, with the exception of the longshoremen and Beat poets in San Francisco, most of the Bay Area and Northern California was nominally Democrat, but practicing Republican. Bill Hewlett and Dave Packard were basically the opposite, the two positions being almost indistinguishable along the political spectrum.

But the sixties changed all of that. The cultural, and literal, warfare of the decade demanded that people chose sides—and Packard, with his speech, publicly cast his lot with conservatives and Republicans. Hewlett did the same, but not on a public stage.

In doing so, the two founders put themselves in a position they had never been before in the thirty-year history of the company: in philosophical opposition to a large percentage of their employees. As long as Bill and Dave had never taken a strong stance on politics, it hadn't mattered to HPers what their politics were. But now everything had changed: nothing divides people so deeply as religion and politics, and Bill and Dave had just broken one of those taboos.

In their minds, the two men probably believed they had no other choice. By the late sixties, it seemed as if civilization itself was about to tear itself to pieces. Hewlett and Packard saw their society, their community, and, most of all, their company at risk and saw no other choice but to speak out and fight. And perhaps they were right; but from that moment on, thousands of HPers who didn't share their politics might still respect and follow them—but never really admire them again.

One person who was watching was the newly named secretary of defense. And when Mel Laird called, Dave Packard could guess what was coming. As requested, he put together a list of likely candidates. Recalled Packard, "I sent him some names of people he could consider, and he called me back and asked me to meet him in Washington. So we met at the Baltimore airport early one evening. We drove to his transition headquarters at the Carlton Hotel and discussed some of the things he wanted to do when he took office.

After a few hours of discussion, he said he wanted me to join him as deputy secretary."[61]

Packard was intrigued, and told Laird that he would need a few days to think about it. He flew home to California and spent the next week considering the offer. He discussed it with his wife and family, Bill Hewlett, the directors of HP, and several friends with experience in the Defense Department. Lucile, in particular, thought her husband needed a change and suggested he go. The opinions of the others are unrecorded.

Packard knew that taking the job would mean enormous sacrifices. For one thing, he would have to donate to charity all of the income from his HP stock, as well as any increases in its principal. He would have to leave his best friend and partner, and walk away from his beloved company during a crucial time in its history. And he would have to work for an institution he didn't particularly like, the Pentagon, and report to a president he didn't admire, Richard Nixon.

Packard called Mel Laird and told him that he would take the job as deputy secretary of defense.

Why did he accept? Packard himself was never very clear on his decision. The money, though it would amount to millions, seemed to matter little in Packard's decision. He would say later that there were some charities that he had wanted to support and this was a good way to do it.

Nor did leaving Bill Hewlett in charge of their company seem to matter. Whatever Bill's doubts were about running HP himself after all of these years, Packard, who had run the company solo, had none about his old partner: "I knew that Bill Hewlett could manage the company just as well as I could and that he had a strong team of management people to support him."[62]

On the other hand, it may have been true, as some senior HP executives hinted at the time, that Dave Packard had always felt a little guilty that Bill Hewlett had gone off to war while he, the big college letterman, had stayed home to mind the store. Now the bugle had finally called for Packard, and he wasn't going to shirk the call.

But in the end it may have been just patriotism and a sense of duty. The HP Objective of *Citizenship* had called on the company to be a good corporate citizen—and by extension, it expected HPers to be committed and serving citizens as well. And thousands must have done just that, serving in local governments, on school boards, and volunteering at thousands of nonprofit organizations. One local election in Colorado in the early 1970s would actually embarrass HP because *three* of its Loveland employees would run for the same city council. Even HP vice president and old friend Ed Porter had served five terms as Palo Alto mayor—and brilliantly, too, during one of the most eventful periods in the city's history.*

Packard too had served, most notably on the Stanford board of trustees, but on industry groups as well. But this was the big one, the most important call to public service in his life, and Dave Packard, as everyone knew he would, signed on. His country was at war, it needed him, and he did his duty.

In answering the call, Packard also did the same for Hewlett-Packard Co. HP, until now just another large company on the periphery of the political and cultural war dividing the country, was now in the center of the fight. It had chosen sides: for the next five years, to its friends it would be seen (to its chagrin) as an extension of the Defense Department, and to its enemies, like that anarchist at the beginning of this chapter who would one day work for HP, it would come to represent (to its horror) a pillar in the military-industrial war machine.

That it was neither made no difference. Not to the protesters. Not to the radicals who would try to firebomb Bill Hewlett's house and burn down the Palo Alto hotel in which Laird and Packard were meeting, and not to the fringe group that would, long after the end of the Vietnam War, set off a bomb at an HP building on Page Mill Road in the mistaken belief that "smart scopes" (oscilloscopes) were components of "smart bombs."

Packard spent the month before the inauguration tying up loose ends and meeting with Laird to strategize a plan for the department. And then he was gone, not to return for three long years. By then, the company, and the world, he came home to was profoundly changed. HP would be fighting for its life in a stalled industry within a collapsing economy.

There were tears in Bill Hewlett's eyes when he announced Dave Packard's departure to his fellow HPers. At Hewlett-Packard, the sixties had ended early. And though in the next decade, Bill and Dave's last at the helm of the company, HP would see some of its greatest successes and noblest achievements, Hewlett-Packard's golden age was over.

Chapter Six:
Bastion

In the early seventies, for a special Hewlett-Packard twenty-fifth anniversary issue of the HP magazine, *Measure,* Fred Terman was asked to talk about his two most famous students.

Terman wrote just four paragraphs. Three were reminiscences of the early days of HP. But in the final paragraph, the old professor suddenly switched direction:

> People have asked me, in view of HP's immense success, whether Dave and Bill were born businessmen. I'd have to say no, but at the same time I'd point out that they had the knack—and still have it—of learning what they needed to know, of taking a new job and tackling it with all kinds of determination and enthusiasm. This is contagious. It affects the people around them and is the true essence of leadership.[1]

After a quarter century of continuous dual leadership, Hewlett-Packard Co. entered the seventies with just one active founder—and it wasn't the one celebrated for his decisive leadership.

When Dave Packard left for Washington in early 1969, he may have been the only HPer without any doubt that Bill Hewlett could run the company by himself. His confidence wasn't shared by many others.

Hewlett-Packard, from the company name right down to the annual report photos (where the towering Packard would sit in a chair to be at the same height as the short Hewlett), had always operated on the belief that the two founders were essentially interchangeable. Their superhuman ability to always seem to agree on everything only underscored that. As Art Fong, who knew them almost as long as anyone, would recall, "It seems that they had this intuitive knowledge of what each other was thinking that was truly amazing. I don't exactly know what it was, but it was like the [unspoken] communication between a husband and wife."[2] Others would draw the parallel to two experienced parents, who long ago learned never to make decisions regarding the children without first conferring with each other and presenting a united front.

But, like parents or spouses, Hewlett and Packard had different personalities, and had carved out their own distinct roles at the company they founded. Those roles did not always match their public image. Aristocratic and eloquent to the world, Packard was in fact the tougher and more decisive of the two men in the day-to-day business struggle. By comparison, the gruff and plainspoken Hewlett was often the consensus-builder. As the Silicon Valley magazine *Upside* would accurately describe them:

> The commanding, sometimes gruff Packard was the person who made the tough decisions when they had to be made. He is not afraid of controversy and has been known to pound tables to make a point. Packard is also a visionary and strong strategic thinker.
>
> Hewlett, on the other hand, is a shirt-sleeved engineer with whom anyone would feel comfortable talking. He ensured that the company's concern for the individual was not overlooked. Together, Packard's and Hewlett's different styles provided the tension that made HP such a strong company.[3]

If physically they were Mutt and Jeff, philosophically Hewlett and Packard were good cop and bad cop, tactics and strategy, operations and the executive office. Not surprisingly, then, with Packard gone to Washington, some doubted that Hewlett could run HP just fine by himself. Hardly anyone was sure that he would have the long-term vision, or even the short-term flexibility in the face of a sudden market shift, to keep the company at the top of the high-tech world.

But, as he had in those early days in Terman's lab, Hewlett once again proved to be a sleeper, with a mind more formidable than anyone, even his admirers, guessed. He quieted any doubts forever with a quick series of moves so strategic and innovative that they are still studied in business schools— and, like Packard in the 1940s, made observers wonder whether Hewlett could have built HP by himself.

Just what Bill Hewlett accomplished in his thousand days alone at the top of HP is astonishing. Between 1970 and 1981, a decade marked by two recessions, rampant inflation, and a gas crisis, nearly 30 percent of the companies on the Fortune 500 fell completely off that list.[4] During that same period, Hewlett-Packard grew from a 16,000-employee company with annual sales of $365 million to a $3.6 *billion* company with nearly 67,000 employees.

It was one of the greatest surges by a mature business ever seen. In the face of just about every obstacle the world economy could throw in its path, HP in the seventies managed to grow at a compounded rate of 23 percent, with net profits growing at an even faster compounded rate of 27 percent. By the end of the decade, Hewlett-Packard would have 26 manufacturing plants around the world, and 160 sales offices in 65 countries.

But those numbers told only part of the story, because during that same decade, HP turned itself from a mostly American company into a global firm with international sales beginning to surpass its domestic sales.

Even more incredibly, during this period HP managed to transform itself from primarily a test and measurement company to a computer company. And it accomplished this without a single layoff, and with employee morale at stratospheric levels. A 1979 survey found that 93 percent of all HP employees would recommend it as a place to work, and that 83 percent said they felt personally responsible for contributing to HP's success—the latter figure 25 percent above the national average, which the survey specialists described as "mind-boggling."[5]

In other words, in one of the most challenging economic environments of the second half of the twentieth century, Hewlett-Packard Co. managed to change its business, invert its market, quadruple its size, grow at the rate of a start-up company, not lay off a soul, *and* enjoy one of the highest employee satisfaction ratings ever recorded.

And it all began under the solitary watch of Bill Hewlett, the man who wasn't sure he could run the company by himself.

Hewlett's Shining Hour

When Dave Packard left HP for Washington in January 1969, he departed secure in the knowledge that the economy was vibrant and the demand for electronic instruments strong.

A year later, everything had turned upside down. Nineteen seventy was the first year that the modern high-tech industry faced the bad end of what would become a quadrennial cycle of boom and bust. Until then, almost from the recession at the end of the Second World War, the electronics industry had enjoyed nearly continuous growth, even vaulting over the downturn at the end of the 1950s thanks to a burst in demand for new consumer products such as color television.

But a new factor was now setting the pace in high tech: semiconductors. The chip industry (and soon the rest of the economy) marched to the pace of

Moore's law, that vaunted doubling of chip performance every eighteen to twenty-four months. Moore's law drove the perpetual innovation and exponential improvements in performance that have characterized tech ever since, but it also brought with it regular, even predictable intervals of shortages, double-ordering by anxious customers, overproduction, and collapse.

This boom-bust cycle—in the form of a sudden drop in chip orders—made its first appearance in late 1970 and bottomed out two years later. This downturn was then exacerbated by a number of other downward economic trends: the winding down of both the Vietnam War and the NASA Apollo program (which devastated the aerospace industry), the shift of the great baby boom demographic bulge from teenaged consumers to young adults, a shakeout at the low end of the desktop calculator industry (which had filled with more than a hundred U.S., Japanese, and European companies intent on tapping into a bubble in demand), and, ultimately, a general economic exhaustion after the go-go sixties.

Hewlett-Packard, as one of the biggest beneficiaries of the boom, was hardly immune from the penalties of the bust. Bill Hewlett, in response to Packard's departure, had formed a kind of operations troika at the top of HP, consisting of himself, Ralph Lee, and Ed Porter. Both Lee and Porter were already company vice presidents, and both had come out of manufacturing, but they were of very different personalities—and Hewlett had chosen them precisely for those differences. Porter, Bill's childhood friend and a former mayor, was an affable diplomat and negotiator—an "outside" guy. Lee, by comparison, was a tough guy (those on the receiving end of one of his budget-tightening episodes would call him "Bill and Dave's hatchet man"), decisive, and a classic "inside" guy. In retrospect, it seems obvious that Hewlett had cleverly constructed out of these two men a surrogate Dave Packard—all while reserving to himself the power to overrule them.

When the 1970 recession hit, it was this trio that had to find a way to get HP through it intact, with as little damage as possible, and ready to exploit the upswing on the back end.

As with the recessions that followed, different companies responded to the challenge in different ways—almost always in congruence with their character and culture. For most companies, that meant round after round of devastating layoffs. Certainly that's what happened in the aerospace industry: a massive layoff at Sunnyvale's Lockheed Missile and Space, still the area's largest employer, almost knocked flat the newborn Silicon Valley, and Lockheed itself was never quite the same again.

HP's response, as might be expected, was to find an innovative solution that would keep the company on a strong financial footing while still preserving the tenets of the HP Way.

That solution, like the answer to many technical problems in the company's history, didn't come quickly or easily. But in the end, HP—and Bill Hewlett in particular—found it.

HP historian John Minck may have been on hand to see the event that sparked Hewlett's most famous personnel innovation:

> One of my friends had begun reporting to a new manager who had been hired in from Ampex Corporation, presumably for some of his systems expertise. Nineteen-seventy was not a good year for high-tech. HP fell into a bit of a recession, and the word came down from top management to trim 10 percent off operating costs.
>
> My friend got called into his boss's office and was told that he was fired. That was the Ampex way of controlling costs: hire and fire as the profits allowed.
>
> This kind of employee treatment was unheard of at HP. Luckily, my friend didn't take it lying down, but using HP's "Open Door" policy, he marched up to Bldg. 3U and told Bill what had happened.
>
> Bill rescinded the order on the spot. The word got back to the Ampex guy's division manager, since it also appeared that my friend's performance reviews might have been doctored to justify the lay-off. I think HE might have been the one let go.[6]

Hewlett, the most empathetic of bosses—and the least profligate with human capital—probably hadn't even considered that ordering an across-the-board cost cut would lead some of his managers to simply fire personnel rather than tighten belts. Now he had to move quickly. He immediately prepared a memo and had it distributed throughout the company. It is reproduced here in full because of the insight it offers into the leadership style of Bill Hewlett:

July 16, 1970

From: Bill Hewlett
To: See Distribution

SUBJECT: Evaluations & Terminations

An increasing number of cases are coming to my attention in which employees are being terminated with little or no warning that their performance has been unsatisfactory. In some cases, evaluations have been glowing up to the time that an individual is released.

There just is no excuse for this. It is not humane. It is not HP-like. It is not justified. I would like you to be guided by the four following points:

(1) The individual affected had had advance warning through written evaluations and has been advised constructively on how he/she should improve.

(2) Wherever practical, assure the employee is given an opportunity for other placement where he/she might make a greater contribution. Employee placement is a function of supervisors and Personnel and not a function of the employee to be turned loose to find his own job someplace in HP.

(3) If termination is the only alternative, Personnel must be fully advised and believe the case is satisfactorily documented, and the decision has the approval of the general manager concerned.

(4) Before any adverse action is taken, it should be well thought out. We must recognize that each of our people represents an individual with problems, families, etc.

Signed: Bill H.
WRH:dlt

It is not humane. It is not HP-like. It is not justified. Bill Hewlett may have been the only CEO of a Fortune 500 company ever to write a memo like this. Indeed, as a manager, "humane" should probably be William Hewlett's epitaph.*

But reasserting a sense of corporate decency didn't solve the problem of a deepening downturn. On the contrary, bleeding away profits violated the first HP Objective. So Hewlett now faced a serious dilemma; he was caught between the requirements of the HP Objectives and the demands of the HP Way.

Somehow he had to cut expenses corporate-wide in order to preserve the profits the company would need to come out of the recession strong and competitive; yet he had to implement these cuts in a structure that didn't end up in pink slips, revenge firings, faked personnel reports, managers getting rid of promising future candidates for their jobs, and all of the other destructive nastiness that attends corporate cutbacks. There was almost no example out there in the business world of such a solution, the business partner on whom he could sound out ideas was three thousand miles away and dealing with his own full plate of troubles, and his subordinates, rather than being a source of new ideas, were looking to *him* for answers.

The solution Bill Hewlett found that squared this circle is the most celebrated of his career. Even at the time, it was covered in newspapers and magazines around the world, which rightly saw in it a new way of managing employees during hard times. And, looking back, it was Bill Hewlett's most brilliant innovation as a business executive, the management equivalent to that moment of genius thirty-five years before when he put the light bulb in the oscillator.

Hewlett's solution was simplicity itself, but the implications were immense and far-reaching. Simply, he asked every HP employee, from himself to the graveyard-shift janitors, to take off work every other Friday. Company VP John Doyle dubbed it "the Nine-Day Fortnight."

In announcing the plan, Hewlett also explained the reasoning behind his decision—his way of making sure that it wouldn't be abused. It was the essence of Bill Hewlett, and of the HP Way: "Usually in business, it is the little guy on the line who takes it on the chin, while management and higher-ups stay at work. It is only right that everyone share in the pain, up and down the line."[7]

Only sales was exempt from the new schedule, because its task remained that of maximizing revenues. All other HP offices—manufacturing, headquarters, R&D—shut down for the day every other Friday.*

The response inside Hewlett-Packard was unforgettable to anyone who worked at the company during this period. Recalled Minck, "The employee loyalty that resulted from this common sense plan was wonderful to see. Many employees actually came in to work on those Fridays, even though the production lines were shut down."[8]

Inside HP, where many employees had already resigned themselves to an inevitable layoff, the Nine-Day Fortnight plan produced an upwelling of gratitude, even love, for Hewlett-Packard—and Bill Hewlett in particular—that would carry the company through the next two decades, and would attach to Bill Hewlett for the rest of his life. Once again, the founders had come up with the perfect HP fork: a pragmatic solution that also had a humanitarian heart. Hewlett had managed to cut costs, but HP employees saw a company that would sacrifice itself before it sacrificed its people.

Outside the company, the reaction was, arguably, even more intense, especially in Silicon Valley. At a time when it seemed that every day the *San Jose Mercury-News* carried stories about bloody mass layoffs in the high-tech industry, when supervisors were being told to come up with lists of employees to be cut, and rich CEOs didn't seem to be compromising their own lives one iota, here, once again, the shining company on Page Mill Hill had found a way to protect its "family."

Hewlett's plan shamed executives everywhere who claimed they had "no choice." It also, in that complex way of all major Bill and Dave initiatives, managed to be enlightened and pragmatic at the same time. The plan, by convincing employees to take a 10 percent pay cut to save the jobs of other HPers (and perhaps themselves), managed to simultaneously cut overhead, preserve the company's intellectual capital, increase morale, earn billions of dollars worth of good publicity, position the company for the market turnaround, embarrass the competition, *and* be one of the best recruiting tools HP ever found.

Needless to say, a year later, when the economy finally recovered, Hewlett-Packard came out roaring. In fact, by the time Packard returned in early 1973, Hewlett and his team had, in the face of a recession, still managed to grow the company at the typical 15 percent per year during the three years Dave had been gone, increasing HP's annual revenues from $326 million to nearly $480 million. But even better, the company had developed and brought to market its single most famous product: the HP-35 calculator.

D.C. Dave Packard

Dave Packard's time inside the Beltway was one of almost continuous frustration. But it also made him a national figure. Given the success Bill Hewlett had back in Palo Alto, Packard's sojourn in Washington, though perhaps the least satisfying of his career, could only be accounted as a PR coup for both the man and his company.

As he would do during every shift his in career, Packard prepared for his new post at the Defense Department by studying every book he could on the topic. One historical anecdote that stood out to him was of recent vintage: just seven years before, during the Cuban Missile Crisis, Robert McNamara, Kennedy's defense secretary, had found himself in a dispute with the Joint Chiefs of Staff. Though the JCS officially reported to McNamara, when the secretary approached the admiral in charge with instructions on how to conduct the blockade, he was rudely told to go back to his office and leave the decision-making to the professionals.

Packard, though temperamentally the opposite of the notoriously technocratic McNamara, as a Republican the political opponent of the liberal former secretary, and emotionally drawn more to military officers than to politicians and government bureaucrats, nevertheless found himself agreeing completely with McNamara's position. "I think Bob McNamara was right. He should have had a say as part of the administration about how the blockade was to be handled."[9]

This assertion of common sense over any other consideration—including politics, sympathy, or precedent—would characterize Dave Packard's career as deputy secretary of defense. It would create many admirers across the country, but make many enemies in Washington.

It started out well. Secretary Melvin Laird had told Packard that he wanted to run the DoD with what he called "participatory management." As this vision seemed a philosophy congruent with the HP Way, Dave was optimistic that he could spark a cultural revolution in government the way he and Bill had in industry.

The first step, as it had been at Hewlett-Packard, was to build the family. To that end, Dave, with Bill, invited the Joint Chiefs to join them in a deer hunt at the San Felipe ranch—an event that would become an annual ritual. Though in future years these trips would be more formal and gracious, that first year Packard was intent on creating some shared experiences.

Each of the chiefs bagged a deer—and then came the work: they were expected to help with dressing the animals, cooking dinner, and washing the dishes, just as Bill and Dave had always done. The flag officers happily joined in. Sometime over the dirty dishes a friendship was formed between the chiefs and the founders that would last, like the annual hunting trip, long after Packard returned to Palo Alto.

But politics isn't business, and on the battlefield of procurement Dave Packard quickly found that his friends at San Felipe ranch would be bitter enemies in the halls of Congress and on the evening news. He also learned that doing the right thing can make enemies even among your erstwhile allies.

Packard arrived in Washington in early 1969 with some strong opinions about the relationship between the military and industry. Hewlett-Packard had been a long, though not particularly happy, defense contractor. And, as chairman of the Industry Advisory Council to the Department of Defense (a group of twenty-five industry executives, including another business legend, Walter Wriston of First National City Bank, that met three times per year at the Pentagon), Packard already had strong opinions about the world of military procurement. None of them were good.

The particular object of Packard's ire was a program called "total package procurement." Packard recalled, "Under that plan contractors who wanted to bid on military weapons were required to bid for the entire job of developing, testing, and manufacturing them. This might be a good theory, but it was simply impossible to make a bid on a weapons system that had not yet been designed."[10]

Proof of this fatal flaw in total package procurement was everywhere by the time Packard arrived in Washington. Indeed, almost from the moment he started on the job, he found himself embroiled in one scandal after another relating to the process: "Almost all of the programs under the total package procurement policy were in trouble, and we had to figure out how to deal with them."[11]

And it wasn't just the total package model that was flawed. Thanks to the Vietnam War, the DoD bureaucracy, already swollen from the cold war, was now almost paralyzed with indecision. According to aviation historian Charles Bright, beginning in 1947 "power [had] been increasingly centralized in the Pentagon, and within it the Office of the Secretary of Defense. The evidence points to increasing paralysis as a result. In the early seventies, even routine contract matters might call for fifty written concurrences."[12]

Packard would later say, in his diplomatic mode, that "there are a great many people in the department . . . it just takes a long time to get anything done, even some of the most simple recommendations." More candidly, he would tell Congress that he would just like to "give the contractor a contract without all of this damn red tape."[13]

As if this wasn't enough, Packard had little time to clean up the mess. Lockheed, one of the biggest defense contractors, was on the brink of bankruptcy, thanks to cost overruns on its giant new C-5A transport. At the same time, the military needed to get under way procuring a fast new fighter, featuring the latest electronics technology, to replace the Vietnam War workhorse the F-15, itself an example of cost overruns and bureaucratic compromise.

Packard thought he had a solution to the bureaucracy problem. But before he could address it, he had to keep alive those big companies victimized by the old system—Lockheed in particular. In early 1970, Lockheed, $3.1 billion into the still unfinished C-5A project, realized it would be paid only $2.6 billion by the government. That represented a potential final project loss of at least $650 million—enough to put the company into Chapter 11.

The subsequent chain of events, according to military historian Marcel Knaack, began with a letter:

> On March 2, 1970, Daniel J. Haughton, Chairman of the Board of Lockheed Aircraft Corporation, in a letter to Deputy Secretary of Defense David J. Packard, acknowledged Lockheed's worsening financial plight. Work on all of Lockheed's defense contracts would cease unless the company received between $600 and $700 million, most of it for the C-5A program.[14]

Haughton went on to say that Lockheed could not wait for the usual appeals process to get its money, but needed immediate interim financing to keep working. He admitted to some "deficiencies" on his company's part, but blamed total package procurement ("imprudent and adverse to our respective interests") as the real cause of Lockheed's predicament.

Privately, Dave Packard, the always financially conservative business-man, was disgusted that Lockheed could have ever gotten itself into such a predicament. Publicly, as deputy secretary of defense, it was his duty to find an acceptable resolution that would keep the military's most important new transport on track. After ten months of continuous negotiation, Packard met with Senator John C. Stennis (D), chairman of the Senate Armed Services Committee, and laid out what he saw as their options. According to Knaack:

> Prolonged litigation, said Packard, would leave Lockheed with "insuffi-cient cash and inadequate commercial credit to finance the continued operation of vital defense programs." Moreover, the company needed ad-ditional government funding and bank support to forestall bankruptcy; and Lockheed's failure, because of the intricate relationship among Lock-heed and other defense contractors and suppliers, could set off a disas-trous chain reaction in the American aerospace industry.[15]

As Packard saw it, there were two possible solutions. The first was to give Lockheed the disputed amount—now at $758 million—to keep it alive, then sue the company later to get back some fraction of that amount based on total aircraft deliveries. The second scenario was to convince Lockheed to drop all litigation immediately in exchange for $560 million, the company having to eat the remaining $200 million shortfall as a loss. Packard preferred this solu-tion because it ended the matter forever and let both the DoD and Lockheed get back to work. Both Laird and Stennis respected Packard's judgment enough to go with his preference.

Not surprisingly, Lockheed's Haughton responded hotly, calling Packard's plan to force his company to lose $200 million as an "excessive and unwar-ranted penalty." But he wasn't up against a government bureaucrat; rather he was squaring off against his superior in the business world. Packard didn't re-spond, but merely waited.

Unfortunately, Dan Haughton wasn't the other important figure upset about Dave Packard's decision. Senator William Proxmire (D), the U.S. Sen-ate's self-declared watchdog of government overspending, had been carefully tracking the C-5A almost from the beginning. Even while the negotiations were going on between Packard and Lockheed, Proxmire had brought up a vote in the Senate to kill the C-5A program altogether.

When Packard's plan was finally made public, Senator Proxmire erupted in disbelief, calling the deal a "bail-out" of Lockheed. It was a description that instantly stuck in the public's mind—and still does.

Dave Packard, who had simply tried to make the best out of an ugly situation, preserve an important new aircraft in production, and keep the aerospace industry solvent, all while trying to reform the Defense Department, found himself attacked from every side. The right saw him as betraying the free market itself: why should the government be propping up private corporations, no matter how big, to protect those companies from their own stupid business decisions? This was socialism.

The left, furious at the war and anyone connected with it, saw the Lockheed "bail-out" as a paradigmatic example of the government and the defense industry cozying up in a secret cabal. Showing how enduring this latter theory is, here is an extract from an academic paper from 1975 that was still being carried on the Web site of a UC Santa Cruz professor in 2006:

> In 1970, for example, Lockheed Aircraft Company, the nation's largest military contractor, was almost bankrupt. Lockheed's chairman, Dan Haughton (a member of IAC) and his banker, Walter Wriston of First National City Bank (also an IAC member) decided to visit Deputy Secretary of Defense David Packard (chairman of IAC). Wriston led a contingent of bankers to Washington to meet with Packard, and shortly thereafter the Administration proposed a $250 million loan guarantee to bail out Lockheed and its creditors.[16]

Later, when the C-5A played a crucial role in the final evacuation of Vietnam, then went on, with its descendants, to become the warhorse transport of the U.S. Air Force for the next three decades, these disputes were largely forgotten. (Lockheed, ironically, would go on to be awarded, by the Defense Department, the David Packard Award for Excellence in Acquisition.) But Dave Packard himself, though vindicated by events, would never fully escape the stigma of the Man Who Bailed Out Lockheed.

Packard, who had never known this kind of criticism, was stunned. But he had known what he was getting into, and didn't take it personally. It was also part of Dave's personality, once he had the facts and made up his mind, to charge on through no matter who disagreed with him. He was given a forum on the floor of Congress and in the press to respond to the charges. And, besides, he was David Packard, the man whom even heads of state looked to for advice—he knew who he was and didn't sweat the attacks on his character.

But Lucile had none of those advantages. This wasn't like the early days at HP, when she could participate in her husband's victories and failures. Now she was expected to put on a brave face, attend all of the right parties, and pretend she was unaffected by the unprecedented attacks on her husband. She paid a terrible price for her powerlessness—none of it, to his credit, lost on her husband. Packard recalled:

> The Washington years were also hard on the family. In the first few weeks, Lucile lost sixteen pounds. As she said at the time, "Each morning when I turned on the radio, they'd be saying something terrible about you, and that spoiled breakfast. Then at noon when I'd listen again it would be worse, and that spoiled lunch. Then you'd get home and tell me what an awful day you'd had and that spoiled dinner. So when was I supposed to eat?"
>
> After a while, she just stopped listening to the radio.[17]

Seeing this cost to his family, Packard resolved to get himself and his family out of Washington as soon as possible. But before he could leave, he still wanted to accomplish what he had come to Defense to do: replace the total package procurement process with a more rational weapons procurement program that produced the highest-quality and the most realistic price in the shortest time to delivery. He also knew that he would have to move quickly, as the pressure was building for the creation of a " 'hot,' small, and affordable" fighter that could fill the gaps left by the oversized and overloaded F-15.[18]

As part of his self-education in the history of the Defense Department, Packard had studied the DoD's counterparts in other countries. That research, and his own experiences as a defense contractor, convinced him that there was not only a better way, but that it had already been tried and mistakenly abandoned.

One of the most telling characteristics of both Bill and Dave was their boundless curiosity. For example, when Packard was asked to sit on the local school board, he immediately drove to Sacramento and spent an entire day at the state department of education, peppering the astonished staffers there with questions—not exactly typical behavior of a corporate CEO.

What Packard learned in his research about procurement was that, before World War II, the War Department had operated under an entirely different procurement system, one that paid aeronautics companies to create competing prototypes, and then selected the best candidates. The results had been literally earthshaking: the P-38, the B-17, the P-51, and the B-29. This system, because it rewarded the creation of cutting-edge design shops—such as Kelly Johnson's legendary "skunk works" at Lockheed—also led to the most innovative period in aviation history.

In the United States, all of that had been slowly lost in the postwar DoD bureaucracy. Total package procurement had been designed to take the waste

out of the program (by eliminating the competition between different aviation companies), but replaced it with a system that presented a single set of
specifications and expected competitors to bid blindly on the contract—
a process that took the onus of responsibility off the government and put it
on the backs of aerospace companies. Meanwhile, Packard's research told
him that in France, the Dassault Company had been able to build a new
fighter prototype from scratch and deliver it to the French military for just
$25 million—little more than a rounding error in the total cost of a full-
blown fighter contract.

After consulting with Dr. John Foster, the director of research at Defense,
Secretary of the Navy Barry Shillito, and a number of others, Packard decided
to bring back the old process. He decided that a prototype program should be
set up to produce not one but two prototype fighter planes and let them compete against each other.

"Fly before you buy," the phrase used to describe the process, was quickly
picked up by the media—to Dave Packard's dismay, as it would take too long
to actually build the prototypes and conduct a true fly-off.[19] And though
Packard felt obliged to publicly backtrack from the term as too ambitious,
"Fly before you buy" was such a simple and appealing notion that it perma-
nently attached itself to the project, and remains to this day the title of the
process.

But there was still one big problem. History also taught Packard that
prototype-based programs, especially with competitions attached, while usually more creative and efficient than total package procurement, were often
at least as expensive—an interesting parallel to new product creation at HP
itself.

However, this wasn't Dave Packard's company—and he got a glimpse of
the battle to come when Congress responded to his initial discussions about
the idea by wanting to take the money for the prototype program out of the
overall budget it had already approved. Such a notion ran smack into the
pressure coming from the White House. Almost from the day he had been
named deputy secretary, Packard had been a member of a task force, led by
Secretary of State Henry Kissinger, and including the likes of CIA director
Richard Helms and James Schlesinger from the Bureau of the Budget (and the
man who, as the next secretary of defense, would one day implement
Packard's plan). One of the first assignments of this task force was to find
ways to cut the defense budget to pay for the Nixon administration's domestic
programs.

Thus, even as he was cutting the defense budget on one hand, Dave
Packard was calling for added expenditures (Lockheed, prototyping) on the
other.

Few government officials could have navigated through this seeming contradiction—and perhaps only David Packard could have done so in the midst of the scandal-ridden Nixon administration.

The good news was that on the administration side, Packard's work, especially with Lockheed, had earned Dave considerable respect from both Secretary Laird and the president. For them, if Dave Packard needed more money to make his program real, he would get it.

Congress was a different matter. But here too, Packard's reputation worked to his advantage. Earlier in his tenure as deputy secretary, he had found himself embroiled in a matter in which two southern textile mills that supplied the military had consistently fallen short of their minority hiring goals. This had been going on for a long time—in fact, the Johnson administration had punted the problem in hopes of embarrassing its successor—and now it fell in Dave Packard's lap.

His solution was classic. Packard remembered how HP had "expended considerable effort . . . to increase the opportunities for the people in East Palo Alto, a predominately black community."[20] The effort had been largely unsuccessful until Packard heard about a Philadelphia organization called Opportunities Industrial Center (OIC), and its leader, the Reverend Leon Sullivan. OIC had been especially successful in helping gain employment for minority industrial workers in that city—so Packard contacted Reverend Sullivan and proposed the creation of OIC West. Then, to assure that the program would work, he also contacted all of the corporate CEOs in the Palo Alto area and invited them to join HP in hiring the program's graduates. It proved a great success, not least because most of the CEOs were honored even to be approached by David Packard.

Now Packard decided to do the same thing with the controversial southern mills. He contacted all three—perhaps not surprisingly, he personally knew two of the CEOs—and made a proposal: he would let them continue to serve as defense contractors, but only if they agreed to join a similar hiring program and show adequate progress in the years to come. It was a typical Packard move, finding a short-term practical solution that achieved a longer and larger goal.

Unfortunately, that wasn't how it was perceived at first by Congress. What Senator Ted Kennedy saw was that the Defense Department had gone ahead and retained contracts with three southern companies with a history of discrimination. He called Packard to give testimony before his subcommittee and explain his actions. But in the end, even Senator Kennedy agreed with Packard's solution—especially after Minority Leader Everett Dirksen showed up on Dave's behalf to intone that Packard "is right as rain."[21]

Dave Packard's eminently pragmatic fix to this problem was not lost in the hallways of the Capitol. He was now seen as a clever businessman who brought a new and innovative high-tech approach to seemingly intractable bureaucratic problems. And so when Packard finally brought his prototype competition acquisition model up for congressional approval, it was his reputation more than anything else that won the day.

Not long afterwards, the Defense Department embarked on the Light-Weight Fighter program, which culminated in a competitive "fly-off" between two prototypes, the McDonnell-Douglas YF-16 and the Northrop YF-17. In the end, unexpectedly, *both* won: the F-16 became the top fighter for the air force, while the YF-17, renamed the F-18, the jet of *Top Gun*, was the dominant navy fighter for a generation.

But by the time of the fighter fly-off, Dave Packard was long gone from Washington. He left behind a considerable legacy. His tenure at Defense was seen at the time as a shining example of how a smart, entrepreneurial business executive could bring new ideas and new life to even the most hidebound government bureaucracy. Today, looking back, military historians consider it one of the most successful and influential performances by any deputy secretary in the last fifty years—hence the DoD's decision to name its highest procurement award after Dave Packard.

Packard's three years in Washington did something else as well: it opened the door to later generations of Silicon Valley executives to serve inside the Beltway, from sitting on task forces to giving congressional testimony, even to running for elected office. And after Packard's accomplishments, Washington would henceforth look to Silicon Valley for new ideas, business expertise, and new blood.

But for Dave Packard, those years in Washington were an exhausting and frustrating sidetrack in an otherwise happy career. In the years to come, he would sit on a number of government commissions, always trying to streamline the DoD bureaucracy, improve interservice communications, and establish common defense industry standards and protocols. In his final years, he liked to think that in some small way he had helped to transform the U.S. military from an organization riven by rivalries, communications breakdowns, and dysfunctionality during the Vietnam War to the efficient, coordinated fighting force of the Gulf War.

As for Packard himself, describing his Washington years in his memoir, he would say that now he understood what President Eisenhower meant when he warned of the dangers of a "military-industrial complex"—a remarkable comment that positioned him very close to his greatest detractors.

A more accurate description of Packard's disgust with his time in Washington came when he was asked by a *Business Week* reporter what he thought was his greatest accomplishment at the Pentagon. "Well," Packard replied, "I gave up smoking."

But Packard's real last word on the matter, a quote that would be reprinted many times in the years to come, came in response to yet another reporter's question about how he had found his time in government. "Working with the Washington bureaucracy," he replied, "is like pushing on one end of a forty-foot rope, and trying to get the other end to do what you want."

The Engineer's Engineer

Because they so often conferred before making decisions—to the point that they eventually could intuit each other's responses—it is easy to assume that Bill and Dave managed in the same way, with the same attitudes and goals.

But, for all of their common interests, they were not the same man. Packard's time in Washington offers a rare glimpse in the HP story of how Hewlett managed differently from his partner.

Packard, as seen throughout this story, was a tough, unsentimental businessman, with a basic decency toward his employees that translated into a kind of corporate noblesse oblige. His was a zone strategy: under Packard, HP entered new markets very carefully, but once in them flooded the market with superior products across the board, especially at the profitable high end. His lateral moves were typically small: a standard HP move under Packard was to own a particular market, take on a new one nearby (such as patient and fetal monitoring), then find a way to link them together with a high-end multiuse product (patient management systems for nurses' stations).

As a business strategy, Packard's style was relentless and intimidating. Throughout the 1950s and 1960s, HP seemed to move across the instrument world in a carefully coordinated attack on a wide front, continuously enveloping and overrunning more narrowly focused competitors.

But this strategy, powerful as it was, had a major weakness: it was vulnerable to time and innovation. With the former, the risk was always that over time the market would mature, prices would fall, products would become commoditized, and profits would disappear. Packard met that challenge with his complete lack of institutional nostalgia—he cared for employees, not products. Packard was prepared to abandon *any* HP business the moment it began to lose its profitability. HPers, in fact, learned to hide old company inventory—as Bill Terry did with the early company instruments, including the 200A, that would eventually become the heart of the HP museum—before Packard ordered them sold for scrap or tossed in a Dumpster.

As for innovation—the very real threat in high tech that some revolutionary new technology will instantly render one's entire business obsolete—Packard protected HP in two ways: by diversifying the company's product line across almost the entire breadth of the instrument business, and by funding a world-class R&D operation, under the redoubtable Barney Oliver, to constantly scour the world for the potential new technical competition. These new competitors Packard either bought, beat to market, or outflanked.

Still, none of these strategies solved the larger issue of the test and measurement industry itself growing old and unprofitable. In some ways, that challenge was beyond David Packard—he was radical, but not a revolutionary.

But Bill Hewlett was a different story. His lifelong love of technology, and his perpetual search for the Next Big Thing, made him a risk-taker in a way his partner never was. Given a choice, Hewlett would always throw deep, hoping for a tech touchdown. Though both men were far too complicated to encompass in a single image, it nevertheless might be said that for Dave Packard, technology was the means by which he achieved his business ambitions, while for Bill Hewlett, business was the vehicle by which he realized his technology dreams.

By the same token, for Hewlett it often seemed that other HPers were fellow members of an immense new product design team, all working together as compatriots and professionals toward a common goal.

Needless to say, the Bill Hewlett business strategy had some very serious vulnerabilities, the most obvious being that every one of these leaps into the technological unknown could also prove to be a jump into business oblivion. If Packard's HP risked being insular, Hewlett's had the danger of being overextended and misdirected. But together, as long as the two men could get along (which they seemed to do almost effortlessly), it was a near-perfect combination.

Less obvious is that separately, for short intervals, and under the constraints of the HP Way, both Dave's and Bill's individual business styles could also be extraordinarily effective. Packard proved that during the Second World War. Now, in the early seventies, during the three years his partner was in Washington, Bill Hewlett showed that his strategy worked just as well. In fact, those three years under Hewlett alone would prove to be the most innovative and exhilarating in Hewlett-Packard company history.

Time to Dream

Bill set the tone early. Even as the recession raged, and the company cut back to the Nine-Day Fortnight, Hewlett instituted what would be the partners' last important proactive personnel innovation at HP. Never official, it was nicknamed the "G-Job," or "government work." John Minck explains, "The idea was that every engineer was to be allowed to spend up to 10 percent of their paid work time on product concepts—not in the official plan—that might result in a saleable product. This was to include necessary model shop time for building materials, or purchased parts if needed."[22]

The reality was that Hewlett was essentially offering back to his employees time for which they were largely idled by the recession anyway. Moreover, most HPers who were still busy for the entire day likely added their "g-time" after hours anyway. But the gesture was deeply appreciated by Hewlett-Packard employees, and had some stunning results. Implicit in Hewlett's decision was a very special kind of social contract: I've saved everyone's jobs—now invent us out of these hard times.*

HPers across the company responded enthusiastically. Even Barney Oliver tried his hand at a new product idea. The result was a radically new solid-state amplifier for home stereo systems that featured noise, hum, and distortion lower than almost any other stereo amplifier at any price. Because it didn't fit with the company's current business strategy, the amplifier was never offered to the public, only to HP employees, who could buy kits from a special in-house run of front panels, enclosures, knobs, and printed circuit boards. It proved so popular that at least two production runs, totaling about two hundred amplifiers, were completely sold out. Today, a real "Barney Oliver Amp" costs collectors a tidy sum on eBay.

A second g-time invention also came from Barney Oliver, who seemed to take the set-aside time as a personal challenge. In this case, the idea came from an HP salesperson in Chicago who, over a drink one night, happened to mention to Oliver that one of the biggest frustrations facing test engineers was the need to cut a power wire to determine the current going down it. There had to be a different way, said the salesman.

Intrigued, Oliver went back to HP Labs and, with the assistance of one of his researchers, came up with what would be the HP 428A probing ammeter. Thanks to a built-in circuit that could measure the magnetic field produced by a passing current, the HP 428A merely had to be clamped over the intact wire. It proved to be a successful and enduring product.

But that was just the beginning: another engineer at HP Labs, reading about the need by banks for high-speed check processing, rejiggered the probe into a flat reader, and used it to detect the magnetic ink code on a passing check. This invention too sold in huge numbers.

But the biggest g-time invention, the one that changed modern civilization, would come later, in the mid-seventies, when a young HPer at the company's new Advanced Products Division in Cupertino, Steve Wozniak, would use HP time and tools to invent—the personal computer.

HP's Greatest Product

In a very short time, Bill Hewlett had created a maverick innovative environment at Hewlett-Packard. Now it began to pay off. The middle-aged company suddenly felt young again—and ready to stir things up.

The opportunity came soon thereafter.

The four years since the introduction of the HP 9100 desktop computer had seen major changes in the calculator industry, and not just at Hewlett-Packard. At HP, the Loveland, Colorado, division (where the desktop computing operation had been transferred) had continued to evolve the original 9100 design into a new generation of much more sophisticated scientific desktop calculators.

This 9810/20/30 family was not only capable of much more powerful computing than the original 9100, but was also able—thanks to the HP-IB interfacing protocol—to operate multiple peripheral devices, or be plugged directly into laboratory or factory automation systems. This quickly made HP desktop computers the new workhorses of labs and assembly lines around the world—and, as originally planned, helped to further spur the sale of compatible HP test and measurement instruments.

But if HP owned the high-end desktop business, the low end—the descendants of the original four-function adding machines—was a near-chaos of dozens of competitors all scrapping for market share and facing oblivion in an inevitable shakeout. Among the players in this market were not only industry veterans such as Texas Instruments and Friden, and newcomers such as Bowmar, but a whole new generation of Japanese electronics companies—notably Sharp, Canon, and Sanyo—that saw these high-volume, low-priced devices as a way to break into the U.S. consumer electronics business.

The result was high tech's first consumer electronics bubble, with each competitor trying to capture customers with lower prices, smaller designs, and superior marketing. By the end of the 1960s, some of these companies even had secret design projects under way to build true handheld calculators. By 1969, TI was able to show a prototype four-function calculator, code-named "Cal-Tech," that would even fit in one's pocket. At about the same time, Sharp announced a new "portable" calculator that would use the newest generation of large-scale integration (LSI) logic and memory chips. Moore's law had come to calculators—and, ironically, calculators were about to come to the home of Gordon Moore himself, Intel Corp.

It was an also-ran in the calculator wars, the Japanese company Busicom, which unconsciously sparked the creation of the so-called product of the century and changed the high-tech world forever. Busicom had struggled to keep up with its bigger competitors even during the good times. Now, as the downturn loomed, its executives concluded that the company's only hope of survival was to bet everything on one roll of the dice: convince a U.S. chip maker to come up with a custom calculator chip set with the smallest possible number of chips. If this could be done, Busicom might be able to leapfrog its competitors both in downsizing the product and cutting costs.

The company approached two U.S. semiconductor makers, Mostek and Intel; and while the former would eventually become Busicom's supplier, it was Intel that made the revolution. A team that included Ted Hoff, Stan Mazor, Federico Faggin, and Busicom's own Masatoshi Shima set out in October 1969 to build a four-chip package that would perform all of the functions of a basic calculator and more.

It took them a year, but the result, the 4004, proved to be more than just a chip set for a calculator. It was, in fact, the first microprocessor, the long-dreamed-of "computer on a chip," and, billions of units and a dozen generations later, the defining invention of the modern world. Within months after completing the 4004, Intel created the 8-bit 8008 and, in 1972, the epochal Intel 8080, the direct ancestor of the Pentium family and almost every other microprocessor on the planet. Luckily for history, Busicom didn't want the 4004 and reverted the rights to Intel—a decision that has proven to be worth (to date) more than $100 billion to Intel.

None of these changes were lost on Hewlett-Packard. Tom Osborne had not forgotten the comment Hewlett had made that day they showed the 9100A to An Wang: that he wanted the next machine to be "a tenth the cost, a tenth the size, and be ten times faster than the HP 9100." Instead, the 9800 family had stayed the same size, and about the same price, and grown at least one hundred times more powerful.

But even if Osborne had forgotten Hewlett's challenge, Bill Hewlett had not. Osborne recalled, "I knew he was serious, but we were kept hostage by the lack of low-power integrated circuits."[23] Without those chips, it seemed impossible to build a multifunction, battery-powered, handheld scientific calculator. But that didn't keep Hewlett from regularly asking about the progress of the project: "I was visited regularity by Bill Hewlett who wanted to know why we were not working on the calculator he had prescribed. The pressure cooker would have been hotter had Mr. Packard not been in Washington at the Department of Defense. Nonetheless, when he did visit the labs, he asked the same question."[24] Luckily for the oppressed Osborne, in 1971, before Dave Packard came home to make his life even more miserable, he came across an article in a trade magazine. It described how Mostek was using a new fabrication process called ion implantation to create chips that required only a tiny fraction of the usual amount of current to operate. (Ironically, Mostek was building these chips for the next—and final—generation of Busicom calculators.) With these chips, Osborne knew he could build a handheld 9100. On the very day he read the article, he went to Bill Hewlett and told him that now, three years later, HP could finally build the calculator Hewlett wanted.

Then, as company legend has it, Osborne asked Bill what size he thought the new calculator should be. Hewlett pondered for a moment, then pointed at the chest pocket of his white, short-sleeved dress shirt. Small enough to fit in that pocket, he said.

Osborne had his marching orders. He quickly contacted the team he wanted to design the device, his old friend Paul Stoft and the HP Labs design team led by Tom Whitney.

> I knew I would have a bit of trouble getting the project staffed because Paul Stoft, Tom Whitney, and Tom's engineers were hard at work on a briefcase-sized something-or-other. This was one of a very few times that I used whatever power I had to pressure Paul and Tom to change their minds about what they wanted to be doing for the next couple of years. I told them that if they were sure we could not do a shirt pocket calculator, then they would have to explain their reasons to Bill Hewlett—because I had already told him that we could do it. During the next few days, they decided that it just might be possible.[25]

It was a remarkable moment. In less than a week, an outside contractor presents a radically new product, based on a largely unproven technology, to the CEO of a $500 million firm with 20,000 employees, gets an immediate green light, and then redirects one of the company's top design teams to take on the project. The phrase "agile corporation" wouldn't be invented for another quarter century, but Hewlett-Packard during this era already personified it.

It was only after the team was assembled and under way that Osborne and his group made a wonderful discovery. Over at HP Associates, the company's components division, another team had just spent two years working with a Phoenix company named Unidynamics to create the keyboard and display for a radically new calculator design. This team had spent two years coming up with a number of innovations, including an inexpensive photoconductor keyboard of spectacular reliability, and a low-power LED display that would be magnified by an optical screen, all part of a larger effort to help Unidynamics come up with a four-function calculator (with some added functions hidden in memory for future use) the size of a pack of cigarettes for just $200—half the price and size of the competition's best.

HPA gave the client everything it asked for—only to have Unidynamics suddenly and without warning cancel the project. The reason? Unidynamics never explained, but it is likely that its market research had estimated a total market for the new calculator of just 10,000 units. In fact, given that it would have been a year ahead of the market, Unidynamics likely would have sold as many as 100,000 of the planned calculator. Historian John Minck, who was part of that team, explained what happened next—and offers a glimpse of how the HP Way's philosophy of trustworthiness affected even the company's internal communications:

> Once we confirmed that the project was clearly cancelled, we felt we were released from our self-imposed HPA rules about revealing any sales details to other HP entities. We always held such information strictly confidential during our contract periods. In the components business, such technical and business details were sacrosanct. If another HP entity should discover any such details about a competitor, we would lose all credibility.[26]

This is a very long way from the standard business practices of the rest of Silicon Valley during this period.

Now unleashed from any commitment to Unidynamics, Minck drafted a memo to HP Labs that laid out the nature of the planned calculator and the breakthroughs HPA had already accomplished to help realize it. Serendipitously, one of the scientists on the routing of that memo, dated January 27, 1970, was Paul Stoft. So, twenty months later, when Tom Osborne came calling with the idea for a pocket scientific calculator, Stoft already knew that half of the technical obstacles to such a device were already solved.

Looking back, Osborne would describe the creation of this new calculator as one of the happiest times of his working career:

> The HP35 project was just plain fun. We knew it would work (the algorithms were similar to those in the HP 9100) so we spent a lot of time deciding whether the arithmetic keys should be on the right or the left, and whether the "+" key should follow the convention of adding machines

and be placed in the lower right corner, or whether it should be located where it is most convenient. As I recall, we did not seem to be the least bit worried about the fact that we were going to be the first people to have non-standard key spacing. After all, if the thing was to fit in a shirt pocket, the keys had to be crunched together.

. . . The [calculator's] design-to-production cycle was incredibly short for a product of that complexity. We got the official go ahead on Ground Hog's day (Feb. 2) and demonstrated working machines to the Board of Directors in August. I still do not know how it happened in such a short time. I remember being busy, but I do not recall having had any major hang-ups.[27]

Perhaps not for Tom Osborne, but over at HPA the calculator team had to break through one problem after another. One of the biggest came with the realization that Whitney's team would only be willing to pay $1.05 for each digit on the LED display—and that it would cost HPA $5 each to build them.

The only solution was to upgrade HPA's Gallium Arsenide Phosphide lab to produce cheaper chips. But that promised to be a $500,000 investment—more than that team had ever asked for at one time. And that would need approval from Bill Hewlett himself.

What the HPA didn't know was at that moment their odds of getting approval just got infinitely lower. With initial estimates that the new scientific calculator might cost as much as $350 to build, almost double the average price of standard calculators currently on the market, Hewlett had ordered a market research study on potential sales for a high-end calculator. The results weren't heartening—even at $395, the proposed calculator was likely to generate sales of just 1,000 units per month as best. Bill Terry, who was now vice president of the HP Instrument Group, recalled:

One day the phone rang and Hewlett says, "We've got this calculator going on at HP labs." So I went up and talked to Bill and he gave me the market research report that suggested we shouldn't do it. [It's going to cost] twenty times more than a slide rule.

Then, Bill said, "I *want* one of these things."[28]

That was it. Looking at market research that offered an even worse prediction than the one that had scared off Unidynamics, his partner a continent away, at the head of a company dragging itself out of recession, Bill Hewlett had made the decision to spend HP's talent and fortune on a project that might, even if it proved possible to build, never find customers.

It was Hewlett's riskiest and bravest business decision. And it is likely that he was the only person at HP who could have made it. Even Dave Packard, with his preference for playing within his game, likely would have killed the project (though once he heard that Bill had made the decision, he stood behind his partner 100 percent).

But Hewlett during this period, like Steve Jobs at Apple a decade later, was so perfectly attuned to HP's market that their interests and desires were almost congruent: at that moment, Bill Hewlett knew that if he liked some new piece of technology, such as this calculator, hundreds of thousands of other scientists and engineers out there would too.*

Did he make the right choice? History says it was a decision of genius. But in the context of the HP Way and the HP Corporate Objectives, it could also be deemed foolhardy and dangerous. But that's why Dave Packard was there: to keep Bill Hewlett from chasing new ideas for their own sake. Just as Bill was there to make sure that Dave remained open to new ideas.

Now that Hewlett had made up his mind to pursue the calculator project, there would be no stopping him. The goal now was to remove any obstacles in the path of Whitney's team getting the prototype built.

Meanwhile, the nervous HPA team held one last meeting before presenting its proposal for a new $500,000 lab. Beyond the potential sales of the new, improved LEDs to the calculator group, the division's marketing people had convinced themselves that there might be another, outside, market for the stand-alone displays. How big? They had no idea. Finally, division manager Dave Weindorf announced abruptly, "What the hell, let's make it a proposal for a cool three-quarters of a million."[29]

The team quickly rejiggered the numbers and, the next day, went to see Hewlett. Like the founders of the division had a dozen years before, they had prepared an elaborate presentation justifying both the project and its price tag. And like Packard had then, Hewlett now waved them off. According to Minck:

> We had our arguments well-honed and practiced. . . . [But] after five minutes of preliminaries, presenting our executive summary, Bill stopped us, saying, "I've got another meeting, so is there anything else important that I should know? If not, let's go with it."
>
> It was by far the easiest project I have ever sold.[30]

Now it was up to Tom Whitney and his crew, notably Dave Cochran, the unsung hero of the project, who was in charge of designing all of the "algorithms" (the simple mathematical steps that produced the complex functions) for the calculator. As for Tom Osborne, unlike the 9100, his involvement in the actual circuit design of the new calculator was minimal. Rather, he focused on what functions the device should feature and making sure the final design would lend itself to what he saw as its natural follow-up: a programmable calculator.

Yet even choosing the functions for the calculator proved complicated, largely because of the endless meddling of both Hewlett and Barney Oliver. It continued right up until the moment Whitney had to send the final integrated circuit masks to the semiconductor fabricators. Finally, in exasperation, Whitney sent a memo to all concerned saying that he had reserved a meeting room for the entire day, and the group would meet to "freeze the keyboard functions to everyone's satisfaction."[31]

It did, in fact, take all day to reach an agreement; but at last everyone signed their signature to the document. Exhausted, Whitney walked back to his office to put the final touches on the paperwork in preparation for sending it off in the morning. He arrived to find the phone ringing. It was Barney Oliver: "I've got another idea."

"Too late," said Whitney and hung up.

Almost instantly, he had second thoughts. Oliver was, after all, not only the most brilliant person at HP, but also his *boss*. So he quickly put in a call to Bill Hewlett to explain what had just happened.

Go with the signed paper, Hewlett told him.[32]

That August, the prototype Osborne demonstrated to the HP board of directors, like the 9100 before it, was basically a finished but empty calculator case with a cable coming out of the top to a larger box containing the actual working components. But it was enough to amaze the board, and thrill Bill Hewlett.

Later, in a meeting with marketing, Hewlett went over possible names for the calculator. The brainstormed titles ranged from the mundane (The Math Marvel) to the silly (Captain Billy's Whiz Bang Machine)—four pages of names in all, and not one of them a winner.[33] Finally, Osborne turned to Hewlett and asked, "Do you have any preference?"

> Bill looked at the machine for a minute or so and said, "Let's call it the
> HP 35." It sounded OK to me, but why the 35? He smiled and said, "Well,
> it has 35 keys."[34]

And that was it. The HP-35, according to *Forbes ASAP* magazine one of the twenty products that changed the modern world, had its name. To those involved in its creation, the calculator seemed like an almost mystical experience. Osborne recalled, "Looking back, it seems as if the HP-35 had a life of its own. It simply chose HP as its birthplace."[35]

Retailing a Revolution

Creating the HP-35 calculator was one thing; selling it was another. Within Hewlett-Packard there were serious doubts, even among the legions of HPers who quickly fell in love with the little marvel, whether there would be enough of a market for the device to escape serious losses, much less break even. Not only did the market research predict failure, but the very eccentricity of the HP-35, a product of all those internal battles over functionality, argued against public acceptance as well.

For example, the HP-35 featured tiny keys in a nonstandard pattern, as well as a computational language, called Reverse Polish Notation, that sounded like a joke. RPN was, in fact, an extremely efficient way to string together multiple operations without the need for traditional parentheses, equal signs, and other formatting. But it was also counterintuitive to anyone (that is, every one of HP's engineer customers) who had grown up with traditional arithmetic. For example, in RPN, 2 + 2 = became 2 2 +. It was as if Alexander Graham Bell had invented the telephone and then demanded that people only speak Hittite when they used it.

And yet none of that seemed to matter, because once they saw the HP-35, people simply *had to own it*. It was the first great example of digital consumer product hysteria, an augur of what was to come with video games, digital watches, the Macintosh, Windows, and iPod. Orders for the HP-35 poured in so fast that manufacturing at Hewlett-Packard was quickly overwhelmed—creating shortages that only fanned the flames of demand. A secondary market appeared of people who were lucky enough to have scored an HP-35 early, and were now reselling it at inflated prices. People sold their cars, fudged requisitions, and skipped meals to buy an HP-35. On college campuses around the world, a market HP had considered minor for such an expensive tool, ownership of an HP-35 was the zenith of cool in the engineering and science departments.

So great was demand for the HP-35 that even a black market formed for machines that had been stolen off lab tables and office desks—even ripped right out of the hands of astonished owners. The theft rate was so great at NASA and other big research laboratories that those organizations began putting the HP-35 into locking cradles fixed to tabletops—the 1970s equivalent of the books chained to walls in medieval libraries. When the U.S. Army refused to honor purchase orders for such an expensive item, the scientists at the White Sands Proving Ground, seeing extra money still in the training budget, merely announced a new course in "Reverse Polish Notation Scientific Computers." The tuition fee: $500, which included a new HP-35 "training tool."

But the HP-35 was more than just a precious novelty. It is hard to gauge just how great was the *cultural* impact of the calculator on both HP and, frankly, the modern world. For thousands of young people, the HP-35 was a glimpse of just how miraculous high technology had become. Here was an invention they could hold in their hands that had as much computing power as the million-dollar, room-sized computers they had seen in movies, such as had been used just a decade before to put a man in space.

Even Tom Osborne found himself overwhelmed. On a visit to Washington, he stopped by the Smithsonian to take a look at ENIAC, the first important American digital computer, built in the early 1940s to compute artillery trajectories. With 18,000 vacuum tubes, it was the size of a house—so big that technicians ran around in bathing suits inside its glowing racks replacing tubes that burned out on average every twelve minutes. As he read ENIAC's performance specifications, Osborne was staggered with the realization that the little HP-35 he had in his coat pocket was more powerful, and immensely more reliable, than the behemoth in front of him.

The HP-35 would eventually join ENIAC on display at the Smithsonian.

One young man in Silicon Valley who was especially affected by the HP-35 was a brilliant young computer programmer named Steve Wozniak. Woz had just dropped out of the University of Colorado at Boulder and was attending a local junior college just a few blocks from his old high school and trying to get his life back together. He had built a celebrated four-function calculator while still in junior high school, and now, seeing the HP-35—"I just drooled seeing that thing"[36]—he had an epiphany. Though it had long been assumed that he would follow his father in working at Lockheed, Wozniak decided that his future belonged with Hewlett-Packard, working on calculators and computers.

Though none of the others would go on to invent the personal computer, thousands of other young people were drawn into the sciences by the ease with which the HP-35 could cut through what had been laborious calculations. In the meantime, two of the most venerable of all technology businesses, with centuries of enduring success behind them—slide rules and books of scientific tables—died seemingly overnight. The HP-35, John Minck would write, was "not only a prestigious personal possession, but an amazing drudgery beater. It made better engineers, and it made them faster and more efficient."[37]

The prediction had been for, at most, 1,000 HP-35s sold per month. The reality was an order of magnitude greater: 10,000 per month, and the number would have been even higher had HP been able to build them. In the end, it would take eighteen months for Hewlett-Packard to finally catch up with demand—and by then, the company had the HP-35's nearly as famous successor already in the pipeline, ready to set off another rush. By the time the scientific calculator finally merged into the PC in the early 1990s, the HP-35 and its descendants would sell more than 20 million units for Hewlett-Packard, making them the most popular products in the company's history. Said Bill Terry, "Bill was willing to take a risk—and boy was he right."[38]

Selling Uncertainty

For good and bad, the HP-35 also taught Hewlett-Packard something about consumer marketing and retailing. Thanks to the efforts over the course of thirty years by Noel Eldred, Russ Berg, and Dave Kirby, as well as the company's veteran PR, advertising, and marketing professionals, HP knew how to sell technology to technologists about as well as anybody.

But the breakout of the HP-35 changed everything. Before that, the height of clever marketing at the company had been Barney Oliver's inspired decision to send, preintroduction, HP-35s to fifty Nobel Prize winners. A few months later, the company looked up to find itself selling calculators to college kids, even teenagers. And HP had little idea of even how to *talk* to these consumers.

On the sales side, salesmen, marketing types, even group VP Bill Terry fanned out to talk to retailers and learn something about selling to consumers. They got an earful. Remembered Packard:

> Bill Terry vividly recall[ed] going to Macy's department store in San Francisco. Macy's, at that time, was interested in building an electronics department. Bill remembers showing the calculator, eliciting interest, striking a deal on the price, then starting to talk about order and delivery schedules.
>
> At that point the Macy's manager placed both hands squarely on the table in front of him, looked Bill in the eye, and said, "You young boys don't understand. I don't sell anything unless I have it in the store." That was our initiation into the consumer market.[39]

HP had always been either a contract supplier of equipment or a one-off catalog seller. Now it had to learn how to build for inventory, to keep retailers' shelves replenished, and to budget for returns. It was training that would serve the company well in another twenty years with inkjet printers and personal computers.

Meanwhile, HP advertising also found itself in a brave new world of consumer promotion: student discounts, back-to-school promotions, expensive consumer media print advertising, packaging, point-of-sale promotion, four-color brochures—all of the standard tools for promoting to mass audiences. It was not something HP took to easily, and it would be many years before the company's advertising looked like more than tweaked-up trade press marketing.

HP corporate PR faced its own challenges. The good news was that the HP-35 didn't need much promoting: the world's media came to Hewlett-Packard for stories on the little miracle. But for the first time, the company found itself barraged with requests for review models, donations, sponsorships of everything from America's Cup yachts to dirt-bike racers, and free gifts for the rich and famous. For thirty years, the only people who had requested free HP instruments were trade magazine reporters who were often as technically astute as HP's own engineers. Now, HP public relations found itself dealing with reporters who took review machines and never returned them, or, in one case, plugged it into the power cord of his electric shaver, blew up the calculator, taped it into a standard envelope, and mailed it back to HP demanding another one.

Public relations learned to be patient and as accommodating as possible to all of these requests. Still, it did draw the line at sponsorships—mostly because Kirby and his team were fearful of an image on the nightly news of the sole surviving remnant of a burning land speed record contender or the floating shard of an exploded hydroplane bearing the HP logo.

It was only after the HP-35 had been on the market for a few months that HP public relations began to hear some extraordinary stories about the little calculator—and quickly began to turn those tales into a series of popular press releases. It seemed that, thanks to the overengineering of almost every part of the HP-35, especially the keyboard and the high-impact plastic case, the calculator was astonishingly durable. Stories began to come in about HP-35s being bounced off the backs of motorcycles at seventy miles per hour, dropped into a bucket of molten lead, frozen in a pond over the winter—and when finally retrieved, even as a twisted lump of plastic, having an uncanny ability to still work.

This only added to the HP-35 legend, especially when HP PR began to distribute these survival stories to the media. The success of these releases led Kirby and his team to embark a series of "application" stories about how the HP-35, and later, other HP products, were being used in unusual real-life applications from determining medication dosages in emergency rooms to calculating flight paths of bush pilots to directing the operations of giant earthmoving equipment.

These features, which would eventually number in the hundreds (and would be Hewlett-Packard's most enduring contribution to the PR profession), enabled HP to be the first high-tech company to reach beyond the electronics trade press into the mainstream media. Before long, stories of the HP-35 and its descendants were appearing in everything from *Time* magazine to the *National Enquirer*.*

Meanwhile, over at HP Labs, the HP-35's creators were also learning some important lessons from their little machine—mostly about duplicity. Dave Cochran, the algorithm expert, found himself at gatherings with potential future competitors from Bowmar and Texas Instruments, equally clever and competitive mathematicians, whose reputations rose and fell in their profession with whoever came up with the most elegant and powerful equations. But at the same time, all were also scouting competitive information for their employers. Minck recounts:

> It became a kind of chess game. They might tell about a new algorithm idea, but might salt-in traps and false leads to put the other company on the wrong track. Naturally, there were advantages to be gained in talking together since, often, it established industry standards and processes, and it was an arcane art. Yet, all information had to be taken with huge caution. Did we gain more than we lost? Knowing Cochran, I suspect we gained a lot more.[40]

Tom Osborne, as the best-known name connected with the HP-35 project, found himself in an even brighter spotlight. As the HP-35 was being finalized, heedful of his promise to Bill Hewlett to put the power of an HP desktop computer in one's pocket, Osborne took it upon himself to fight for certain specifications in the calculator that would lend itself to a more powerful follow-up machine. In particular, he intended for this next calculator, unlike the HP-35, to be fully programmable.

Calculating Opportunities

The astounding success of the HP-35 not only immediately green-lighted Osborne's follow-up plan, but also drew a host of competitors hungry for a piece of the huge new market. In the end, three different calculator models would enter the design phase. Two of them, the HP-45, a more powerful version of

the original, and the HP-55, a programmable calculator, were already anticipated by the analysts, customers, and competitors.

But it was the third, the HP-65, that Osborne knew would be the company's next great product, and the linchpin of HP's future dominance in the
calculator business. What made the HP-65 revolutionary was that it was not
only programmable, but it featured a tiny magnetic card reader. Users could
simply feed a narrow strip of plastic, containing a complex application program (that is, a series of mathematical equations, rather than a computer's
programming code), into a slot in the side of the HP-65 behind the display,
and the calculator would then be programmed to perform the operation.
Even better, users could write their own programs, run a blank strip through
the HP-65, and preserve their application for future use.

There was simply nothing in the world like the HP-65, and Osborne knew
it. He decide to protect the crown jewels, even if it meant violating the HP
Way: "By that time, everyone in the calculator business was aiming at HP. I
knew they would be second guessing what we were doing, so at a convention
at which I was a speaker, I somewhat intentionally misled the competition by
telling them that to just have a programmable calculator was inadequate. The
programs had to be easily loaded into the machine."[41]

So far, so honest—but then Osborne decided to send the competition on a
wild goose chase. To the assembled, he dissembled: "Keying them in once is
OK, but successive loadings should come from a magnetic media, like an ex-
ternal tape reader (at the time we were designing an internal card reader into
the HP 65). When we introduced the HP 65 with its tiny internal mag reader,
I could hear the competitor's projects fall by the wayside."[42]

If anyone at HP knew beforehand about Osborne's planned misrepresentation, they didn't stop him. It wasn't in the spirit of the HP Way, but it
worked. If anything, the HP-65 made an even bigger explosion on the market
than the HP-35. Consumers were now prepared for something new, and the
HP-65 delivered. Even the $695 retail price didn't scare them away—on
the contrary, demand had now become so inelastic for HP calculators that the
higher price merely made the calculator more exclusive and desirable.*

The HP-65 was destined for the Smithsonian too. And with good reason.
It was not only a masterpiece of compact, reliable design, but it radically
enhanced the productivity of professionals from scientists and engineers to
doctors and educators. It also brought, for the first time, the power of programming into the everyday working world—thus setting the stage for the
personal computer. So influential, in fact, was the HP-65 that it became emblematic of the entire electronics industry in the early 1970s. And, if anything,
the hysteria surrounding it—thefts, cooked books, students selling their pos-
sessions to own one, reporters scamming "review" copies—was even greater.

And HP's PR, advertising, and marketing operations, now with some experience, had a field day getting the story out.

As was standard practice at HP, as the HP-35 had rolled out of HP Labs and into manufacturing, the company had created a new division to manage it. HP's Advanced Products Division was located a few miles from headquarters in Cupertino, in an anonymous leased building across the street from HP's new computer division campus.

If the computer operation was classic HP, from the cubicles to the standardized building and grounds, APD was anything but. In retrospect, it was the prototype of the next generation of Valley entrepreneurs, and one that still survives at places such as Google and eBay: offices filled with toys and tchochkes, endless practical jokes, all-night work sessions, active rebellion against company dress codes and management hierarchies—all of the Triumph of the Nerds corporate culture that would soon capture the world's imagination a few blocks away at the newly founded Apple Computer.

This wasn't a coincidence. One of the new young hires at APD was Steve Wozniak, who quickly used his salary and employee discount to buy an HP-65—the calculator he would sell (along with Steve Jobs's VW van) to finance the founding of Apple. And Apple itself was a company that Wozniak and Jobs self-consciously modeled after those things—the HP Way, the spirit of innovation, and the culture of APD—they most admired at Hewlett-Packard. (Jobs, in fact, was so much in thrall of HP that he presented Woz's credentials as his own—including a fabricated claim that he worked on the HP-35 project—to get a job at Atari.) Wozniak recalled, "It was just something magic. Designing the products, laying them out, doing the software work—and we were all part of the same thing, working together. And we knew while we were working together that we would take care of each other— and boy that sure influenced my thinking."[43]

Wozniak worked for HP for less than four years. Yet the experience never left him—and years later, for all of his fame from his time at Apple, he seemed to gravitate back to Hewlett-Packard as representing one of the happiest times of his life. This is somewhat surprising, given that his tenure there was marked first by sleep deprivation and distraction, and then by the most disappointing experience of his early career.

One reason Wozniak was so happy at APD was that he was able to work with a childhood friend, Bill Fernandez, the now all but forgotten third player in the creation of Apple Computer. The other was the HP-65, a machine that instantly captured his heart:

Woz, who was naturally inclined toward finding the most economic and compact solution to any electronics design problem, found the HP-65 a revelation. "It's got this little chip and serial registers and an instruction set," he would later recall thinking. "Except for its I/O [input/output] it's a computer, the love of my life." Studying the HP-65's design, he got his first clue that it might now be possible to enter that middle ground of computation from the other direction as well.[44]

Happy with his work and life, Wozniak rented an apartment and settled into what he hoped to be a long and rewarding career as a Hewlett-Packard technician—and in time, with luck, an engineer. As a hobby, he set up at home a Dial-a-Joke phone line, and through it met a woman and soon thereafter married her. In every way, Steve Wozniak looked to be an up-and-coming member of the new, third generation of HPers.

But it wasn't to be—and though what happened next was certainly unique, it still offers a glimpse into the changing nature of the electronics industry, entrepreneurship, and Hewlett-Packard's growing struggle to remain relevant in this new business world.

In Wozniak's case, as everyone knows, he ran into a Pied Piper, another childhood friend named Steve Jobs. Jobs was manipulative, brilliant, obnoxious, and a born entrepreneur. And he too had had his brush with Hewlett-Packard. While still in high school, Jobs had taken some Stanford courses taught at HP and open to the public. There he had made his name as a fearless (and tireless) questioner of instructors after class.

At age sixteen, not long after he had met Wozniak and began helping him build an early (failed) computer, Jobs gave the first glimpse of his future self when, the team being short of components, he got on the phone and called Bill Hewlett to hustle free parts:

> Hewlett, a great engineer and an even greater entrepreneur, was at this point one of the most powerful businessmen in America and on the way to becoming a multi-billionaire. Forty thousand people reported to him from HP divisions and sales offices in nearly one hundred countries.
>
> It speaks volumes that, even as a teenager, Steven Jobs could detect a soft touch in Hewlett and then contact him directly (and even more volumes that Hewlett would answer the call). Once he had Hewlett on the line, Jobs made his pitch. Remarkably, though also characteristically, Hewlett agreed. [He] was never one to turn down a student.
>
> But once Steve Jobs scored, he wasn't about to stop there. He also pitched Hewlett for a summer job at HP. He got that too, ending up on the assembly line at HP's plant in Cupertino, building computers. The experience was so compelling that Steven even tried to design a computer of his own—a notion he quickly abandoned as too difficult.[45]

Now, after a sojourn at an ashram in India, Jobs was working at the hot new video game company, Atari. Moreover, he had talked its flamboyant founder, Nolan Bushnell, into letting him design a computer game. Bushnell didn't think the odd young man could pull it off, but sensing a kindred entrepreneur, he decided to give him a chance.

But Jobs had an ace in the hole: Steve Wozniak, who was already spending many evenings after work in the Atari game room trying out new products. Jobs had just four days to create the game, to be called "Breakout," and having no real ability to actually create such a product, he prevailed upon his friend to help him. As Woz already had a day job at HP, he agreed to work in shifts: Jobs would work all day, and Woz all night.

In the end, to Bushnell's astonishment, Jobs delivered the game. No mention was made of Wozniak's role; nor did Jobs honestly split the money he was paid for the project. Nevertheless, a partnership was born.

Two threads—his work at HP on programmable calculators, and, beginning with Atari, a growing interest in programming for consumer applications—were beginning to knit together in Wozniak's life. Within months the third, and most crucial, thread would appear. Around the San Francisco Bay Area, a growing number of young people, obsessed with computers thanks to university data processing centers, time-share terminals, and not least, HP desktop computers, were beginning to talk with each other about the prospect of building their own computers.

In due time, the most committed of these computer fanatics formed an organization called the Homebrew Computer Club. It met each month, first in yet another Silicon Valley garage, this one also a few blocks from Stanford, then eventually in a lecture hall at the Stanford Linear Accelerator offices. There they swapped notes, helped each other through design bottlenecks—and ultimately showed off their newly built computers to one another in an ongoing game of intellectual one-upmanship.

Wozniak was drawn to this crowd (Jobs had moved to Oregon) and soon became a mainstay of Homebrew, the go-to guy for the really tough design problems. He seemed to have a genius, no doubt enhanced by his work on calculators, for being able to find the cheapest, simplest, and smallest design solutions, solutions that awed even his peers.

It was inevitable that Wozniak would once again (he'd tried once before in high school) build his own computer, and that he would show it to Homebrew. He spent much of his spare time in the second half of 1975 preparing to do just that. Jobs, now back in the Valley, saw Woz's work and, sensing a business opportunity, spurred him on.

Thanks in no small part to his HP "g-time," Woz finished what would be the Apple I prototype that December. But before he took it to Homebrew, he decided to first show it to his bosses at Hewlett-Packard in hopes that HP might decide to build it.

As it turned out, he wasn't the only Homebrewer at APD: his workmate Myron Tuttle was also working on a personal computer prototype—one that even contained the same second-rate microprocessor that Woz had bought on the cheap. When Tuttle saw Wozniak's design he instantly recognized that it was far superior to his own, and offered to help Woz present it to their supervisor.

In January 1976, the two young men, along with a third technician, made the presentation to their boss. This is how Wozniak remembered that meeting thirty years later:

> As soon as Steve Jobs suggested, "Why don't we sell a PC board of this computer?" I said, "I think I signed something, an employment contract, that said what I designed belongs to Hewlett-Packard." And I loved that company. That was my company for life.
>
> So I approached Hewlett-Packard first. Boy, did I make a pitch. I wanted them to do it. I had the Apple I, and I had a description of what the Apple II could do. I spoke of color. I described an $800 machine that ran BASIC (an early computer language), came out of the box fully built and talked to your home TV. And Hewlett-Packard found some reasons it couldn't be a Hewlett-Packard product.[46]

Tuttle would remember the meeting slightly differently: "It was one of those informal meetings. It wasn't a big deal. We just sort of asked for five minutes and showed Woz's board. We were told, 'HP doesn't want to be in that kind of market.' "[47]

From this has come the Silicon Valley's legend of HP's Great Lost Opportunity. The young hippie genius in its midst came up with the most valuable invention of the age—and hidebound old Hewlett-Packard, with its white shirts and skinny black ties, had looked at this bearded freak with his hand-built motherboard and dismissed him out of hand.

The truth is much more complicated, as anyone who walked the halls of the Advanced Products Division in 1976 would have known.

The fact was that the entire building was full of mavericks, many of them far more unusual than Wozniak—and their new product plans always got a hearing. Indeed, at that moment the division was a hotbed of new ideas, thanks to the announcement that APD would be leaving Cupertino and moving to Corvallis, Oregon. With the next generation of calculator designs already under way, and the division distracted with an imminent move (with all that it entailed regarding selling and buying homes, transferring equipment, finishing the new Oregon facility), operations at APD had slowed considerably from the mad rush of the year before, and employees spent their empty hours coming up with new inventions.

In fact, it can be said that Silicon Valley would not see anything like HP's Advanced Products Division until—Apple Computer itself.

Thus, by the time Wozniak made their presentation, it is very likely that APD management had already seen similar proposals, and already come to some conclusions. It is also probable that both the computer division across the street in Cupertino and the desktop computer division in Loveland, Colorado, were also contemplating the same idea.

That this was indeed the case is suggested by the supervisor's remark: the decision that HP "doesn't want to be in that kind of market" was not likely made by a divisional department supervisor, but had been made earlier by senior management after extensive consideration. Wozniak and Tuttle, unknowingly, had walked in late to the conversation.

In fact, there were very good reasons why HP wasn't prepared to take on a brand-new consumer market in personal computing, the biggest being that the company was still learning how to sell calculators to that same market, how to set up a viable distribution system to retailers, and how to deal with millions of technically inexperienced customers. HP simply couldn't afford at that moment to throw another new product category into the mix.

But the decisive arguments against the claim that Hewlett-Packard was too out of touch to recognize a brilliant new idea like the Apple I, are other HP products of the era, especially those coming out of APD. Both the HP-35 and HP-65 were revolutionary products, in many ways much more innovative than the Apple I, which was essentially a budget minicomputer featuring some inspired design work. On top of that, even as Wozniak was making his pitch, APD had another product in the works, a calculator-watch, code-named Cricket, that was even more radical in its ambitions than Woz's prototype.

Finally, there is one last factor to be remembered. As brilliant as Steve Wozniak's design was, there were other, nearly as brilliant, personal computer designs coming out of places like the Homebrew Computer Club. And most used better processors, such as the Intel 8080, and were thus far more powerful. In the end, what made Apple unique was not Wozniak, though his contributions were considerable, but the marketing savvy and charisma of Steve Jobs. And Jobs was not in that January meeting; on the contrary, he was trying to pull Wozniak the other way.

All of that having been said, the ultimate truth about that historic meeting was that, however lackadaisical the supervisor may have seemed, word of young Steve Wozniak's invention reached the top of the company, indeed to Bill Hewlett himself.

At the end of April Wozniak gave up and filed a formal memo to HP's legal department requesting a release of his technology (followed a few days later by a schematic of this "Microprocessor System," with the footnote, "Apple Computer Co. is a partnership of myself and Steve Jobs founded to market PC boards"). Over the next two weeks HP's general counsel, J. C. Chognard, ran Wozniak's request past every HP division. There were no takers. Wozniak got his release. It was Hewlett himself who signed it.

To the last moment, Steve Wozniak still believed that he would find a way to work with his friend Steve Jobs and continue to be an HPer for the rest of his career. But in the end, he couldn't do both, and the new company offered him a chance to be his own person and follow his computer dreams. In a symbolic moment, he sold his most cherished possession, his HP-65, and invested it as his share in the founding of Apple Computer.

———

Did HP make a mistake in passing on the Apple I prototype? A decade later, when Apple had captured the world's imagination with the Macintosh computer and one of the most successful IPOs in business history—and Woz's design was properly acknowledged as one of the great technology inventions—it certainly seemed so. HP was still struggling to find an attractive PC design and a workable business strategy, and was looking to become a perennial also-ran in the business.

But three decades on, when the myth of the Lost Opportunity is fixed in the public's mind (if they remember the beginnings of the PC industry at all), the answer is very different. HP at last found its footing in personal computers and had passed Apple in industry market share by the mid-1990s. By the thirtieth anniversary of that fateful meeting, HP was now the world's second largest personal computer maker, its market share four times that of Apple, and its total revenues and profits over those intervening years far outstripping that of its more notorious competitor.

Lost in the Woods

If Hewlett-Packard made a major mistake with its Advanced Products Division in the mid-1970s, it wasn't with Steve Wozniak, but rather in moving the operation to Corvallis, Oregon.

This was standard procedure at the company. Between HP's computer operations in Cupertino (expected to grow rapidly), APD across the street, and the company's instrument operations less than a mile away in Santa Clara, the area was, for headquarters, getting too crowded.

The move to Corvallis was Ralph Lee's idea. He believed that expanding into more rural locations would be good for employee morale. For a man notorious for dismissing other people's radical plans as "a dim bulb idea", Lee didn't recognize one of his own. In Lee's defense, Corvallis *seemed* an excellent location for a major HP manufacturing division: big enough to support a facility with a thousand employees, but small enough where HP could be a major player in town. Oregon State University was in town, and a medium-sized city, Eugene, with the University of Oregon, was just an hour's drive away. Moreover, in keeping with the company's tradition of "twinning" plants, HP already had a small medical operation located nearby in McMinnville.

The move must have seemed the perfect solution to Bill Hewlett when he signed off on the proposal. But he had made a dreadful mistake. The Advanced Products Division was part of the HP family, but it was also a product of the unique environment of Silicon Valley. With its maverick style and eccentric workforce, APD was Hewlett-Packard's outpost in the Wild West show that was the Valley in the 1970s, a world the rest of HP was largely insulated from.*

Though APD drew its sustenance from HP's infrastructure and the HP Way, its imagination lived outside the company in the singular ecology—cutthroat competition, high risk, and runaway entrepreneurship—that had emerged in Silicon Valley. There were hundreds of new companies out there now, spawned by the disintegration of Fairchild Semiconductor and the rise of the semiconductor industry, then by the inexpensive and powerful chips those new companies produced. APD may have inherited the HP-35 and HP-65 from corporate R&D, but the division had run with those products, taken the company into an equally successful line of financial calculators (notably the hugely influential HP-80), and now had a remarkable second generation of calculators waiting in the wings.

In its brief tenure in Cupertino, APD had been a source of both wonder and dismay for the rest of Hewlett-Packard. It seemed spectacularly creative, but also disorganized, disrespectful, and, many thought, unprofessional. In other words, it was very Silicon Valley—and might have been a great asset to the company in the years to come. But that wasn't to be.

The move to Corvallis cost the division much of a year lost to distraction—the year in which an underused Steve Wozniak found time to invent, in the personal computer, the world's biggest ($230 billion by 2007) electronics industry. But the move itself, when it finally happened, went smoothly—almost too smoothly. APDers, weary from the traffic and climbing real estate prices of Silicon Valley, went up to Oregon that summer and, like generations of fair-weather Oregon tourists before them, found what they thought was an undiscovered paradise: green meadows, pristine forest, burbling creeks, and fluffy clouds in an azure sky. Even better, the price of a three-bedroom tract house in Sunnyvale would buy a small estate on several acres in Corvallis. Even the food was cheaper.

Though some people in the division decided to stay in the Valley, taking advantage of HP's program of helping to find jobs in other divisions, many more packed up and left for Oregon. They arrived and set up shop in the shiny new standard HP building, this one set deep in the woods, and excitedly made plans to continue the revolution they'd begun in Cupertino.

And then the rains came.

It was the bicentennial year. Back in Silicon Valley, an historic consumer electronics boom was under way in digital watches, calculators, and video games—and, for those with the vision to see it, the biggest boom of all, personal computing, was just being born. It was the natural place for the mavericks of HP's Corvallis division to be. Instead, they looked out at the endless rain under leaden skies from offices that had to be brightly lit all day against the gloom, and realized they had made a terrible mistake. In less than a year after the big migration from Cupertino to Corvallis, a steady stream—including some of the division's most important intellectual capital—began to flow in the opposite direction.

HP Corvallis had one last chance to return to its old glory, to produce yet one more revolutionary calculator product that would put it back in the vanguard of the industry. It was the Cricket, a calculator as powerful as the HP-65, but stuffed into the form of a wristwatch.

Designated the HP-01—a singular honor that HP had held in reserve for many years—and introduced in 1977, it was yet one more tiny miracle of HP innovation. Users could pull out a tiny stylus, so well integrated into the wristband as to be invisible, and punch the twenty-eight tiny keys, each of them not much bigger than a pinhead. In an astounding feat of industrial design, HP engineers had managed to stuff *six* chips and *three* batteries into this tiny case. The software was just as remarkable: the HP-01 could solve sophisticated arithmetic problems, serve as a stopwatch and two-hundred-year calendar, convert between different measurement systems, even dynamically compute time-based operations on the fly.

At $695 for the gold-plated version, it was expensive, but no more so than the better Swiss watches of the era—and it promised to confer on its owners the cachet HP-35 buyers had enjoyed three years before. HP Corvallis kept the HP-01 hush-hush for maximum impact at introduction, corporate advertising geared up for a major ad campaign, and corporate PR organized in San Francisco the first big new product press conference in the company's history.[48]

When the big day came, the press conference was jammed with reporters. The wire services carried the announcement of the HP-01 around the world. HP employees throughout the company schemed how to get on the short list of discount purchasers of the first HP-01s to come off the manufacturing line . . .

. . . And then, nothing.

The HP-01 never took off, remaining (albeit briefly) an object of admiration, but never a serious subject of purchase. It looked beautiful, functioned superbly, and enjoyed the usual HP reliability. But there were too many reasons not to buy it: the buttons were too small for older eyes, the case was so big that shirt cuffs couldn't be pulled past it, and the HP-01 was so heavy that even HPers joked that it would slowly make that arm longer than the other.

In time, the HP-01 would become a joke, a case study in engineering for its own sake without due consideration for the desires of the potential customer. It would also be a prized collectible on eBay. But in 1977, no one was laughing in Corvallis—or on Page Mill Road.

HP hadn't been alone in misreading the digital watch business. Half of the semiconductor companies in Silicon Valley had been burned chasing the lower end of the same market. Gordon Moore for years wore a Microma digital watch to remind him to never let Intel dive into the consumer market again. But failure and recovery are part of daily life in Silicon Valley. Up in Corvallis, the HP-01 wasn't just a product failure, but a cultural failure as well. The division would produce a number of superb calculators in the years to come, but it would never take such a risk again. And, as the calculator business faded away in the face of the new personal computer world created by its lost child, Steve Wozniak, HP Corvallis was reduced to a supplier of inkjets for HP's printers.

The sad irony of the APD/Corvallis story is that for twenty years, Bill and Dave, against one obstacle after another, had fought to bring the culture of the HP Way out into the larger community, and had consistently failed. Now, with the cultural revolutions of the sixties largely over, a new culture, this one based on technology and entrepreneurship, was beginning to emerge. In the Advanced Products Division, HP had the vehicle to take center stage in that new community; Bill and Dave had Apple before there even was Apple. And they sent it off to get lost in the Oregon woods.

Alpha Bit Soup

If Hewlett-Packard's calculator program seemed blessed from the beginning, just the opposite was true for the company's other big product initiative.

As noted, the HP 2116A minicomputer, introduced in 1966 as an adjunct to the company's instrument family, had proven to be an unexpected success, not just because of its low price (starting at $25,000) but because it was built to meet the stringent environmental standards of the company's instruments.

Two years later, HP announced its follow-up, the model 2000A Time-Shared Basic System. Like the 2116A before it, it was basically a 16-bit version of the 12-bit Digital Equipment PDP-8 computer, a design it had inherited with its 1964 purchase of Data Systems, Inc.[49] As the name suggested, the 2000 ran BASIC programming language software applications and could support as many as thirty-two time-sharing users.

It proved to be an even bigger success than its predecessor, mainly because schools were attracted both to its use of a popular language and its ability to serve a classroom full of computer terminals. According to computer historian Bob Green, "Heavy sales of the 2000 brought the computer division of HP its first positive cash flow, and with it the urge to 'make a contribution.' The engineers and programmers in Cupertino said to themselves: 'If we can produce a time-sharing system this good using a funky computer like the 2116, think what we could accomplish if we designed our own computer.' "[50]

What came out of this dream was the Omega project—that ill-fated 32-bit computer plan Dave Packard killed for being too ambitious and costly, and that had led computer division employees to sport black armbands at its demise. The cancellation of Omega had been expensive in other ways too: it cost HP several of its best computer scientists.

If a handful of the Omega team leaders left HP after the project was canceled, the rest, taking advantage of the company's move-not-fire philosophy, quickly accepted an invitation to join a follow-up project. This one was called Alpha, perhaps because it was to be the opposite of its predecessor. Alpha, chartered to create a 16-bit computer, was already under way when Omega was canceled—so when the Omega engineers arrived, they were essentially told to keep doing what they were doing, but figure out how to stuff those features into a 16-bit architecture. In a sense, they were being asked to do with computer architecture what the HP-35 team had been told to do with calculator hardware.

Ironically, the additional time now given to the Alpha team to integrate the new team members and get the computer to market resulted in an even *more* ambitious design than either the original Omega or Alpha. According to

Green, "As a result, the software specifications for this much smaller machine were now much more ambitious than those for the bigger Omega. They proposed batch, time-sharing *and* real-time processing, all at the same time, all at first release, and all without a front-end processor."[51] By comparison, the original Omega was planned to only offer batch processing, with time-sharing (using a front-end communications processor) as a possible add-on for later release. Now with Alpha the team proposed to do much more.

Within HP one of the best-known "Dave stories" involves Packard, upon his return from the Defense Department, reimmersing himself in HP by touring the company and getting presentations on new products in the works. It is very likely that story was born out of Packard's first encounter with the Alpha project. This is that story, as told by blogger, and ex-HPer, Katherine Lawrence:

> The Division General Manager made his presentation: During the first two years of introduction, the product would lose money. The third year would be break-even, and then the rewards would flow in.
>
> The head of marketing got up and delivered the same strategy. People in the room noticed that Packard grew ever more grim.
>
> The third presenter, the head of Product Management was half-way through his presentation when Packard stopped the meeting and quoted them the HP Way [more precisely, Corporate Objective #1]. "HP makes a profit," [he told them], "What have you people been doing while I was away?"
>
> He then ordered everyone out of the room, save for the senior-most members, and according to legend, spoke his mind to them.[52]

Not surprisingly, the Alpha project was scaled back to stay on budget. Unfortunately, the team still tried to keep as much of the original functionality in the computer as possible—and to do so came up with some odd technical solutions. One of these, which allowed for both positive and negative data addresses, would eventually lead to disastrous bugs in Alpha's proprietary MPE operating system.

The Alpha computer, now named the HP model 3000, was formally announced to the world at a trade show in the fall of 1972. The press carried the report that HP had now entered the computer business with a serious competitor to midsized IBM and DEC computers, and potential customers saw "a fancy cabinet of pizza-oven doors, available in four colors." The base price was $250,000, and prospective users were promised that the HP 3000 would support sixty-four users with 128 KB of memory (a sizable capacity at the time). Writes Green:

The first inkling I had that the HP 3000 was in trouble came in an MPE design meeting to review the system tables needed in main memory. Each of the ten project members described his part of the MPE and his tables: code segment table, data segment table, file control blocks, etc. . . . When the total memory-resident requirements were calculated, they totaled more than the 128 KB maximum size of the machine.[53]

Faced with such a problem, Bill and Dave, the supreme business realists, would have instantly cut back on the 3000's targeted capabilities. But HP had a group organization now, with dozens of divisions and hundreds of departments underneath. Specmanship of individual products was now outside their purview; they trusted that individual managers would make the right decisions. This was the HP Way.

And this time, it failed. Desperate to succeed, the entire team fell into self-delusion. Writes Green:

[The MPE] wouldn't fit, so everyone squeezed. The programmers squeezed in 18-hour days, 7 days a week trying to get the MPE to work. Managers were telling their bosses that there was no problem, they just hadn't had a chance to "optimize" the MPE yet. When they did, the managers maintained, it would all turn out as originally promised.

So, marketing went on selling the machines to the many existing happy users of the HP 2000. As the scheduled date for the first shipment approached, the Cupertino factory was festooned with banners proclaiming: "November is Happening."[54]

The division hit its target date, November 1, 1972, shipping the first HP 3000 to a loyal HP customer, the Lawrence Hall of Science in Berkeley. But the computer sent was a pile of junk. It wasn't even finished, missing some key components. It also supported only two users, not the sixty-four that HP had promised. And if that wasn't insulting enough, the computer crashed every ten to twenty minutes. It was a $300,000 paperweight.

Lawrence Hall was angry, but not as furious as Bill Hewlett and Dave Packard when they heard about the dead-on-arrival 3000 from an article in *Computerworld* magazine. It was the first piece of truly bad press Hewlett-Packard had experienced in thirty-three years in business, and the two founders, seeing the edifice they had constructed, the bastion of quality products and good customer relations, suddenly at risk, reacted ferociously.

First, without hesitation, they pulled the HP 3000 from the market and endured the additional bad publicity that ensued. This alone was a remarkable move for a Silicon Valley company: a few years later, Apple went ahead and shipped the first Apple IIIs knowing that a flaw in the mounting of its microprocessor would cause many to be dead on arrival. Intel famously went into denial mode, even to the point of blaming customers, before finally admitting the Pentium software "bug."

That wasn't how Bill and Dave worked. Every customer in the first shipment of HP 3000s was contacted and their computers picked up and returned to Hewlett-Packard. In their place, when the application was computer-critical, HP delivered a free 2000 to tide the company over.*

Meanwhile, inside HP's computer division, Bill and Dave unleashed hell in the form of Paul Ely, one of the hottest young executives in the company's well-run Microwave division. Ely was made division general manager and told by Bill and Dave to do whatever it took, within the bounds of the HP Way, to fix the mess.

Hewlett and Packard didn't make this appointment lightly. They knew what they were about to deservedly inflict upon the HP 3000 team. Among the new generation of HP superstars, Ely was the loudest, the brashest, and the toughest. With the exception of senior VP Ralph Lee, he more than anyone at HP provoked real fear in the people who worked for him. Everyone knew that, with the HP 3000 team, though he might be constrained from mass layoffs, Ely was not afraid to consign miscreants to the outer darkness of far-off HP service offices, or make their lives so miserable that they quit the company. Recounts Green:

> Once the HP managers realized the magnitude of the 3000 disaster, the division was in for a lean time. Budgets and staffs that had swollen to handle vast projected sales were cut to the bone. Training, where I worked, was cut in one day from 70 people to fewer than 20. HP adopted a firm "no futures" policy in answering customer questions [about upcoming products and delivery dates].
>
> [Ely] was strictly no nonsense. Many people had gotten into the habit of taking their coffee breaks in the final-assembly area, and kibitzing with the teams testing the new 3000s. Ely banned coffee cups from the factory floor and instituted rigorous management controls over the prima donnas of the computer group.[55]

The chaos and upheaval in the computer division now cost the company even more talent. Tom Perkins, the senior executive who had been central to the killing of the Omega project, announced his departure, taking with him a number of managers and scientists, including Mike Green, one of the designers of the 2000A, and James Treybig, one of the company's brightest young management stars.

This team of ex-HPers eventually moved down the street and founded Tandem Computer, the most HP-like of all the Silicon Valley companies—right down to the beer busts. Perkins eventually became a famous venture capitalist. Treybig, famous for being the only entrepreneur in Valley history to hit every revenue target on his initial five-year business plan, as Tandem CEO openly expressed his admiration for the HP Way. Thus there was a wonderful symmetry when, thirty years later, with HP's purchase of Compaq Computer (which had bought Treybig's company in 1997), Tandem at last returned to the company from which it sprang.

Meanwhile, at the HP computer group, it took several months of near twenty-four-hour days, with an uncompromising Paul Ely holding the whip hand, but eventually the programmers had managed to reduce the number of crashes in MPE from forty-eight per day to just two. They also managed to bring the number of concurrent users up from two to eight—still not what had been originally promised for the HP 3000, but enough to make it a real product. Writes Bob Green, "Marketing finally took a look at what the 3000 could actually do, and found a market for it as a replacement for the IBM 1130. HP no longer sold the 3000 as a souped-up version of 2000 time-sharing. Instead, they sold the 3000 as a machine with more software capability than an IBM 1130 that could be available to a number of users at once, instead of just one."[56]

HP public relations and advertising were brought in and given the un-precedented assignment of introducing the same product for a second time—only now aimed at a different market. And it seemed to work—right up to the moment when users began complaining that their 3000 seemed to crash ex-actly every twenty-four days.

It turned out to be a design flaw in the 3000's internal clock. When the computer ran continuously for twenty-four days (2^{31} seconds), the clock reg-ister would overflow and the system would automatically reset itself back twenty-five days. Tellingly, no one had noticed the problem before because no HP 3000 had yet been reliable enough to run that long. That was the good news—at least the computers were becoming more reliable. The bad news was that it meant another fix, and more bad publicity. One of the first to hear of this new problem was Ted Workman, an MPE product specialist for HP in the southern U.S. region: "I instructed the clients to do a cool start once a week, and grimaced when/if they asked me why. I cannot remember what I told them, but it was not [the truth]: 'The original designers of MPE never thought the operating system would stay running for 25+ days in a row!' "[57]

Once more HP went back to the drawing boards. This time, most of the installed 3000s were fixed in the field. And once more, the grumbling advertising and PR people had to go back to the press with yet another new product announcement.

But this time it worked—sort of. The HP 3000 that finally emerged after all of these fixes was now a solid, reliable computer. This time the HP engineers got it right, including a proprietary operating system (MPE) that was a miracle of reliability. But the 3000 still was just a shadow of the machine that had first been promised to customers. Fulfilling that promise wouldn't occur until 1975 and the introduction of a second-generation computer, the so-called HP 3000 Series II. This new machine—at Hewlett's demand almost completely backwards-compatible with the Series I to let those poor, beleaguered customers finally get the computer they wanted—at last had the software, the performance, and the reliability claimed in the original promotion three years before. Only the dream of concurrent real-time processing had been abandoned as unrealistic, and it would still be another seven years before a later-generation 3000 would finally support sixty-four users. But, at last, the HP 3000 worked. ABCNews.com:

> It was about this time my 20 year old self joined HP PR. I remember driving down from Palo Alto to Cupertino with a couple of the older guys from the office, and asking them what the meeting was for.
>
> Oh, they replied, we're getting ready to introduce the HP 3000.
>
> Really? I asked. But hasn't that already been done?
>
> Yeah, three times, they grumbled. And those stupid bastards still can't get it right.
>
> I didn't have to ask any more questions to appreciate that the 3000 had become a very sore point at Hewlett-Packard. Bill and Dave were furious. The future of the computer group and its employees was on the line. And my little circle of PR guys was bracing for another humiliating presentation to the press.[58]

The press was indeed skeptical. But, in the end, the HP 3000 proved itself. In 2003, thirty-one years after it was first announced, Hewlett-Packard finally announced the retirement of the HP 3000. After its rocky start, it had gone on to become the cornerstone of HP's entry into the mainstream computer business, which in time would lead the company into PCs and printers—and turn HP from a $5 billion company to a $50 billion one. As an article this author wrote for ABCNews.com, "That it has survived so long—and that its retirement is being met with goodbye parties all over the world, the biggest in Roseville, Calif. and Monterrey, Mexico—is testament to the extraordinary quality of the 3000's architecture and quality. It ranks with the

IBM 360, the DEC VAX, and the Apple II as one of the greatest computers ever made."[59]

The incredible success of the HP 3000—the estimated 200,000 units sold may have produced as much $40 *billion* in revenues for HP during those three decades—was also a testament to the will of Bill and Dave and the tenacity of Paul Ely. Hewlett and Packard, in the face of revelations that the most important new product initiative in the company had fatal flaws, the news of which might have seriously damaged the company's reputation, had opted for public admission, withdrawal of the product to get it fixed, and restitution to customers. In other words, at the moment when it was most challenged, Bill and Dave had maintained the HP Way.

Ely, for his part, had taught the company something else: companies are not democracies, and the HP Way is not a suicide pact. The inherent danger with building an organization on trust and teamwork is the potential for wishful thinking and mass delusion. When the HP 3000 team discovered there wasn't enough memory in the HP 3000 to hold its operating software, everyone had just put on a happy face, trusted each other to solve their corner of the problem, and then assumed it would all work out. It didn't, and it took a tough leader, in the form of Paul Ely, to go in, turn the place upside down, and demand real, measurable results.*

Revolution, Inside and Out

In retrospect, the major events at Hewlett-Packard in the early 1970s—the political turmoil at Stanford, Packard's time in Washington, Hewlett's leadership, the HP calculator project, and the HP 3000 computer—can be seen as testing the boundaries of the company, its leadership, and its core philosophy.

The family company of the fifties that had reached out to become the community company of the sixties, only to be burned by an unexpected social revolution, now in the seventies began to test its own edges. Was the HP Way still viable? Were there limits to its application? What was the role of leaders in a company built on openness and equality? Who were HP's real customers—engineers, or consumers now as well? And if the latter, what did the company owe these newcomers—did it have the same responsibility to everyday users as it did to professionals?

In their actions and their decisions during this period, their last as day-to-day leaders of the company, Bill and Dave sent a whole new set of important messages.

One was that, when it came to employees, the HP Way was a *social con-*

tract, not a sophisticated form of paternal benevolence. The early seventies may have been the years when Hewlett-Packard rolled out flex-time to its U.S. operations, but it was also the period when, at least for the HP 3000 team, the company made daily life a living hell for employees who had failed to live up to their responsibilities. Under Bill and Dave, you *earned* the HP Way.

The second lesson was that Hewlett-Packard was a *company*—not an instrument company. HP entered the decade as a largely U.S. maker of test and measurement instruments; it ended the decade a largely international maker of data processing equipment. The only common thread was a spirit of innovation, the HP Way (with its commitment to employees), and the Corporate Objectives (with their commitment to customers, community, and success). Everything else was expendable—including, as Packard showed by going to Washington, the founders themselves.*

The third lesson, and the most subtle, was that Hewlett-Packard had *boundaries*. Bill had Dave may have entered the sixties believing the Hewlett-Packard culture and the HP Way would change the world, but by the mid-seventies they seemed to accept that would never happen, and were just content to maintain HP itself as a bastion of their humanistic standards. They would teach by example, and if the rest of the world—even just their industry—chose not to follow, then so be it. There would be no more great human resources innovations at HP after flex-time; henceforth, the great challenge would be to try and preserve, against manifold challenges inside the company and out, what HP had already accomplished.

The brief but eventful history of calculators at HP was also a lesson in boundaries for future HPers. The story of the HP-35's development was a reminder that even a mature company could—and should—take great risks, even to the point of changing its entire trajectory. But, at the same time, Packard's decision to kill the Omega project and Hewlett's choice to turn his back on the Wozniak computer were reminders that risk-taking was not just about recognizing opportunity, but being realistic about both the competition and HP's own capabilities in those other disciplines beyond engineering: marketing, sales, and distribution.

Unfortunately, this third lesson was the least well taught by the founders—largely because this was one of the rare areas in which Bill and Dave disagreed, and thus gave mixed and contradictory messages. Hewlett, for one, appeared much more willing to pursue cool new technologies and products for their own sake, while Packard seemed interested in new products only in terms of the revenues they could generate and the new markets they could penetrate.

The truth was that the two men really weren't that far apart in their philosophies. It was Packard, after all, who had driven the development of many of the company's most important new product lines over the previous forty years; and it was Hewlett who walked away from the personal computer because it was too much of a marketing challenge. By the same token, it was Packard who never looked back, and was most willing to abandon old HP businesses to pursue wholly new opportunities; while Hewlett had implemented the Nine-Day Fortnight in a single-minded quest to maintain HP's profit margins.

A shrewd observer might well have spotted, as many HPers did in the years to come, that there was indeed an underlying lesson about boundaries offered by the two founders in their final years running the company. It was that Hewlett-Packard, to not only endure but thrive, must remain perpetually innovative—even at the expense of abandoning beloved products and entire industries that had become synonymous with the company—but that this innovation must *never* be allowed to take on a life of its own. Rather, innovation must *always* be disciplined by the marketplace.*

Unfortunately, Bill and Dave had left enough ambiguity in these lessons that there was room for others to draw an entirely different message—and enough of these people would run Hewlett-Packard over the next quarter century to put the very survival of the company at risk.

What was this other message? Take the HP-35 story. Wasn't it also a case study in pursuing a brilliant new technology without concern for what the eventual demand would be—indeed, a technology so innovative that it was impossible to even *know* what the demand would be? And wasn't that a license to pursue technology for its own sake and worry about the business side later? And hadn't Dave Packard done essentially the same thing with the 9810?

By the same token, in sticking with the HP 3000, despite one disaster after another, wasn't Packard sending a message to the future that if you had a solid product and good business plan, you should stick with it all costs? Similarly, hadn't Hewlett taught, with the Wozniak episode, that the company should stay away from radical jumps into unproven markets?

The answer to all of those questions was no. But it wasn't a clear answer. Worse, much depended upon the subtle dialectic of Hewlett and Packard themselves. Though one seemed to embody technological radicalism and the other business conservatism, those roles weren't fixed: Bill and Dave often unexpectedly switched. What did remain fixed through all of the years, and through all of the crucial business decisions, was that the two men, whatever their starting points, *always* moved toward each other, always approaching a common ground.*

This was the secret of their success, why they always seemed to think alike, and why—to others at least—they never seemed to disagree. After nearly forty years of working together, Bill and Dave automatically moved to that center point, and made that shift so quickly that to the outside world they seemed in a kind of perpetual, almost superhuman, concurrence. Reinforcing that reputation was the fact that the two men had learned early on to keep quiet with others until they had reached that personal accord.

In the years to come, Hewlett-Packard would be at its best when it repeated this process, when these opposing natural tendencies in the company found a way to converge. And the company would be at its worst—which happened more often as the years went on—when the two forces pulled the company in opposite directions. Then the hidden danger of the HP Way would appear: unbridled innovation, marketing overreach, and management paralysis. By their character, their toughness, and their pragmatism, Bill and Dave had never let this genie out of its bottle. Future HP leaders wouldn't be as successful.

The Other HP

Calculators and computers weren't the only stories at Hewlett-Packard in the 1970s, only the most important ones. HP was still a test and measurement company, and the Instrument Group had its own great successes during those years.

The seventies was the decade in which the company first promulgated the HP Interface Bus for networking instruments to computers and then drove it to become the world's standard. These years were also the great transitional years of testing, in which computer logic, then the computer-on-a-chip, the microprocessor, began to be designed into traditional instruments, giving them for the first time the "intelligence" needed to perform automatic operations, conduct sophisticated analysis, and even be programmed for different tasks.

Hewlett-Packard had been born in the first test and measurement revolution, and now, forty years later, HP led the second, and likely the last, one. Throughout the decade, the company's Instrument Group tackled one market after another, consolidating all of the product threads that had been developed over the previous half century, adding digital control, and turning what had been a vast array of scopes, meters, and monitors into a handful of multipurpose "analyzers."

These analyzers—the first one for microwave networks, the second for chemical tests, and the third for digital logic (and thus a tester for the device that made it possible)—were incredibly sophisticated for the time. In many ways they were the finest product creations in Hewlett-Packard history, the zenith of the instrument maker's art, and the cornerstone of all technology manufacturing in the future—but they also signaled the end of the era. Instruments would remain a vital and valuable industry in electronics, but they would never again rule, either in high tech or at Hewlett-Packard.

In fact, across the company—in medical products, gas chromatography, mass spectrometry, microwave devices, printers and plotters, optoelectronics, laser measurement and surveying tools, and all of the other product divisions scattered around the planet—Hewlett-Packard in the mid-seventies showed remarkable creativity. It was as if a thousand ideas were sitting in a thousand offices, just waiting for the recession to end. Because HP had kept all of its employees, none of that inventiveness was lost. When the economy again returned, it was if gates opened everywhere at once at Hewlett-Packard and the company surged out of every doorway.

In 1971, HP had been a $375 million company, with 16,500 employees. Six years later, it was $1.4 billion company—one of the ten largest U.S. manufacturers—with 35,000 employees. Those revenues would double again by the end of the decade.

Though little-noticed at the time, this was not only an amazing burst of creativity from a company heading toward its fortieth anniversary, but also a stunning example of world-class management. If the message they left for the future was imperfect, the example Bill and Dave set in the present was unforgettable. And this time the world noticed.

The seventies saw the first real widespread reporting in newspapers and magazines of business as personalities and lifestyles. This included the first lists of the "best-run companies" in America, the top executives, the "best places to work," and the best "corporate citizens." Hewlett-Packard, to the surprise of many East Coast readers who had barely heard of the company, seemed to top every list every year. It seemed impossible that a firm so innovative, and growing so fast, could also have the most enlightened employee practices *and* the least rigid management structure. Yet that's what the surveys said.

Closer inspection only seemed to make Hewlett-Packard even more paradoxical. It seemed to operative effectively with the most liberal work culture, but also the most conservative business practices. It was a huge "family" company full of traditional workers, yet seemed more innovative and more agile than most of its smaller, more entrepreneurial neighbors in Silicon Valley. And, most incredibly, it seemed to function with inverted management structure, yet at the same time seemed less chaotic and more monolithic in its decisions than the most autocratic of corporations.

Not surprisingly, these seeming contradictions soon provoked two decades of business school case studies, feature articles in magazines such as *Fortune* and *Business Week*, and ultimately books, the best-known being the mammoth best-seller *In Search of Excellence*, which pointed to HP as a model for restoring America's competitiveness, and the classic *Built to Last*, which described how the HP Way had been crucial to the company's durability, and David Packard's own *The HP Way*, ostensibly an autobiography but really a memoir, written primarily for future generations of HPers on how he and Bill Hewlett had created and preserved the HP culture.

The irony of all of this attention was that it finally arrived just as Hewlett-Packard was withdrawing its efforts to export the company's culture to the outside world. That work would now be done not by the founders, but by journalists and academics. And if the company they probed and analyzed seemed somewhat diffident to their queries, it was not (as many reporters supposed) because the HP Way reinforced privacy and distance from outsiders, but because Hewlett-Packard had long since given up missionary work and was content to preserve its cherished culture at home.

Departures

On October 1, 1976, Noel Porter died. He was just sixty-three. Bill Hewlett's childhood best friend and Stanford classmate, Packard's lab partner, Hewlett-Packard vice president, and one of the most successful mayors in Palo Alto history, "Ed" Porter's death sent a shock wave through HP—and nowhere was it felt more deeply than in the offices of the two founders.

The death of a friend and contemporary is always a time for taking stock; and an early death is a reminder that life can be unpredictable and its end can come at any time. It is also a time for taking stock of one's own legacy.

Ed Porter, though far less famous than his two illustrious friends, had left a considerable mark. Not only had he played a crucial role in the founding of Hewlett-Packard Co., and later, as a vice president, in the company's success, but arguably he had accomplished even more in his life outside of work. As a member of the Palo Alto city council, then the city's mayor, he had been instrumental in the creation of both the Stanford Industrial Park and, soon after, the Stanford Shopping Center, both archetypes of intelligent, dignified planning that would be imitated all over the world. Porter also played a key role in the building of the Palo Alto/Stanford Hospital, it too paradigmatic in its field—and, perhaps appropriately, where Ed Porter died.

There were other acts as well, smaller but no less enduring. One of these was the donation to the Episcopal diocese of Northern California of a parcel of land on Lake Tahoe. For a half century, Camp Noel Porter has served as a retreat for thousands of people in hundreds of nonprofit organizations.

Ed Porter had died while still on the job, never having enjoyed a second of what would have been, thanks to a fortune in HP stock, a rich and rewarding retirement. That he was the same age as Hewlett and a year younger than Packard was not lost on anyone at HP, including the founders themselves. As the company had grown older, and with it the earliest employees, HP, with the founders' approval, had set age sixty-five as the informal company retirement date.

But there had always been questions as to whether that date applied to Bill and Dave themselves. After all, strictly speaking, they weren't exactly employees, but *founders*—and with their immense stock holdings (enough to now make them among the handful of U.S. billionaires) they were also as close as a publicly traded company could have to *owners*. Their names were on the door, and on every product the company shipped, and, thanks to the glowing publicity of the last few years, they had come to embody the Hewlett-Packard Co. Other entrepreneur-CEOs had found themselves snug up against an "official" retirement date and decided (officially) that the company still needed them and (privately) that they could not give up the work by which they defined themselves.

Not surprisingly, then, the approach of their presumed retirement date created considerable disquiet within and without the company. Outside, investors and analysts, customers and suppliers wondered if the two men, so perfect in their performance so far, might fumble the transition like so many other famous business executives before them. Bill and Dave had always presented themselves as dispensable, just two men among 60,000 equals; this would be the test.

Inside the company, understandably, the concern went much deeper. There had never been an HP without Bill and Dave. And though the two men had always, in the spirit of the HP Way, entrusted others to make vital company decisions, they had also always been there to clean up the mess when those decisions went wrong, even overrode those decisions when they posed an obvious threat to the company's health. Who would play that role when they were gone? And who had the presence and the reputation to represent Hewlett-Packard on the world stage?

It was the classic fear of a company about to lose its founders—and not even the comforting world of the HP family could fully ease the fear of impending disaster.

Most of the attention now focused on Hewlett. Packard had, in fact, turned sixty-five the year Porter died. But ever since his return from Washington, he had served as chairman of the board, and though he still was intimately involved in the daily activities of the company, there was no official retirement age for board members. Hewlett, on the other hand, was company CEO and president, and his sixty-fifth birthday would be in 1978. He seemed happy in the job and certainly the company was thriving under his leadership. So why retire?

The simple answer was trust, that centerpiece of the HP Way. At every step of the way, Bill and Dave had set the same rules for themselves—even when no one demanded it of them—as they did for every other HPer. To suddenly award themselves a special dispensation on retirement age would be to deny everything they had said in the past, and to state that they were indeed special players in the HP family. That Bill and Dave actually were unique didn't matter: the HP Way depended upon them behaving as if it weren't so.

But there were other, personal forces at work on Bill Hewlett as well, to which no other HPer besides Dave Packard was privy. The death of Ed Porter wasn't the only reminder to the two men that time was growing short. Fred Terman, their mentor and teacher, had begun to visibly fail after the death of Sibyl. Bill and Dave continued to honor Terman by keeping him on the board, but his presence at the meetings became increasingly problematic—he would drift off, or demand endless explanations, or get off topic. As time went on, he also began to grow confused—one HP employee was stunned to hear him, arriving in the HP headquarters lobby for a meeting, inquiring of the receptionist about "zeppelins."

But the most devastating intimation of mortality was even closer to home. On February 9, 1977, Flora Hewlett, Bill's beloved wife of thirty-eight years, the mother of their five children and grandmother of their twelve grandchildren, died of breast cancer. As dedicated to her work as her husband, she had attended a board meeting of the Stanford Board of Trustees just days before her death.

It was a hard blow for Bill Hewlett. Flora had been his rock, the centerpiece of his private life, the one person who knew his weaknesses and had compensated for them. But in a way often found with widows and widowers, the fact that the marriage had been, by all accounts, a happy and deeply satisfying one made it easier for Bill to deal with the loss.

If there had been any thoughts in Bill Hewlett's mind about staying on at the top of HP, Flora's death ended them. It was time for him to move on to the next, and final, phase of his life.

But who would replace him?

By the mid-1970s, Hewlett and Packard had created a senior management team that was strikingly eclectic. A handful of the postwar team—Barney Oliver in the labs, the baleful and intimidating Ralph Lee in operations (once, when a media trainer was brought into HP to train senior management to get along better with the press, Packard scratched Lee's name from the trainee list, saying, "It'd be pointless"), Bruce Wholey in corporate services, and Ray Demere in manufacturing—were still with the company. To this core had been added the men who had joined the firm in the 1950s or early 1960s: the small and impeccable Bob Boniface, who ran marketing, the voluble and profane Al Oliviero in sales, Bill Doolittle in international, and jolly Ed van Bronkhorst in finance.

In recent years, Bill and Dave had begun adding to the team the stars of the new, third generation of HP managers: smooth and competent John Young, the company's hottest rising star and newly named executive VP; the supremely competent Dean Morton in medical products; and maverick Bill Terry from the instrument group. Just behind them was the fiery Paul Ely, who had just turned around the computer group—and reporting to Ely, the most junior rising stars in the company, led by the sly Ed McCracken and hardworking Bill Krause.

Though the youngsters, still in their early thirties, were too young to lead a billion-dollar corporation, all of the other executives were considered in play. There didn't seem even a remote chance that Bill and Dave would go outside the company for a CEO: both men had always promoted from within the company, believing that only a longtime HPer could fully appreciate the company's complex culture. Moreover, it would have been an abandonment of the HP Way—if Bill and Dave didn't trust HPers with their company, then everything they had ever said would be shadowed by doubt.*

But what would they do? Would the founders pick from the first generation, buying three or four years while the real candidate got a little more seasoning? Or the second generation? But which of them had the breadth of skill and, more important, the personality, to lead the company?

And the third generation? Would Bill and Dave put a forty-year-old in charge of the company, with the prospect of that person perhaps leading the company until the end of the century? The stars of the third generation also seemed to exhibit a major flaw: with the exception of Terry, and perhaps Morton, most seemed less interested in Hewlett-Packard than in their own career development; they were less trusting and "family" than they were ambitious gunslingers. Many HPers, including a number of second-generation company executives, quietly feared that, were this crowd to come to leadership of the company too quickly, it would sacrifice the HP Way for the sake of short-term success.

As always, Bill and Dave kept their own counsel. Even the chapter on management succession in Packard's *The HP Way* is uncharacteristically vague on how the two men reached the most important personnel decision of their careers, other than to restate the obvious, that "management succession is especially critical at the upper levels of the organization."[60]

But one young employee in the PR department (the author) got an early clue as to who would be Hewlett's heir apparent. Invited with his supervisor to attend an executive meeting in the boardroom adjoining Bill's and Dave's offices to make a presentation on the theme for the company's next annual report, the young man, despite being intimidated by the roomful of corporate vice presidents, did manage to notice something unusual: while the others were chatting, John Young put each foot in turn up against the side of the beautiful wood table and casually pulled up his socks.

Only later did he appreciate the meaning of that gesture. Recalled Packard:

> Long before we reached retirement, Bill and I had been thinking and talking about who might succeed us. John Young was our choice for many reasons, and in 1977, the president's title passed to him. Bill remained as CEO, and I as chairman. This provided a good transition to the time when Bill retired in 1978 and John Young became CEO in addition to being president.[61]

The formal announcement of the promotion to a Hewlett-Packard employees was just as prosaic: just a couple of paragraphs announced Young's new title. No grand celebrations of the end of Bill and Dave's forty-year tenure at the helm of the company they had founded. No long list of Hewlett's and Packard's achievements. Just a simple announcement, no different from one noting the promotion of an employee to division newsletter editor.

It was classic Bill and Dave. But behind the simple announcement, a momentous change had taken place at Hewlett-Packard. Though the company would soon race to even greater heights, this announcement would be looked back upon as the end of HP's golden age. Though no one knew it yet, neither Hewlett-Packard, nor any other company, would ever have such a two-decade run again.

What HPers and HP watchers did agree upon at the time was that Bill and Dave were now gone forever from the daily operations of the company. But in that they were wrong. One extraordinary day a dozen years in the future, the two founders, now very old men, would come roaring back to save the family one last time.

Chapter Seven:
Legacy

Now, for the first time in nearly forty years, Bill Hewlett and Dave Packard were no longer in day-to-day control of the company that bore their names.

When they had started HP, Franklin Roosevelt was president, Palo Alto was a town of 5,000 souls, and the world's most powerful computer, Harvard's Mark 1, was fifty feet long, five feet tall, weighed five tons, and was capable of about three computations per second. When Bill and Dave left the leadership of Hewlett-Packard in 1977, Jimmy Carter was president, Palo Alto had grown to a population of 50,000, and the newly introduced Intel 8086 (whose descendents would power HP personal computers) was the size of a fingernail and capable of 4 million computations per second.

Few high-tech executives had ever led their companies through so much technological and societal change. And it is hard to imagine how anyone will ever do so. In the Addison garage, the two young men worked in a world of vacuum tubes, radios, and slide rules; as old men, they retired into a world of semiconductors, the early Internet, and personal computers—much of it their creation.

Just as remarkably, Bill and Dave bookended their years at the company with intervals of spectacular creativity: their first years and their last were arguably the most innovative for the two men. On the day Bill Hewlett stepped down as CEO of HP, he was not only the most vital person at the company, he was also, as evidenced by both the Nine-Day Fortnight and the HP-35 calculator, the most innovative as well. No one has come close to matching that achievement since.

None of this was lost on the other men and women who now led the thousands of high-tech companies, big and small, in Silicon Valley and elsewhere. The pioneers of electronics, such as Charlie Litton and Cy Elwell, were now dead and mostly forgotten, their achievements part of the dusty old world of crystal radios and vacuum tubes. But Bill and Dave were not only still around, the last surviving entrepreneurs of the world before semiconductors, but still at the top of the game.

For these younger entrepreneurs—from the middle-aged men running the chip companies to the post-adolescents building personal computers and video games—Bill and Dave were the gold standard. They had done it all, from entrepreneurs in the ur-garage itself, to small businessmen, to leaders of a public corporation, to CEOs of the valley's first billion-dollar company, to business titans ruling a global empire, to (in the case of Dave Packard) a statesman operating on a global stage.

Many of these younger executives had started their careers assuming, often by watching Bill and Dave, that each of these steps was comparatively easy for a smart and ambitious person—and they had learned to their dismay that the path was both long and treacherous. Many had already failed at least once. And all of that combined to make their respect for Hewlett and Packard ever greater. Those two guys, they realized, had not only already negotiated every step of the career path they intended to follow, often doing so first, but they had also done so with breathtaking grace. Indeed, they often set the bar so high that those who followed found it impossible to reach. Even in the virulently competitive world of high technology, even as people measured their own careers against those of Hewlett and Packard, many privately admitted that matching Bill and Dave was beyond their reach. No amount of revenue or percentage of market share would ever match a company that had invented a dozen entirely new industries; no amount of laudatory *Business Week* cover stories would ever match a company whose employees set historic records for loyalty and commitment, and no number of trips to Washington would ever equal having a *medal* for quality named after you.

Hewlett and Packard had set out the steps to a successful business career in the second half of the twentieth century—and then, by example, had shown just how to take those steps well. They were the grand old men of high tech now, and in the years to come it would be a rare executive who didn't at least attempt to follow the path that Bill and Dave marked for them.

But if Hewlett and Packard were old men now by Silicon Valley standards, by the actuarial tables they were still comparatively young. How would they spend the years they had left to them? Would they remain partners or, after all of those years, would they go their separate ways? Would they withdraw from public life, or immerse themselves even more deeply into it? Would they still secretly run Hewlett-Packard, reducing John Young to little more than a puppet?

But the biggest, unspoken question of all was whether Bill and Dave would devote the rest of their lives to actions that would further burnish their reputations—or would they, like Poniatoff and Shockley, wander off into strange obsessions or the misuse of their great wealth that would cast an eternal shadow on the sterling careers that had come before?

The answer, as those closest to the two men would have predicted, is that in the years that followed their retirement from Hewlett-Packard, Bill and Dave created a legacy of good works—and one legendary act of corporate restoration—that in the minds of many is even more illustrious than their working years at HP. In the process, once again, they set a professional standard (and a capstone career step) that those who followed could only look upon with awe—and struggle to match.

Corporate Diplomacy

The first thing Bill and Dave did upon retirement was, as a show of trust, leave John Young alone.

In Hewlett's case, this was inevitable; he needed time to deal with the repercussions of his wife's death. But for Packard, HP's chairman of the board, the solution was yet another of his classic HP fork moves: he would travel to a far end of the earth—and create new business for Hewlett-Packard.

He would go to China.

In his autobiography, Packard devotes an inordinate amount of space— five pages—to his dealings with China. That's more than he spends on HP going public, the Sonoma meeting, even the company's entry into the computer business. Obviously it represented an important milestone in his life, one that is largely lost upon the book's readers. Then again, there is almost always a hidden lesson in Packard's actions—and this one may have been his case study in how to find meaning in a career after you've graduated beyond day-to-day management. It is Dave Packard, freed from business tactics to focus on corporate strategy, and, at last, bringing a little of the HP Way onto the world diplomatic stage.

The invitation came to Packard as a result of his membership in an organization called the Committee on the Present Danger. This group, which had been first formed in the early 1950s to combat Soviet expansionism, had been restarted by Democratic senator Henry "Scoop" Jackson in the mid-1970s because, in Packard's words, "[We] felt we were not strengthening our military capacity fast enough to counter the rapid buildup in the Soviet Union."[1]

The committee included a number of past (and future) government defense experts, including General Brent Scowcroft, arms negotiator Paul Nitze, and diplomat Max Kampelman—as well as Dave Packard, one of its few businessmen—and its work would ultimately set the ground for much of President Ronald Reagan's successful cold war policy. Nevertheless, as Jackson's involvement suggests, the committee tried to be nonpartisan—to the point that it even delayed its formal creation until after the Carter inauguration.

It wasn't long before the Chinese government, faced with its own Soviet threat on its northern frontier, invited the committee to visit and discuss common interests.

The invitation couldn't have come at a better time for Dave Packard. And, in November 1977, the committee traveled to Beijing. From there, the group toured the country, listening as their hosts described China's security threats. Apparently the tour went well, because the group was invited to return.

Meanwhile, newly retired secretary of state Henry Kissinger had also recently visited China—and gotten an earful from the leadership complaining that the Carter administration was not being responsive to their entreaties, especially regarding trade. Kissinger quickly wrote down a short list of names of U.S. business leaders he suggested the Chinese call. Leading the list was David Packard, who recalled, "I was tremendously excited by this invitation. Finally, I saw an opportunity for a substantial business conversation with the Chinese. In great haste, I assembled a special delegation: just myself, Lucile, and Chi-Ning Liu, an engineer at HP who was the son of a Nationalist Chinese general."[2]

The seemingly casual, but in fact carefully considered, composition of this little contingent offers a glimpse into the mind of David Packard. The message he gave his Chinese hosts was that this was a personal contact, not an official U.S. mission (though indeed Packard may well have been carrying a diplomatic message that he would never disclose, even to posterity). And the presence of Lucile signaled that Dave was perfectly willing, if the formal agenda went nowhere, to treat the entire trip as merely a vacation for an elderly businessman and his wife.

Meanwhile, the addition of Mr. Liu sent all sorts of complex signals. For one thing, Packard was bringing his own translator, showing not only that he was serious about any potential discussions, but that he would not be surrendering any advantages to his hosts. That he chose to bring the son of one of Chiang Kai-shek's generals into the land of Mao was Packard's reminder to his hosts that he was no sympathizer to their ideology or their policies.

It worked. Just as it had been said that only a rabid cold warrior like Richard Nixon could safely lead the political rapprochement with Red China, so too, it seemed, it would take a conservative Republican businessman (and former deputy secretary of defense) to open the China business market without being accused of being soft on communism.

The trio spent the first week visiting the tourist spots in Beijing, while Dave awaited a call. "I did not have any idea about whether we were making any progress."[3] Then, at the end of the week, everything changed. Suddenly, the three found themselves attending a reception and dinner at the Great Hall of the People held in their honor. Packard wrote, "I immediately knew then that we were getting somewhere."[4]

For the next week, while Lucile toured the historic sites that just days before she'd been told were closed, Packard and Liu joined their host, Ye Zhen-hua, vice chief of R&D for the People's Army, for a tour of local military factories.

One was a manufacturing facility for antiaircraft guns, "using 1950s technology, about which I knew a great deal. . . . There were about 4,000 people at this facility, and we were the first Americans ever to visit. It was obvious to me that what they were building would be entirely useless in modern-day combat, but I didn't say anything at the time, except to compliment them on their workmanship."[5]

The next tour, of a turbine engine plant, offered the same obsolete technologies. Packard regularly complimented his hosts on their fine work—even as he recognized most of it was a quarter century out of date, "and I told my guides that I would happily arrange some meetings in the United States so that they could learn about our work in related fields."

Both parties had played their parts perfectly. Packard knew what his hosts wanted, and he now patiently waited for the moment when they would make their pitch. It came a few days later, as the trio prepared to leave. The hosts approached Dave with a proposal: "They said they wanted to form a joint venture with Hewlett-Packard. I said that was OK, but I wanted to know what the rules were going to be. They said I could make the rules."[6]

It wasn't long after the Packards returned to Palo Alto that the Chinese government set up a special corporation to deal directly with Hewlett-Packard. It also sent to the States a dozen engineers and managers to study HP's business practices. After this group dutifully toured HP's Palo Alto facility, Packard—obviously relishing his retirement—decided to have some fun with his visitors. He invited the group to join him at the ranch in Merced to watch the cattle being branded—and to try some Rocky Mountain oysters.

There is no record of the Chinese visitors' reaction to the taste of fried bull testicles. Next, as if to drive home just how well capitalism rewarded successful and hardworking entrepreneurs, Dave and Lucile invited the group down to their Big Sur estate, just south of Monterey. What happened next was classic Dave Packard: As hosts, we got there ahead of our guests and realized that we didn't have any chopsticks in the house. So I went out into the shop and made a dozen sets of chopsticks out of redwood. When our guests arrived, they asked me to autograph their new handmade chopsticks, which I did. And they took them back to China as souvenirs.[7]

Needless to say, this was not how the party officials and nomenklatura back home behaved. And for the young Chinese engineers, many of whom had just survived the Cultural Revolution, the week with Dave Packard must have been an experience they never forgot.

By 1983, the ties between Hewlett-Packard and the Chinese government had grown so strong that the Chinese invited the entire Hewlett-Packard board to China for a meeting. That in turn opened the door for HP to do business in China—first as a supplier of electronic instruments, and soon after as a domestic manufacturer with several HP factories in the country. As with Japan two decades before, Hewlett-Packard Co. through one of its founders had pioneered one of the world's largest, but closed, markets.

Giving an Example

A constant refrain from nonprofits and the media in Silicon Valley beginning in the early 1990s was that the Valley's newly minted tycoons had not given back to the community even a tiny fraction of what they had taken out.

It wasn't long before the national media picked up the story, suggesting that high tech's billionaires were greater cheapskates than their counterparts in the rest of the business world, and especially in comparison to the great tycoon philanthropists—Rockefeller, Carnegie, Getty, and so on—of the past.

The one counterexample the media used as a cudgel against all of the other techies was, of course, Bill Hewlett and Dave Packard. By then, Bill and Dave, measured by the size of their benefactions and the funds in their foundations, were among the greatest philanthropists in U.S. history. Why, columnists asked, couldn't high tech's other CEOs be as enlightened as Hewlett and Packard? *Computerworld* commented:

> The lesson of Hewlett's life seems lost on so many current technology people, for whom the urgency of Internet time—that relentless compression of real time—shoves all other considerations aside. Hewlett and Packard were competitive, all right, but they didn't value paranoia above other qualities, as some modern executives seem to do. What's missing today in Silicon Valley and across the U.S. is any sense of community. No corporate or political leader can create it. They can only encourage it, by deed and example. Hewlett and Packard lived it.[8]

Interestingly, the person who leapt to the defense of these purported tightwads was Bill Hewlett. When asked by the *San Jose Mercury-News* why others weren't following him and Dave into good works, Hewlett replied that they were being judged unfairly. "Give them time . . . you forget that Dave and I didn't start giving away our fortune until we were 50 years old. Before that, we were too busy running our company. Just wait: they'll come around, too."[9]

Hewlett was, in fact, being both disingenuous and calculating in making such a statement. Though he and Dave didn't really begin the philanthropic work for which they became famous until after they had retired from HP, both had been making donations of time and money, especially to Stanford, almost from the day they left the garage. As early as 1964, the Packards founded the David and Lucile Packard Foundation with $100,000 of their money. Two years later, the Hewletts followed suit with the William and Flora Hewlett Foundation.*

Both men were, in fact, in their early fifties at the time, which enabled Hewlett to be truthful in his diplomatic remark a quarter century later. But 1964 was also just seven years after Hewlett-Packard went public—and given the much more accelerated pace to IPOs in the personal computer and dot-com eras, that would have required the next generation of Valley leaders to step up to the charity bar in their early forties. Not many did.

But if Bill Hewlett was publicly cutting the younger generations some slack, his secondary message gave them no excuse: you *will* become philan-thropists at some point in your career. It is your duty. And that, of course, was also one of the HP Objectives: *Citizenship*. Hewlett's remark, often repeated, "Never stifle a generous impulse," underscored the challenge to his profes-sional peers.[10]

Hewlett and Packard also gave those that followed an example of just how big that contribution should be: not merely enough to impress people with-out great wealth, but commensurate with one's actual wealth. The Packard Foundation, for example, funded during David's and Lucile's lifetimes with more than $1 billion, swelled after their deaths to more than $4.7 billion, with an annual grant budget of more than $500 million. Forty years after it was founded, the foundation was still the sixth wealthiest institution of its kind in the United States.

Through this legacy, Dave Packard also continued to surprise. Anyone who dismissed him as a relic of another time, or merely a reactionary business tycoon, had to explain the fact that he and Lu decided to target their good works at such nontraditional targets as population control, environmental protection, preschool education, and universal health insurance for children. Once again, Dave Packard had proven to be more radical than the radicals he dismissed as deluded dreamers. It was his last lesson on how to make even the most ambitious dreams real.

As for Bill Hewlett, he and Flora created a foundation that would end up, four decades later, with that endless symmetry between the two business partners, almost exactly the same size. It too was dedicated to global environmental and education issues, but it also added global development and, showing Flora's influence, the performing arts. (Their children would go on to create another institution, the Flora Foundation, dedicated to supporting programs in the spirit of their mother's interests and her life.)[11]

With the creation of the two foundations, Bill and Dave also took the last step in what would be regarded as the ultimate high-tech career: garage entrepreneur, start-up executive, company president, CEO of a public corporation, billionaire tycoon, government official, global diplomat, and world-class philanthropist. They did it first, they did it best (that is, they triumphed at each step), and in the process they, largely unconsciously, threw down the challenge for all to follow. It was a ridiculously high bar to set, but that didn't keep hundreds from trying.*

It is also impossible to quantify the full impact that Hewlett's and Packard's own philanthropic activities have had on the world over the last half century. The more than $1 billion their two foundations have given away is only a fraction of the overall impact of their example on those who emulated them. By making philanthropy of some kind an almost mandatory next career step for high-tech tycoons, Bill and Dave have likely already influenced ten times that amount to be given to good works around the world—the single most important nongovernmental source of philanthropy of the last half century.

Not everyone followed, but those who shared Hewlett's and Packard's attitudes almost always did. At Intel, for example, all three of the troika who built that company ultimately created major foundations. One, Gordon Moore, the Valley figure most like Bill Hewlett, endowed a foundation (also dedicated to environmental causes) nearly as large as Hewlett's and Packard's. William T. Coleman, the founder of BEA software, would credit the example of Bill and Dave when he gave $250 million—the largest gift in the history of higher education—to the University of Colorado.

But it was the dot-com generation of entrepreneurs who really took Hewlett's and Packard's example to heart. The real innovators were Pierre Omidyar and Jeff Skoll at eBay, who didn't even wait to go public, but set aside stock options in the very first days of the company with the express purpose of creating a corporate foundation at the IPO. They would go on to create their own large personal foundations. Their model, in turn, was adopted by Sergey Brin and Larry Page, the two founders of Google—and when that company went public, it instantly also endowed a billion-dollar foundation.

Ironically, the one tycoon who most closely followed Hewlett and Packard's lead was also the one who appeared least like them, the richest private citizen in the world: Bill Gates. Though little noticed, Gates's philanthropic career has resembled a supercharged version of Bill's and Dave's: from major grants to Stanford's engineering program to the creation, with his wife, Melinda, of America's largest foundation ($28 billion), in this case dedicated to the especially ambitious dream of ending AIDS in Africa.

Until Bill's and Dave's retirements, both foundations had operated at a fairly low key. But now, with greater free time and the opportunity to liquidate some of their HP shares, both Hewlett and Packard began their philanthropic activities in earnest.

For Bill Hewlett, one of his first tasks was to bring his old partner back to Stanford. During the turbulence of the late 1960s, when student protesters at the university had all but called him a war criminal, and school administrators, to Packard's mind, had failed in their duty to maintain control, Dave had largely pulled away from his beloved alma mater, narrowing his gifts almost exclusively to the athletic department and the conservative Hoover Institution.

Hewlett, on the other hand, despite the fact that his house had been firebombed, never gave up on the university. Recalled former Stanford president Richard Lyman, "Packard pulled back some of his giving. But Bill never stopped, and I think Bill was instrumental in bringing Dave back into the fold."[12]

Hewlett had the perfect vehicle to turn Packard: a new engineering building at the school for Fred Terman.

One of the most admirable decisions the two men made early in their careers with regard to their charitable efforts was to never name anything again solely after themselves (an act of modesty that, perhaps not surprisingly, has rarely been followed by others). This agreement had a liberating effect, as it enabled Bill and Dave to either honor others or to more closely link their contributions to the larger community.*

Their first major joint contribution was an example of the former. Fred Terman, more frail and confused by the day, was nearing the end of his remarkable life. Happily, before it was too late, the world had begun to recognize his great contributions to electronics, to the creation of Silicon Valley, and to Stanford University. In October 1976, President Ford awarded him the National Medal of Science "for his principal role in creating modern electronics and his ability to document his knowledge so that it could be effectively communicated to his many students who now populate the worlds of industry, academics and public service."[13] Six months later, his fellow Stanford faculty members and school administrators gave him an honorary dinner at the Bohemian Club.

Now it was Bill and Dave's turn to give their old teacher the ultimate thank-you. In October 1977, Terman was invited to attend the dedication ceremony on campus of the new $9.1 million Fredrick Emmons Terman Engineering Center, built from gifts by Hewlett and Packard. Standing before the crowd at the ceremony, Hewlett recalled, "Many years ago we were walking out of the old Engineering Building and Terman said he was looking forward to the day when I gave my first million dollars to the laboratory. I remember this, because at the time I thought it was so incredible."[14]

Fred Terman would live another five years, largely withdrawn from public life. Though he rarely left the house, except to be driven on small errands, he still attended HP board meetings, from which—though he was no longer really participating—he seemed to derive great satisfaction. So great was his pride in "the boys" and the company they had built that late one night, in his confusion, he drove over to HP and announced to a surprised security guard that he was there for the board meeting. He was politely told that it wasn't until the next morning, and escorted home.

In those last years, Terman was still regularly visited by his old students, Bill and Dave. The great men would sit patiently while the old man reminisced about their days together in the electronics laboratory. Art Fong would often stop by as well to drive him to IEEE chapter meetings and serve as another indulgent listener.

On November 21, 1982, Fredrick Terman died in his sleep of a heart attack at his home on the Stanford campus. At his memorial service in January, David Packard, one of his two most famous students, read Terman's eulogy.

Packard Unleashed

During this period there is something almost superhuman about David Packard's activities. It was as if, now unleashed from the constraints—conflict of interest, public image, influencing the stock price—of running a company, he was finally free to pursue all of his interests, and had the money and time to do so. Indeed, he almost seemed to be in a hurry.

Thus, even as he was beefing up his foundation's endowment and helping build the Terman Engineering Center, he was also looking for other, even bigger opportunities to give his money away. And the new ideas came from the most unlikely directions. The best-known came over a pitcher of margaritas.[15]

Packard had asked his children to come up with a family project. Daughter Nancy Burnett, who, with her husband Robin Burnett, worked as a marine biologist at Stanford's Hopkins Marine Station in Pacific Grove, came up with the idea of rehabilitating the dilapidated and mostly abandoned buildings—notably Knut Hovden's cannery—along Monterey's famous Cannery Row. This once lively area, made famous by John Steinbeck's novels, had fallen into decay after the sardines abandoned Monterey Bay.

What to do with these buildings became the subject of a brainstorming session over margaritas at the Burnetts' Carmel Valley home. Besides the couple, the meeting was also attended by two of their fellow researchers, Chuck Baxter and Steve Webster. Somewhere in the course of the conversation, someone—though no one remembers quite who—said the word "aquarium." The rest quickly agreed.

Robin Burnett then wrote up a proposal for a "Monterey Bay Aquarium" and sent it to his in-laws. They loved it. So did Julie Packard, Nancy Burnett's sister and a marine biologist as well—she immediately signed on to be part of the project.

The original idea was for a small facility. Said Webster, "We were thinking of remodeling a little, and inviting people in to see some fishes and invertebrates."[16] But when it was discovered that the old Hovden Cannery building was little more than a rusting shell facing imminent collapse, the original plans were scrapped for something far more ambitious. They would build a world-class facility from scratch.

Dave Packard was more than just the benefactor of the aquarium. He was, in fact, all over its creation, seeming to take enormous pleasure in poring over blueprints, suggesting new features, and, most of all, getting his hands dirty. At the foundry he set up at his Big Sur home, Packard cast handles in the shape of sea otters for the macro video exhibit. He also designed and helped build the wave machines in the habitat areas—visitors would often see an elderly giant in overalls down on his knees with a wrench tightening plumbing joints and checking motor drives.

Every Friday afternoon, David and Lucile would arrive at the Hopkins Marine Station to review the latest plans with the aquarium's architects and exhibit specialists. It was on one of those afternoons, in 1981, while looking at plans for the tidepool exhibit on the first floor, that Packard glanced over at the adjoining exhibit: a presentation of the Monterey Bay shoreline as it would be experienced walking from the rocky beaches of Big Sur to the sand and sea grass of Elkhorn Slough.

Packard studied the design for a moment, then said, "That's fine, but where are the birds? You need birds."

Everyone assembled was taken aback. Recalled Webster, who would go on to become the aquarium's senior marine biologist, "None of us had even considered birds. We were all fish and invertebrates and seaweed people."

The room had not been designed as an aviary, and at that moment no one was even sure it could even work in that role. But they did as Packard asked. Recalled Webster, "It turns out the aviary is one of the most popular exhibits at the aquarium. We didn't think of it, but he did."[17]

When the Monterey Bay Aquarium opened its doors on October 20, 1984, it was a $55 million, state-of-the art facility, one of the finest of its kind in the world. Though the initial feasibility study had predicted 300,000 visitors the first year, 2.1 million showed up—and they have continued to come, revitalizing the Monterey economy and restoring Cannery Row to one of the nation's leading tourist destinations.

But Dave Packard didn't stop there. The aquarium was an appealing place to visit, and a wonderful educational experience for young people—both worthy accomplishments. But Packard, as he had been all of his life, was about research, innovation, and contribution. And so, while the other people involved in the aquarium project were congratulating themselves on a job well done, Packard, twice the age of everyone else involved, was already rushing on to the next cool thing.

Back during his days as deputy secretary of defense, Packard had been involved in one of the strangest of all CIA programs of the era: the secret recovery of part of a sunken Soviet submarine from the ocean floor under the guise of a deep-sea mining operation. This recovery effort involved the *Glomar Explorer*, a special ship built by Packard's fellow, but infinitely more eccentric, billionaire, Howard Hughes.

At the Pentagon, Packard had oversight of the *Glomar Explorer* and, according to marine biologist Marcia McNutt, "by necessity became familiar with the prospects and limitations of deep-sea work. He was proud of that operation and enjoyed telling guardedly cryptic stories about it later on."[18]

One of the exhibits at the Monterey Bay Aquarium was images of creatures from the deep ocean in the nearby, 3,000-foot-deep Monterey Trench, taken with a broadcast-quality underwater video camera custom-built by an aquarium engineer. It wasn't long before this camera had caught the attention of undersea researchers, and in 1985 the camera was mounted on the manned submersible *Deep Rover*. The result was groundbreaking footage of the jellyfish and other fragile creatures—many seen for the first time—living in the darkest regions of the ocean.

So successful was this work that the aquarium created a research wing specifically to make new ocean discoveries that in turn could be displayed in exhibits.

But Dave Packard wanted more than that. In late 1986, he convened a panel of some of the world's leading oceanographers to discuss the prospect of establishing a full oceanographic research institute on Monterey Bay. The panel's report said that should such an institution be built, it should have "a clear identity distinct from that of other oceanographic institutions and a reason for being that leaves no doubt that the institute occupies a mostly vacant niche of importance." In other words, the message to Packard was: "Go ahead and do it, but make it different from everyone else."[19]

Dave Packard took the advice to heart. A few months later, in May 1987, the Monterey Bay Aquarium Research Institute (MBARI) was formally incorporated as an independent entity from the aquarium itself and dedicated to advancing research in oceanography. To create that "clear identity," Packard mandated the institute to advance the *technology* of underwater research, which had hardly moved in the previous two decades.

In particular, Packard called on the institute to focus on sending instruments, not people, into deep water, and to study undersea creatures in situ, sending information back to shore, rather than scooping up samples and dragging them back to the lab. Said McNutt:

> Thus, demonstrating the utility to research of ROVs [remotely operated vehicles] equipped with high-quality cameras and a suite of *in situ* sensors became the first assignment for the young institution. In [Packard's] own words, MBARI was to "Go deep. Stay long. Take risks. Ask big questions. Don't be afraid to make mistakes; if you don't make mistakes, you're not reaching far enough."[20]

It was the HP Objectives brought to undersea research. For a quarter century, Dave Packard had tried time and again—and been frustrated every time—to bring the Hewlett-Packard business model to the outside world. Now, to his great pleasure, it had found a second home in this most unlikely place.

And he didn't stop there. Next he brought the HP Way to the institute as well. He broke with the traditional academic model, in which scientists only tried to solve problems for which they had the tools, and instead enforced a peer-relationship structure between the institute's scientists, engineers, and operations people.

In this format, scientists would devise important research questions, regardless of whether the technologies to find the answers were available—and the engineers would then take on the task of building the platforms and instrument systems to get the job done. Meanwhile, the operations people would maintain and operate the resulting tools during the actual experiments. As at HP, this system was designed to be self-correcting: scientists wouldn't restrict their ideas to what they thought could be done, engineers wouldn't build systems merely for their own sake, with no practical application, and operations people would actually understand what they were doing the experiments for.

It wasn't easy, but it worked—as the old corporate radical, Dave Packard, knew it would. Said McNutt, "MBARI's sometimes difficult three-way partnership of the science, engineering, and operations cultures remains one of its chief distinguishing features."[21]

Next, Packard went after that old bugaboo of corporations, information management. In 1989, he announced, "Deep-water research involves immense amounts of data. I have the impression that much more time is being spent in collecting the data than in looking at it and analyzing it. We believe that situation can be greatly improved."[22]

That meant bringing data processing power—something Packard knew well—to the archiving, indexing, and presentation of MBARI's extensive information collection. In one area in particular—the digital annotation of video materials from undersea footage so that researchers can compare images from multiple sources—literally revolutionized deep-water research. Said McNutt, "Packard established a fourth leg of the stool: science, engineering, operations *and* information dissemination."[23]

For the employees of the Monterey Bay Aquarium Research Institute, it was all quite overwhelming—and to an outsider, the story bears an amusing comparison to a Hall of Fame coach deciding to devote his energies to a high school team. McNutt said:

> As had been the case with the Aquarium, Dave Packard was personally involved with the research at his new institution. . . . He frequently dropped in unannounced at laboratories or shops to check on the progress of projects ("Management by Walking Around," he called it). He never failed to demand a justification from the project personnel whenever he thought something should have been done differently. As is sometimes the case with forceful personalities, the staff did not always know when he was asking questions versus giving an order.[24]

There were other echoes of HP as well. Just as Hewlett had begun to steer the company away from government contracts in the 1970s because they tended to straitjacket innovation, so too did Packard eschew federally funded grants at MBARI, believing they would distract the institute from tackling big questions and would stifle creativity. Instead, he provided both the start-up costs and the entire annual operating budget for the institute for the rest of his life—an underwriting that was continued after that by the David and Lucile Packard Foundation.

As he had shown over forty years at HP, Packard continued to employ his prodigious and technical mind to understand the work being done by his researchers. A well-known marine biologist was visiting him at the Big Sur ranch in 1989 and was surprised to discover on his reading table a textbook on plankton. When he asked about it, the seventy-seven-year-old Packard began to grill him on the subject.

Also similar to HP was Packard's treatment of institute employees as an extended family. As with the company in the early days, MBARI people were invited to the Big Sur house, and joined Packard on hunting and fishing trips. Said McNutt, "Packard never failed to let the staff know how much he appreciated their efforts. . . . He thus developed a loyal and devoted following. His legend looms large at MBARI to this day."[25]

As always, Packard refused to look back. On the plane flight home from an awards ceremony in Los Angeles, Bill and Dave were joined by their wives and Chuck House, now a distinguished Silicon Valley leader and educator, and member of the Computer Design Hall of Fame. When House began reminiscing about the old days at HP, the others enthusiastically joined in—except Dave Packard. He listened with increasing irritation until he finally interrupted the happy conversation. "That's enough of that," he said. "Let's talk about finding squid." Packard still hadn't given up on his dream of creating a new generation of deep-sea research vessel—in his words, "the most advanced ship of its time." By 1990 he set MBARI to work on it—or, rather, them: the *Western Flyer*, named after the ship used by John Steinbeck and Doc Ricketts, was a twin-hulled host ship crammed with computers, remote cameras, and a state-of-the-art control room, as well as the *Tiburon* (Spanish for "shark"), its remotely operated vehicle. It was the *Tiburon* that was the most revolutionary: it employed electric motors to minimize noise and disturbance, and a variable buoyancy system (rather than thrusters) that enabled it to hover just inches off the bottom without stirring up sediment. The result would be some of the most extraordinary deep-sea images ever taken.

Building and operating the two vessels was not only an immense undertaking for a small operation like MBARI, but was too much for the institute's current facilities. So Packard bought it a new $20 million home, on four acres farther north on Monterey Bay at Moss Landing.

In late 1995, just as the institute was moving into this new facility, MBARI launched the *Western Flyer*. Dave, now eighty-two, was there to christen the ship. He would live long enough to take one ride on the *Western Flyer* and to see the *Tiburon* completed.

At an age when most of his peers were either dead or long retired from active service, David Packard, in a bravura performance of leadership, shrewd investment, and relentless innovation beyond the abilities of the most talented executives half his age, had built a new world-class institution *and* revolutionized an entire scientific field. In the process, he had now proven himself as one of the century's great managers in all three social sectors: commercial, government, and nonprofit. It was a record no other American of the era could match.

As a postscript, it is interesting to note that the presence of Dave and Lucile Packard in the Monterey area during those years had a transformative effect beyond just Cannery Row. As Julie Packard told a local newspaper, "It was clear that . . . there were big needs here and not so many donors."[26]

Between their own behind-the-scenes support and that which followed from the foundation, Dave and Lu's legacy in that community ranged from local arts groups to the preservation of natural habitat. The latter included the purchase of thousands of acres of land in Elkhorn Slough, Big Sur, and the Salinas Valley to be protected from development. According to Gary Patton of LandWatch Monterey County, "Ten years out, you might not notice much difference. But 30 years from now, you would be seeing hotels on the beach and all sorts of defacement along the Big Sur coastline. Looking back at it 50 years from now, you would say it made all of the difference in the world." There was much more. As reported by the *Monterey County Weekly:*

> Over the years, Packard money has pumped through numerous local agencies and groups, from California State University Monterey Bay to local school districts, from Natividad Hospital to the Big Sur Land Trust, from the Monterey Symphony to the Carmel Bach Festival and Pacific Repertory Theatre.
>
> Stephen Moore, founder and artistic director of Pac Rep, a 20-year grant recipient, jokes that there would be no Monterey County without the Packards' help.
>
> We might as well hang a sign, "Welcome to Monterey County, sponsored in part by the David and Lucile Packard Foundation."[27]

The Ultimate Alum

One of the interesting ironies of Bill's and Dave's retirement years is that, as if to round out their life experiences, they each crossed over into the other's area of strength. Thus, Dave Packard, the ultimate businessman, spent his last years immersed in the science and technology that had been central to his life back in the Stanford days but secondary thereafter. Meanwhile, Bill Hewlett, the engineer's engineer, began to devote his life to supporting the only area where he'd ever been a less than a success (and Packard an almost effortless success): education.

Where Packard seemed to roar out of the gate from the moment he was freed from the daily operations of HP, Hewlett took longer to get rolling. Not only did the loss of Flora occupy his life for the years immediately following 1977, but so did health problems. He had a minor heart attack in 1979 that slowed him temporarily, but posed no major medical threat—though it did spread fear throughout Hewlett-Packard, where HPers had long assumed the two founders were larger than life.

In 1978, just a year after Flora's death, Bill married Rosemary Bradford, whom he had met skiing. This surprised many HPers, but not those who understood how often the survivors of long, happy marriages quickly re-marry. Rosemary Hewlett, who also brought to the marriage five grown children, seemed to bring back to Bill's life the comfort and stability he needed, and it wasn't long before the Bill Hewlett of legend was back in action.

Where Dave moved outward into new ventures, Bill seemed content to bring his experience and wealth to bear on improving those institutions that had always been part of his life. And none more so than Stanford University.

Stanford had been, after all, the professional home of his late father. The university had also been willing to take on young Bill when he was struggling with his studies and his career choice. And, of course, it had been at Stanford where he had met Fred Terman and Dave Packard and set the course of his ex-traordinary life. Bill Hewlett and Stanford would be intimately connected for an astonishing eighty-five years.

Now he would pay the school back. And by the time he was finished, *Stanford Magazine,* in appreciation of his work, would declare Bill Hewlett to have done more for the university than anyone since founders Leland and Jane Stanford back in the late nineteenth century.[28] More than anyone, it was Hewlett, in support of Terman's vision, and in partnership with Packard, who turned Stanford from a sleepy college for rich California kids into one of the world's greatest, and wealthiest, universities. Said Hewlett's former secretary Mollie Yoshizumi, "Mr. Hewlett was very passionate and very emotional about Stanford. Mr. Packard and Mr. Hewlett had very strong feelings that it was be-cause of Professor Terman and Stanford that they wound up with this very successful company."[29]

Walter Hewlett, his son and a Stanford doctorate, offers another clue: "I think the most important thing was that Stanford was making a worthwhile contribution to society." Like Packard in Monterey, Bill Hewlett believed that at Stanford he could continue that most important of HP's Objectives.

It is estimated that Hewlett, Packard, and their respective foundations have donated nearly $400 million to Stanford—a figure that continues to grow by the year. Given the magnitude of that number—one of the greatest in the history of educational philanthropy—it can be said that one of Bill Hewlett's most important contributions to Stanford was in convincing Dave Packard not to give up on his alma mater during the dispiriting protest days of the late 1960s. Whatever his own feelings at the time, Packard, as always, trusted his lifelong business partner—and in the years to come would once again become a passionate supporter of the university.

Bill Hewlett's support of Stanford was careful, subtle, and often anonymous. Arguably, he understood the university better than any of the successive generations of administrators he dealt with, and knew precisely how to obtain a desired result.

> Bill Hewlett's relationship with Stanford went much deeper than pockets. He was in many ways like a father to the University, supporting it in good times and bad—sometimes indulgent, sometimes strict, always unconditionally loving. Not that he ever publicly depicted himself in an authoritarian role. By all accounts, he remained a down-to-earth and even shy man, whose contributions to the campus were frequently anonymous and who looked more like a suburban weekend fisherman than a titan of industry.[30]

In practice, this "fatherhood" of Stanford meant that Hewlett almost never made unrestricted donations, and rarely made gifts alone. His donations were often in the form of matching funds. Walter Hewlett said, "He didn't want to be the only person giving a gift. He felt it was not right. And he didn't want to be the sole determining factor in whether something succeeded or not."[31]

He was also just as likely to refuse an entreaty, as various Stanford University presidents learned to their dismay. In the words of one of them, Gerhard Casper, "He was clearly somebody who was being asked for money a lot by lots of people. I was completely clear that if I asked him for support, he might say 'No,' or 'This is too much.' I think he was concerned that Stanford not take him for granted. I certainly did not."[32]

For these presidents, one of the initiations connected with taking the job at Stanford was the first meeting with the formidable Hewlett and Packard. It wasn't lost on these individuals that a bad first impression, even a misspoken word, might jeopardize the entire financial underpinnings of the university itself.

Casper, for one, never forgot that first meeting. Hired from the University of Chicago, he found himself being driven directly from the press conference to his first meeting with Bill and Dave. "It was like going to meet two mythical beasts," Casper recalled. Then Hewlett walked into the room, wearing a pair of shorts and looking like a suburban grandfather at a family barbecue. From that moment, Casper knew everything would be all right.

But, just as he had been at HP, Hewlett mixed grumpy toughness and rigorous intellectual discipline with disarming moments of great warmth and insight into human nature. For example, in 1989, when the Loma Prieta earthquake damaged the sandstone Stanford quad, especially the Memorial Church, Hewlett quietly offered to make an anonymous $3 million gift—almost one-third of the total needed—on condition that the work begin immediately. Said Professor Robert Gregg, who was then dean of the church, "I think he understood that the sooner the centerpiece monument was returned, the sooner people would have a sense that we were back in operation."[33]

Not long after his appointment, Gerhard Casper found himself in a car with Hewlett racing to a meeting in the East Bay. Bill casually offered him $1 million in discretionary money, says Casper, "for me to do whatever I wanted to." Casper gratefully accepted—and spent the money on initiatives for undergraduate education.

Many of these acts were never known to the general public. For example, in 1985, Hewlett's cardiac physician Christopher McGregor decided to move back to the United Kingdom. McGregor, a heart transplant expert, had reached an agreement with the British government that if his first three transplant surgeries there were successful the government would consider supporting a new center. Hewlett agreed to cover the cost of those first three cases—which totaled several hundred thousand dollars. They were successful, and the resulting transplant center in Newcastle-upon-Tyne became one of the largest in Europe.[34]

Through it all, those who dealt with Hewlett—and Packard as well—during these years were struck by how little they resembled the standard image of either a billionaire or a captain of industry. People now used terms such as "humble" and "unaffected" to describe them. It was as if, having briefly tried the life of conspicuous consumption in the 1960s, the two men had found it so unsatisfying that they bounced back even further than where they had begun. There were no castles or racehorses or great yachts. For Bill and Dave, the only indulgences left seemed to be ranchland and giving their money away—and people, especially HPers, loved them for it.

Here is how Herant Katchadourian, the biology professor to whom Hewlett once confided that he might have followed his father into medicine, described the older Bill Hewlett to *Stanford Magazine*: "If you didn't know him, it could be difficult to separate the person from the purse. But when you got to know him, what was so impressive was how this man was so untouched by his fortune. He would have been the same person even if he did not have the fortune."

And this, from David Pierpont Gardner, former president of the William and Flora Hewlett Foundation and of UC Berkeley:

> In his personal life he lived modestly for one of his position, preferring to raise his five children in Palo Alto, to center Hewlett-Packard's corporate interests within the city, and to participate in its civic affairs and in the work of his beloved Stanford. He drove himself to work and occupied the same office (seemingly with the same furniture) for more than forty years. . . . His wants were remarkably simple and he did not seem to be in any way the object of his professional life. He told me once that he did what interested him as an engineer and "the money just happened along."[35]

Finally, from his son, Walter Hewlett: "My dad didn't want to be distracted by the money he made. He was too interested in other things. He never forgot where he came from and who he was."[36]

But these comments didn't just come from family and friends. HPers who lived in Palo Alto grew accustomed to seeing Bill Hewlett driving around town in a company Ford Taurus station wagon, or bumping into Dave Packard in paint-spattered overalls buying wood screws and nails at the local Orchard Supply Hardware store. Packard only reluctantly gave up driving his beat-up Olds Toronado when HP security experts insisted that he get a new car and driver, and take a different route to the office each day.

Perhaps the most amusing, and telling, story about Hewlett's growing simplicity comes from Gardner (and is confirmed by Walter Hewlett):

> I recall one conversation involving Bill, his son Walter, and me at his home following a review of our upcoming meeting of his foundation's board. Bill could not shop for a Christmas present for his second wife, Rosemary, owing to an operation from which he was then recovering. He asked Walter to shop for the gift he wanted: a pair of binoculars for Rosie's bird-watching.
>
> He gave Walter a hundred dollars for the purchase. Walter, who knew a great deal about binoculars and optics, suggested that his father might prefer one of the better German or Japanese binoculars that would cost not a hundred dollars, but six to eight hundred dollars.
>
> Bill was having none of this, and the matter was "discussed" for some twenty minutes. Finally, in exasperation, Bill said, "Walter, here is two

hundred dollars. It is more than enough for a decent pair of binoculars. Please go buy it."

All this after just settling on proposals to spend some $15 million of Bill's money at our next board meeting.[37]

A Calculating End

Bill and Dave had left a Hewlett-Packard racing forward with terrific momentum—and, by all appearances, the right new CEO at its helm.

In the eleven years between Bill Hewlett's retirement in 1978 and the company's fiftieth anniversary year in 1989, HP grew from $1.9 billion in revenues, with 42,000 employees, to $11.8 billion in revenues and nearly 100,000 employees. In between, the company introduced a major new minicomputer family, the 32-bit HP 9000, the first so-called "desktop mainframe." It would become the mainstay of HP's computer business, first as part of the emerging "client-server" architecture that would define corporate computing in the 1980s, and in its last years as part of the Internet server revolution.

Also during the 1980s, the computer group would embark on the most expensive R&D project in the company's history: that of developing a whole new computer architecture based upon the RISC (reduced instruction set computing) technology recently invented at Stanford. RISC, because it used a smaller operating "vocabulary," was intrinsically faster than the more commonly used CISC (complex instruction set computing), a characteristic HP used to its advantage in a series of computers and very high-end PCs featuring its RISC "Precision" architecture.

At the other end of HP's computer business, the company finally introduced its first personal computer, the HP-85, in 1980. With its built-in thermal paper printer and tiny display, it was closer to the company's existing desktop calculator line than what Apple was building a few blocks away, but it was a start.

Three years later, HP introduced the company's first "real" PC, the HP-150. It was a solid machine, with one interesting feature: a touch-screen system by which the user could quickly manipulate data by simply pointing a finger near the surface of the display. The company sold tens of thousands of HP-150s, but mostly as part of larger packages of company instruments or minicomputers. The rest of the world was much more interested in the latest generation of IBM PCs and was anxiously awaiting the announcement of the Apple Macintosh.

There may have been many good reasons for Hewlett-Packard not to jump into personal computers when Wozniak offered up the Apple I—but six years later, when the company had at last made the commitment to compete in that market, there was no excuse for a computer that, touch screen aside, was not more innovative than its competitors. This was, after all, the company that had set the tech world on its ear a decade before with the first scientific pocket calculators. In retrospect, it was an early clue that, for all of the company's impressive business success, all was not right at HP.

A year later, HP introduced a follow-up version of the HP-150 that was more powerful and reduced the touch screen to an option. It was an improvement, but Hewlett-Packard would not be a serious player in personal computers until the arrival of its IBM-compatible Vectra line later in the decade. By then, it would be an also-ran in the field—and would spend two more decades catching up. In its desperate attempt to make up that lost ground, the company would often compromise or abandon many of the dictums about mass marketing to consumers, event sponsorship, attacking the competition, compromising quality for price, and choosing market share over profit margins that it had adhered to for the previous half century.

Meanwhile, the rest of HP seemed to chug along, producing solid if largely uninspiring new products that often succeeded because of the company's reputation for quality, because of the company's long history with key customers, and because of the network advantages of interconnecting with the HP Interface Bus. HP's Instrument Group, the most venerable and reliable part of the company, continued to march along, maintaining its market dominance and generating solid profits, but it was now a mature business, long past the days when it could produce the kind of explosive growth that had once propelled HP. Rather, it was slowly becoming a secondary business at Hewlett-Packard.

Calculators, too, though just a few years before the most exciting business at HP, were quickly become a minor contributor to the company's growth. There were several reasons for this, most of them not in HP's control. As with any hot new business, scientific and business calculators quickly drew a host of new competitors—in this case, both Japanese calculator companies, such as Casio, and U.S. makers of low-end calculators, such as Texas Instruments. Both saw the profit margins that HP's calculators were producing—and responded by adding more and more functions to their calculators, while sacrificing quality in exchange for a bargain. These companies bet that there were hundreds of thousands of potential customers out there who wanted an HP calculator, but would settle for something nearly as good for half the price.

They were right. And though this didn't really cut into Hewlett-Packard's current customer base, it certainly carved off large regions of its potential customer universe. But even that arrangement might have proved profitable for all of the competitors in the scientific/financial calculator business had not Texas Instruments, enamored with the controversial Boston Consulting Group learning-curve pricing model, decided to price bomb the market in hopes of capturing dominant market share.

And it did just that. But it was a Pyrrhic victory: TI made itself the industry leader, but so damaged the profit structure of the industry, and so truncated the normal time span from early adopter to commodity product, that by the early 1980s high-end calculators were all but dead as a healthy business. HP continued to produce a couple more generations of its regular and programmable calculators, but it was already looking for an exit strategy.

The company thought it found the answer in 1982 with the HP-75C, its first "handheld computer." It was basically a highly programmable HP desktop calculator in a small (but nearly two-pound), pocket-sized form. It could also manage peripherals, such as a cassette memory drive and a printer. But it wasn't enough to revitalize an aging industry.

Hewlett-Packard would continue to produce these handheld computers, culminating in 1991 with the $700 HP-95LX, an exquisite palmtop personal computer that featured a simple word processing program, a financial calculator, and an innovative wireless infrared link to transfer data to an HP desktop. Impressive as it was for the time, and though the company sold $50 million worth of the device the first year, the HP-95LX was basically the end of the line.

In handheld computers, Hewlett-Packard had managed to be both too early and too late. Too late to keep the world interested in calculators—TI had ruined that market, and consumers were now distracted by the much more interesting offerings coming from the desktop computer industry. Too early by a decade for the handheld/laptop computer paradigm to be firmly established. In the meantime, given the choice, and a limited budget, customers bought PCs over supercharged calculators. Other than the cheap versions sold in drugstores, the calculator era was over.

Future Imprint

But as had always been the case at Hewlett-Packard, just as one business faded, the company invented another one to take its place.

Few technology companies have ever accomplished this; most rise and fall with the market they were founded to pursue. A few famous companies have managed to make the shift once or twice: Intel from memory to microprocessors, Apple from personal computers to consumer entertainment devices,

Motorola and TI from instruments and radios to semiconductors. IBM is justly celebrated for having, over the course of nearly a century, made the jump from office machines to computers to information services.

But Hewlett-Packard is unique. It began as an instrument company, became a computer company, then a calculator company, and, beginning in the late 1970s, the world's leading printer company (and even later, one of the world's biggest PC companies). And this doesn't even include its dominance in smaller markets, such as analytical devices, optoelectronics, and medical monitoring systems.

These were head-snapping changes in business direction; yet, unlike most of these other great companies, HP managed to make these turns without having been made desperate by business reversals, without a sweeping management coup, and without massive layoffs.

How did the company do it? The answer seems to lie in HP's inverted business structure and the trust that was the central tenet of the HP Way.

As with every other company in the world, it was HP's employees who were the closest to customers, who understood their changing needs, and who had the best chance of identifying interesting new technologies and solutions for those customers. What made Hewlett-Packard different, at least during its first half century, was that the company *listened* to these line employees. A new idea, even from outside contractors like Tom Osborne, or brand-new, post-adolescent hires like Steve Wozniak, got a fair hearing—and if the idea was judged interesting enough, it quickly moved up through the organization. And being a company of engineers, the one thing HP did best was take new technological ideas and turn them into real products.

As a result, even into the 1980s, HP remained a surprisingly agile company for business of its age and size. And nowhere was this better proven than in its jump into the printer business—an idea that began in one of the most remote of the company's operations and quickly came to redefine the entire organization.

In 1990, when President George H. W. Bush visited the Hewlett-Packard printer division in Boise, Idaho, he publicly congratulated the company's engineers there for the invention of the computer laser printer. Though the president's comments weren't really accurate, it was easy to understand how he might have made the mistake: by then HP had become so synonymous with printers, and had dominated that market for so long, that it was hard not to imagine it as the industry pioneer.

In fact, work on laser printers had begun at Xerox's Palo Alto Research Center (PARC) just up the hill from HP headquarters in the late 1960s. This was during that fabled period at PARC when researchers devised not only the laser printer, but the personal computer, windowing software, bit-mapping displays, the computer mouse, indeed, almost every part of the modern PC industry—and then proceeded not to capitalize on any of it.[38]

In the case of the laser printer, perhaps because its underlying technology was a cousin to its main photocopier business, Xerox did manage to get a model out the door: the Xerox 9700, an ultra-high-end (120 pages per minute) monster designed to support mainframe computers and priced at $350,000. One company that saw the Xerox 9700 and decided to give chase with a low-cost version was the Japanese camera and optics company Canon—and by 1982 it had introduced a desktop laser printer called the LBP-10. Canon then quickly went to work on a follow-up printer, the LBP-CX, featuring the revolutionary new CX printer engine.

But Canon had a problem: it knew little about the computer business, especially how to sell into the data processing community. So it came to Silicon Valley looking for partners. It had three in mind: Diablo, Apple, and Hewlett-Packard.

Diablo, ironically a subsidiary of Xerox, was the best choice. It was already the world leader in letter-quality daisy-wheel printers and had recently embarked on a program of putting its label on OEM products from Honeywell (dot-matrix printers) and Sharp (color inkjet printers).

But Diablo declined, giving it the unenviable record of losing twice in the soon-to-be giant industry it founded. It seems that Diablo already had a deal in the works with another subsidiary, Fuji-Xerox in Japan, for what it thought was a superior printer.

Chastened, the Canon delegation next crossed the Bay from Fremont to Palo Alto and visited Hewlett-Packard. HP, the team reasoned, might be interested because it was already spending a lot of money reselling under its own label (OEMing) Diablo's daisy-wheel printers (and dot-matrix printers from other sources) in support of its computer lines. They almost failed there as well, largely because they ran smack into a growing, and dangerous, attitude at HP—spawned in part by the HP Way—that anything not invented at the company couldn't be very good. Luckily, the CX engine was so indisputably superior to anything on the market (its 300 dot per inch resolution was wonderfully clear), and HP was so desperate to get out from under its dependence upon Diablo, that the Canon delegation met with a positive reception. They left with a deal to provide the CX to Hewlett-Packard.

As with all fundamentally new technologies, especially those rarities that entered HP from the outside, the CX engine passed through HP Labs for testing and design, before being assigned to a division for completion, manufacture, and marketing. The division chosen, Boise, Idaho, proved to be serendipitous because it was led by the most interesting new executive in the entire corporation: Richard Hackborn.

By 1983, Hackborn was already well-known inside of HP for his brilliant analytical mind. Wrote the *New York Times*, "Sometimes, subordinates say, he will closet himself in his office for a few days and write a long letter that in compelling logic outlines the company's strategy in a particular area and the reasons for it. These missives then become the marching orders for his troops. Mr. Hackborn is famous within Hewlett-Packard for laying out all elements of a strategy in a single mind-boggling chart or slide."[39]

Outside of HP, Hackborn had also become somewhat famous, if only pseudonymously. One of the biggest business best-sellers of 1976 was *The Gamesman* by Michael Maccoby. The hero of this nonfiction look at corporate leadership was a character named Jack Wakefield, who exemplified a new breed of executive "who views business as a game, adapts rapidly to change and excels at crafting strategies and motivating teams to win."[40]

In profiling Hackborn the *Times* reporter Andrew Pollack was also among the first outsiders to recognize the maverick side of Hackborn as well:

[Hackborn] is also considered one of the less conventional executives at Hewlett-Packard. Fiercely loyal to Hewlett-Packard, he is also somewhat detached, operating his own Idaho fiefdom and avoiding the bureaucracy at corporate headquarters in Palo Alto, Calif. . . . Instead of working in Hewlett-Packard's sprawling factory here [in Boise], Mr. Hackborn works a couple of miles away in a tiny suite of offices in a business-oriented shopping center, near an insurance company, a dentist and an optometrist.

Brilliant, focused, opportunistic and a risk-taker, Dick Hackborn—as many HPers noticed—seemed cut from the same cloth as the founders themselves. And he seemed to have the same knack for spectacular success. Others had looked at Canon's CX engine and, while recognizing its qualitative improvements, had not seen anything sufficiently compelling to adjust their business model. But Hackborn looked at the CX and saw the future, a family of products that—if he moved decisively—could not only create a gigantic new market, but *own* it.

Years before, Bill Hewlett had explained to him his theory of "Never try to take a fortified hill, especially if the army on top is bigger than your own." Hackborn had never forgotten—and now he saw exactly that terrain lying before him in the printer business. The high ground in established impact printer businesses—dot matrix, daisy wheel, and so on—had already been taken by other companies and was now well defended. Yet when Hackborn looked to the horizon he saw an even bigger hill, low-cost laser printers, still empty. If he could get there first, HP might end up controlling the entire field.

And that is precisely what he did, in one of the most impressive examples of product management in Hewlett-Packard history. Said Hackborn later, "We focused on the hills that weren't fortified yet."[41]

In May 1984, just a year after it first saw the Canon CX engine, Boise introduced the HP LaserJet printer. It was destined to become the largest dollar-volume product line in the company's history. It took off so fast that by late 1985 HP already controlled 85 percent of the desktop laser printer business, and, by the time the CX-powered LaserJet was replaced by the more powerful SX-powered LaserJet II, Hewlett-Packard had sold an estimated 500,000 units. Better yet, the printer was so popular in the business computing world that many dealers were willing to sign up and promote the HP-150 and Vectra personal computer lines just to get their hands on the LaserJet.

The LaserJet's success was well earned. At $3,500, it was one-tenth the price of many of its competitors. It was also small enough to sit on a desk, comparatively quick in its output, and, best of all, it was astonishingly reliable. This last resulted from a design breakthrough by HP: it put the printing technology in the replaceable cartridge, rather than building it into the printer itself. That meant that every time you replaced the (rather expensive) cartridge you were actually upgrading the printer—a distinct improvement over having to call in a technician to tear apart the printer whenever the print quality degraded.

There were also bigger, structural reasons for the LaserJet's success. In 1984, thanks to the Apple Macintosh and Adobe PageMaker software, business technology was quickly abandoning word processing to embrace simple desktop publishing, with its wide array of fonts, charts, and images. Traditional impact printers couldn't handle this new output, but a laser printer could, brilliantly. By rushing the LaserJet to market quickly, and then supporting it with a wide range of programs in HP's proprietary PCL (printer control language), Hackborn essentially blew apart the upper end of the computer printer industry, then gathered up the pieces and reassembled them in HP's image.

That was just the start. Now that he controlled the high ground, Hackborn decided to sweep the rest of the field. That meant taking on the low end of the printer business, the world of thermal, simple impact, and most of all, cheap dot-matrix printers. Though it would take a little longer to perfect, Hackborn knew he already had the weapon to take that market as well.

As early as the late 1960s design engineers at various companies around the world had come up with working versions of just about every way to put marks on paper—except one: shooting dots of ink onto the paper's surface in a controlled pattern. This technique promised to be not only one of the fastest and most precise, but also potentially the cheapest. Thus it became a kind of holy grail in the printer world.

The problem was the sprayer: how to get it to squirt exactly the same size drop every time, at the right target, and not drip or quickly gum up. Over the years, a number of research teams at different companies had tried and failed to come up with a solution. In 1979, HP Labs decided to take on the challenge. It assembled a design team with the specific task of understanding the fluid dynamics of a workable inkjet.

The team quickly determined that the solution likely lay with using an offshoot of semiconductor (and computer disk drive head) technology called thin-film. But from there things got complicated. It was not immediately obvious how to get the ink to project from the thin-film surface across the gap to the paper.

As legend has it, the answer came one day when a team member was waiting for the office coffee maker to finish percolating—and realized that he was looking at an answer. Heat. If they got ink boiling and bubbling in a controlled way, the popping bubbles of vaporized ink might in turn shoot a droplet through a nozzle onto the paper.

As it turned out, this was a classic example of a revolutionary invention that seems deceptively simple as an idea and incredibly difficult in execution. The problem was that every time they built and ran such a device it seemed to destroy itself.

Figuring out what was going wrong fell to team member John Meyer. What he eventually discovered was that as the bubbles being created by the process collapsed they acted like a jackhammer on the circuitry. The solution, Meyer realized, was to move the bubble off the surface of the resistor chip.[42]

It was a true breakthrough, proving once again that no company on earth was better at finding practical solutions to apparently impossible technological problems. Unfortunately, it would also be the last great technical breakthrough at Hewlett-Packard in the twentieth century.

The HP Labs team would spend nearly four years improving inkjet technology, dealing with one technical problem after another involving print heads, inks, residue buildup on the cartridge resistor surface, and so on. Once the project was given the formal go-ahead from corporate, it was code-named St. Helens, officially because that volcano's recent eruption resembled the action of the inkjet head—but no doubt unofficially because working on all of the technical challenges was like surviving a natural disaster.

Despite all of its problems, for those HPers who got an early glimpse of the technology, it was nothing short of a miracle. According to John Minck:

For some years in the 1980s, Barney [Oliver] set up a practice of holding an annual HP Labs Technology Show. This was intended to show the employees just what a diverse and dramatic series of R&D projects were under way in his Labs. . . .

About a year before the ink-jet printer was introduced, HP Labs just showed a technology demo, with a print head driving back and forth, and printing a line of alpha characters.

Most of us could hardly believe our eyes when we were told that the engineers had succeeding in blasting millions of tiny droplets of ink out through microscopic holes in a process that happened in microseconds. For us engineers, it was hard to conceive that tiny amounts of liquid could be made to move that fast. But there it was, writing in front of our eyes.[43]

The work on inkjet printing had been originally targeted toward the creation of a cheap, portable X-Y plotter. But by the time the HP Labs team had finally perfected the process enough for full-scale manufacturing, it was obvious that the new PC printer market was much more interesting. And that's why it was transferred in 1983 to Boise and Dick Hackborn.

In April 1984, a month before the LaserJet, HP Boise introduced the ThinkJet ("thermal inkjet") printer to worldwide attention. Unlike the sophisticated LaserJet, the first ThinkJet was a pretty primitive machine. It printed only 96 dpi—too crude for letters—used only black ink, and required special paper. But, compared with daisy-wheel printers, it was blindingly fast (150 characters per second), extremely quiet and small, and, best of all, it only cost $495. It wasn't yet good enough to compete directly with the best dot-matrix printers on the market. But it was good enough to be profitable in certain niche markets now, and had the potential to be much better than any of its counterparts in the future.

As with the laser printer, the HP inkjet printer and Dick Hackborn was one of those rare marriages in tech—like Steve Jobs and the iPod—of a great technology with a great marketer. Hackborn knew that the key to his strategy to dominate both the high and low ends of the printer business depended upon getting inkjet technology through a couple of generations of improvement— and he drove both the HP Labs and Boise to get there.

It wouldn't be enough to improve the print quality of the ThinkJet, Hackborn realized, though that would be part of it. So would plain paper printing. But to really separate HP from the pack, and steal away current dot-matrix users in the process, there had to be something more: low-cost color printing on the desktop.

HP's competitors in printing had already considered color, which would have added considerable cost to dot-matrix printers—only to have customer surveys universally come back with the answer *No*. Hackborn didn't believe it. So HP rephrased the question in its survey to instead ask prospective customers if they would be willing to buy a black text printer that could be occasionally used to print color images—all for only a marginally higher price. The answer was a resounding *Yes*.

The Gamesman had found his edge. John Meyer recalled, "Hackborn told the inkjet business guys 'Go do color.' "[44]

Once again, it fell upon the team at HP Labs to come up with the technical solution. The team had already begun experimenting with using the inkjet to print, like a professional offset press, the three basic color runs, one after another. It produced some adequate images, but the process was too cumbersome for consumer applications.

Meyer was picked to lead the team because he happened to have the unlikely combination of a PhD in physics and work experience in photolithography—the kind of lucky break HP had long been famous for. He and his team went back to the drawing board. The result was a proprietary software HP called Architecture for Color Imaging, which instructed the print head, in real time, to shoot combinations of red-green-blue (RGB) ink dots to produce the color image. Said Meyer:

> The [resulting images] didn't look like much in the beginning, but often things that turn out good don't look like much in the beginning. That, to me, is one of the fundamental things that HP Labs has got to be about. . . .
>
> The thing that was remarkable was that there was no "expert" in the process. . . . We took a lot of what I knew, which was about how to build colors by hand, and put it together with a lot of color science and imaging science and created the intelligent printer driver from that software program—and that's been the basis for the drivers for all of our color printers since then.[45]

Now Hackborn was ready to make his move. For the next decade, HP stunned the low-end printer market with one new inkjet model after another. In 1986, Boise introduced the QuietJet and QuietJet+, both with near-letter-quality 192 dpi resolution. A year later, it introduced the $1,395 PaintJet, the first full-color graphic printer. It quickly captured market leadership. Nineteen eighty-eight saw the arrival of the DeskJet, with laser-quality imagery on plain paper. A year later, HP introduced *three* new printers, the DeskJet+, the DeskWriter, and the PaintJet XL. The DeskJet 500, introduced in 1990 for just $729, quickly became the world's best-selling printer.

And on and on. Under Hackborn, HP Boise upgraded its printer generations so quickly that competitors barely had time to react to one model before its superior replacement appeared. From HP's official history: "In 1991, a mere seven years after entering the market, HP had taken on and was soundly trouncing the competition. An industry insider at the time noted that if you wanted an inkjet product you had your choice: HP, HP or HP."[46]

By the time the *New York Times* traveled to Boise in 1992 to profile the fifty-four-year-old Hackborn, HP's printer sales were estimated at $2.5 billion, at nearly 20 percent of HP's total revenues—and this was *before* the inkjet line fully gained traction. That year, HP printer sales would reach $3 billion. Meanwhile, as much of the rest of HP suffered through a malaise and high tech through a small recession, "strong printer sales" the *Times* noted, "continue to contribute and were cited as one reason the company's net income is up an astounding 49 percent in its most recent quarter."

So successful had Hackborn been with HP's printers that by the time the *Times* reporter arrived in Boise, he had been promoted to company vice president and put in charge of turning around HP's long-troubled personal computer business. As a measure of the respect with which he was held by the company, when Hackborn demanded that he manage his new assignment from Idaho, Hewlett-Packard acquiesced.

Not surprisingly, throughout HP it was whispered that Dick Hackborn had already been picked to become John Young's replacement five years hence when Young retired.

As it turned out, those rumors would be answered in a matter of months. Bill and Dave were coming home.

Young in Retrospect

Assessing the fifteen-year tenure of John Young at the helm of Hewlett-Packard has always been problematic. For all of the achievements on paper—and they are impressive—there still remain the imperfect finish and final judgments of the founders. That ambivalence toward the Young era still echoed at HP a quarter century later.

Young was, after all, Bill and Dave's handpicked choice as their successor. And his appointment as president (and a year later, CEO) of a giant corporation at such a comparatively young age—just forty-five—surprised the industry. It also surprised much of Hewlett-Packard: in picking Young, Hewlett and Packard leapfrogged the entire second generation of HP executives—men who had spent as many as thirty years in loyal service to the company—to name instead the superstar of HP's third generation.

It may have been a classic Bill and Dave play, ignoring the predictable spoils appointment for the radical, long-term play, but it didn't go down entirely easy on executive row in Palo Alto. No one doubted that John Young was qualified—his had been one of the great careers at HP—but there would always remain the question of whether he had the character and the temperament to fill Bill's and Dave's shoes. No doubt part of this was the natural reaction of an employee population that had never known anyone but the founders at the head of their company. But as the years passed, other, more realistic questions were raised about the quality of Young's leadership.

Still, there is no question that John Young accomplished remarkable things as CEO of Hewlett-Packard Co. When he was named president in 1977, HP was a $1.4 billion company, with 35,000 employees. When Young retired in 1992, Hewlett-Packard's annual revenues had reached $16.4 billion, and the company employed 92,000 people.

In other words, during that fifteen year interval, despite the fact that HP was now one of the largest corporations in the world (it joined the Fortune 50 in 1988), Young still managed to grow the company at nearly its historic rate under Hewlett and Packard.

Meanwhile, during those fifteen years, Young also presided over a number of important new product creations at the company, including laser and inkjet printers, the model 9000 computers, RISC computing, the first successful HP personal computers, and palmtop computing. On the business side, he led the company into China with China Hewlett-Packard (CHP), the first high-tech joint venture in that country. He also took HP onto the Tokyo stock exchange, implemented corporate recycling and energy efficiency programs, opened a second major company research lab—this one in Bristol, England— and, most visibly, directed the building of a new HP corporate headquarters just down the hill from the old one.

This was no mean accomplishment, especially in the face of oil price shocks, rampant inflation, one of the worst recessions in tech history, and while managing a huge, ungainly company burdened with two almost mutually exclusive main product groups and passing through its half-century mark.

But John Young was used to success. Like Packard, his life had been one of few mistakes and fewer failures. Like Packard, he even looked the part: with his cleft chin, square jaw, and thick hair, he looked like the central casting version of a corporate CEO. Since joining HP in 1958, he had served as regional sales manager, then in corporate finance, then marketing manager of the Microwave division, and finally Microwave division general manager. He did all of them brilliantly.

Thus, except for actual lab research, Young by the age of thirty-one had already punched all of the tickets at HP to jump to senior management. As already noted, that call came five years later, when he was named a vice president of the company and assumed leadership of the Electronic Products Group, which included instruments, measurement systems, and components. Only six years later, he jumped again. This was the big one: executive vice-president and a member of the HP board of directors.

Through all of this, Young wasn't a beloved figure, but neither was he disliked. Rather, his rise through the company seemed inevitable. He was just too smart, too ambitious, *too* perfect to go anywhere but the top. And he seemed so destined to lead HP that no one really begrudged him his success when that call to the presidency arrived just three years later.

But all of that perfection came at a cost. What Young seemed to lack, at least at the distance most HPers saw him, was that touch of humanity they saw in Bill and Dave. It was difficult to imagine him pulling up a stool at the next lab bench and helping solder wiring on a new prototype like Hewlett would, or pounding on a table and demanding respect for the lowliest HP employee, as they knew Packard would.

Some of this was not John Young's fault. To be seen as too aloof and political is the fate of all corporate types who follow founding entrepreneurs. Professional managers don't get to the top by exhibiting the personal eccentricities and maverick behavior that make the founders, with their unassailable stock holdings, so endearing. (Of course, they usually don't do as much damage through capriciousness, either.)

In fact, to those who knew him well, Young did have the common touch. He was, by all accounts, a loving husband and father. And despite his image as a moderately animated statue, some HPers saw another side. Recalled HP historian John Minck, who worked with Young both in the Microwave division and at corporate:

> John was a knowledgeable manager. He practiced Management by Walking Around religiously, visiting production operations regularly, and learning of current problems.
>
> One morning, just after we arrived at work, John and I were chatting over a cup of coffee. One of the production process managers came up, and urgently told John of a possible problem that had happened about 10 p.m. the previous night. It seemed some excess acidic chemicals had inadvertently released into the Palo Alto sewer system.
>
> John said, "No problem. I know all about it, and it was taken care of. The city was notified. I was here last night, and learned of it when I was down having coffee with the night crew."[47]

But few HP employees ever saw this side of Young. Though he logged many more miles in the eighties than the older Bill and Dave had in the seventies visiting HP plants around the world, the impact of all of this attention was just not as great. Once again, this was not entirely Young's fault: at this point in their careers, Bill and Dave carried with them the penumbra of legend everywhere they went; Young was merely the CEO. A visit from the founders would be the stuff of conversation and reminiscence for years to come. And Bill and Dave knew it. By now they were the consummate corporate actors. They knew exactly how the little friendly gesture by Packard to a young employee or low-level secretary, or a spirited new product assembly competition between Hewlett and a couple of division executives, would pull together the "family" more than any formal directive. It came easily to them; it had been the way Bill and Dave had always worked, and it was a natural extension of their characters.

It was none of those things for John Young. He was a sales and marketing expert, not a technologist. He was drawn to the big strategy, not the small gesture. And his personal warmth did not translate easily to the theatrical stage of corporate leadership. A Bill and Dave visit brought a connection to a half century of HP glory; a John Young visit meant racing to meet revenue targets.

What *was* Young's fault was a series of choices that actually amplified his appearance of detachment from the daily lives of HPers. One was his decision to reduce the number of personal appearances he made around the company and to substitute a corporate-wide television network through which he could make major company announcements, such as earnings and profit sharing.

In theory, it was a reasonable decision: Hewlett-Packard had grown so large and far-flung that maintaining the traditional personal contact of the Bill and Dave era was becoming both difficult and a threat to Young's productivity as CEO. But in practice, it only increased the emotional distance between headquarters in Palo Alto and the rest of the company. John Young was now just a talking head facing a camera thousands of miles away.*

But that miscalculation was minor compared with what would be one of the most enduring decisions of Young's tenure as HP CEO: the construction of the new corporate headquarters.

Once again, this decision was made for all of the right reasons. The original headquarters building, with its distinctive sawtooth roof and impressively prescient "green" architecture, was beginning to look old. Moreover, as HP had become a multibillion-dollar corporation, so too had its headquarters operation seen a commensurate growth (too much, some HPers complained). With insufficient facilities at the old headquarters to hold them, these operations were scattered in rented offices all over that part of Palo Alto. Both financial prudence and managerial control argued for the construction of a new, centralized headquarters facility.

Hewlett-Packard had the land for it: even as they were helping Terman create Stanford Industrial Park, Bill and Dave were already reserving a large enough parcel of land to deal with years of future growth. Though HP had grown even faster than the founders had imagined, and its manufacturing plants were now scattered across almost every major city of Silicon Valley, as well as a dozen states and a score of nations around the world, the company had kept undeveloped a large parcel adjacent to and just down the hill from the old headquarters.

It was here that John Young built HP's first new headquarters in thirty years.

Ground was broken in 1979, and the building, at 3000 Hanover Drive, was completed on schedule two years later. It was, and is, a beautiful structure: a low-slung bronze wedge that conforms to the topography so well that it can almost be overlooked by those driving down Page Mill Road, so well nestled into the hillside that it seems much smaller than it really is. This new HP headquarters, in its modesty and sense of civic responsibility, was a far cry—and, in that regard, a distinct improvement—over the triumphant, and unmistakable, old headquarters.

But it was also gloomier and more claustrophobic than its predecessor, lacking the soaring spires, the walls of glass, and the natural light that had made working in the older building such an uplifting experience.

Worse, there is a "law" in Silicon Valley, first formulated around this time by a local journalist, that "whenever a company builds a new headquarters, short its stock."[48] The reasoning was that when a company decides to construct a new headquarters, most of the people who run the company—the people who will work out of the new building—are inevitably distracted from their real work by such considerations as who will get the best view or the corner office or be stuck near the bathrooms. And then, of course, there are all of the dislocations of the move itself.

But the biggest danger of a new headquarters is that—always for very good reasons—it becomes the occasion for the senior executives to make their work environment even more exclusive than before. That is what happened at Hewlett-Packard; indeed, witnessing just those events at HP had given the reporter the idea for the law.

The changes, by the standards of most Fortune 50 companies, weren't extreme—an elegant glass-curtained office for John Young, an executive washroom, and private dining room—but by HP standards they were shocking. It was hard to argue against the notion that the chief executive of a $10 billion corporation should have a private dining area to meet with world leaders and other distinguished guests; but it was also hard to forget sitting in the old HP lunchroom and having Bill and Dave, trays in hand, come sit on the bench beside you. And in light of that that memory, both John Young and headquarters seemed even farther away. "Galactic Headquarters" was the nickname some HPers gave the place.[49]

Still, as underscored by the impressive growth numbers HP exhibited through the eighties, none of these compromises to the company's culture seemed to slow HP by even a step. John Young may not have been as warm as Bill and Dave, but when it came to running the machinery of a giant, modern corporation, he was arguably a better pure businessman than either of them. And under his management, HP became a more efficient, better-structured company than it had ever been before. If it had lost some of the upside potential that came with the mercurial decisions of its founders, it also lost the downside risk of spectacular failure as well. And if Hewlett-Packard abandoned some of its excitement as a radical innovator of new markets, new employee programs, and new community service initiatives, it also became much more efficient at driving industry standards, rationalizing HR operations around the company, and serving its communities through systematic underwriting of nonprofits, pollution control, and giving its managers leave to serve in the public sector.

Young himself was a classic example of the balanced, socially engaged chief executive. While running HP he also served as chairman of President Reagan's Commission on Industrial Competitiveness and its successor, the Council on Competitiveness. He was also national chairman of Junior Achievement and a founding director, and later president, of the Malcolm Baldrige National Quality Award. And in his retirement he served on the President's council of Advisors on Science and Technology, the Advisory Committee for Trade Policy and Negotiations, the Business Council, and the National Academy of Engineering.

All of this extracurricular activity certainly helped give Hewlett-Packard Co. a presence—as a company—in Washington it had never before known, even when Dave Packard was at the Defense Department. Young turned HP from a highly successful West Coast corporation into a pillar of the American business establishment. A half century after the plucky little company began in the Addison Avenue garage, it was now a leading indicator of national economic health, and a barometer of the state of the world economy.

But these same traits for organization, efficiency, structure, and stability that worked so well for Young during his first decade as CEO of HP, in time began to take their toll on the company. Almost from the day of his appointment, Hewlett-Packard began to bleed talent, especially those individuals who exhibited maverick, unorthodox, or entrepreneurial behavior. They could sense that the old, unpredictable HP, the family that took even its black sheep and prodigal sons to heart, was disappearing—to be replaced by a more standardized HP "type." And as the years went on, the more the company seemed to expel these nonconformists—politely, of course, and by their own volition—even though they were many of the same folks who had helped bring the company to greatness.

The first to go were the senior executives who looked at Young's management style and his comparative youth and realized they could never get along for the twenty years until he retired and they at last had a shot at his chair. And once they looked around, often for the first time in their careers, they realized that a résumé that included senior management at HP was like gold in booming Silicon Valley.

Thus, by the end of the 1980s, an entire vertical swath of management at HP's Computer Group was gone: group vice president Paul Ely to Convergent, division general manager Ed McCracken to Silicon Graphics, and division marketing manager Ed Krause to 3Com. The loss of each was, in its own way, devastating. Krause was a potential corporate vice president of marketing. McCracken, brilliant and calculating, was the John Young of the next HP generation, a fast-rising superstar who by his late twenties was already being whispered about as the company's future CEO.

But the loss of Ely was the worst blow. Much of the power of the Bill and Dave partnership was their complementary personalities. They filled in each other's weaknesses—and just as importantly, trusted each other to do so. Fiery, difficult and unpredictable, Ely was the antithesis of the cool, smooth, and rational Young. But what might have been a perfect match of opposites failed, perhaps because the two men were just too far apart, their visions of the future of HP were simply too different. As a result, the two men never really got along, and worse, they never really trusted each other's judgment.

Thus, when the time came for John Young to appoint his number two, HP's executive vice president, he made the single biggest mistake of his career. From that moment, Hewlett-Packard turned onto a trajectory that would ultimately lead to a corporate crisis and the end of Young's career as CEO.

Nice Guys

In choosing an executive vice president, Young essentially had two choices: with Ely off the table, he could take a senior executive from either the Instrument Group or from HP's second-tier divisions (such as Medical, Analytical, or Opto). A third and more interesting choice—reaching deeper into the management ranks, as Bill and Dave had with him, to pick out an up-and-comer like Hackborn, McCracken, or a young manager named Lew Platt who was beginning to make waves in large computer networks—was not in Young's personality.

The head of HP instruments was Bill Terry. Approximately Young's contemporary, Terry was passionate, often fiery, a tech romantic, mischievous, and unconventional. He had done a great job in keeping the aging HP Instrument Group relevant, but seemed to have little interest in computers. And computers were obviously HP's future. Terry was also too rough around the edges, *too Hewlett*, for the new HP with its elegant headquarters and global diplomacy.

Instead, in 1984 Young picked HP's other group vice president, Dean Morton, as HP's new chief operating officer. In 1990 Morton was made executive vice president and appointed to the HP board of directors. Together with Young, the two men comprised Hewlett-Packard's chief executive office, in charge of overall company management.

Morton was a gracious and thoughtful manager, and one of the most intelligent people at Hewlett-Packard. He was roundly admired by his fellow executives for his calmness, his competence, and his strategic thinking—all traits that, in later years, would make him one of the most desired and respected corporate directors in high tech. His problem wasn't lack of ability, but lack of difference. John Young had picked as his executive officer not someone who complemented his strengths and weaknesses, but *amplified* them.

This was a fatal error. Young may have been a superb businessman, but he was also, at heart, a consensus-builder. But that wasn't what HP needed. The HP Way took care of that; HPers naturally built consensus. Ironically, for such a family company, what HP always required was a bold, but ultimately constrained, decision-maker—a risk-taker who set ambitious goals and then entrusted the company with the task of reaching them. Put metaphorically, the Hewlett-Packard family needed a strong father, and John Young was perennially the golden boy, the overaccomplishing oldest son.

With a strong and decisive technologist as COO, either Young or Morton could have likely maintained Hewlett-Packard's momentum into the late nineties and their own retirements. Instead, they had each other, and that was the wrong combination. In the short term—a product generation or two— HP could survive, even thrive, with a John Young at the helm. But high tech was too fast-moving, too rough-and-tumble, and too unforgiving of prudence to let HP coast on its history and reputation for long. And by the end of the eighties, it was becoming increasingly apparent to HPers, as well as a few astute outsiders, that something was going wrong at Hewlett-Packard. The company that had always been able to regain its youth by reinventing itself now suddenly seemed old and slow and confused.

Nowhere was this more apparent than in HP's workstation business.[50] The company had been one of the first to introduce a computer workstation, the HP 9000 Series 90, way back in 1982—not long after Apollo introduced the first workstation, in the same year as the first Sun workstation and two years before DEC. With its huge size, immense distribution network, and reputation in desktop calculators, HP should have crushed the competition and owned the market. Instead, exhibiting the arrogant and solipsistic "Not Invented Here" attitude that was beginning to infect every division of the company, it wasted time trying to do everything itself.

Thus, while Sun and Apollo, working with much smaller budgets, simply put together new models using off-the-shelf components, notably the powerful new Motorola 680X0 processor, HP decided it would design its own chip, to be called the Focus II. On paper, the Focus II was a better chip than the Motorola—but on paper was pretty much where it stayed, because after burning precious months, HP dropped Focus and adopted the Motorola processor.

In fact, HP's Computer Group already had in-house the perfect processor for the job: the PA RISC chip, a product of its massive RISC program for minicomputers. Unfortunately, given the increasing balkanization of the computer group, the RISC chip program was zealously guarded by the HP 9000 team and wasn't made available for design into workstations. Compounding this, the 9000 RISC program itself ran into software problems and was delayed by two years, until November 1986.

Thus it wasn't until May 1987 that HP finally introduced a RISC workstation. Two months later it was trumped by a Sun RISC workstation of equivalent power at almost half the price. It wasn't until March 1991, ten years after HP began its RISC program, that the company finally introduced a truly competitive RISC workstation.

Not surprisingly, Hewlett-Packard, which for fifty years had consistently dominated every market that it had either pioneered or entered very early, now found itself fourth in a four-company race.

The company responded with a move that foreshadowed its darkest years ahead: it went out and bought one of its biggest competitors, Apollo, for $500 million. Wrote *Upside* magazine:

On paper this move made HP look much stronger. HP and Apollo together held the number-one position in the workstation industry in 1989 in both revenues and installed base. Below the surface, other problems persisted and some got worse.

This lack of coordination, which had long plagued HP's computer units, was magnified with the addition of Apollo. "Sometimes the Apollo people in Massachusetts did not know what the Fort Collins [Colorado] people were doing," says Carolyn Griffin, a senior analyst at International Data Corp. "In order to make a decision they often had to go up three or four levels to get someone who had responsibility for both product lines."

Thus, HP often did not take a systems approach in its workstation design, which resulted in products that did not offer top performance. "The workstations were put together from a bunch of different parts built by different divisions," says an HP employee. This approach also led to delays and even some interdivisional rivalries. "One of the things we recognized was that HP was doing an awful lot of fighting with each other," the former Apollo employee adds. "We said, 'Hey, the competition is Sun Microsystems, not Cupertino versus Fort Collins.' "[51]

It was a measure of just how lumbering and uncoordinated the company had become that in 1990, a year after the purchase of Apollo, which had made it number one in the workstation market, it had already fallen to a distant number two.

There were a few bright spots in the company. Dick Hackborn was working his magic in Boise—and doing his best to stay away from headquarters. In Cupertino, Lew Platt, a transfer from the Medical Group, was fighting to rationalize the structure of the Computer Group and bring HP back into the personal computer business. And Bill Terry was still keeping the aged Instrument Group rolling along, its profits serving as a cash cow for the rest of the company, and its people acting as the enduring repository of the HP Way. (Literally, in the case of Terry, who, having saved the old company instruments—including an HP 200A—in the early 1980s, now became the chief defender of the new company archives. HP, it seems, was not only becoming unsure about its future, but also losing its grip on its past.)

But with increasing bureaucratic inertia at the top, these heroic efforts at the division level were increasingly stymied. Hewlett-Packard was becoming too thick with layers of management, too risk-averse, and too slow to move. Even the HP Way, that dynamic philosophy of interpersonal relations at the company, was becoming more ossified by the year. By 1990, a dozen years after Hewlett's and Packard's retirements, a whole new generation of employees—nearly 60,000 of them—had joined the company without ever having known life under the founders. To them, the HP Way was reduced to a handful of dictums: no layoffs, flex-time, profit sharing, coffee breaks, Management by Walking Around.

Even the very heart of the HP Way, trust, had been seriously compromised: with so many layers of management, it was almost impossible to set general objectives at the top that were reduced to explicit orders by the time they reached the rank and file. "The HP Way under John Young," said analyst

Peter Rogers, "is to get a consensus ahead of time. It never happens. He is more of a politician than a businessman."[52]

And there was no indication that the situation was going to get anything but worse:

> Under President John Young's leadership, HP lost the balance that had made the company so successful in its earlier years. The firm swung too far in the direction of consensus decision-making. His management style led to such organizational quagmires as a matrix management system and a proliferation of committees and meetings.[53]

Wrote business author Richard Pascale, who was at the time preparing a case study on HP, "The combination of John Young, who is a smart cookie, but is non-confronting, with a COO [Morton] who is very genteel doesn't give you the same kind of power you had with Hewlett and Packard. These guys have a difficult time with contention."[54]

Michael Maccoby, who wrote about Hackborn in *The Gamesman*, looked back to the two founders to explain what had been lost: He told *Upside* magazine, "Hewlett was a craftsman, and Packard was a gamesman. The power of HP lay in the combination of the two."

Wisdom and Reward

But where were Bill and Dave?

For one thing, they were busy with their lives. The two foundations. The Monterey Aquarium and Institute. The new facilities at Stanford. Scholarships and fellowships. Managing their various properties and ranches. Sitting on committees and boards. For men now in their seventies—and, in Hewlett's case, suffering from medical problems—they were extraordinarily busy. They were also spending more time now with their families, including a small army of teenaged grandchildren.

It was also the time in their life for honors, as befitting two of the wealthiest and most influential men of their time. Their official biographies each carry long lists of these awards and titles. A sampling:

———

David Packard—Trustee of the Herbert Hoover Foundation, the American Enterprise Institute, and the Hoover Institution. Vice chairman of the California Nature Conservancy in 1983, and from 1983 to 1989 a director of the Wolf

Trap Foundation in Vienna, Virginia, an organization devoted to the performing arts.

Appointed in 1985 by former president Reagan to chair the Blue Ribbon
Commission on Defense Management. Member of the (beloved to conspiracy
buffs) Trilateral Commission from 1973 to 1981. From 1975 to 1982, a member of the U.S.-USSR Trade and Economic Council's committee on science
and technology. Chairman of the U.S.-Japan Advisory Commission from
1983 to 1985. Member of the President's Council of Advisors on Science and
Technology from 1990 to 1992.

Active in the Business Roundtable and founding vice chairman of the
California Roundtable. Director of several business organizations, including
Boeing Co., Caterpillar Tractor, Chevron Corp., and Genentech Inc. Director
of Beckman Laser Institute and Medical Clinic. Founder and chairman of the
Monterey Bay Aquarium and Monterey Bay Aquarium Research Institute.

Awarded honorary degrees of doctor of science from Colorado College;
doctor of law from the University of California, Catholic University, and Pep-
perdine University; doctor of letters from Southern Colorado State College;
and doctor of engineering from the University of Notre Dame.

———

William Hewlett—Awarded by President Reagan in 1983 the National Medal
of Science, the nation's highest scientific honor.

Trustee of Mills College and Stanford University. Member of the San
Francisco regional panel of the Commission on White House Fellows.

Director of the Kaiser Foundation Hospital and Health Plan from 1972 to
1978, and the Drug Abuse Council in Washington, D.C. Honorary trustee of
the California Academy of Sciences, member of the National Academy of Engineering and the National Academy of Sciences and fellow of the American
Academy of Arts and Sciences. Trustee emeritus of the Carnegie Institution of
Washington.

Chairman of the William and Flora Hewlett Foundation, which he established with his late wife, Flora. Director of the Monterey Bay Aquarium Research Institute.

Honorary doctor of law degrees from the University of California at
Berkeley, Yale University, Mills College, Marquette University, and Brown
University; honorary doctor of science degrees from the Polytechnic Institute
of New York and Kenyon College; honorary doctor of engineering degrees
from the University of Notre Dame, Dartmouth College, and Utah State University; and an honorary doctor of humane letters from Johns Hopkins University. Honorary doctor of public policy degree from the Rand Graduate

Institute, and honorary doctor of humanities degree from Santa Clara University. Honorary doctor of electronic science degree from the University of Bologna in Italy.

————

And these awards and honors are just from their early retirement years.

As always with advanced age, Bill and Dave were also busy dealing with the diminishments and losses within themselves and those closest to them. In Hewlett's case, there were ongoing health problems: the weak heart and the first of what would be a series of strokes that would mark the rest of his life. He was also learning to cope with a new wife and the extended family she brought with her. His strength was limited these days, and his face had grown softer. The gruff and curt Bill Hewlett had evolved into a warmer, gentler man.

Meanwhile his intellect, if anything, seemed *more* acute. The dyslexic student who had to memorize everything by ear, now, after a half-century of watching the behavior of people under the pressure of daily business, seemed to have distilled it all into a deep understanding of human nature.

For example, when HP's printers developed a quality problem, manager Rick Belluzzo was hauled in front of the Hewlett-Packard board of directors—including Bill Hewlett—to explain the situation. Recalled Belluzzo, "I said that we had a range of tens of millions of dollars of exposure here—and [as for] Bill, I couldn't even tell if he was paying attention."

But then, Hewlett suddenly turned to Belluzzo and asked, "Rick, what have you learned from this experience?"

Belluzzo was taken aback. Hewlett didn't attack the younger man for his error. He never even raised his voice. Instead the two men talked like compatriots, dispassionately analyzing a difficult problem. And when Bill was satisfied that Belluzzo understood what had gone wrong and how to fix it, he gave him only a single ultimatum: "Make sure your No. 1 responsibility is to take care of our customers."

That was it. Belluzzo left the room a changed man. It was a moment he never forgot.[55]

If Hewlett grew kinder in his old age, Packard became less and less patient with human foolishness, especially self-delusion. Unlike Hewlett, his health remained strong, and so, as always, he seemed an iron man. His face had now grown longer and more jowly, his hair thinner, and his great height was reduced now by a slight stoop. But his voice, always deep, had become a rumble, like sound emerging from deep rock.

Indeed, in his final years, there seemed something elemental about David

Packard—as if he had been so successful and so famous that those things didn't mean much to him anymore, except as tools to accomplish his goals. He had never been a sentimental man—and now his attention seemed focused on getting things done with the minimum of wasted effort. At an age when most men stop to look backwards, Packard was still searching for opportunities to make a difference.

One way was devote more time to his family. But even here, his actions were still strategic; he still played the Packard "fork" with genius. Thus the project to spend more time with his daughters resulted in the creation of a national institution in the Monterey Bay Aquarium. And, in the process, Julie and Nancy also got to work beside him, apprenticing to him on how to become major civic leaders. Susan, meanwhile, trained with her father to become a director of HP, a trustee at Stanford, and chairman of the family foundation. David Woodley Packard, whose life had always led him in the opposite direction of his forever forward-looking father—into classics and antiquities—now, with his father's blessing, took on the challenge of historic film preservation, becoming one of the most important figures in that field. But in the years to come, he too would begin to show his father's entrepreneurial gifts (and politics)—pulling away from the increasingly left-leaning family foundation, he would create the more conservative, $1.5 billion Packard Humanities Institute. And in 2002, he would team up with Walter Hewlett to fight for the survival of their fathers' company, showing a talent for business strategy that few knew either son had.

But the most effective family partner to Dave was his wife, Lucile. Here, at the end of their lives, the two were again working together as closely as they had in the early years of their marriage, when Lucile was doing HP's books, delivering gifts to new company parents, and convincing her husband to hold company picnics and beer busts. Lucile had also been largely the impetus behind the creation and expansion of the great foundation that bore their names—and had acted as its director during the years when Dave had been busy running HP or working in Washington (and, some complained, it was her influence that had turned the foundation away from Dave's conservative politics).

Now, even as her own health began to fail—she would fight cancer for six years—Lucile found time not only to help her children create the aquarium, but embarked on the biggest project of her own career: a brand-new children's hospital at Stanford, to serve as an adjunct to the university's own giant teaching hospital.

Lucile had always been as entrepreneurial as her husband, and the many years of watching him in action, advising him, and then managing the foundation had trained her to be, if not the equal of Dave, still a brilliant executive in her own right.

The Lucile Packard Children's Hospital, as it would be named in her memory, was a $60 million project. Lucile was relentless in her drive to get it built, and to build it right. Even as her health faded, she toured the country, visiting twenty other children's hospitals to research best practices. Recalled Diamuid McGuire, community affairs director at the hospital, "She was concerned about everything from the color of the upholstery of the furniture to the broad medical direction of the project."

Those who worked with her noticed that Lucile, despite being both the chairman of the project and its underwriter, always managed using a combination of consensus and decisiveness, a style remarkably like her husband's. Recalled Charles Anderson, who would follow her as chairman of the hospital, "I've seen in the course of my career many chairmen of the board. She was probably the most effective in that role I've ever known. She was neither domineering nor was she so self-effacing so as not to exercise leadership. She operated on the basis of getting the consensus views of the people who were involved in these activities."[56]

Lucile Salter Packard died, at age seventy-two, on May 31, 1987, at the Packard family home in Los Altos Hills. Ground was broken on the Lucile Packard Children's Hospital in 1988, and the hospital officially opened in 1990 to universal acclaim. Fifteen years later, it had become one of the world's leading hospitals for children, especially those with unusual care requirements, and was staffed by 650 physicians and nearly 5,000 staffers and volunteers. In the minds of many in Silicon Valley, Lucile's hospital, more even than Hewlett-Packard Co. itself, was the Packard family's greatest contribution to its home community.

Lucile was gone, as were most of the men and women with whom Bill and Dave had started their adventure all those years ago in the Addison garage. Time was running very short, and Dave Packard knew it. He was a physical giant who had lived now long beyond his three score and ten—making a widower's life now in a land few very tall men ever reached. Yet his mind had lost nothing; it still presented challenge after challenge to him—and all the while he knew the big projects would never be finished under his watch. He was one of the greatest leaders of his time, and he was in a hurry to use that gift while there was still time.

There is a classic story that captures the David Packard of this period. Asked to sit on the board of Genentech, Dave had realized that he didn't really know enough about genetic engineering to give good business advice to the company. So, sitting down at his home in Los Altos Hills, he wrote up a long list of books that he needed and sent his handyman down the road to the Stanford University bookstore to buy them.

A few weeks later, at the board meeting, when the CEO inquired if Mr. Packard would like to add anything, Dave reeled off a series of questions on recombinant DNA so scientifically arcane and penetrating that the company executives had to send for their lab people to get the answers.

This was Dave Packard at *eighty* years old.

He would soon need every one of his skills, and those of his business partner, to investigate, and then deal with, an immense problem that had been growing for years, but only now was he beginning to recognize. It was HP itself.

The Great Return

The distraction of their retirement lives was actually the lesser reason why Bill and Dave didn't spot the growing dysfunctionality at Hewlett-Packard Co. earlier than they did. Far more important was the HP Way itself, and the mutual trust that powered it.

As chairman of the board, Dave Packard was acutely aware of the dangers of his position. He had seen too many companies paralyzed by a founder-chairman who interfered too deeply into the work of his successor. Packard had resolved not to do that, not least because it violated the principles of the HP Way.*

As Packard saw it, his task as chairman was to help John Young formulate the company's long-term strategy and oversee the results of that strategy's implementation. It was not to second-guess his successor on tactics, product development, and the day-to-day management of the company, because that would violate the core principle of entrusting your subordinates to exercise their own judgment on achieving the company's objectives, and giving them the maximum freedom to do so. Only if that subordinate was failing in some serious manner to achieve those goals was the manager obliged to intervene.

For all of the structural problems that were eating away at Hewlett-Packard in the late 1980s, on paper the company was still healthy and strong. Between 1988 and 1989, for example, its revenues grew 21 percent, from $9.8 billion to $11.9 billion, and employment jumped from 87,000 to 95,000. As long as Young was hitting his revenue and profit targets, and the company wasn't suffering any scandals or obvious employee unhappiness, Packard saw no reason to interfere with its daily operations.

But as the 1990s began, the situation on the ground at Hewlett-Packard had begun to change for the worse. The indecisiveness and inattention of the preceding years, fueled by an economic downturn, began to surface. Wrote the *San Jose Mercury-News* afterward:

> In the late 1980s, as if reflecting the growing age of its founders, Hewlett-Packard began to slowly rot from the inside. The world was changing fast, entire product categories, such as the once dominant minicomputers, seemed to evaporate overnight. Only the most nimble firms managed to survive by dancing ahead of events. Meanwhile, sclerotic, flat-footed giants like Wang, Data General and DEC—HP's toughest old competitors—were sunk or left crippled in the water.
>
> The clock was now ticking on Hewlett-Packard, and HP acted as if it didn't care. The entire company seemed bloated and out of touch, its employees buried in endless meetings. Products were late or inconsequential, marketing programs were half-hearted or misdirected and the best talent was bailing out for more exciting opportunities elsewhere. Even suppliers seemed to have caught HP's disease, consistently delivering components late or incongruent with the original orders. . . .
>
> Hewlett-Packard Co. was dying.[57]

Growth in 1990 was just 11 percent to $13.2 billion. Only some of that could be blamed on the economy, and the company still managed to maintain its profit margins by letting attrition reduce its ranks to 89,000.

Now Packard began to notice. For those who were paying attention, these financials were a subtle warning about a fundamental weakness of the HP Way: its dependence upon trust broke down when faced with subordinates who were honestly fooling themselves.

Packard's good friend President Ronald Reagan was saying at that very moment about the Soviet Union, "Trust but verify." The great check and balance to "trust" in the HP Way were Management by Walking Around and the freedom of all employees when they weren't being heard to take their message to the top.

Now, with his company beginning to stumble, Dave Packard started listening closely and, if not yet walking around, at least asking some penetrating questions.

The catalyst for what would privately be called by HPers "the Great Return" was a note from an unnamed low-level secretary out in one of the many divisions, one of the thousands of veteran HPers who believed in the HP Way and who had most suffered from the changes of recent years. She had written to Packard because, as she said in the note, he and Bill had always said that their doors were open to everyone at the company:

[It was] a note that never would have been sent to the chairman of any other company, a note that never would have been read and believed by any other corporate chairman, that turned Hewlett-Packard around.

The note was simply a complaint by this HPer that she was wasting all of her time in meetings instead of getting anything done, and that this problem seemed endemic to the entire company.

Packard, and Hewlett with him, saw much more.[58]*

The note was a tiny cry for help from a small, distant corner of the HP family. But the patriarch heard it—and now he began to act. After expressing his concerns to Bill Hewlett, the two old men began to ask questions, study reports, interview key individuals inside and outside the company. *Upside* magazine wrote in June 1991:

> During last year Packard and Hewlett started "walking around" once again. Both spent time visiting with various HP employees to learn first hand the reasons why HP's computer business was having problems.
>
> "We spent some time with Bill Hewlett last year around Christmas," says a mid-level HP employee in the company's workstation operations. "The meeting was held to give the employees an opportunity to discuss their operations with the co-founder."

The two founders also held meetings at the senior management level for the same purpose. Often they brought in the author Richard Pascale, whose recent book *Managing on the Edge* had criticized HP for what he saw as too much decentralization and consensus management, and not enough smart, quick decision-making. Being engineers talking to engineers, Bill and Dave didn't just appeal to the HP Way or to nostalgia for their own leadership days, but marshaled the best empirical arguments to support their case.

Bob Sadler was a management consultant to HP who had just found himself in considerable trouble. For a decade he had put on two- and three-day workshops for companies, typically attended by about twenty-four managers and executives, on managing change in a highly competitive business environment.

In 1990 he had been invited to give the workshop at HP. It had gone over so well—HP having become a textbook case of a company fighting change—that he was contracted to put on as many as thirty of the workshops over the course of the next year at HP divisions around the world. Suddenly, Sadler found himself with a lucrative full-time job working with Hewlett-Packard—and then just as suddenly, it was all at risk.

On the third day of a workshop in Palo Alto, he recalls, "we were working with one of the project leaders to mitigate some of the issues that were stalling his project. . . . The major issue was related to a person who was an informal leader and was resisting the change. That wasn't uncommon: most projects [at HP] had a similar issue."[59]

> The leader had tried everything that was suggested. The change project was critical to the future of the IT function. The business case for the change was obvious and one person was holding up progress. No amount of time and attention was enough to get him to step aside. He was acting as if he worked in an academic environment where the bottom line didn't matter.[60]

Finally, Sadler had had enough. He suggested that the recalcitrant employee either be transferred or "laid off" from the company. This, in turn, led to "an intense discussion in which the participants bemoaned the fact that it was very hard to remove people at HP."

> It was a conversation that broke out by the third day of *every* workshop that I delivered at HP. I said that I didn't believe that it was that hard to remove people at HP because I had seen it done. Then, I suggested either removing the person or canceling the project.
> Canceling the project was not an option. The leader left the workshop believing that he should remove the person.[61]

But so ossified had become what had once, under Bill and Dave, been a social contract among HP employees that even certain terms had now become taboo. That night, Sadler received a call from the manager who had contracted him. She was furious: her boss had learned "that I had used the 'L word'—*layoff*—in my workshop. And I was never to do that again."

When Sadler said that he didn't understand, that the same topic came up in every one of his workshops, he was ordered to read the company's materials on "The HP Way," which included the Corporate Objectives. There, he was told, he would learn that "letting someone go was not an option." Sadler had, in fact, read the materials:

> I said I was sorry, but I didn't see anything in the material that said that the company couldn't lay anyone off; that the closest thing in the HP Way was "Respect for Individuals."
> The manager said I could not conduct the workshops any more

unless I complied. I said I couldn't comply because the question of irrational resistance to change would always come up and I would have no credibility if I couldn't deal with it honestly.

So, my scheduled workshops were canceled.[62]

A week later, Sadler drove down to Monterey—to the aquarium—to put on another HP workshop, this one off the main contract. He assumed it would be his last for Hewlett-Packard.

Never having been to Monterey, he arrived several hours before the kick-off dinner, and decided to use the time to tour the aquarium's exhibits.

I was standing at the Wave Tank, observing the action, when someone standing next to me began talking about what was going on in the tank. I assumed he was a docent, and I didn't look at him for a while.

He was very knowledgeable about the microbiology of the tank. He described the importance of the wave action on the rocks to the entire food chain and ecosystem. I was impressed with what he knew and the way he communicated. Then, he said, "I know this tank because I built it in my garage."

That's when I looked up—and realized it was David Packard.[63]

Packard too had come early to look around the aquarium. Sadler introduced himself. When Packard learned that he was a specialist in organizational and cultural change in organizations, he invited Sadler to join him for a cup of coffee in the aquarium café.

There they talked for a long time. Sadler recalled that Packard "asked questions with intense curiosity and played my answers back to me with great clarity. By the time we had this conversation I had met [and interviewed] hundreds of HP managers and executives. I told him that change was taking too long, not because the culture had become too complex, but because the culture had developed attributes which were increasingly dysfunctional."[64]

Packard wanted more. He wanted evidence to support Sadler's claim. Sadler pulled out research, cultural studies, that measured a dozen critical behaviors at HP and compared them to world business norms. Put simply, in terms of constructive behaviors, "HP was still doing well but was probably coasting on its prior momentum and excellent brand name."

Worse, on destructive measures, the data showed that "HP would resist change, but hide that resistance. Executives wouldn't know that a change project was going to fail until it had failed."

Dave was visibly angry about what this data was saying. He hammered the table with his fist and said, "Damnit! That's exactly what I've been hearing and I don't understand it!"

I hesitated for a moment and said, "It gets worse."

"I'm all ears," he said. I remember that exactly because he did have big ears and I thought he might be mocking himself a little.[65]

Sadler next laid out the results of yet another pair of measurements, one measuring perfectionism and the other oppositional tendencies. The first suggested that HP was now so obsessed with creating perfect products and marketing strategies that it was almost paralyzed, waiting forever for that last bit of polish before it could move forward. At the same time, the oppositional numbers suggested that too many people at the company now saw their role in the company as one of finding flaws. "Meetings were a forum for showing off an ability to find flaws instead of a forum for creating and buying into solutions."

I told him the HP Way was now interpreted as "job for life." There were no negative consequences for negative behavior. I told him that people felt that HP was a family and that the family would take care of them and that now an "entitlement mentality" was firmly in place.

Packard flinched at my choice of words. . . . Then, I told him about my experience with the workshop and that I had been removed for recommending that someone be replaced for standing in the way of a critical change.

He pounded his fist on the table again and said "Damnit! I've heard things have gotten bad, but I had no idea how bad. And that's not true, by the way. We fired people for not delivering. I don't know where this idea is coming from!"

Packard asked Sadler for the name of the person who had killed the contract, and wrote it down. "Packard calmed down. He sat reflecting for a moment. Then, he said, 'I haven't paid much attention to the company lately, but Bill and I are going to have to get very active for a while. You just keep doing what you're doing and saying what you are saying.'"[66]

Packard thanked Sadler for the information and left. That night he incorporated some of the data into his speech. A week later, Sadler was rehired.

Three months later, John Young "retired." Dean Morton retired as well.

It was all done with great sensitivity and dignity. Young had, after all, enjoyed one of the most successful careers ever seen at HP, and as CEO he had grown the company's revenues eightfold—a spectacular achievement by any measure. Luckily, the timing was perfect: he would turn sixty in 1992, a perfect retirement milestone.

Young's departure as CEO was handled so smoothly that most of the press treated it as a standard corporate transition. Only one enterprising reporter, Eric Nee of *Upside* magazine (and later of *Forbes* and *Fortune*) even noticed that something unusual was going on. But for his story, "Dave & Bill's Last Adventure" (complete with a caricature of the two old men back in the Addison garage tinkering on a new HP personal computer), the story of the Great Return—what one writer would later describe as "one of the most heroic acts in modern business"—would never have been known to the outside world. That was how Bill and Dave preferred it. In *The HP Way*, Packard would recognize Young's retirement with a single-sentence compliment for his having done an "outstanding job."[67]

John Young, not having to carry the stigma of a forced departure, would go on to great success as the head of a number of nonprofit organizations and government task forces. One of his roles was especially far-reaching: filling in temporarily as CEO of Novell Corp., he hired his replacement, Eric Schmidt, and trained him in the job—lessons that proved useful when Schmidt was named CEO of the hottest company of the new century, Google.

Dean Morton, whose intelligence and knowledge of HP were greatly admired within the organization, would remain associated with the HP family for years to come; in a validation of his talents, he was asked to serve on the board of both the Packard Foundation and the Monterey Aquarium. In addition to serving on the boards of Clorox, ALZA Corp., and KLA-Tencor, he would become a trusted mentor and adviser to one of the most successful women CEOs in high tech, Carol Bartz of Autodesk.

Instead of a vindictive termination, Bill and Dave had preserved the careers of two brilliant and vital men who would go on to make important contributions to the industry and to society.*

For the months between Bill and Dave's return and John Young's departure, Packard (and to a lesser degree, Hewlett) managed the company from behind the scenes, plotting the restructuring of the organization and searching for a new CEO. After Young's departure, they continued to stay on the scene for a number of months, completing the work they had done. Wrote the *San Jose Mercury-News*

Thus, at an age when rich old men retire to their country homes and resist any threat of change, Packard and Hewlett set off a revolution in the giant company they had once built. . . .

Before they were done, Hewlett-Packard had been all but turned upside down. Decision-making had been streamlined, recalcitrant managers retired, customer service improved, relationships with suppliers revitalized (the problems there turned out to be HP's own fault), and the company had been turned again into an aggressive force.[68]

What followed was remarkable, even by HP standards By the mid-1990s, a lean, revitalized Hewlett-Packard was the fastest-growing large corporation, and had the highest profit margins, in American industry. It not only dominated the printer business, but was now carving out large chunks of those markets, such as workstations and PCs, where just a few years before it had been an also-ran.

Two octogenarians had come out of retirement and saved a multibillion-dollar corporation—and the livelihoods of tens of thousands of people around the world. Though hardly recognized at the time, and still little known today, it was one of the greatest closing acts in business history.

Hail and Farewell

Just how close Hewlett-Packard came to disaster during that period will never be known. What is certain is that, had Dave Packard not listened to the letter writer—and later to people like Bob Sadler—and waited until real structural problems appeared a few years later, it would have been too late. Perhaps not for HP, but certainly for Bill and Dave. Their timing hadn't failed them this one last time.

The immediate task now was to find a new CEO. The two primary candidates—Dick Hackborn and Lew Platt—remained, their stars now even brighter with printers and computers enjoying explosive growth in the restored HP.

On paper, both men looked like winners, and perfect candidates to lead the resurgent company. Both had been with the company for decades, both were true products of the company's culture. And both had managed operations that were bigger than most companies.

But the reality, as always, was more complex. To his credit, Platt, at fifty the younger of the two, was an engineer; he understood technology, not just the business—and though he had come from medical instruments, he seemed to have picked up computers quickly. He was also well-organized, capable of making sure that the operations of the giant company would run smoothly. Best of all, he was a man of deep integrity: fair, honorable, committed to his people. Some of this empathy came from his own life experiences—he was a single father, having lost his wife to cancer a decade before—but it was also integral to his character. Platt exemplified the very best of the HP Way.

But the fear with Platt was that he was not a strategic thinker, not a vision- ary. According to *Upside*, "Platt is a meat-and-potatoes man, someone you wouldn't be surprised to find heading up a machine tools company in Toledo, Ohio. 'He's real down-to-earth,' says a manager who works for Pratt. 'Some- one who's much more hands-on than many I've seen. He sits down with the troops and says what's happening.' "[69]

The magazine went on to say that while every HP manager it interviewed had given Platt high marks as a manager, none had given their unconditional support to the idea of him as HP CEO. The *New York Times*, while noting Platt's success with turning around the computer group, damned him with faint praise by saying that he wasn't "as vivid" as Hackborn.

By contrast, Dick Hackborn was everything one could ask for in a strate- gic executive. He was brilliant, audacious, and clever—and he had a gift for enlisting talented people to join him in his latest corporate crusade. He had taken a me-too product at a backwater HP division and created one of the most exciting and celebrated businesses in all of electronics. In that respect, he was, of all the thousands of employees at Hewlett-Packard, the most like Bill and Dave.

But there were also many reasons to worry about Dick Hackborn as HP CEO. There was about him, always, an odd ambiguousness about Hewlett- Packard. He professed to be a true HPer, but seemed to despise everything about HP corporate—to the point that he seemed to do his best to never visit Palo Alto. He remained in Boise even after Platt moved to headquarters.

In many ways, with his relaxed style, willingness to delegate responsibility, and commitment to innovation, Hackborn seemed to embody the HP Way. Yet privately he was heard to complain that he had been given neither the for- tune nor the fame that had come to those entrepreneurs—Bill Gates and Steve Jobs—he considered his equals in the PC revolution because he was buried in a giant company.

But the greatest worry about Hackborn among other HP executives was that the Gamesman didn't always know when the game stopped, that it wasn't just an intellectual exercise, but that people's livelihoods were at risk. They knew that while Hackborn was hugely respected within the company— almost worshipped—he was rarely loved.

As the genteel but heated race for CEO approached its conclusion, some HPers hoped for a return to the past. Dick Watts, director of HP's worldwide sales and distribution for computer systems, told the *Times*, "Dick is the strategist; Lew is the consummate professional communicator to customers and the team. I figure that since their initials are H-P, they should just take over as a tandem."[70] Others thought only Hackborn could maintain the aggressiveness that had finally returned to HP after the lost decade. Meanwhile, those who knew Hackborn better prudently suggested that he would make a perfect COO under a more reliable CEO like Platt.

In the end, it came down to Dave Packard. And he went with audacity. The call went out for Dick Hackborn to come to down to Palo Alto and meet with the chairman.

Why Hackborn? Packard never explained his reasons. But he rarely made any decision at HP without a larger, often implicit message to the rest of the company. In offering the position to Hackborn, Packard was obviously saying that Hewlett-Packard was never again to lapse into inertia, or to choose the safe path over the riskier but more promising one.

But it was also a profession of faith in the people of Hewlett-Packard. *Hackborn will give you the opportunity*, he was saying to them. *You give him the heart.*

Dick Hackborn arrived at the old HP headquarters in Palo Alto, where Packard still kept his old office, in spring, 1992. He was in Packard's office for nearly an hour, then left. Packard, who had grown hard of hearing, initially thought Hackborn had said yes—only to be told the opposite was true.

A stunned Dave Packard emerged, turned to those nearby, and shook his head. "He didn't want the job."

Dick Hackborn, the crown prince of Hewlett-Packard, the entrepreneur who wanted to be as famous and rich as his entrepreneurial peers, had turned down one of the most influential and financially rewarded corporate jobs in the world to stay in Boise, Idaho.

So it would be Lew Platt after all. The news was met throughout the company with both surprise and satisfaction. Platt had the reputation of being a true HPer, a manager who watched out for his people.

But could he keep HP's renewed momentum going? Or, without a long-term strategy, would the company sink back into the introversion and inertia of the recent past? Packard did what he could to create a balance, packing the board with the kind of mavericks—Terry and Hackborn among them—who would, with luck, keep Platt's eyes on the horizon.

But beyond that, there was little Packard could do. He sensed that his time was running short now. The management of the company that he and Bill had created and run for fifty-five years would now have to be handed over to those who would lead it into the new century. The future of Hewlett-Packard Company was theirs. On September 17, 1993, David Packard officially stepped down as chairman of Hewlett-Packard Co, turning over the position to Platt.

Never again would H and P be part of HP. From two young men in an unheated, dirt-floor garage, the Hewlett-Packard employees now numbered 92,000 scattered around the world in a $20 billion company. In his final address to the company's senior management, Dave Packard chose to say goodbye by quoting from a poem that had been popular in his childhood but now long forgotten.

It was "The Deacon's Masterpiece, or, the Wonderful One-Hoss Shay," written in 1858 by Oliver Wendell Holmes. It is perhaps the earliest, and one of the best, allegories ever written about the lures—and the dangers—of technology. In it, a small-town deacon in 1775 resolves to build the best one-horse chaise carriage in town.

Recognizing that carriages always break down because of a single weak point, the deacon decides to build his chaise from materials of all equal quality, such that no component will break down first:

> *Now in building of chaises, I tell you what,*
> *There is always somewhere a weakest spot,—*
> *In hub, tire, felloe, in spring or thrill,*
> *In panel, or crossbar, or floor, or sill,*
> *In screw bolt, thoroughbrace,—lurking still,*
> *Find it somewhere you must and will,—*
> *Above or below, or within or without,—*
> *And that's the reason, beyond a doubt,*
> *A chaise breaks down, but doesn't wear out.*

To defeat nature itself, the deacon builds his chaise out of the finest materials he can find, such that no part is better or worse than any other, a creation without a visible flaw. The resulting carriage is, indeed, "The Deacon's Masterpiece," so superior to any other carriage in town that as the years pass and the other carriages begin to break down and fall apart, it seems ageless.

Twenty years pass. Then fifty. Then seventy-five. And the chaise outlived generations of its counterparts, even its creator. And, "but for a flavor of mild decay," it seems as sturdy and perfect as the day it was built.

Then, on the morning of its hundredth anniversary, the town's parson decides to take the chaise for ride while he composes a sermon. He is halfway through his composition when the horse suddenly stops. The chaise shudders for an instant—and then completely disintegrates, leaving the stunned parson sitting on a rock.

> *What do you think the parson found,*
> *When he got up and stared around?*

The poor old chaise in a heap or mound,
As if it had been to the mill and ground!
You see, of course, if you're not a dunce,
How it went to pieces all at once,—
All at once, and nothing first,—
Just as bubbles do when they burst.

What final message Dave Packard meant to send to his lieutenants with this poem has been the subject of speculation ever since. Computer science students at Colorado State University are regularly assigned to come up with possible explanations. Was it a warning about technology and the notorious tendency of HP engineers to waste time trying to create impossibly perfect products? Or, conversely, was it a call to engineering glory—that if every part of a product was built to the highest possible standards it might last nearly forever—until, *pop,* it crashed all at once and for all time?

Another theory is that Packard was talking about Hewlett-Packard itself. Was HP, the greatest company of the age, so well designed that it could last a century or more? Or was he saying that, no matter how well conceived, no company could last forever—and HP had already thrived for more than fifty years—without regularly being rebuilt? Was this a warning that Hewlett-Packard might one day seem to be running just fine—then suddenly disintegrate?

One possibility that no one considered at the time was that Dave Packard might have been talking about himself. "But for a flavor of mild decay," Packard at eighty-one seemed as strong and healthy as ever. Like the deacon's chaise, it seemed as though he might live forever. But Packard knew better. It was time to go.

The Last Word

But David Packard wasn't yet done. He had one last task to do for his HP family.

For twenty years there had been talk of a Hewlett and Packard book, one that would combine a history of the company with the founder's musings on the HP Way, their principles of management, and the processes by which they made key decisions in HP's history. There had, of course, been numerous in-house publications on the HP Way and Objectives, and the company's culture had been described in numerous magazine articles, academic papers, and books. But other than a couple of video interviews, and a few speeches, there was really nothing from the founders themselves, no first-person record of what it was like to be Bill and Dave during all of those years.

Now, as the last project of his long career, Dave Packard decided to tell that story. It would be by him alone—a stunning departure from all of those years of the "perfect" partnership. But Bill Hewlett was fading. The first of a series of strokes had a put him in a wheelchair, and there was some question whether he had the endurance to take on another major project. But there was also something more: Packard had a story he wanted to tell, and he was impatient to tell it. It would be his name on the book, and ostensibly his autobiography—but as the title, *The HP Way*, and subtitle, *How Bill Hewlett and I Built Our Company,* showed, Dave Packard would share equal credit with his partner on every page.

To write the book, Packard assembled a small team: himself, Dave Kirby (who was brought back from retirement), and Karen Lewis, HP's archivist. They spent the next six months on the book. Packard, who was increasingly ill from a persistent infection, established the structure for the book, set the key points, and gave the pair their deadlines. Kirby and Lewis would do most of the writing—a straightforward task for Kirby, as he had crafted Packard's written voice for thirty years.

But if Dave Packard was doing little of the actual writing, he was still very much in charge. It proved to be a frustrating experience for Kirby and Lewis, who wanted a richer, more elegantly written book, a compendium of anecdotes from Packard's life combined with the lessons he had learned over his remarkable career.

All they got was the last. They may have written *The HP Way*, but in the end it was the book Packard wanted, and in his voice—not even his spoken word, which was often funny and profane, but the structured, plain exposition of an engineer with no time to spare.

The HP Way is a quixotic, sometimes frustrating book. Anyone expecting a chronology or a collection of interesting stories is doomed to disappointment. The book doesn't even have an index. Instead, except for opening sections on Dave's and Bill's very different childhoods and on the founding of the company, most of it is structured around each of the HP Corporate Objectives.

It is very unusual narrative structure. Whenever anecdotes appear, they are always told to illustrate one of the Objectives. The result is that a story about inkjet printers from the early 1990s appears a dozen pages before another about company picnics in the early 1950s, which in turn precedes a disquisition on the creation of flex-time in Germany in the 1960s. It takes every bit of Kirby's skill as a prose stylist to create the transitions that hold the tale together. Anyone expecting a straightforward and standard autobiography by a business titan is destined to be very surprised by *The HP Way*. To the very end, Dave Packard remains a maverick.

But Packard never broke the rules without a deeper purpose. Only with closer study of the nonlinear narrative is his strategy revealed: *The HP Way* is an autobiography in name only; what Dave Packard has really written (as the title says) is a book about the creation of—and a career lived within—the HP Way. It is not really about how Bill and Dave created HP, but, as the chapter structure shows, how HP and its people created them.

In its pages, Bill and Dave are learning as they go along, just like every other HPer. They make mistakes, they triumph, they come up with great ideas, and they adopt better ideas from others. What humor there is in the book comes at Packard's expense, some comeuppance by a person lower on the HP organizational chart but far higher in experience and wisdom. Packard doesn't diminish what he has accomplished, but neither does he ever suggest that he ever did it without the help of others, especially his partner. It is one of the humblest books ever written by a successful CEO.

But the ultimate message that Packard wanted to convey in the book was that, whatever the titles and the awards said, his career had been one subordinated to the HP family and the HP Way, and not vice versa. Only his duty to his country trumped his sense of duty to Hewlett-Packard Company and its people. And though he could not speak for Bill, implicit in the narrative was that this sense of duty was true for Hewlett as well.

Though many scratched their heads when they first read it, that didn't keep thousands of HPers, and thousands more non-HPers, from turning *The HP Way* into a best-seller, and one of the biggest business books of 1995. More important, quixotic as it was, the book endured. Read once and put on the shelf, *The HP Way* often found itself pulled down again and read for a second time during the dark days at Hewlett-Packard at the beginning of the twenty-first century. Then, perhaps as Packard had planned, it provided both succor and hope. *This is the way it was,* Packard seemed to say in its pages, *and this is how it can be again.*

David Packard

The HP Way was all that Dave Packard had left. And completing it took its toll on his now fragile health.

In the early planning stages of the book, Kirby called upon one of his old staffers (the author of this book) to come in and advise on the book's structure. The young intern who, twenty years before, had nervously found himself flanked on a lunchroom bench by Bill and Dave, was now middle-aged and a veteran journalist.

Waiting in the old company boardroom, adjoining Packard's office, he was taken aback by what he saw:

> The door opened. At eighty, David Packard was shockingly old, as very tall men seem to be. His voice was an even deeper rumble, like thunder, and having just recovered from an infection, he moved carefully and with great fragility.
>
> It would have been heartbreaking, but for his mind. There, he hadn't lost a step.
>
> He was still gracious, but tougher now, almost curt, as if there wasn't much time left to waste on delicacies. The legendary David Packard and the real man now seemed detached from one another, as if the myth was ready to break free and take wing.
>
> The last I saw of him was out the boardroom window. He was outside now, hunched in a cold wind, taking instructions as always from [his long-time secretary] Margaret Paull. Then, an ancient king in his blessed kingdom, he set off alone to face his last challenge.
>
> As always, he did it right and he did it well.[71]

David Packard died on March 26, 1996, at age eighty-three. He died, of pneumonia, at 11 p.m. at Stanford University Hospital, surrounded by his children. The news, carried by wire services and network news, raced around the world. At Hewlett-Packard divisions around the world, HPers openly wept. At *Reason* magazine, editor Virginia Postrel wrote that among Americans, David Packard was second only to Ronald Reagan as a world figure. The *San Jose Mercury-News* reset its presses to create a special section devoted to the Packard legacy.

That morning, Robert Boehm, archivist for the Hewlett Family Library, drove up to the Hewlett house in Portola Valley to work on some documents. He found the house quiet, with the family members talking in hushed tones. "I went through the kitchen and saw Bill Hewlett sitting his wheelchair at the table in the breakfast nook. Just sitting there staring. I have never seen a sadder-looking man."[72]

For a moment, Boehm considered walking over and speaking to the grieving figure, but couldn't bring himself to do so. No one else could either. "Someone on the staff later told me that Bill had been sitting at that table since very early morning—and that he continued sitting there for hours."

The memorial service was held three days later at Stanford Memorial Church.[73] The twelve hundred attendees—from the governor of California to loyal HP rank and file—were handed a program as they arrived that featured on its cover a sepia-toned photograph of Packard driving his tractor on the ranch and looking back at the camera. The caption read:

David Packard, 1912–1996. Rancher, etc.

On the back was a photograph of a smiling Lucile Packard, captioned *Dave's Sweetheart.*

The crowd quietly filed into the church and filled the pews. Then an elderly figure in a wheelchair was wheeled up the center aisle. There was murmur of recognition as every head turned to watch Bill Hewlett pass. He was helped out of the wheelchair and into the front pew, where he sat with his wife, Rosemary, and members of the Packard family.

The emotional forty-five-minute service was presided over by Robert Gregg, dean of the church. David Woodley Packard told the audience that his father had written a letter to the family saying "very sternly" that he didn't want a memorial service when he died. But later, when pressed on the subject, he had "grunted" in reply—which the family had decided to take as an affirmation.

Packard then pointed at the program, saying that those who knew his father would understand why they had chosen the cover picture. He then noted the photo of Lucile Packard on the back page: "My father and my mother were each other's sweethearts, and they're together again."

Stanford provost Condoleezza Rice said of Packard that he "had a belief in human potential that was unshakeable." Lew Platt added that only now that he had served for three years as CEO of Hewlett-Packard did he really understand just how remarkable a company HP was—and that the greatest lesson he had learned from Dave Packard was to "apply common sense consistently."

Former secretary of defense George Shultz rose to say "I've seen him at ease, I've seen him under pressure. He was always the same. Dave was a decider, not a ducker. He knew what he thought, and he made decisions that worked.

"Honesty, leadership, learning. To me, that's David Packard. I salute him for his vast accomplishments. I thank him for all he has taught me. I grieve at the loss of this great, patriotic American."

Family, Hewlett-Packard, Stanford, Washington. Each part of Dave Packard's life had been represented but one: friend. With Hewlett unable, that task fell to Packard's old college buddy Morrie Doyle, who recalled a happy trout-fishing trip the two men had taken along the Lewis and Clark Trail just five months before. He closed by reciting the Irish blessing that begins, "May the road rise up to meet you . . ."

The crowd filed out to a nearby reception, accompanied by the music of Turk Murphy's Band, one of Packard's favorites. Then, after tears and reminiscences, they returned to a Hewlett-Packard and a Silicon Valley that, for the first time, would be without David Packard.

Aftermath

Lew Platt served as Hewlett-Packard's chairman and CEO until 1999. He remained, until the end, beloved by HPers for his dedication to the family of HP and his deeply felt belief in the HP Way.

Under Platt's watch, Hewlett-Packard would continue to dominate the printer business (through such popular products as the all-in-one OfficeJet), stake out a major position in laptop computers (the Omnibook), and finally become a major player in PCs through the hugely successful Pavilion family. He proved wrong all of his old classmates at Wharton who had tried to keep him off their project teams because they thought him too slow to keep up.

Platt also turned out to be an innovator in personnel policies. Thanks to his own personal understanding of what it was like to balance both a job and family at home, he led HP to become a pioneer in telecommuting—in the process making Hewlett-Packard the most "virtual" of the world's large corporations.

And, in the ultimate recognition of HP's half century of continuous success, the company was selected to join the list of the thirty Dow Jones leading industrial stocks, the ultimate honor in American economic life.

Lew Platt had lived up to all that had been expected of him. By the midnineties, morale at the company had returned to its historic highs. The momentum that Bill and Dave had created for the company with the Great Return was maintained all the way through 1996, when HP's annual revenues passed $38 billion.

But by then, the fears about Platt's lack of strategic skills—that he might become John Young redux—were also beginning to be proven accurate. And no one understood this more than Platt himself. As the years passed he felt more and more that the task of running HP was getting away from him, that he was in over his head.

It was during this period that Platt and the HP board reached an extraordinary decision: HP would spin off its measurement, components, chemical analysis, and medical businesses—in other words, the original Hewlett-Packard—into a new company. It would be called Agilent Corp, and the group's current executive vice president, Ned Barnholt (who had replaced the retired, now HP director, Bill Terry), was tapped to be Agilent's first CEO. Though HP's venerable instrument operation, at less than $8 billion per year, now represented only 15 percent of the company's business, the announcement came as a shock. After nearly sixty years as a single family, this felt like a divorce.

A man of deep integrity and great loyalty to the HP family, Platt would never do anything to hurt the company and the people he loved. And so when in 1999 company revenues fell for the first time since the end of the Second World War, he essentially fired himself and retired. He was only 58, but looked much older, a situation not helped by a not-so-secret two-pack-per-day cigarette habit that helped him deal with the stress of the job (one story that circulated around HP at the time was that the company had to regularly replace its corporate vehicles because they all reeked of Platt's cigarette smoke). His departure was met with sadness throughout the company—which only grew as HPers experienced what came after.

The last years at Hewlett-Packard had taken a lot out of Platt, and when he took the job of CEO for the Kendall-Jackson winery, it was seen as a well-earned hiatus from the high tech wars. But before long he was back in action, becoming chairman of Boeing, whose board he had joined about the time he left HP.

Boeing was a long way culturally—and, it proved, ethically—from Hewlett-Packard. Lew Platt found himself dealing with company executives being sent to prison and accepted the resignations of two CEOs, both of them enmeshed in scandals.

It proved to be too much. In October 2005, just hours after meeting with some old friends from HP, Lew Platt died of a brain aneurysm. He was only sixty-four.

Platt's sudden retirement from HP put the company once more in an executive crisis. As it was assumed that he would stay as CEO for at least a few more years, no one had yet been groomed as his replacement. So, among the HP board members, a search committee was formed. It included, among others, Dick Hackborn, now slated to become HP's new chairman.

The presence of the Gamesman, HP's Mr. Inside/Outside, proved decisive. Hackborn, whose distaste for headquarters politics hadn't diminished, now had his chance to destroy it. For the first time in company history, HP decided to look beyond its walls for a senior executive—indeed, for the most senior executive in the company.

Hackborn already had the next step plotted as well. He championed a young woman executive, Carly Fiorina, who had become something of a superstar at Lucent, a huge new conglomerate originally created from the systems and technology unit of AT&T. Founded in just 1996, Lucent was already well into what would be a $46 billion acquisition spree. This swashbuckling style had made it one of the biggest stories of the telecom/dot-com boom of the late nineties—and again later, after the bubble burst, for various scandals involving foreign bribes and stock pumping.

Fiorina had made her name at Lucent taking the company public in a particularly successful IPO, and had most recently served as group president of the company's global service provider business. Known as a brilliant self-promoter, Fiorina was regularly in the news—and that, combined with her high position in one of the hottest companies of the decade, regularly put her at the top of the list of the most important businesswomen in the United States. She was also a Stanford graduate.

Hackborn saw in Fiorina the perfect instrument to shatter the status quo at Hewlett-Packard and turn the company into his vision of what it should become: clever, high-profile, and agile. That she was also a woman—and would thus shock the still mostly male executive ranks at HP—was a bonus. He would be her mentor, and together they would lead Hewlett-Packard into the twenty-first century.

"I could see he was dazzled by her," fellow director Patricia C. Dunn recalls. "He was really excited about her vision for the company. She had a feel for the company's strengths and weaknesses. It corresponded with his feelings." Hackborn expressed mild concern about Fiorina's lack of a technical background, but that wasn't a top-priority worry for him. "We may be getting one of the top two or three CEOs of our generation," Hackborn declared. "She could be the next Jack Welch."[74]

So impressed was Hackborn with Fiorina and her potential that he pushed her through a successful vote over any in-house candidates and, it was reported, more than a hundred other non-HP candidates (including Paul Otellini, who would go on to become CEO of Intel Corp.). What Hackborn never seemed to have noticed is that in hiring Fiorina, he had repeated John Young's mistake of teaming up with a person too much like himself. And if a company run by two nice guys was at risk of losing momentum, one run by two self-obsessed game players was a company unmoored and without a soul.

Some board members questioned whether an outsider, no matter how brilliant, could come in at the top of a giant corporation with such an enduring and subtle corporate culture and actually assimilate those attitudes and mores quickly enough to be an effective leader. Hackborn, who himself had never been a great expositor of the HP Way, dismissed those concerns as secondary. To seal the vote, he guaranteed that he would stay on as HP chairman to teach Fiorina the company culture and act as a check on any wayward moves by the new chief executive.

Hackborn's guarantee finally swayed the board, and Carly Fiorina was tendered an offer to become HP's fifth president.

Not surprisingly, Fiorina's appointment was met with international acclaim. Hidebound old HP had regained its lost youth. In hiring a woman CEO—and thus making her the most powerful businesswoman on the planet—in the public's mind HP had gone from an anachronistic old dinosaur to an exciting new trendsetter. And, after sober and weary Lew Platt, Fiorina's first public appearances, showing a handsome and telegenic young woman with a quick mind and an abundance of energy, were especially refreshing. Any demurrals from HPers about her lack of experience in either tech or the HP culture, and from Lucent employees about her careerism, were either waved aside as sour grapes or lost in the roar of the general acclaim.

Not long after Fiorina's arrival at Hewlett-Packard, she was invited up to meet Bill Hewlett at his house in Portola Valley, in the hills above Palo Alto.

The meeting began poorly. Fiorina and her husband, as had many before them, got lost on the way and arrived late. Obviously anxious over both the meeting and her tardiness, Fiorina rushed into the house and only made the most perfunctory hellos to those assembled, including Arjay Miller, former president of Ford Motor Company and dean of the Stanford Business School. She also didn't take the time to make any small talk with Hewlett family members or the house staff.

This was a mistake, as most of the people there were prepared to warn Carly that, because of his strokes, Bill Hewlett was having difficulty assimilating large volumes of verbal information at one time.

Instead, once she learned that Hewlett was outside, sitting in his wheelchair beside the pool, Fiorina "bounded" out to join him. She pulled a chair up next to him, and as others followed and gathered around, she leaned over and proceeded to regale the old man with what a great honor this was for her to head the company he had started, how she would be true to HP traditions—while, of course, making some needed changes. She told Hewlett that she had once been a secretary across the street—and now she was head of one of the greatest companies in the world.

At this point, Hewlett said something inaudible to the listeners present, but for the word "here." Jeremy Hackett, Hewlett's nurse, was used to interpreting the old man's words.

Someone asked Hackett, "Did he say something?"

"I think," said one of the guests, "that he asked 'Did you have trouble getting over here?'"

"No," the nurse replied, "He said, 'Get me the hell out of here.' "
Bill Hewlett was quickly whisked away.[75]

William Hewlett

A few months after Dave Packard's death, HP's Middlefield Road division in Mountain View, at the suggestion of one its employees, Donna Solis, led a campaign to plant an oak tree in Dave's memory at their site.

The ceremony, which was kept private from the public, drew several hundred people from the division, several senior HP executives, members of the Packard family, and Bill Hewlett.

Jo Ellen Sako, who would spend twenty-four years at HP, worked at the division. She recalled:

> Bill Hewlett spoke. He was in a wheelchair, but appeared to insist that he stand to make his speech, rather than sit. It seemed difficult for him to stand. Although he was using a microphone at the podium, I could only hear a murmur of his voice and see his mouth moving; I could not make out a single word. It was so sad because there he was, doing everything he could to stand up and speak—and I believe that only those immediately next to him were able to appreciate what he said.
>
> In the courtyard afterwards, Bill sat in his wheelchair. He was accompanied by his wife, his nurse, and the person who had driven them over—and they sat nearby and watched while we employees gathered and waited to meet Bill.
>
> After the first brave individuals lined up and began taking photographs, the rest of us realized it was okay and the line extended out into the parking lot. There must have been three hundred people in that line.
>
> I don't know how long it took for all of us to meet Bill; maybe two hours. He shook hands with each person, looked them in the eye, asked their name, and either said something or asked a question that was unique and personal—not just the pat "Pleasure to meet you." It was a sunny and warm day, yet I heard later that Bill refused to leave, even at the urging of his companions. He was going to stay until he met every person in line.[76]

Sako admits to being so awestruck that she recalls little of her conversation with Hewlett. But she does remember a second conversation a few moments later.

Susan Packard Orr was standing alone in the courtyard, looking away from the crowd around Bill towards the building. She was very tall, like her father, and I remember thinking it must be very hard for her to be there so soon after her father's death.

I wanted to approach her, but also didn't want to disturb her—when a fellow employee, Rich Luerra, stepped up to introduce himself and speak to her. He explained that he had starting working for HP when he was very young—and he wanted to thank Susan for both her father and Bill starting such a company and providing a place for people like him to work.

Susan took his hand, looked him straight in the eye, and said, "No, no. *We* should be thanking *you.*"[77]

Burdened with ill-health, Bill Hewlett now largely withdrew from public life. Privately, he remained engaged, and deeply committed to Stanford and the work of the foundation. Improving education now became the paramount activity of his last years. Wrote *Stanford Magazine:*

In an address at a 1995 event honoring him and Packard, Hewlett expressed concern about the rising cost of higher education and emphasized the importance of Stanford sustaining its need-blind admissions policy. "The answer, of course, is more and more fellowships and scholarships," he said. David Glen, a major gifts officer at Stanford, says "hundreds of students" have benefited from scholarships Hewlett helped fund, including some that carry other donors' names. Moreover, "there are about 50 faculty walking around on this campus because of Bill Hewlett's fellowships."[78]

One of those fellowships, a faculty chair in the medical school, was named for Albion Walter Hewlett. It was a son's last tribute to a father for the brief but important time they had together.

Hewlett's contributions to Stanford weren't only financial. He also served as an adviser and mentor to a generation of Stanford leaders, most famously Condoleezza Rice, who undoubtedly found his advice useful not just at the university, but later as national security adviser and U.S. secretary of state. In the patient and kind Hewlett, she was lucky to have her first experience of a world figure.

The strokes were coming more often now. But a steady stream of old friends made the recoveries endurable. One regular visitor was Art Fong, himself approaching eighty, who kept Bill company the way he had a decade before for Fred Terman. They often talked about the old days, when they and the company were young and there was a world to conquer.

Professor and Hewlett Foundation trustee Herant Katchadourian, an old friend, would come by to take Hewlett on drives—sometimes all the way to the San Felipe ranch, the place where Bill was always the happiest. On these trips, they would often stop at some hole-in-the-wall diner for a bite to eat. Katchadourian always insisted on paying, saying, "Please let me take care of it; I don't think you can afford this place." Hewlett would smile and agree.

Finally, at one of these lunches, Hewlett had had enough, and insisted on paying—only to discover that he had no money on him. Laughing, Katchadourian covered the tab and teased his friend, "What's going to happen to you without friends like me?"

"I don't know," Hewlett replied sheepishly. "I guess I'd be homeless."[79]

Despite his growing physical frailties, Bill Hewlett's mind remained strong, as did his pride. His driver once found him sitting at an HP personal computer. The display was suffering an electrical short that was scrambling the image—and a frustrated Hewlett was smacking it on the side with his hand, as if to knock some sense into it. "Mr. Hewlett," said the driver. "That's a delicate machine. It can't take that kind of treatment."

"It can if it has my name on it," Hewlett replied, giving the computer another whack.

Once, while recovering in the hospital, Bill was visited by Sandra Kurtzig, who would often come to keep him company. Two decades before, Kurtzig had been a young woman with young children and a master's degree in aeronautical engineering that she had put on hold to be a mom. Bored one day, she sat down at the kitchen table while the kids played and began to write the code for what would be one of the first important minicomputer-based inventory control programs. As she had written this software for the HP 3000, she decided to show it to Hewlett-Packard. Hewlett loved it and offered HP's support. So did Paul Ely, who saw a way to sell more machines, and agreed to let Kurtzig and her new company, Ask Computer, incubate inside HP Cupertino.

Ask would go on to become a $400 million company and Kurtzig one of the first women executives to ever take a U.S. company public. She had never forgotten HP's trust, and though now a busy tycoon herself, found the time to visit the man who had believed in her.

Anxious about Hewlett's condition, she made small talk about how she had stopped beforehand at some office under renovation. As she walked across the parquet floors, workers had shouted at her to remove her high heels so that she would not leave marks.

"Let me see your heel," Hewlett said from his hospital bed. A pause and then, "How much do you weigh?" Kurtzig answered, then listened in surprise as Hewlett—one day after a stroke—tried to calculate whether the pounds per square inch she exerted on the floor would have been enough to make an impression.

The garage genius still had a problem to solve.[80]

Hewlett's last appearance in the news was a poignant one. In late November 2000 a fire broke out at the Hewlett home, trapping Bill, now bedridden, on the second floor. The three-alarm fire blazed for more than three hours, and caused more than a million dollars' worth of damage, but firemen managed to rescue Hewlett by passing him out, on a rescue stretcher, through a window. Happily, no one was hurt.

One constant visitor to Bill Hewlett during the last years was Gerhard Casper, the former president of Stanford. The two men had grown close during the days when Casper was running the university, and the friendship had grown only deeper after Casper's retirement.

Casper would often push Hewlett in his wheelchair on tours of the Stanford campus while they talked. And when even that became too taxing on the old man, Casper visited Hewlett at his home. Near the end, during one of these visits, as the two men sat side by side, Hewlett grew silent, then reached over and gripped Casper's hand: "He held my hand tightly for a long time. Then he suddenly turned to me and said, 'Gerhard, the curtain has fallen.' "

Casper, recounting the story on the news of Hewlett's passing, was momentarily overcome, then pulled himself together long enough to add, "I was just in love with that man."[81]

William Redington Hewlett died in his sleep on January 12, 2001. He was eighty-seven. In an editorial (by the author), the *Wall Street Journal* would call his first encounter with Dave Packard on the football field at Stanford in 1930 "the most momentous meeting of the modern world" and describe Bill Hewlett as "the soul of the HP Way."[82]

He's still with us. In Silicon Valley, more than ever, if you want to see William Hewlett's legacy, you need only look out the window.[83]

A second oak tree would now be planted at the Middlefield division.

The memorial, held at the Stanford Church, took place on Saturday, January 20.[84] As with his old partner, the church was filled to capacity, and Dean Gregg led the prayers. But in keeping with Bill Hewlett's personality, the memorial was kept humble and simple: there were no lavish decorations, merely a line of thin candles along the back wall of the church. Classical organ music echoed off the walls and out the great doors across the quad to where Fred Terman's lab had once stood. On the old football field, where Bill and Dave had first met, the organ notes were tiny wisps, half heard in the cold air.

In the pews, mourners carefully held the program they would save for their grandchildren as the last moment of an era. On its cover was a photograph of Bill Hewlett with the familiar amused twinkle in his eye, and inside a quote from one of his grandchildren:

> In the end, his greatest gift to future generations was not the compass he could build with his hands, but his moral compass. Its cardinal points were knowledge, modesty, justice and hard work. He was true to himself and an example to us all.

One after another, friends and family stood to talk about Bill Hewlett. Walter Hewlett, Arjay Miller, former dean of Stanford's Business School, Herant Katchadourian, family friend Maggie Lacey Schneider (who joked that the reason Bill had married his second wife, Rosemary, beyond their common interests, was that her house had something Bill had always wanted: a garage).

David Woodley Packard read from letters and e-mails Hewlett-Packard Co. had received from around the world following the death of Bill Hewlett, and of his own father four years before. The most memorable had come from a man who described traveling in Singapore: "I asked the cab driver to take me to HP, and he said, 'You mean the holy place?' "

Then, before they shuffled out to face a Silicon Valley without its founding fathers, the congregation arose as one and sang one of Bill's favorite hymns, "O God, Our Help in Ages Past."

> *O God, our help in ages past,*
> *Our hope for years to come;*
> *Be thou our guide while life shall last,*
> *And our eternal home.*

Afterword:
The Last Gift

The Carly Fiorina era at Hewlett-Packard was a catastrophe. Bill Hewlett had been able to escape her, but the rest of HP quickly discovered that it could not.

Looking back, she seemed to epitomize a time and a type: the CEO as superstar—driven, media-savvy, addicted to the big power play, always choosing the grand gesture over the little touch. It was a phenomenon of the go-go years of the late nineties and the turn of the millennium—and that quickly grew ugly and stale in the face of the dot-com bust, 9/11, and the scandals of Enron and WorldCom.

It had all started out so well. Fiorina, in a private meeting with Dick Hackborn, had argued that she would only take the job of CEO if Hackborn stayed on as chairman and her mentor.[1] This was not only what Hackborn had promised the board, but it also appealed to his own private ambitions.

Said Michael Maccoby, who had written about Hackborn twenty years before in *The Gamesman* (and had apparently grown increasingly skeptical of his business style), "Dick's very political, but without really putting his skin in the game. He probably felt he could use Carly to do all the things he didn't want to do."[2]

But Fiorina proved to have a mind of her own—and within months, Hackborn was openly worrying at board meetings about her performance. Recounted *Business Week*, "Hackborn fretted . . . about three issues, say sources: Fiorina's refusal to delegate operations, her tendency to make bold promises, and the exodus of trusted execs. 'As Carly drove strong people out of the company, Dick got quieter and quieter' in HP circles, says longtime colleague Bob Frankenberg, who helped Hackborn build HP's PC business in the early '90s."[3]

But whatever his private concerns, Hackborn publicly supported Fiorina, first in her failed attempt at a big play by trying to buy the 31,000-employee consulting firm PricewaterhouseCoopers—a deal that fell through when she tried to lower her $17.5 billion offer—and then in her $19 billion tender to acquire troubled 65,000-employee PC giant Compaq.

While other board members (and legions of HPers) worried that the Compaq deal was just a rebound reaction by a CEO bent on being seen as a major mergers-and-acquisitions player, Hackborn supported Fiorina to the point of lobbying key investors and holding gatherings of select HP and Compaq board members. In board meetings, he used his legendary presentational skills to show how, under Fiorina's vision, HP (PCs and peripherals) could be the third leg of a troika with Microsoft (software) and Intel (chips) to rule the electronics world. All of this despite Hackborn's professed concern about Fiorina's ability to run HP.

And yet for all of his privately voiced concerns about Fiorina's leadership, and despite his promise to the board when she was hired, after just a year, Hackborn—gamesmanship not being associated with either fidelity or constancy—voluntarily stepped down as HP chairman to take a regular board position, and handed over the chairmanship to Carly Fiorina.

Now almost nothing could stop her. Not even HP's employees, though they came very close.

If Fiorina made the boardroom of HP a place of growing concern, she had turned Hewlett-Packard itself into a place of dread and desperation for the nearly one hundred thousand HPers. Their one hope was that, somehow, she would learn the HP culture and internalize the HP Way before she did too much damage to the company.

But within weeks of her arrival, Fiorina made it very clear that she not only had no intention of understanding the HP Way, but that she considered it an anachronistic philosophy that was acting as a drag on the company's ability to compete in the new century—and that she intended to destroy it.

But not all of it. Latching on to the Addison garage as a powerful and iconic marketing tool, Fiorina used it in television and print advertising, and even had a replica built to use in the ads and to display at HP as a kind of shrine. Bill and Dave had left the garage without a glance back, but sixty years later Carly Fiorina fixated upon it as a quick ticket to her own high-tech respectability. Many HPers (and outsiders) saw this as a cynical ploy, and were furious that the Addison garage, the unofficial symbol of Hewlett-Packard, had been reduced to a design element.

That resentment only grew when employees began to notice that, thanks to a new marketing directive, the very name "Hewlett-Packard" began to disappear all around the company, to be replaced by the simple and anonymous "HP." It seemed as though Fiorina, even as she was wrapping herself in the Bill and Dave legend, was also doing her best to drop the real Hewlett and Packard down the memory hole.

Sometimes the anger turned to laughter, as when Fiorina inaugurated a new corporate marketing message—*Invent*—that seemed, for such an ostensibly progressive CEO, to be little more than a throwback to IBM's *Think* of the 1950s. Given that Fiorina was already becoming notorious for ignoring the latest research from HP Labs and focusing on competing in a nearly commoditized business like PCs, her public promotion of innovation seemed particularly risible—the joke was that the only thing Carly had ever invented was the *Invent* logo. Gallows humor was becoming a way of life now at Hewlett-Packard—or, more accurately, "HP."

It only got darker from there. In June 2001, Fiorina asked all HP employees to either voluntarily take a pay cut or additional nonpaying vacation time to help the company save money. It was reminiscent of one of the most celebrated moments in Hewlett-Packard history, the "Nine-Day Fortnight" of 1970. In the spirit of the HP Way (which Fiorina failed to notice), HPers responded: 80,000 employees signed up for the program, creating an expected savings of $130 million for the rest of that fiscal year.

It should have been an equally famous moment, the one that finally cemented the relationship between the new CEO and her company. Instead, one month later, Fiorina announced the impending layoff of 6,000 HPers—leaving, in the words of the *Palo Alto Weekly,* "some employees feeling they'd fallen for a bait and switch."

This was the biggest betrayal of all. Since the days when Hewlett-Packard was just a hundred employees in the Redwood Building, there had never been a mass layoff at the company. It was part of the social contract at the very heart of the HP Way: HPers shared equally in the company's good times and bad. That's why they had lined up to sacrifice for its greater financial good. Now Carly Fiorina had destroyed all of that; she had torn up the contract.

Fear and mistrust were now beginning to define the daily work environment of HP—and nowhere more so than at corporate headquarters in Palo Alto.

Jo Ellen Sako, who still worked at the Middlefield division, had always recalled a story, told by her uncle, about his stopping by HP headquarters in the 1960s to raise money for the local Boy Scout camp. Uncle Frank had simply walked into headquarters and "started walking around asking people where to find Bill Hewlett's office.

"And, without even asking who he was, or even if he worked there, HP employees gave him directions. He always was amazed by that."

Once he got to Hewlett's office and told the secretary his purpose, Frank Sako was ushered right in. "Uncle Frank said that Bill listened to him, asked how much he needed, and wrote out a check on the spot."

Forty years later, Jo Ellen Sako took some family friends up the hill to HP headquarters to give them a tour. Despite her badge, she was turned away from the executive offices. "It was like an armed camp in there." A few months later, after twenty-four years at Hewlett-Packard, Jo Ellen Sako took an early retirement. "I had always thought I would die with the company," she said sadly.[4]

Civil War

Now Fiorina began to pile on the indignities. Wrote the *Palo Alto Weekly*:

> The way the layoffs were handled rankled employees and bred distrust, according to insiders. Lower-level managers, who had been asked to give their input in the layoff decisions, were disgruntled when these recommendations were disregarded.
>
> Furthermore, [said Carl Cottrell, former head of HP Europe], managers had to "be the executioner" in departments other than their own, preventing a department's own manager from breaking the news to laid-off employees. It was a process some called "cold." Employees also saw little rhyme or reason about who got the pink slips. Even high-performing employees weren't spared, leading remaining employees to speculate that Fiorina simply wanted to show them who's boss.
>
> "She's feeling like HP employees are stuck in their ways, and she wants to rattle that. She wants to put fear in our hearts, and she's done that," said an employee who didn't want his name used."[5]

From 1999 through 2002, as Fiorina made one sweeping move after another, the employees of Hewlett-Packard Co. could do little more than reel from the blows, pray they kept their jobs, and write their résumés in case they didn't.

Those who didn't bail out early quickly discovered that there was no place else to go. The dot-com bubble burst in the spring of 2000, throwing Silicon Valley into its worst recession in almost thirty years. One thousand new Internet companies died, and even the most established companies in the Valley were temporarily crippled. There were no new jobs in the Valley—and, at the bottom of the bust, so many people were leaving town that there weren't even any U-Haul trucks to rent in the Bay Area. Wrote ABCNews.com,

> Almost every HPer I talk to, young or old, newcomer or veteran, wants out. That there hasn't already been a rush to the exits is only testimony to how bad the downturn has been in Silicon Valley. But "wait until the

economy comes up around here," says a local executive. "Watch what happens to HP when folks can find jobs elsewhere."[6]

Unable to leave, and faced with the prospect of imminent layoff, many HPers felt trapped—and increasingly bitter. It was not unusual during these months to hear second-generation HPers, men and women who were lifted up by their fathers to shake Bill's or Dave's hand at the company picnic, say that this was no longer "their" HP, that the HP Way, the reason many had dedicated their careers to Hewlett-Packard, was dying before their eyes.

Worst of all, they had no recourse. There was no way for disgruntled HPers to voice their opinion to the people at the top, no line of communication, no Dave Packard to read their e-mails, and, given the apparently arbitrary nature of the layoffs, the very real possibility that they would be fired for speaking up. As time went on, it became increasingly difficult even to actually *see* Fiorina anywhere but on television or on a stage. Said former HP vice president Al Bagley, "She isn't around like she ought to be. I don't think she is as comfortable walking around inside [the company] and hearing what people really think. She's got a lot to learn."[7]

But Fiorina also had her defenders. There had been many people inside and outside the company who had come to believe, by the time of Carly's arrival, that not only had HP grown old and slow and lost its edge, but that even its famous culture might be anachronistic in the faster world of the Internet and e-commerce. In this view, veteran HPers were unhappy not because they were being treated unfairly, but because they were resistant to change—thus their growing anger was proof that what Fiorina was doing was right. Said Stanford professor Charles O'Reilly, "HP developed a culture for engineers at a time when life-cycles of products were longer. In the last decades, product life-cycles became shorter and profit margins lower. . . . The infrastructures were built for a different market. They were consensus-oriented—and built for a different strategy."[8]

Also working in Fiorina's favor was the recession itself. Every major technology firm was hurting at this point, and most were laying off thousands. What might have been a more obvious contrast had these cuts and reorganizations occurred during healthy economic times now looked like one more sad, but inevitable, cutback in an industry-wide trend.

Fiorina, while admitting that HP management "did not do a good job of implementing those decisions," also argued that the characterizations of her as arbitrary or vindictive were unfair—that she had warned employees that the short-term pay cuts might have to be followed by more serious long-term actions, that HPers hadn't been laid off merely based on job performance but on the criticality of their work to the company's new strategy, and that she had used a world-class career outplacement firm to handle the layoffs judiciously.

Certainly no one could fault Fiorina's commitment or her energy. She often put in fifteen-hour days at HP, and during those hours was a whirlwind of activity, racing from meeting to press interview to sales call to sales conference. Perhaps the most famous image of her during this era shows her under the spotlights in front of an audience of thousands, sharing the stage with singer Gwen Stefani of the rock group No Doubt. Fiorina looks as much the rock star as Stefani. It is the perfect iconic image of the superstar CEO of the era—and looking at it, one is left wondering, as HPers did at the time, what any of this had to do with Hewlett-Packard.

As early as 1999, Fiorina had told *Forbes*, in a response to rumors that as many as 25 percent of HP's employees might be laid off, "I'm not sure about that, but if one-quarter of the people in HP don't want to make the journey, or can't take the pace, that's the way it has to be."[9]

If anyone had expected her attitude to change after extended contact with the HP family, they were disappointed by her comment to the same magazine two years later: "People should depart with dignity, but don't confuse that with the departure being an inappropriate choice."[10] *Forbes* went on to note that a recent survey of 8,000 HP employees had found widespread dissatisfaction, citing poor communication and inefficient implementation of changes— an astounding reversal of morale for a company that just a few years before had the highest employee satisfaction numbers on the planet.

A growing tide of resentment was building within the company. HP was quickly becoming a company where employees—and even managers— believed that it was their duty to defend the firm from its own CEO.

It all came to a head in the fall of 2001. Fiorina, chastened by the collapse of the PricewaterhouseCoopers deal, appeared to immediately rush off in a zeal to acquire—and soon thereafter entered into merger talks with Compaq. In truth, the move was neither as arbitrary nor as impetuous as it seemed: believing that HP was about be crushed between IBM and Dell, Hackborn and Fiorina had decided that if they couldn't make an acquisition in services to take on Big Blue, they would make a move in computers against Compaq.

The merger, which would make HP an $87 billion monster, was publicly announced on September 4, 2001—just a week before the world turned upside down.

Even when they heard management's reasoning for the HP–Compaq merger, tens of thousands of HPers remained unconvinced. Many saw it as one more, and the biggest yet, insult to real HP employees by their carpetbagger CEO—some arguing that Fiorina was just padding her résumé with a mega-merger before she moved on to an even bigger company like IBM or GE, or maybe even into politics. In looking to a competitor to solve HP's problems, they believed, Fiorina was saying that HPers couldn't turn the company around by themselves, that they couldn't—as HP always had in the past—innovate their way out of hard times.

Others pointed to Compaq's own business troubles; it was in even worse shape competitively in the personal computer market than HP, more desperate for help, and even more dysfunctional and demoralized than HP itself. How would the union of two troubled companies produce a single company that was innovative and dynamic enough to take on a thoroughbred like Dell Computer?

Moreover, in buying Compaq, Fiorina seemed to be committing HP to a future dedicated to slugging it out in the printer and PC businesses. But both businesses were becoming increasingly commoditized, their profit margins falling. That was a game played best by Asian mass producers such as Samsung, with their low domestic wages. Was this the future of HP? How could a company of technologists and engineers possibly compete in that arena? And why should it?

But the most immediate concern facing HPers was how the company could possibly absorb 65,000 Compaq employees. And even if it could, what of the company culture, of the HP Way, would ever survive?

Then an astonishing thing happened: HPers, including even retired employees, discovered they had a voice—and a platform on which to use it.

Bill Hewlett and Dave Packard had given HP three things: the HP Way, a sense of family, and ownership of the company. It was this third that HPers now realized was their most powerful weapon. It was Bill and Dave's last gift to their fellow HPers, and now those HPers were going to use it to try and save their company.*'

An acquisition as great as the Compaq merger could not be executed merely by CEO fiat. It required a proxy vote by shareholders—and, thanks to a half century of the company's employee stock purchase program, nearly half of HP's outstanding shares were in the hands of private individuals. This, HPers realized, was their last channel to express their views to management and the public.

They weren't the only people thinking this way. The Hewlett and Packard families, still the largest private shareholders in the company (18 percent), were equally disgusted by what they saw as Carly Fiorina's reckless dismantlement of their fathers' legacy. In November 2001, Walter Hewlett and David Woodley Packard met and agreed to lead a proxy fight against Fiorina in the name of the HP Way. They quickly gathered a small army of current and former HPers willing to fight for their cause.

There was no little irony that the scions of the founding families, two men who had never before shown much interest in working for their fathers' company, seemed to suddenly find their calling in defending Bill and Dave's achievements. In fact, they showed an aptitude for the fight and an understanding of business dynamics that proved they had inherited more than the family names.

The challenge seemed to catch Fiorina and her team by surprise. That perhaps is why she made two nearly fatal errors. The first was to react personally. What would have been a traditional, dignified proxy fight suddenly turned very ugly when, on January 18, 2002, Fiorina sent a letter to stockholders characterizing Walter Hewlett as a "musician and academic" who had "never worked at this company or been involved in its management."

This was not only inaccurate (Walter, besides being a software developer and chairman of the Hewlett Foundation, was also a director of HP) but incredibly foolhardy. Generations of HPers could remember young Walter hanging out in the labs at HP doing his homework; they knew he was a voice on the board of directors for the HP Way. He was more HP than Carly Fiorina could ever be. And to launch an ad hominem attack against him—when the challenge by the Hewlett and Packard *fils* had to date been conducted impersonally and with dignity—was seen by HPers as yet one more assault by Fiorina and her lieutenants on the HP Way.

But the response from the CEO's office to this backlash was both clever and unexpected:

> [Fiorina] recast herself as a brave woman, alone on a podium, crusading for the dreams and aspirations of her entire company. If people thought she was vulnerable, all right, she was. Before her opponents fully realized what had transpired, she had turned that appearance of vulnerability into her greatest asset. In a major speech she declared, "To the skeptics who say it won't work, it won't sell, it won't succeed, it's not the HP Way, I say, 'You don't know the people of the new HP.' "[11]

Then, having brilliantly turned around her first mistake, Fiorina now stumbled into a second, even bigger one. This time her error was to publicly suggest that Walter and David Woodley had no real plan for the company, only a misguided nostalgia for the good old days now long gone.

But the sons saw this one coming. Despite pressure from Fiorina and fellow board members to come up with a formal alternate plan to fix HP, Walter Hewlett demurred, assuming that it was a trap to make him and David Woodley Packard look as if they were plotting a coup. Instead, he publicly stated that the only alternative "plan" was that HP should execute its historic business strategy better and not move forward with a hastily conceived acquisition. Privately, he told friends of his fears that Fiorina was trying to emulate Cisco's John Chambers and his "move fast, fix it later" philosophy.

Meanwhile, sensing a bloody battle ahead, the new Hewlett and Packard partnership gathered together a team of veteran Silicon Valley corporate mergers and securities attorneys.[12]

For individuals who were reputedly out of touch with the realities of the business world, Walter and David Woodley's stated goals were remarkably reasonable: restore the Hewlett-Packard culture of trust, get out of commoditized products, focus on high-margin goods, and reassert HP's talent for invention to innovate the company out of its current doldrums.

For many HPers, the plan was a lot like the one they had in their own minds for HP—and what they thought Bill and Dave would have come up with as well. More proxy votes rallied to the contesters' side.

Fiorina fought back with the most powerful weapon she knew—Bill and Dave. As George Anders wrote in the magazine *Fast Company*:

> In her most audacious move, Fiorina began invoking the early careers of Hewlett and Packard as a justification for the HP-Compaq merger. With the late founders' heirs strongly opposed to the merger, it seemed mind-boggling that she could lay claim to the patriarchs' intentions. She latched onto a legendary Packard quote—"To remain static is to lose ground"—and made it the centerpiece of two-page newspaper ads.
>
> And not only did she appropriate the founders' language for her cause, but she also scripted dialogue for them, using her new ideas for the company as their text. Fiorina created plausible—but unsubstantiated—conversations from long ago, in which the founders spoke her language. Her tactics infuriated Packard's son, David Woodley Packard, but she didn't back down. She had framed her message.[13]

In the days before the vote, the HP proxy fight was the biggest business news story in the world. Analysts predicted that the vote would be very close, with individual shareholders and the Hewlett and Packard families lining up on one side, institutional investors on the other. Few dared to pick the outcome.

The press joined in as well. At *Forbes*, publisher Rich Karlgaard titled his column "Vote Carly," writing that "Fiorina's foibles do not make her wrong about the merger. She and Hackborn are right, and they should be supported." The *Wall Street Journal* editorial page took just the opposite position.

At 6:30 a.m. on March 19, 2002, the doors opened at Flint Center on the campus of De Anza Community College in Cupertino—a well-worn auditorium that because of its unique location had managed to be the site of two historic events in high tech: the Apple Macintosh introduction and the HP proxy fight.

Many shareholders had arrived long before the scheduled time and a line had already formed to file in. What followed was one of the most unusual corporate annual meetings Silicon Valley had ever seen. Reported CNetNews.com:

> Institutional approval of the $20 billion deal has done little to quiet the ranks of upset workers, retirees and other individual shareholders who packed the Flint Center in Cupertino, Calif., filling hundreds upon hundreds of rows of seats—some even perching in the balcony seats. Shareholders flew from as far as France to attend Tuesday's meeting and speak out against the merger—an indication of how passionate many voters felt and how much work could lie ahead if the merger goes through.
>
> A chorus of angry investors booed Fiorina and yelled "No!" when she said most employees were in favor of the merger. By contrast, board member Walter Hewlett, son of HP co-founder William Hewlett, received standing ovations before and after a five-minute speech reiterating his opposition to the merger.[14]

The odds seemed against the Fiorina camp: with the founding families in opposition, she would have to take 61 percent of the remaining share votes. But immediately after the vote, a confident Carly declared victory. What Fiorina knew, and everyone else would learn a month later when the final tally was announced, was that she had taken the institutional shareholders (who almost never vote against a sitting CEO) and Compaq's individual shareholders (who loved the idea of jumping to HP).

It was a victory, but a Pyrrhic one. Looking at the vote totals, it became apparent that almost no one at Hewlett-Packard had voted for the Fiorina plan. After three years at the top of HP, Fiorina had managed to marshal almost zero support from her own employees.

This was something Wall Street could not fail to notice.

There were also rumors of vote buying and other shenanigans on the HP corporate side—stories that seemed even more plausible when a voice mail was leaked to the press that had CEO Fiorina saying to HP chief financial officer Bob Wayman, just two days before the proxy vote, that in the case of major institutional shareholders Deutsche Bank and Northern Trust, HP "might have to do something extraordinary for those two to bring them over the line."

Based on this and other reports, Walter Hewlett brought suit against Hewlett-Packard. HP responded by refusing to renominate Hewlett to the HP board. The Hewlett and Packard era of HP was now officially ended after sixty-three years.

On April 30, a Delaware judge dismissed the Hewlett lawsuit. Walter Hewlett announced that, for the sake of the company, he would not contest the decision.

The HP proxy war was over.

Ding Dong

Carly Fiorina had won. But in the process the old HP had lashed out one final time and given her reputation a fatal wound.

The real message of the proxy vote was that Fiorina had failed in the single most important task of a CEO: that of enlisting employees into the company's vision of the future. Instead, by the thousands, HPers had repudiated everything she stood for. They had booed her at the annual meeting. And they had shown remarkable cohesion in working for her opponents.

She had won, but the business world would never look at her the same way again. The rising corporate superstar now looked faded and out of touch, her vaunted energy a performance only in the service of herself. And when Compaq CEO Michael Capellas, considered one of the major assets of the merger, quickly dove out of the newly merged company, Fiorina looked even more like a sucker in the deal.

In truth, there were some good things to be found at Compaq—a large customer base, a strong position in memory, and the remnants of that most HP-like of companies, Tandem Computer—but not enough to warrant the near-destruction of Hewlett-Packard, and nothing a healthy and energized HP couldn't have invented itself. As the coffee mugs offered on one Web site said, "Walter was right." Wrote ABCNews.com:

> In the last three months, HP employees have shown themselves to be as passionate, intelligent and creative as ever. They don't need Compaq; they need to be untethered. They need to be trusted—or this won't be the last battle. They have found their purpose again.
>
> The question is: has Carly Fiorina learned this lesson too? Does she appreciate that the business philosophy she considers tired and obsolete has proven to be her strongest opponent? Or that in calling for the company to trust her she has embraced the very culture she decries?[15]

Carly had won the battle, but she had lost the war. And everyone seemed to know it but her. Even the Gamesman understood. Dick Hackborn had been Fiorina's biggest cheerleader on the board during the Compaq merger, but now he grew impatient with her decisions and management.

His reputation too had taken a drubbing in the last few months, as he was seen not only as the man who hired Fiorina, but also her leading supporter. As one longtime colleague at HP told *Business Week*, "I like Dick, but he screwed up. He should resign."[16]

Now Hackborn seemed resolved to make Fiorina toe the line and fix the mess she had made of Hewlett-Packard. From this moment on, Carly Fiorina would be on borrowed time at HP.

The awful irony of all of this was that had Fiorina dropped her prejudices and looked around her, she would have gotten a magnificent lesson in the power of the HP Way she so despised. Despite all of her attempts to destroy it, the HP culture and the HP family had survived. And faced with the opportunity of the proxy fight, HP employees had mobilized almost overnight and taken on the senior management and all of the hired guns of one of the world's biggest corporations—and almost beaten them.

Now, in the months ahead, while she was distracted with boardroom politics, publicity tours, strategy development, and the other demands of merging two giant organizations, she would entrust—for the first time—the employees of HP with a distasteful task of their own: to assimilate tens of thousands of Compaq employees, all of them unschooled in HP's culture and many of them arrogantly assuming they were arriving to take HPers' jobs.

It was a task no employee should ever be asked to do. And many outsiders, including some die-hard HP supporters, assumed that it was impossible. Yet HPers, though many grumbled privately, did the job, and in record time. In the process, they made Carly Fiorina look like a better strategic manager than she really was. That too was the HP Way.

There is no record of Fiorina ever recognizing or rewarding this achievement.

After the proxy fight, Hewlett-Packard seemed to settle down and get back to work. The two sides were tired of fighting and there were the daunting details of the merger still ahead.

This common cause seemed to do wonders for the company. Within four quarters, Hewlett-Packard had returned to profitability. And partly through layoffs of redundant employees (18,000 of them, less than many feared), partly through cost-cutting measures, HP also managed to cut $3 billion—$500 million more than its goal—from expenses. It was a $57 billion company now, number 13 on the Fortune 500, with more than 140,000 employees. The

San Jose Mercury-News ran a postmortem on the HP-Compaq merger with the headline "The Verdict: So Far, So Good."

But in the one measure that counted most to shareholders, stock price, the story was very different. With the proxy fight, Wall Street had lost its faith in Carly Fiorina—and by extension, Hewlett-Packard. The cost-cutting, the lay-offs, the successful assimilation of Compaq, the return to profitability—none of this good news resulted in more than a temporary bump in HP's deeply depressed stock price, which was down 33 percent one year after the merger was announced.

Wall Street wasn't being stupid or vindictive, but realistic. Fiorina had proven she could win a proxy fight, absorb a major acquisition, and slash her way to productivity, but little more. Her employees didn't believe or trust in her, her board of directors (including her mentor) was turning on her, the company had come up with no new product breakthroughs since her arrival, and Dell Computer, the target of the merger, was stronger than ever.

Sure, HP was back, but not as back as some of the other big names in high tech. Even Agilent, the old HP Instrument Group that had spun off down the street in 2001, and nearly died when the economy collapsed even before the company got fully under way, was now coming back—and doing so with a corporate culture based squarely on the HP Way.

Throughout 2004, HP seemed to struggle along. The employees hunkered down and tried not to get fired. Thanks to time, the merger, and layoffs, only a small fraction of the company now remembered what it was like even in the Lew Platt era. A job at HP, which had once been among the most coveted in American business, was now a job just like (and maybe a little worse than) everywhere else.

Carly Fiorina implemented one plan after another, all while cutting back on everything from employees to the coffee cups in the lunchrooms. Yesterday's news, she was all but out of the public eye now for months at a time. She remained optimistic, convinced that her strategy would soon pay off—but it was increasingly apparent that she was now on a razor's edge. One bad quarter and both the board of directors and Wall Street would turn on her.

Everyone on the HP board knew that the director who would lead the coup d'état would be Dick Hackborn. Wrote *Business Week*, "Hackborn's anxiousness eased after the merger. But as HP began to miss its financial targets in 2003 and 2004, Hackborn 'became increasingly outspoken,' says [an HP] insider. 'Carly viewed [HP's performance] as getting better, requiring less urgency than the board viewed as necessary. Dick was the key figure in this debate.' "[17]

In the fall of 2004, HP (and former Compaq) director Tom Perkins, one of Silicon Valley's most distinguished venture capitalists, and an outspoken critic of Fiorina, abruptly retired from the board in frustration. The end was near. And when HP's numbers fell for the last quarter of calendar 2004, that was it.

Just before the January 2005 board meeting, director Patricia C. Dunn, flanked by Hackborn and director (and former Reagan adviser) George Keyworth III, presented a memo to Fiorina outlining a list of concerns about her management of the company. It also included a demand that she shift operating authority for HP out to her division heads.

It was, of course, an unacceptable request—and was meant to be. Fiorina refused to comply. On February 7, in a symbolic gesture, Tom Perkins was invited back on the board. The next day the board of directors of Hewlett-Packard Company fired Carly Fiorina as chairman and chief executive officer of the company.

Dunn, a vice chairman of Barclays Global Investors, was named the new chairman of HP, and CFO Bob Wayman was named interim CEO.

Fiorina was gone, but the damage wasn't undone, at least not within the HP board of directors. The internal schism, created first by the proxy fight and then by the final battle over Fiorina's leadership, had turned the board against itself, creating an environment of mistrust, paranoia and calculated leaks.

The subsequent struggle to heal those wounds and plug those leaks (most of which, it turned out, came from Keyworth), would lead new Chairman Dunn to embark on an investigation that would eventually cross the line into illegally obtaining employee private phone records and the hiring of investigators to pose as reporters from such publications as The New York Times.

The story finally broke in late summer, 2006. Within weeks Dunn, outside counsel and Silicon Valley legend Larry Sonsini, and others were the subject of front page stories, hauled before a Congressional subcommittee, and in the case of Chairman Dunn, indicted. Just as HP was finally regaining its old glory, it had to face the most ignominious moment in its long history. The long-suffering HPers were appalled, but were ultimately resigned to the new reality of life at Hewlett-Packard.

But that was still far in the future. For now, when the news of Fiorina's firing reached the rest of HP, spontaneous cheering erupted in company plants from California to France to China. HP employees around the world gave each other high-fives and hugs. At HP's Boise plant, employees raced off to the nearest supermarket to bring back armfuls of Hostess Ding Dongs ("the witch is dead"). HP's e-mail system and phone lines were jammed with happy messages between employees and congratulatory notes from outsiders. On the Internet, in the newly emerged blogosphere, postings were filled with vituperation and obscenities about Carly Fiorina and what she had done to the world's greatest company.

A few hours later, when the formal announcement hit the wires and it was learned that Fiorina would walk away from HP with a $28 million severance package, there was a momentary flash of anger—until people decided the money was worth it to see her gone.

After five devastating years, the Carly Fiorina era at HP was over at last. The question now was: what was left of the old HP?

Bill and Dave

On December 6, 2005, a clear and mild Tuesday morning, police cars and television camera vans converged on a quiet Palo Alto neighborhood.

As the police put out the sawhorses to close the street, and the camera crews erected their satellite booms, the first visitors began to arrive. By 9 a.m., the flow of people had turned into a flood. Standing on the sidewalk in front of an elegant but unassuming old house, young people in business suits checked the names of the arrivals on a clipboard, then pointed them not toward the house, but down the alleyway beside it.

The visitors, some youthful with the crisp walk of corporate professionals, others ancient and leaning on a cane or the arm of another, made their way through a gauntlet of reporters and cameras, past the state historic marker that read "Birthplace of Silicon Valley," and down the driveway to a humble garage.

Before long the press of the crowd was so great that one could only flow with it into the garage for a quick glimpse of a few boxes of vacuum tubes, some machine tools, and, on a shelf, an HP model 200A audio oscillator. But that was enough: the little garage on Addison Avenue was not a place for a tour, but for reassurance. The younger visitors looked around in amazement: could Silicon Valley—could the modern world—really have started in this little room? Could those thousands of giant corporations, and millions of careers, the computers crawling around on the surface of Mars and the billions of messages racing around the earth each day on the World Wide Web, all have had their start *here* in this dingy little box with dirt floors, a single bare light bulb, and spiderwebs in the corners?

But the older visitors, as they passed through like pilgrims at a holy shrine, looked as much at the lovingly restored but still worn and uninsulated plank walls as at the historic items. After all these years, after all that has happened, it is still here, they told themselves. Together, we have survived.

Outside, the camera crews circled a businessman who had arrived to join the Packard and Hewlett children and grandchildren in a ribbon-cutting ceremony. For a famously fast-talking and jumpy man accustomed to managing giant corporations and thousands of employees, he seemed a little disoriented to be there.

"It's kind of a humbling thing," said Mark Hurd, the new Hewlett-Packard CEO, pointing at the garage.

In the months since his hiring by HP after a quarter century at NCR Corp., Hurd had moved quickly to unravel much of what Carly Fiorina had built. Instead of grabbing the spotlight, as his predecessor had done, he seemed to shun it, turning down most requests for interviews. Instead, he went to ground. Moving into Fiorina's office, he didn't change anything, saying there wasn't time.

Besides, he was hardly ever there. Instead, he was racing around the world to meet with—and actually listen to—thousands of delighted HPers, even retirees. At the same time, he toured all of the company's major customers—in many cases, the first visit by a senior HP exec in years—and asked for an honest appraisal of how the company was serving them. He didn't like what he heard.

Hired in March, Mark Hurd didn't make a major move until summer. And then he moved quickly.

There was another round of layoffs; 15,000 this time, much of it last residues of Compaq. Next, he froze pension benefits, putting them in line with industry standards, but disappointing many who expected a return to the old HP benevolence.

Next, concluding that HP's internal information processing network was a confused mess, Hurd poached Randy Mott, the man who had built Wal-Mart's famous IT network, and who was now working for rival Dell Computer. It was, as *Fortune* magazine noted, a nice "twofer"—scoring a world-class talent and weakening a competitor.[18]

But Hurd's biggest move was to throw out Fiorina's strategy, the now-notorious "digital, virtual, mobile, personal," and replace it with—basic business: building products, selling them, and servicing them. "We want to get out of the drama business and into the business of business," said Hurd. No more complicated matrix management schemes. Hurd broke up the company's monolithic sales force and assigned the pieces to the three major product groups—enterprise, printers, and PCs—where he believed they would be more responsive to customers. Wrote *Fortune*:

No matter how you dress up his views, he's simply trying to leverage the things HP is already good at. It's as if a new CEO at Procter & Gamble were to demand, "What else can we do here with toothpaste and diapers?"

Indeed, from the avuncular way he lets his rimless glasses perch at the end of his nose to his straight-talk emphasis on fundamentals, Hurd evokes another tech industry turnaround maestro, Lou Gerstner, the former IBM boss who famously said, "The last thing IBM needs right now is a vision."[19]

But many older HPers looked at Hurd and were reminded of someone else: Dave Packard. The same plain vanilla business philosophy, so old now that it seemed new, of putting "profits" first before anything else among HP business objectives.

And when *Fortune* asked Mark Hurd about the fate of the HP Way, he replied that he had read about it and come to his own conclusions: "When things weren't right in the past, they were fixed," he said. "If things aren't right now, we've got to fix them. If that's countercultural to the past few years, so be it. We're just trying to run the fundamentals of a sound business."[20]

Veteran HPers read those words and heard Dave Packard's voice.

By the time of the garage ribbon-cutting, Hurd's back-to-basics approach had begun to pay off. HP's stock was still below its 2000 bubble high, but up 65 percent since Fiorina's departure. Meanwhile, in personal computers, many of the other big competitors, notably Dell, had finally begun to stumble—leaving an opening for a stable, sales-oriented HP to gobble up market share. By mid-2006, it was vying with Dell for industry market leadership.

For all of the good business news, life inside Hewlett-Packard under Mark Hurd was still a long way from the days of Bill and Dave. HP was now again a driven company, but not yet a fully happy one. Much had been lost of the company's legendary culture during the Carly Fiorina years. She had tried to kill the HP Way, but had only managed to cripple it. It still hid in the memories of a few survivors at the company, in the Bill and Dave stories, and among the veterans in HP's lively alumni organization. And if Mark Hurd still didn't quite get it, at least he was listening. And as long as he listened, there was hope that he would at last understand.

There was another reason for hope as well. The world had changed once again. The go-go years at the turn of the century, of CEO superstars, merger mania, and fiscal irresponsibility, had died in a welter of ruined fortunes, dead companies, and criminal indictments. The fantasy of fast moving corporations hip-hopping to glory under the command of media-savvy, charismatic, and quick-thinking dictators had (at least for now) died an ignominious death—and Carly Fiorina had been its poster child.

Now there was a growing realization that, in a new world of virtual corporations, of sudden market births and deaths, of employees scattered around the world and working everywhere from traditional offices to the local

Starbucks, the most powerful organizations would be those that had a strong and moral corporate culture that employees could identify with wherever they were, that empowered them to make important decisions on the spot, and that were driven by ambitious, yet general, business objectives set at the top by senior management that were more tightly defined as they moved down the organizational chart.

And as academics, analysts, and corporate executives pondered this new corporate philosophy, they realized they were looking at a very old one:

The HP Way, rather than being an anachronistic leftover from a slower, quieter age, is in fact the most avant-garde management model ever devised for a large company—and better suited for today than ever before.

The HP Way is not a technique, but an ethos of restraint, responsibility, and most of all, trust. . . . It sounds easy, but the HP Way is nearly impossible to execute because it demands forbearance by the very people most likely to aggrandize power, and almost infinite trust from the people least likely to give it.

When it works, as it did at Hewlett-Packard for decades, the HP Way creates a decentralized, cohesive and intensely competent organization of stunning resilience—and a genius for innovating itself out of hard times. The HP Way resists empire building and eschews flash—which is why it is hated by CEO superstars and dismissed by the press. Yet, in the age of global organizations, independent work teams, and lightning decision cycles, the HP Way is better suited for modern organizations than any other.[21]

Bill Hewlett and Dave Packard had, with the help of two generations of HPers, built the HP Way in a much different era. But the HP Way had survived and remained relevant precisely because they had not built it *for* their time. Instead, it had been devised from a basic understanding of human beings—of duty, family, responsibility, inventiveness, and the desire to succeed and make a contribution. Everything else was secondary, which was why HP regularly revisited and rewrote its Corporate Objectives. But the Way remained unchanged, it would survive the bloodiest attacks (and the worst of scandals), and would be rediscovered again and again as long as people were people.

More than any company or product, this was Bill and Dave's first, last, and most enduring gift to everyone.

The day before the garage dedication, a group of thirty people gathered in a Palo Alto restaurant to watch a video. All had been executives at Hewlett-Packard during the Bill and Dave era. It was a Proustian moment: the faces were familiar—Dave Kirby, John Young, Dean Morton, Karen Lewis, Al Bagley, Bill Terry, and more—but in the intervening thirty years these once young and ambitious men and women had all grown old. Fong, the oldest, was eighty-five. Most were in their seventies. Even the youngest, Steve Wozniak, was now in his mid-fifties.

As they ate lunch, the group reminisced about the past, told anecdotes from their HP days, compared their current health, shook their heads at any mention of Carly Fiorina, and nodded cautious approval of "the new guy." Whatever mistakes had been made in the past were now forgiven. After all, they were family. And, like a family, they mourned all of those who were no longer with them, especially Lew Platt, whose recent and sudden death still shocked them all.

They had been brought together by Hewlett-Packard to be the first to view a new corporate video, produced by an award-winning documentarian, telling the story of Bill Hewlett and Dave Packard. HP had ordered the creation of the video as a way to teach HPers—many of whom had never even known the company during good times—the legacy they were inheriting. Most of the assembled knew it was coming: many had even been interviewed for it. But assembling footage, filming reenactments, and interviewing HP veterans had taken months—and by then, having become accustomed now to disappointments from Hewlett-Packard, many of the veterans assumed the project had been abandoned.

But now here it was, entitled simply "Origins." As the video played, the audience looked on in astonishment. It was all there: the garage, the Redwood Building, company picnics, Packard's challenge to the stunned gathering of corporate executives, Hewlett cutting off the tool bin padlock—everything that they cherished; everything they had assumed had been long forgotten by Hewlett-Packard Co. and the rest of the world.

As they watched, they marveled at the footage of an impossibly young Bill and Dave. They laughed one more time at the Bill and Dave stories. And they scrutinized closely the faces of the interviewees who were not among them—Paul Ely, Tom Perkins, Barney Oliver's successor Joel Birnbaum—for the marks of time and toil. The longer the film ran the louder the audience became. Fearful at first of yet one more insult, one more misrepresentation of the past, they now relaxed, confident that they were at last seeing the realization of what they had long been waiting for. They began to talk back to the screen, add their own side comments, and joke to each other over events a half century gone.

For those few minutes, it was as if time had rolled back. They were young again. Working once more with Bill and Dave. And proud to be part of the greatest company in the world.

Appendix:
Management and Leadership Lessons from Bill and Dave

Source material can be found at the asterisk (*) on the designated page.

Page number

15. The best possible company management is one that combines a sense of corporate greatness and destiny, with empathy for—and fidelity to—the average employee.

24. Most successful people exhibit some larger-than-life characteristic (often it is superhuman work habits). By the same token, most successful people seem to especially dislike other successful people who are most like them.

32. The lesson from team sports: Given equally good players and good team-work, the team with the strongest will to win will prevail.

34. The greatest success goes to the person who is not afraid to fail in front of even the largest audience.

42. Older advisers are good for wisdom from the past, but cannot always be depended upon for advice about the future.

44. *Terman and Hewlett:* Mentors should be chosen for common interests, not for a common personality.

44. The cliché is true: the most difficult and challenging path is also the most rewarding.

47. *Bill Hewlett at Stanford:* Great potential in young talent can often be disguised, especially in those with learning disabilities—and occasionally with real genius. The "slow" learner may in fact be using that time to understand the much bigger picture.

48. *Packard at GE:* Those closest to the action, no matter what their title, typically understand a process (and its flaws) better than anyone else—and would be happy to share that knowledge with anyone who will take the time to ask.

53. *Fred Terman:* Great entrepreneurs typically combine almost obsessive preparation and attention to detail with a wide-open opportunism.

54. Set out to build a company and make a contribution, not an empire and a fortune.

59. Whenever possible, don't quit your job to embark on a new venture. Take a leave of absence instead: leave the door open to returning.

61. *The Varian brothers:* Never be afraid of abandoning one idea—no matter how much time you've invested—if a better one comes along.

65. *Charlie Litton:* Happiness in success comes not with wealth, but in the freedom to be yourself.

66. *The coin toss:* In a good partnership, neither partner worries about who benefits more from random events.

68. In a start-up company, the founders' skills must be complementary and cover all required core competencies.

72. *The Packard garage:* A CEO should look back only strategically, never with nostalgia. What matters is what's next.

75. Price to customer desire. If that doesn't offer an adequate profit margin, then don't offer the product. If it exceeds standard margins, use the difference to finance future innovation.

76. You can't serve two masters or run two different kinds of businesses (for instance, custom work and mass production, or consulting and manufacturing) at the same time.

80. If the logic of your technology and your business argue for it, don't be afraid to take on even the biggest competitor.

81. The best education for an entrepreneur takes place not in a classroom, but in taking on the many different jobs in a new start-up company.

83. It is easy to be loyal to your employer and your mentors, especially if they are good people. It is far more difficult to be loyal to people who need you more than you need them.

84. A great manager never leaves anyone behind.

85. Treat small vendors and new companies—even potential competitors—well. They may become future allies.

85. Poor cash flow—even with a full in-box of orders—is one of the greatest threats to a company. Don't be afraid of debt; but fully understand the difference between short- and long-term debt.

85. Take care of your smallest clients—they may one day be your biggest.

86. *The HP Way:* Sometimes a radical new idea is merely an old idea preserved in a changed present.

87. Diversify early. A company with multiple product lines enjoys a number of advantages, including greater brand recognition, greater strategic flexibility, customer loyalty, and less vulnerability to attacks from competitors.

89.   Employees who are allowed to share in a company's success (through profit sharing, stock plans, etc.) are more willing to make sacrifices during the bad times.

92.   A frustrated employee is a greater threat than a merely unhappy one.

93.   An industry can never reach its full potential until it settles upon standards.

97.   *Helping Litton Labs:* The true test of loyalty is when you have every excuse not to honor it.

98.   Core principles are only valid if they are maintained in times of stress.

101.   At the beginning of a new era, or a new industry, every decision—even the seemingly inconsequential—is momentous and far-reaching.

101.   *Management by Walking Around:* The job of a manager is to support his or her staff, not vice versa—and that begins by being among them.

102.   *Open Door Policy:* A true "open door" policy goes all of the way to the top—but in return requires the employee to pass through every door in between.

104.   *The HP Way:* A great company entrusts *all* of its people, from top to bottom, to do the work that they were assigned, to take responsibility for their actions, and to speak for and represent the company as if they are the owners (which they are) and the founders themselves.

105.   *The Storeroom Incident:* Don't punish employees for having initiative, even if it doesn't fit standard procedures.

106.   Be prepared to forgo extra hiring during good times, even at the risk of losing added revenues, to keep from having to mass fire employees during the bad.

107.   Don't punish employees for having been put in a position beyond their abilities. Relocate them quietly and diplomatically.

111.   *Art Fong:* Common sense and decency, not legality or even tradition, are the best hiring policies.

111.   Investing in new product development and expanding the product catalog are the most difficult things to do in hard times—and also among the most important.

114.   The biggest competitive advantage is to do the right thing at the worst times.

116.   Empowered "families" of employees, under enlightened managers, can perpetually produce near-miracles of invention, quality, and adaptability.

117.   A company that focuses solely on profits ultimately betrays both itself and society.

124.   *The HP Way:* A great corporate culture is a fabric of rules, experiences, myths and legends, relationships, and rituals as complex as any real family—and just as difficult to describe to any outsider.

124. Maintain your personal networks. Never lose track of anyone you may one day want to hire.

125. When possible, hire talented people who are also acquaintances—particularly those whom you have seen firsthand perform well in both good and bad times.

126. *Company picnics:* Smart companies reward the families of their employees for the sacrifices that they too make for the company. These are also occasions for senior management to humanize itself by serving their subordinates.

128. Joint projects outside of work can help partners better understand how each other thinks.

128. Employees are like children; when they don't get the answer they want from one person, they move on to the next. It is crucial then that, like parents, senior executives (especially partners) be in concurrence before rendering a decision.

129. *Annual bonus:* Employees want to be seen as individuals. Personal contact, then, is vital. Take the time to learn as many of their names as you can.

130. *The coffee break:* Set aside time each day for employees (whatever their title) to leave their work and gather together with their fellows.

132. *The Beer bust:* Institutionalize times when employees can step away from their normal work personas, relax, and free their imaginations.

134. No matter how appealing a new idea, if it is not within your core competencies do not pursue it.

135. Introducing products that do not yet exist ("vaporware") is a betrayal both of customers and the company's own values.

139. *Going international:* A corporate culture, when it is fair and humane, takes precedence over a larger culture that is not.

142. *Tektronix:* Never take on an entrenched market or competitor unless you can make a decisive contribution.

143. When entering into a new geographic market, prepare carefully before making a decision. But once the decision is made, move quickly and decisively. Don't hesitate or move piecemeal.

145. Corporate reorganizations should be made for cultural reasons more than financial ones.

146. *HP Objectives:* Corporate objectives are designed to empower employees and constrain management, not the reverse. People naturally want to do a good job. The true goal of corporate objectives is to let them.

148. The HP Corporate Objectives (1966):

  1. *Profit:* To recognize that profit is the best single measure of our contributions to society and the ultimate source of our corporate strength. We should attempt to achieve the maximum possible profit consistent with our other objectives.

2. *Customers:* To strive for continued improvement in the quality, usefulness, and value of the products and services we offer our customers.

3. *Field of Interest:* To concentrate our efforts, continually seeking new opportunities for growth but limiting our involvement to fields in which we have capability and can make a contribution.

4. *Growth:* To emphasize growth as a measure of strength and a requirement for survival.

5. *Employees:* To provide employment opportunities for HP people that include the opportunity to share in the company's success, which they help make possible. To provide for them job security based on performance, and to provide the opportunity for personal satisfaction that comes from a sense of accomplishment in their work.

6. *Organization:* To maintain an organizational environment that fosters individual motivation, initiative and creativity, and a wide latitude of freedom in working toward established objectives and goals.

7. *Citizenship:* To meet the obligations of good citizenship by making contributions to the community and to the institutions in our society which generate the environment in which we operate.

149. In high tech especially, it is vital to be revolutionary, but dangerous to be utopian.

150. A company is not just a business, but a philosophy, a set of values, a series of traditions and customs. It is these deeply held beliefs that guide a company in meeting its objectives.

152. Along with humanity, realism is the single most important trait in a good executive.

153. Always try to finance growth on profits. Long-term debt is a dangerous game. Taking on long-term debt means serving two masters—customers and lenders—whose interests may not be compatible.

154. There is no cultural legacy with acquisitions. The day a company is acquired is the day it adopts the buying company's culture in toto.

156. Even the healthiest corporate culture will be incompatible to large numbers of talented people. This is inevitable, and a company should not compromise that culture just to gain those individuals.

160. *The HP fork:* The best business decisions encompass a personnel component and vice versa. Real management genius lies in the ability to hide shrewd business strategy inside of benevolent employee programs, and enlightened employee benefits within smart business programs.

160. *Employee stock purchase programs:* Helping employees to purchase company stock has multiple advantages:

a. It places ownership of the company in the hands of those most dedicated to its success.

b. It is a prime source of cash without taking on debt.

c. It is both a recruiting and retention tool.

d. It may one day save the company in a decisive shareholder vote.

162. By the nature of their careers, successful executives will inevitably grow apart from their employees, costing them crucial understanding and empathy. There is no easy solution for this, beyond constant contact and regular monitoring of employee behavior.

162. A company's culture is not a suicide pact. There are times when senior executives must intervene, violating their own rules of engagement, to keep the company from spinning out of control.

169. Really listening to employees is not only a way to identify both problems and opportunities early, but also a powerful technique for identifying emerging talent.

175. Over the long term, the interconnection between company products can be as valuable as the products themselves.

176. If you can share your own technology standards to create an industry standard—even at the cost of some short-term competitive edge—you will enjoy an automatic, and nearly decisive, long-term competitive advantage.

177. Senior management hesitation should never be the reason for the delay of an important new product or strategy that already has the support of the rest of the company.

178. *The Omega project:* No matter how thrilling, popular, or complete a new product development project, if it isn't going to succeed, or doesn't fit the business model, kill it—even if it is at the cost of respect, key talent, and employee morale.

178. If it doesn't impact daily operations of the company, be prepared to turn a blind eye to side projects and skunk works. If they work, profess ignorance and give credit to the mavericks.

184. Great companies look for the opportunities that might lead them to success, not weaknesses that might preclude them from success.

185. Eccentric, but talented, people may require atypical, but demanding, employment arrangements.

187. One revolution at a time. If you expect customers to accept a radically new technology, don't demand that they change their behavior as well.

188. As long as it is for a good cause—and legal—a certain amount of employee subterfuge is acceptable (and should be ignored).

189. *The HP 9100A:* At the moment of your greatest victory, you should be preparing for the next battle.

192. When the accomplishment exceeds the agreement, pay the accomplishment.

196. If a corporate tradition has fallen behind changes in the larger society, abandon the tradition.

199. A company that honors entrepreneurs, even if it means losing talent, is more likely to keep such people, or see them return someday, or turn them into allies, than one that threatens and punishes those in its ranks.

202. *Flex-time:* Entrusting employees to set their own schedule has a minimal impact on operations, but an immense impact upon employee morale, loyalty, and productivity.

204. When possible, create industry-wide dominance by combining products in submarkets in which you are already hold leadership.

210. Prepare early for succession, because the need for such a plan may come sooner than you expect.

210. Divide operating groups when they reach a critical mass to maintain the existing culture, and open new opportunities for advancement. But try to keep the new unit physically close to the original to minimize disclocation, transfer of intellectual capital, and maintain identity with customers.

211. Companies, as they grow, vacillate between centralization and decentralization. Therefore, even as the company is decentralizing, prepare for the next centralization—and vice versa.

212. When establishing a new level of management, circumscribe its authority (to constrain ambition), but expand its capabilities (to keep top talent engaged).

216. Don't confuse the apparent risk-taking of most entrepreneurs (which is, in fact, risk aversion in disguise), with the real risk-taking of trying out revolutionary new organizations and strategies when the company is still young and vulnerable.

219. The greatest career challenge facing successful entrepreneurs is reinventing themselves as business professionals.

221. The highest level of corporate leadership moves beyond operational management to *symbolic* management. That is, it consciously chooses acts for their theatrical impact, and as models of behavior for others (even future generations) to emulate.

222. In symbolic management, the best persona is the one most congruent with the true character of the manager himself.

225. *The HP-35 retirement:* Nostalgia for past success can lead you to preserve current failure.

226. *The Chuck House Defiance Medal:* Recognize mavericks for their successes— but only if they support the company's ideals. When possible, use the occasion to humanize senior management—and to remind it of the dangers of doing things only by the book.

227. *Executive luncheons:* Institutionalize regular contact between senior management and regular employees, without the presence of intermediate supervisors and managers.

228. Regularly survey employees to make sure that understanding, not just information, is being conveyed up and down through the organization.

228. *Executive build-offs:* Institutionalize games, competitions, and other activities to keep senior executives aware of what it takes to be a line worker in the company.

229. *Hewlett's hat-wearing process:* Enthusiastically cultivate new ideas as they surface throughout the company. Only later, rigorously challenge their value. This will foster an enduring climate of innovation in the company, yet protect it from pursuing too many dead ends.

232. *Hewlett on creativity:* "Creativity is an area in which younger people have a tremendous advantage, since they have an endearing habit of always questioning past wisdom and authority. They say to themselves that there must be a better way. Ninety-nine times out of a hundred, they discover that the existing, traditional way is the best. But it is that one percent that counts. That is how progress is made."

239. Just because you have built a strong and vibrant corporate culture does not mean that it can, or should be, transferred to the larger culture outside the company's walls.

242. *Packard in Washington:* Companies have a responsibility to the society(ies) that provided the context for their success. By the same token, employees, no matter what their title, owe a larger allegiance and duty to the country in which they are citizens.

250. The best business decisions are the most humane decisions. And, all other talents being even, the greatest managers are also the most humane managers.

251. *The Nine-Day Fortnight:* It is only fair that, during hard times, *everyone* in the company share in the pain, and make comparable sacrifices.

263. *G-time:* Take advantage of slow periods to give back to employees time that wouldn't be used anyway—and let them use their imagination to fill it productively.

269. A great entrepreneur, deeply attuned to a market, may be the single best predictor of the potential success or failure of a revolutionary new product.

275. When a technology product unexpectedly breaks out into the general consumer marketplace, promote and market it there as well.

276. Dissembling to customers is dishonest; dissembling to competitors is smart business practice.

283. Some product groups are as much defined by their surrounding community as by their role in the company. You relocate them at your own peril.

290. When the company makes a mistake, admit it immediately and make full restitution. It may be the only way to retain loyal customers.

292. The inherent danger with building an organization on trust and teamwork is the potential for wishful thinking and mass delusion. Senior management must be prepared to intervene at these moments—even if it means violating the tenets of the corporate culture.

293. A company is not what it makes, but what it is. The only enduring factor is its core philosophy. Almost everything else is expendable.

294. Innovation must *never* be allowed to take on a life of its own. Rather, innovation must *always* be disciplined by the marketplace. This is especially true in a company dedicated to innovation.

294. Successful partners always move toward each other in their decision-making, toward a common ground.

301. The first candidates for succession should always be from the company itself. They alone can fully appreciate the nuances of the corporate culture. Moreover, if you don't trust your own employees with the future of the company, then you have failed as a manager.

309. The tools and techniques of the commercial world largely map over onto the nonprofit world. If you have been a success in the former, you have an obligation to lend your talents to the latter.

310. A successful career in the high-tech world is one that begins with entrepreneurship and moves outward to ever larger communities and ever greater contribution. For example, entrepreneur, start-up executive, company president, CEO of a public corporation, government official, global diplomat, and philanthropy. Each jump requires a reinvention of oneself, but will only be successful if, through it all, one remains true to one's core values.

311. True philanthropy is not self-promotion. Keep your name off your creations; instead honor those who helped to make you the success you've become.

336. Successors to charismatic founders must spend *more* time in personal, physical contact with employees than did their predecessors, especially in the months immediately after the transition when those employees are most likely to feel alienated and abandoned.

348. *John Young:* The chairman of the board needs to exhibit the same kind of trust in his CEO as characterizes the rest of the corporation. Nevertheless, the chairman should not be afraid to intervene quickly and decisively should the long-term health of the company appear at risk.

350. A true Open Door Policy extends beyond the CEO to the directors and the chairman. An employee who has exhausted all other outlets should feel empowered to call directly on the board and receive a fair hearing.

354.   Talented, loyal senior executives who have given years of good service to the company should not be stigmatized for failure, but allowed to transfer or retire with dignity. In many cases, they still have considerable contributions to make to both the company and to society.

379.   *The proxy fight:* The most important legacy founders can give their employees is ownership of the company. Employee shareholders are the last redoubt in the defense of the company and its culture. Giving them the company is the ultimate statement of trust.

Acknowledgments

As every author of history or biography knows, but few readers appreciate, writing one of these books means devoting thousands of hours to your subjects—whether you like them or not. I have experienced the latter, and know all too well that spending months in the intimate literary presence of an unpleasant subject is its own kind of hell.

Just the opposite was true working on *Bill & Dave*. Here were two men who did almost everything right, especially when it came to their duty to others. Even when they made mistakes, they inevitably learned from them. Best of all, as I wrote the book—and I hope as you read it—I found myself in their shoes, running up against some problem or obstacle . . . and almost always discovering that their solution was better than mine. It was humbling, but also very uplifting. Men and women of humanity and character are the hope of the world, and thank heavens we have them.

Unfortunately, it also meant, as I finished the manuscript, that I found myself growing sad. Not just for the two men I once knew, and whom I now know so much better, but because their talents are now gone forever. Certainly Hewlett-Packard Co. has felt their loss. But so has Silicon Valley: no one has yet taken their place, and likely no one ever will. Indeed, though few people realize it, the business world itself feels the loss of Bill & Dave: who, in the last two decades, has taken their place as paragons of innovative and enlightened business practice?

For that reason, I'd like to begin by thanking Bill Hewlett and Dave Packard. Though I met both men, knowing Dave better than Bill, and worked for them briefly at the beginning of my career, it was only in writing this book as a middle-aged business veteran, that I fully took the measure of the two men—and their impact on my own life. I realize now that when I finally became a manager I unconsciously set out to lead by the HP Way . . . and quickly learned the difference between theory and real-life application. This gave me an even greater appreciation of Bill & Dave's achievement.

I had no shortage of source material in writing this book (and help, in the form of Leslie Johnson, in compiling it). HPers, new and old, freshly hired or long retired, are a family. And even when Hewlett-Packard senior management forgot, they still carried the torch of the HP Way. My single most important source for company history, besides HP's own official Web site, was the Hewlett-Packard alumni site. It is a treasure trove of historic information, oral histories, timelines, product descriptions, etc., and I plundered it enthusiastically for this book. One particularly valuable resource was John Minck's unpublished manuscript "Inside HP: A Narrative History of Hewlett-Packard from 1939–1990." A veritable book in itself—and a classic example of a primary source that will be crucial for generations of historians to come—I found myself returning to Minck's writing again and again.

A particular challenge came in telling Bill Hewlett's story. Bill was notoriously untalkative, and besides a few interviews and speeches, there isn't much out there on him—especially compared with the voluminous materials by or about Dave Packard. Happily, this void was filled by the William Hewlett Library and its director, Robert Boehm, who made available to me source materials and photographs, many of which had never been seen in public before. Indeed, I only decided to take on this project when Bill's son, Walter Hewlett, graciously offered to open up the library to me, no questions asked and no strings attached—a decision very much like his father would have made.

I also want to acknowledge a fellow veteran Silicon Valley reporter, Eric Nee, who was the only journalist clever enough to cover Bill & Dave's great return—and who dug up the very rare copy of *Upside* magazine that carried the story. Without his work, that incredible story would have been lost forever.

Writing this book also gave me a wonderful opportunity to reconnect with the people who had once been an important part of my life. Karen Lewis, formerly the HP archivist and now a senior executive at Agilent, made available many of the photos in this book. She also read the manuscript for factual errors. So too did her old *The HP Way* writing partner, and my first boss, Dave Kirby, HP's retired PR director. Getting back together with Dave after all these years was my favorite part of this project. As with many ex-HPers, I feel a deep loss for the old HP. For me, it was working for Kirby. And though my career took me in exactly the opposite direction of HP Corporate PR (indeed, several years when the company wouldn't even talk to me) I've never forgotten those years, nor the men—Ross Snyder, J. Peter Nelson, John Kane—who taught me to be a real writer. I hope this book honors their teaching.

In the end, the people whom I most want to acknowledge are the employees of Hewlett-Packard, past, present, and future. Bill Hewlett and Dave Packard always gave them full credit for the success of the company. Through good times and bad (and lately, very bad) they alone have carried in their hearts the spirit of Bill & Dave. From senior executives to interns, they all had a story to tell me about the company and its founders. Many are my neighbors here in Silicon Valley (Jo Ellen Sako, for example, is the mother of a boy I was coaching in Little League while working on the book), others sought me out when they heard I was writing the book. Some are old friends (whose comment "It's about time you did it" suggested a destiny I didn't know I had). Others were new acquaintances, including Robert Sherbin and Anna Mancini, who straightened me out on some factual errors and a few company myths. Part of the fun was hearing from the powerful men, now retired, whom I met as a nervous new employee just out of my teens thirty years ago—Paul Ely, Al Bagley, Bill Terry, Emery Rogers, Bob Grimm—who e-mailed me or took me aside at the Packard garage re-opening, and gave me words of encouragement.

It was in talking to these HPers, seeing the excitement in their eyes, when they talked about Bill & Dave and the golden age at Hewlett-Packard, that I knew I had to write this book—and to them I am especially grateful.

Finally, no book is ever written solo. Leslie Johnson did crucial research for me on the book. Jim Levine of Levine/Greenberg, convinced me of the worthiness of this book and shepherded it through its sale. Branda Maholtz and Portfolio showed a genius for the carrot and the stick, always staying gracious even as deadlines approached (and were occasionally passed). And, of course, there is Adrian Zackheim, founder and publisher of Portfolio. Adrian and I started out together a quarter century ago—and now, after taking different routes we find ourselves working together again. It's all the better the second time around.

Notes

1 Friendship

1. David Packard, *The HP Way* (New York: HarperBusiness, 1995), p. 13

2. Ibid.

3. Ibid, p. 14.

4. William Aspray interview with John V. Granger, Sept. 20, 1993; IEEE History Center, www.ieee.org/web/aboutus/history-center/index.html.

5. *The HP Way*, p. 4.

6. Ibid.

7. Ibid., p. 7.

8. Ibid.

9. Ibid.

10. Sources for this section include the William Hewlett official biography on the William and Flora Hewlett Web site (www.hewlett.org) and "Technology pioneer William R. Hewlett dead at 87," the formal obituary announcement prepared by the Stanford University News Service (http://news-service-stanford.edu/news/2001/January 17/hewlett-a.html).

11. Source of photograph: William Hewlett Archives, courtesy Walter Hewlett.

12. SFGate.com, April 14, 1999: "San Francisco in the '20s" produced by KRON-4 TV.

13. *The HP Way*, p. 19.

14. "Memorial Resolution Albion Walter Hewlett," www.histsoc.stanford.edu/pdfmem/HewlettA.pdf.

15. Larry Gordon, "Father Figure," *Stanford Magazine*, March–April 2001; http://www.stanfordalumni.org/news/magazine/2001/marapr/features/hewlett.html.

16. Lewis M. Terman, "Recollections of Fredrick Emmons Terman," *SMECC Vintage Electrics*, Vol. 3, Issue 1 (1991); www.smecc.org/the_human_side_of_management-_bill_hewlett.htm

17. C. Stewart Gillmor, *Fred Terman at Stanford* (Stanford, CA: Stanford University Press, 2004), p. 16.

18. Ibid., p. 22.

19. Ibid.

20. Ibid.

21. Michael S. Malone, *The Big Score* (New York: Doubleday, 1985), p. 14.

22. Ibid., p. 15.

23. *Fred Terman at Stanford*, p. 23.

24. *The Big Score*, p. 20.

25. *Fred Terman at Stanford*, p. 66; Arthur L. Norberg, Charles Suskind, and Roger Hahn, "Fredrick Emmons Terman, Interviews," 1975. Joint project of Bancroft Oral History Project and Stanford Oral History Project, published 1984.

26. *Fred Terman at Stanford*, p. 27.

27. Ibid., p. 31.

28. Carolyn S. Tajnai, "Fred Terman, the Father of Silicon Valley," Stanford Computer Forum, May 1985, from an interview by Sandra Blakeslee, Stanford University News Service, Oct. 3, 1977.

29. Ibid., p. 58.

30. Ibid., pp. 59–60.

31. http://www.ibiblio.org/pioneers/bush.html.

32. *The Big Score*, pp. 21–22.

33. *Fred Terman at Stanford*, p. 64.

34. Ibid, p. 65

35. "Recollections of Fredrick Emmons Terman."

35. *Fred Terman at Stanford* p. 65.

36. Ibid., p. 66. Source: "Fredrick Emmons Terman, Interviews."

37. Ibid., p. 65, same source.

38. Ibid.

39. Ibid, pp. 66–67.

40. "Biography revisits Fred Terman's roles in engineering, Stanford, Silicon Valley," *Stanford Report*, Nov. 3, 2004.

41. "Fred Terman, the Father of Silicon Valley."

42. Ibid.

43. Ibid.

44. Ibid.

45. *Fred Terman at Stanford*, p. 95.

46. Ibid. p. 488.

2   Apprentices

1. David Packard, *The HP Way*, pp. 8–10.

2. Ibid., p. 11.

3. Ibid.

4. Ibid.

5. Ibid., p. 14.

6. Ibid., p. 13.

7. Ibid., p. 21.

8. Ibid.

9. Ibid., p. 17.

10. Ibid., p. 15.

11. Ibid.

12. Gerhard Casper, "Uncommon Men," *Stanford Today*, Letter from the President, July–Aug. 1998.

13. *The HP Way*, pp. 21–22.

14. "Hewlett-Packard, the Early Years," Southwest Museum of Engineering, Communications and Computation; http://www.smecc.org/hewlett-packard,_the_early_years.htm.

15. "Fred Terman, the Father of Silicon Valley."

16. Ibid.

17. *The HP Way*, p. 23.

18. Ibid.

19. "Recollections of Fredrick Emmons Terman."

20. *The HP Way*, p. 16.

21. Ibid.

22. Ibid., p. 17.

23. Ibid., p. 24

24. Michael S. Malone, *The Big Score*, p. 29

25. *The HP Way*, p. 24.

26. Ibid., p. 25

27. Ibid.

28. Ibid.

29. Michael McMahon interview with William Hewlett, Nov. 27, 1984; IEEE History Center, www.ieee.org/portal/site.

30. Ibid.

31. Ibid.

32. "Recollections of Fredrick Emmons Terman."

33. C. Stewart Gillmor, *Fred Terman at Stanford*, p. 122.

34. Ibid., p. 123.

35. Ibid.

36. Ibid., p. 26.

37. Ibid.

38. Ibid., p. 27.

39. *The Big Score*, p. 29.

40. Ibid.

41. *The HP Way*, p. 31.

42. *Fred Terman at Stanford*, p. 123.

43. *The HP Way*, p. 29.

44. *Fred Terman at Stanford*, p. 124.

45. *The HP Way*, p. 32.

46. Quotes from Hewlett letter from *Fred Terman at Stanford*, pp. 124–125.

47. Ibid, p. 126.

48. Ibid.

49. "Recollections of Fredrick Emmons Terman."

50. *The Big Score*, p. 54.

51. Ibid.

52. Ibid., p. 55.

53. *The HP Way*, pp. 35–36.

54. Ibid., p. 36.

55.   From "Origins," a video history of Hewlett-Packard, directed by Robby Kenner, 2005.

56.   Ibid., p. 40.

3   That Damned Garage

1.   David Packard, "How Bill Hewlett and I Wound Up in a Palo Alto Garage," *The Scientist*, 1986; http://www.the-scientist.com/articles/display/8678/.

2.   Michael S. Malone, "Silicon Insider: Remembering the HP Way," ABCNews.com, Dec. 8, 2005.

3.   Anonymous source, HP alumni memories, http://www.hpalumni.org/.

4.   David Packard, *The HP Way*, p. 42.

5.   Ibid.

6.   Ibid., p. 43.

7.   C. Stewart Gillmor, *Fred Terman at Stanford*, pp. 127–128.

8.   *The HP Way*, p. 45.

9.   Michael S. Malone, *The Big Score*, p. 32.

10.   *The HP Way*, p. 46.

11.   Source: William Hewlett Library. With permission of the Hewlett family.

12.   Ibid., p. 46.

13.   John Minck, "Inside HP: A Narrative History of Hewlett-Packard from 1939–1990, unpublished manuscript for the HP alumni website (www.hpalumni.org), p. 4.

14.   *The HP Way*, p. 47.

15.   Ibid., p. 48.

16.   "Hewlett-Packard The Start—2," Southwest Museum of Engineering, Communications and Computation. www.smecc.org/hewlett-packard_the_start__-2.htm.

17.   *The HP Way*, p. 51.

18.   Ibid., p. 52.

19.   Michael McMahon interview with William Hewlett, Nov. 27, 1984; IEEE History Center, www.ieee.org/web/aboutus/history_center/index.html.

20.   Ibid.

21.   Ibid.

22.   *The Big Score*, p. 33.

23. "Michael McMahon interview with William Hewlett."

24. Ibid.

25. Ibid.

26. *The HP Way*, p. 59.

27. Ibid., p. 55.

28. "Hewlett-Packard The Start—2."

29. *The HP Way*, p. 55.

30. Ibid., p. 56.

31. Ibid., p. 57–58.

32. "Hewlett-Packard The Start—2," "Microwaves—A New Vista."

33. From an e-mail received in response to author's ABCNews.com column, "Silicon Insider: Remembering the HP Way." Name withheld for privacy reasons.

34. *The HP Way*, p. 136.

35. *The Big Score*, p. 35.

36. Bill Hewlett, "The Human Side of Management," *SMECC Vintage Electronics* Vol. 3, Issue 1(1991); http://www.smecc.org.

37. John Minck, "Inside HP: A Narrative History of Hewlett-Packard from 1939–1990" p. 35.

38. "Hewlett-Packard The Start—2."

39. *The HP Way*, p. 64.

40. *Fred Terman at Stanford*, p. 335.

41. Michael McMahon interview with William Hewlett.

42. Ibid.

43. Ibid.

44. Packard's quotes describing the CEO gathering are from *The HP Way*, pp. 165–166.

4   The HP Way

1. Michael McMahon interview with William Hewlett, Nov. 27, 1984; IEEE History Center www.ieee.org/web/aboutus/history_center/index.html.

2. "Hewlett-Packard The Start—2"; www.smecc.org/hewlett-packard_the_start__2.htm.

3. David Packard, *The HP Way*, p. 131.

4.   Ibid., p. 132.

5.   Ibid., p. 68.

6.   Ibid., p. 70

7.   Michael McMahon interview with William Hewlett.

8.   *The HP Way*, p. 70.

9.   John Minck, "Inside HP: A Narrative History of Hewlett-Packard from 1939–1990," unpublished manuscript for the HP alumni Web site (www.hpalumni.org), p. 31

10.   Ibid., p. 33.

11.   This is exactly what happened to the author, an HP intern, while waiting for a meeting with Dave Packard in 1979.

12.   "Inside HP," p. 6.

13.   Ibid., p. 5.

14.   "Hewlett-Packard The Start—2."

15.   C. Stewart Gillmor, *Fred Terman at Stanford*, p. 328.

16.   Michael S. Malone, *The Big Score*, pp. 48–49.

17.   "Inside HP," p. 31.

18.   These numbers are estimates, interpolated from the company's growth between 1951 and 1956, for which numbers are available. HP never published numbers for 1954. Source: HP Archives.

19.   "Hewlett-Packard The Start—2."

20.   *The HP Way*, p. 78.

21.   Michael McMahon interview with William Hewlett.

22.   Ibid.

23.   *The HP Way*, p. 80.

24.   Michael McMahon interview with William Hewlett.

25.   "Human Resources at Hewlett-Packard," 1992 HP Internal Report.

26.   Ibid.

27.   Michael McMahon interview with William Hewlett.

28.   *The HP Way*, p. 82.

29.   Ibid., pp. 141–142.

30.   Ibid., p. 85.

31.   Ibid., p. 89.

32.   *The Big Score*, p. 65.

33.   *The HP Way*, p. 65.

34.   The price of the stock itself was determined by either the closing average for the full calendar quarter, or the average closing price of the last five days of the quarter, whichever was lower. Source: HP Archives.

35.   Ibid., p. 85.

36.   Ibid., p. 86

37.   Ibid.

5   Community

1.   http://www.processedworld.com/Issues/issue14/14emp85292.htm.

2.   David Packard, *The HP Way*, p. 122.

3.   Ibid., p. 124.

4.   http://hp9825.com/html/hp_loveland.html.

5.   Michael McMahon interview with William Hewlett, Nov. 27, 1984; IEEE History Center, www.ieee.org/web/aboutus/history_center/index.html.

6.   *The HP Way*, p. 111.

7.   Ibid., p. 102.

8.   Michael McMahon interview with William Hewlett.

9.   *The HP Way*, p. 103.

10.   Ibid.

11.   Ibid., p. 104.

12.   Michael S. Malone, "Silicon Insider: HP 3000, RIP," ABCNews.com, Nov. 5, 2003.

13.   http://hp9825.com/html/the_9100_project.html.

14.   Ibid.

15.   Ibid.

16.   Ibid.

17.   Ibid.

18.   Ibid.

19.   Ibid.

20.   Ibid.

21.   Ibid.

22.   Ibid

23.   Ibid.

24.   Ibid.

25.   Ibid.

26.   Ibid.

27.   Michael McMahon interview with William Hewlett.

28.   Michael S. Malone, *The Big Score,* pp. 39–40.

29.   John Minck, "Inside HP: A Narrative History of Hewlett-Packard from 1939–1990," unpublished manuscript from the HP Alumni Web site (www. hpalumni.org).

30.   Ibid.

31.   Ibid.

32.   From "Origins," a video history of Hewlett-Packard, directed by Robby Kenner, 2005.

33.   Source of historical material for cesium clock section: by John Minck, "Inside HP."

34.   *Fred Terman at Stanford,* pp. 484–487.

35.   *The HP Way,* p. 146.

36.   Ibid., pp. 146–147.

37.   John Minck, "Inside HP."

38.   Ibid.

39.   Ibid.

40.   William E. Jarvis, "Three Generations," http://jarvisnapa.com/3Genera tions/102.html.

41.   Ibid.

42.   Ibid.

43.   Ibid.

44.   "Legends," HP video.

45.   *The HP Way,* p. 108.

46.   Paul Swart, "William Hewlett, 1913–2001," *Electronics Times,* January 22, 2001.

47.   Bill Hewlett, "The Human Side of Management," *SMECC, Vintage Electrics* Vol. 3, Issue 1(1991); http://smecc.org/the_human_side_of_management_- _bill_hewlett.htm

48.   Ibid.

49. Ibid.

50. *The HP Way*, pp. 100–101.

51. William Hewlett, "Random Thoughts on Creativity." A good condensed version of the speech can be found at http://www.hp.com/hpinfo/newsroom/hewlett/creativity.htm.

52. Ibid.

53. *The HP Way*, p. 127.

54. The author has done his own part over the years to perpetuate this myth, including in Bill Hewlett's obituary in the *Wall Street Journal*.

55. John Minck, "Inside HP."

56. Larry Gordon, "Father Figure," *Stanford Magazine*, March–April 2001.

57. Ibid.

58. Author conversation with Ned Barnholt, October 2005.

59. *The HP Way*, p. 168.

60. Ibid.

61 Ibid., p. 175.

62. Ibid.

6 Bastion

1. *Measure*, December 1973.

2. Robert S. Boehm interview with Arthur Fong, William Hewlett Archives, 2005.

3. Eric Nee, "Dave & Bill's Last Adventure," *Upside*, June 1991, p. 68.

4. Hal Plotkin, "The End of Hewlett-Packard as We Know It?" SFGate.com, Nov. 19, 2001.

5. "Human Resources at Hewlett-Packard," company white paper, circa 1993.

6. John Minck, "Inside HP: A Narrative History of Hewlett-Packard from 1939–1990," unpublished manuscript for the HP alumni Web site (www.hpalumni.org).

7. Ibid.

8. Ibid.

9. David Packard, *The HP Way*, p. 176.

10. Ibid., p. 179.

11. Ibid.

12. Charles D. Bright, "Costs: Into the Stratosphere," chapter 11 of *The Jet-makers: The Aerospace Industry from 1945 to 1972:* http://www.generalatomic.com/jetmakers/chapter11.html.

13. Ibid.

14. Marcel Size Knaack, "Military Airlift and Aircraft Procurement: The Case of the C-5A," Air Force History & Museums Program (Washington, DC: 1998), pp. 78–79.

15. Ibid., p. 81.

16. Diana Roose, "Top Dogs and Top Brass: An Inside Look at a Government Advisory Committee," Research Consultant, National Action/Research on the Military-Industry Complex. Reprinted from *The Insurgent Sociologist*, Vol. 5, No. 3 (Spring 1975), pp. 53–63. Carried on the Web site of Prof. G. William Domhoff, Sociology Dept., University of California at Santa Cruz (http://sociology.ucsc.edu/whorulesamerica/).

17. *The HP Way*, p. 185.

18. http://www.airpower.maxwell.af.mil/airchronicles/aureview/1985/sep-oct/smith.html.

19. *The HP Way*, p. 181.

20. Ibid., p. 180.

21. Ibid, p. 181.

22. John Minck, "Inside HP."

23. "Tom Osborne's Story in His Own Words," http://www.hp9825.com/html/osborne_s_story.html.

24. Ibid.

25. Ibid.

26. John Minck, "Inside HP."

27. "Tom Osborne's Story in His Own Words."

28. "Origins" video, quote from Bill Terry.

29. Jon Minck, "Inside HP."

30. Ibid.

31. Ibid.

32. Ibid.

33. Source: Bill Terry

34. "Tom Osborne's Story in His Own Words."

35. Ibid.

36. "Origins," quote from Steve Wozniak.

37. "Inside HP."

38. "Origins" video.

39. *The HP Way*, p. 112.

40. "Inside HP."

41. "Tom Osborne's Story in His Own Words."

42. Ibid.

43. "Origins" video, quote from Steve Wozniak.

44. Michael S. Malone, *Infinite Loop* (New York: Doubleday/Currency, 1999), p. 41.

45. Ibid., p. 28.

46. John Boudreau, "Didn't Want to Change the World, Just Wanted to Work on Computers," *San Jose Mercury-News* interview with Steve Wozniak, March 26, 2006.

47. *Infinite Loop*, p. 65.

48. The author was a member of the HP-01 PR team.

49. Bob Green, "The History of the HP 3000," http://www.robelle.com/library/smugbook/classic.html.

50. Ibid.

51. Ibid.

52. Katherine Lawrence, "The HP Way—misunderstood. Bottom line trumps all," http://www.pingv.com/blog/katherine/200508/the-hp-way-misunderstood-bottom-line-trumps-all.

53. "The History of the HP 3000."

54. Ibid.

55. Ibid.

56. Ibid.

57. Ibid.

58. Michael S. Malone, "Silicon Insider: HP 3000, RIP," ABCNews.com, Nov. 4, 2003.

59. Ibid.

60. *The HP Way,* p. 161.

61. Ibid., p. 163.

7 Legacy

1. David Packard, *The HP Way*, p. 72.

2. Ibid., pp. 72–73.

3. Ibid., p. 74.

4. Ibid.

5. Ibid., p. 75.

6. Ibid.

7. Ibid.

8. Dan Gillmor, "The Indelible Legacy of Bill Hewlett," *Computerworld*, Jan. 29, 2001.

9. Michael S. Malone, "Silicon Insider: Good, Hard Work: High-Tech Entrepreneurs Are Setting Out to Make the World a Better Place," by ABCNews.com, Nov. 19, 2003.

10. From the William and Flora Hewlett Foundation Web page: www.hewlett.org.

11. In the interest of full disclosure, the Flora Foundation was a secondary underwriter (via Oregon Public Broadcasting) of the PBS miniseries *The New Heroes*, for which the author was co-producer.

12. Larry Gordon, "Father Figure," *Stanford Magazine*, March–April 2001; http://www.stanfordalumni.org/news/magazine/2001/marapr/features/hewlett.html.

13. C. Stewart Gillmor, *Fred Terman at Stanford*, p. 491.

14. Ibid.

15. The story of the Monterey Aquarium comes from Jessica Lyons, "Big Dave's Legacy," *Monterey County Weekly*, Oct. 25, 2001.

16. Ibid.

17. Ibid.

18. Marcia McNutt, "How One Man Made a Difference: David Packard," presented at the symposium "Oceanography: The Making of a Science," February 8, 2000, Scripps Institution of Oceanography.

19. Ibid.

20. Ibid.

21. Ibid.

22. Ibid.

23. Ibid.

24.   Ibid.

25.   Ibid.

26.   Ibid.

27.   Ibid.

28.   "Father Figure."

29.   Ibid.

30.   Ibid.

31.   Ibid.

32.   Ibid.

33.   Ibid.

34.   Joseph Moriarity, "Devoted to the Heart," *Minnesota Medicine*, Vol. 84 (December 2001); http://www.mmaonline.net/publications/MnMed2001/December/Moriarity.html.

35.   David Pierpont Gardner, "William Redington Hewlett," http://www.hewlett.org/AboutUs/wmHewlettBio.htm.

36.   "Father Figure."

37.   "William Redingon Hewlett."

38.   The source of this history of laser printing is "Early Laser Printer Development," The Printer Works; http://www.printerworks.com/catalogs/cx-catalog/cx-hp_laserjet.

39.   Andrew Pollack, "Hewlett's 'Consummate Strategist' " *New York Times*, March 10, 1992.

40.   Ibid.

41.   Ibid.

42.   "Close-up on Color Printing," interview with John Meyer, April 2004. HP publication: http://www.hpl.hp.com/news/2004/apr-jun/color_printing.html.

43.   John Minck, "Inside HP: A Narrative History of Hewlett-Packard from 1939–1990," unpublished manuscript for the HP alumni Web site (www.hpalumni.org).

44.   "Close-up on Color Printing."

45.   Ibid.

46.   Deborah Hudson, "The Jet Set Turns 20," http://www.hp.com/cgi-bin/pf-new.cgi?IN=referrer.

47.   "Inside HP."

48.   The author, in the *San Jose Mercury-News*.

49.   Eric Nee, "Dave and Bill's Last Advernture," *Upside*, June 1991, p. 40.

50.   Ibid. Source for the workstation history: pp. 41–42.

51.   Ibid.

52.   Ibid.

53.   Ibid.

54.   Ibid.

55.   Anecdote from "William Hewlett," by Jeff Bliss, *Computer Reseller News*, www.crn.com/sections/special/supplement/763/763p45_hof.jhtml.

56.   Lucile Packard obituary, *San Jose Mercury-News*, May 31, 1987.

57.   Michael S. Malone, "The Packard Way," *San Jose Mercury-News*, March 31, 1996.

58.   Ibid.

59.   The quotes are from the author's correspondence with Bob Sadler, CEO, Sadler Consulting, May 2006.

60.   Ibid.

61.   Ibid., emphasis added.

62.   Ibid.

63.   Ibid.

64.   Ibid.

65.   Ibid.

66.   Ibid.

67.   *The HP Way*, p. 163.

68.   "The Packard Way."

69.   "Dave and Bill's Last Adventure."

70.   "Hewlett's 'Consummate Strategist.' "

71.   "The Packard Way."

72.   Author conversation with Robert S. Boehm, August 15, 2006.

73.   The source of the quotes from the Packard memorial service is "Farewell to David Packard," *Palo Alto Online*, April 3, 1996. http://www.paloaltoonline.com/weekly/morgue/news/1996_Apr_3.PACKARD.html.

74.   George Anders, "The Carly Chronicles," *Fast Company*, Feb. 2003, p. 66.

75.   The story, as here presented, was provided by Walter Hewlett. It should be noted that Arjay Miller, who was present at the event, in telling the same anecdote often leaves out the mild obscenity in Hewlett's quote.

76.   Author interview with Jo Ellen Sako, June 5, 2006.

77.   Ibid.

78.   Larry Gordon, "Father Figure," *Stanford Magazine.*

79.   "William Reddington Hewlett."

80.   "William Hewlett," *Computer Reseller News.*

81.   "Father Figure."

82.   Michael S. Malone, "The Soul of the HP Way," *Wall Street Journal,* Jan. 16, 2001.

83.   Ibid.

84.   The details of the Hewlett memorial service come from Jennifer Dietz Berry, "Remembering Bill Hewlett," *Palo Alto Online,* http://www.paloaltoonline.com/ weekly/morgue/news/2001_Jan_24.HEWLETT.html.

Afterword: The Last Gift

1.   Peter Burrows and Ben Elgin, "The Surprise Player Behind the Coup at HP," *Business Week,* March 14, 2005. pp. 36–37.

2.   Ibid.

3.   Ibid.

4.   Author interview with Jo Ellen Sako.

5.   Jocelyn Dong, "The Rise and Fall of the HP Way," *Palo Alto Weekly,* April 10, 2002.

6.   Michael S. Malone, "Silicon Insider: Bill and Dave's Last Gift," ABCNews. com, May 20, 2003.

7.   "The Rise and Fall of the HP Way."

8.   Ibid.

9.   *Forbes,* December 13, 1999. Referenced in http://www.gale.com/bizdev/ biography.htm.

10.   Ibid., *Forbes,* June 11, 2001.

11.   George Anders, "The Carly Chronicles."

12.   This team included Steve Neal and Keith Flaum of Cooley Godward LLP, and Spencer Fleischer and Tully Friedman of Friedman, Fleischer & Lowe.

13.   "The Carly Chronicles."

14.   Dawn Kawamoto and Rachel Konrad, "HP Merger Duel: Fervor Just Won't Seem to Go Away," by CNET.News.com March 19, 2002.

15. Michael S. Malone, "Bill and Dave's Last Gift."

16. Peter Burrows and Ben Elgin, "The Surprise Player Behind the Coup at HP."

17. Ibid.

18. Adam Lashinsky, "Can HP Win Doing It the Hurd Way?" *Fortune*, April 3, 2006.

19. Ibid.

20. Ibid.

21. Michael S. Malone, "Silicon Insider: The HP Way," ABCNews.com, Feb. 10, 2005.

Index